Books by Dennis Bloodworth

The Messiah and the Mandarins (1982)
The Chinese Machiavelli (WITH CHING PING) (1976)
Heirs Apparent (WITH CHING PING) (1973)
An Eye for the Dragon (1970)
The Chinese Looking Glass (1967)

FICTION

Trapdoor (1980)
Crosstalk (1976)
The Clients of Omega (1975)
Any Number Can Play (1972)

THE MESSIAH AND THE MANDARINS

DENNIS BLOODWORTH

THE MESSIAH
AND
THE MANDARINS

MAO TSETUNG
AND THE IRONIES OF POWER

❀ ATHENEUM ❀

NEW YORK

1982

Library of Congress Cataloging in Publication Data

Bloodworth, Dennis.
    The messiah and the mandarins.

    Bibliography: p.
    Includes index.
    1. China—Politics and government—1949-1976.
2. Mao, Tsetung, 1893-1976. I. Title.
DS777.75.B55   951.05   82-45182
ISBN 0-689-11297-1   AACR2

FOR MY WIFE CHING PING

(something towards an unrepayable debt)

The whole of the opposition's error lies in this, that being bound to "guerrillaism" by traditions of a heroism that will never be forgotten, they will not understand that those days are over.

LENIN, 1919

✣ ACKNOWLEDGMENTS ✣

I WOULD LIKE to thank *The Observer* for allowing me to quote from articles about China that I wrote for the Sunday paper and for the Observer Foreign News Service during the twenty-five years from 1956 to 1981 that I was chief Far East correspondent, and the U.S. International Communication Agency for permission to quote from *Current Scene.*

I am also particularly indebted to the biographers of Mao Tsetung listed at the end of this book, to the *China News Analysis* of Father L. La Dany, and to the British and American information and monitoring services in Hong Kong.

I must above all express my appreciation to my wife, Ching Ping, who went through the book with such care and made so many invaluable suggestions to help me see the story through Chinese eyes.

Finally, my thanks are due to Edward de Souza, who so conscientiously typed and checked the manuscript.

❀ CONTENTS ❀

❈ INTRODUCTION ❈

T HIS BOOK is not a biography of Mao Tsetung, nor is it yet another report on Communist China. It is—as the subtitle suggests—a study in irony. The life of Mao and the story of his times provide the background for a tragicomedy of Chinese manners on a grand scale, in which the characteristics of the hero that enabled him to perform the almost incredible feat of "liberating" all China then prompted him to shatter the society he had created.

I have not written for the specialist. My object has been to confront the ordinary reader with an extraordinary paradox, matching the magnitude of Mao's achievement against the enormity of his errors. As an essay on human frailty, the book may have a universal relevance, but Mao was the ideal subject for it, for his frailty cast—and still casts— a long shadow.

Mao Tsetung is not only the hero and the villain, but the villain and the victim of this strange drama. He was the victim of his own skill in war, which persuaded him that his guerrilla strategy held the answers to the problems of peace. He was the victim of a single-minded obsession, a vision of a classless, selfless utopia that became a vice when he destroyed his closest comrades and plunged China into misery and sometimes near-anarchy in order to realize it. And he was the victim of an elaborate charade in which the Chinese leadership and the Chinese masses connived at his errors in order to reserve a facade of solidarity and success. Raised to the status of a demigod, he was trapped by the myth of his infallibility.

The key to Mao lies in his Chineseness, and I have tried to trace the ancient mental reflexes and modern social pressures, the influences of blood and environment that formed this outstanding, unorthodox, and flexible revolutionary—thinker, teacher, poet, soldier, and political leader—and then contrived his inexorable conversion with the passage of years into an old man withered by the dogmatism he had so despised when young.

Traditional patterns of thought and behavior—and the points at which Western logic and Chinese reason diverge—are very much part of the story, for they explain the bizarre conspiracy whereby life in China became a bewildering, often Kafkaesque adventure for twenty years before Mao died. It was an adventure that I covered as Far East correspondent of *The Observer* from the time of my first visit in 1955, and that I have set out to share with the reader in this book—as an incredulous eyewitness of the Great Leap Forward, as an interpreter of chaos during the Cultural Revolution, and as a reporter studying the legacy that Mao had left when I went back to China in 1979 and 1980.

China was torn in two during this entire period by what Albert Sorel has called "the eternal dispute between those who imagine the world to suit their policy, and those who arrange their policy to suit the realities of the world"—in this instance, the contradiction between the messianic message of Chairman Mao and the more pragmatic perspective of the Communist mandarins around him. As a tale of men found morally wanting in the face of political compulsions, the history of this "struggle between the two lines" deserves a fair hearing. But the Maoist era leaves one dismayed by the pitfalls it reveals: the corrupting power of noble aspirations; the hardening of mental arteries that comes with age; the evils of a system that rejects political euthanasia and perpetuates the rule of senescent leaders long after the fading light has started to play tricks with their vision; the principle of solidarity—the Communist or Asian consensus—that silences opposition; the rewritten history that turns man into myth.

The rewriting of history to create a legend around a leader—or subsequently destroy that legend—must trouble anyone who tries to draw an accurate profile of Mao. But if the official facts become flexible, that is still only part of the problem. The author also faces a mountain of conflicting, often ungradable material about the man and his day acquired from sources that range from foreign biographies to Chinese mosquito magazines, and from monitored radio broadcasts to big character posters put up by rival factions of Red Guards during the Cultural Revolution.

But this is not an academic work. I have therefore stepped back and tried to sketch a recognizable likeness of the truth by sifting the evidence and selecting the main features that stood out from all the unverifiable minutiae. Furthermore, I was not writing a blow-by-blow history, but tracing a theme, and I have ignored events and people not essential to that theme.

For the historical background, the early life of Mao, and the account of the Chinese Revolution up to 1954, I have drawn on the accepted biographies (including the short autobiography Mao dictated to Edgar Snow) and on general works and commentaries on the period, Chinese and foreign. For the years from 1955 until the death of Mao in 1976, and from 1976 until 1981, however, most of the material I have used is "live." I have taken it from notebooks I filled during my visits to China, from articles I wrote for *The Observer* and the Observer Foreign News Service over a period of twenty-five years, from contemporary Chinese press and radio monitoring reports, from quotations and intelligence put out by foreign information services, and from the accumulated cuttings and documentation in my files.

A difficulty arises here, because my own articles did not always identify sources of information in detail at the time (editors decline to devote precious space to parentheses like, "According to a wall poster put up in Canton on 10 October 1967 by the *Hold-High-the-Banner-of-Mao-Tsetung's-Thought People's Red Army of National Liberation*"). Since the book is for the general reader, however, I have in any case thought it better not to clutter it with footnotes, or try to identify for him the precise source of every statement and quotation. (A general list of sources is given at the end of the book.) For the same reason, I have kept the number of Chinese names to the minimum necessary, I have sometimes contracted quotations to make the meaning clearer, and when translating from the Chinese I have been more concerned with conveying the sense of the original than with the precise wording. (All obscure Chinese allusions have been omitted.)

Names are spelled in modern Chinese *pinyin*, except for a few that will be more familiar to the reader in their old form. These include Mao Tsetung, Chou En-lai, Chiang Kai-shek, Sun Yat-sen, Kuomintang, and the place names Peking, Nanking, Chungking, Canton, and the Yangtse River.

Pinyin (in so far as names in this book are concerned) is pronounced much as it is spelled, with the following major exceptions:

C   *should be read as* Ts (in Cao Cao)
Q   *should be read as* Ch (in Jiang Qing or Liu Shaoqi)
X   *should be read as a thin* Sh (in Deng Xiaoping)
Z   *should be read as* Dz (in Zunyi)
Zh *should be read as* J (in Zhu De)

The vowels are pronounced as in Italian, but "e" (as in Zhu De) is pronounced like the French "e" in "le."

To avoid confusion between Chairman Liu Shaoqi as head of state, and Chairman Mao Tsetung as head of the Communist party, I have used the convention of calling the head of state "President."

DB *Singapore 1981*

THE POTTERY SOLDIERS

*Though 400,000,000 people are united within one
China, in reality they are just a heap of sand.*
(DR. SUN YAT-SEN ON "NATIONALISM," 1924)

❀ *CHAPTER ONE* ❀

May 1980. The dig is like some antique, bloodstained battlefield on the Day of Judgment, and strangely moving. As workers gingerly scrape away at the soil, column after column of chalk-white men and horses rise from the reddish earth in fighting formation, the vanguard of a legion of silent warriors still waiting to be excavated from the vault beyond who last saw the light more than two thousand years ago. For this ghostly army of terracotta figures, each as large as life, was buried to defend the body of the "First Emperor" of China who died in 210 B.C.

Behind curled mustaches and well-combed beards, the haunting faces are drained of all color as if by death, yet fierce, eager, intensely alive—the lips strongly carved, the eyes often glancing sharply sideways under their war helmets or intricately braided hair. The swordsmen, charioteers, and kneeling archers wear elaborate plate armor and leggings; attendants and footmen, soft belted gowns and laced boots. Every fold is studied.

An official explains that the immense catacomb, discovered in 1974 by peasants sinking a well, is expected to yield six thousand of these heroes, and that archaeologists believe there may be more like it. Somewhere under the persistent drizzle and flat fields of tall millet some twenty-five miles northeast of Xian, the ancient capital of China, there could be further legions of frangible, fired clay, deployed symmetrically to guard a low, enigmatic tumulus in the eye of the complex—the tomb of Qin Shi Huangdi, the Emperor himself.

Heir to one of seven warring states, this ambitious dreamer seized "the chance that comes once in ten thousand years," and, after destroying the other six kingdoms between 230 and 221 B.C. in campaigns marked by a judicious mixture of cold-blooded treachery and single-minded carnage, founded the colossal empire that men called after

3

him—China. Feudalism was stamped flat as the internal barriers that divided fief from fief came down, the corners of the new, unified Chinese realm were drawn together by a net of strategic roads, and the Great Wall rose to guard its external frontiers. Peasants were no longer the vassals of exigent local lords, but tilled their own land and were taxed by the emperor instead. Weights, measures, tools, coins, cart axles, and the written language and laws were all standardized.

But if farmers were favored, moneymaking merchants were hounded down as unproductive profiteers. The laws were strict, punishments prompt and terminal, ordinary folk were made responsible for each other's good behavior and obliged to denounce each other's crimes—or else. Dissent meant death, books were burned, and imprudent scholars buried.

In 1974 the Chinese press claimed that the abominable act of reducing China's literary heritage to ashes had simply been an "inevitable development of the class struggle of that era," and hailed the Qin ruler as a much-maligned reformer who had "accomplished the tremendous task of unifying the empire." For equally inevitable was the comparison with Chairman Mao—the scourge of the feudalist, the capitalist, and the erring intellectual, the champion of the peasant whose military genius had again made China one.

Comparisons may become invidious, however. The grandiose complex of 270 pavilions and palaces and parks built by the self-styled "First Emperor" was the monstrous emanation of a deteriorating mind. A superstitious megalomaniac hypnotized by magnitude and terrified of being diminished by death, Qin Shi Huangdi was simultaneously dogged by fears of assassination and obsessed by his search for the elixir of life. In consequence, this marvelous maze of mansions served three practical purposes. It pandered to his greed for glory as a self-appointed god, and meanwhile he could both sleep in safety and obey his astrological charts by hurrying secretly down its covered corridors from palace to palace, never spending two consecutive nights in the same one (to reveal his movements was to die).

If his palace was designed to preserve him in life, his tomb was designed to preserve him in death. A silent tree-covered hill of sandy soil whose summit has been softened by twenty centuries of rain, it has not yet been opened, but may tell us tomorrow whether ancient accounts of the vast stone-lined chambers beneath its surface are true. Within the terraced "Mound of Qin," it is said, the entire Chinese empire was laid out in relief, its mountains and plains fashioned in bronze, its rivers mimicked in flowing mercury, the huge toy precise in its detail down to cities and palaces and gardens worked in jade and gems.

The Emperor's body, confided to a boat-shaped sarcophagus, was supposedly left floating on a river of quicksilver forever. But from the outset its condition could have had little about it to suggest the evergreen fragrance of immortality. For in 210 B.C. Qin Shi Huangdi fell ill and died while on a progress a thousand miles from the capital, and, for their own ignoble ends, conniving counselors pretended he was still alive, "reporting" to—and even "feeding"—the disintegrating corpse in its carriage on the long road back, while carts filled with rotting salt fish followed behind to mask the smell of human corruption.

How long had the mind begun to decay before the body? Doctors who believe that the alternating flashes of firm logic and fatuity in aging statesmen may be attributable to atherosclerosis (which can starve the brain of oxygen) asked the same question in 1980 when filing past the rigid cadaver of Mao Tsetung in its mausoleum in Peking. For the pathetic remains in their pompous setting were already discolored and bloated, and as his public image as an infallible genius began to dissolve along with his noticeably biodegradable body, it became evident that the embalmers of his legend had been no more successful than the embalmers of his legs.

But the splendor of a culture that could respond to the inane delusions of the First Emperor with a tomb to rival that of Tutankhamen, guarded by an earthenware army thousands strong, went far towards inspiring the "First Chairman" two thousand years later. And the splendor is unquestionable.

Pliny recounts that in the first century the Chinese were already selling fine-cast iron as well as silk to envious Romans incapable of guessing how either was fashioned. Their technical superiority was to continue down the centuries, so that twenty-two years before William the Conqueror hit the beaches of Sussex, their armies were using both floating and dry compasses, and well before the English longbow won the Battle of Agincourt in 1415, Chinese ships driven by treadmill paddle wheels and armed with trebuchets smashed an invading armada of six hundred vessels with salvos of explosive bombs.

In Christ's day they assembled rigs that could drill two thousand feet down for brine, practiced acupuncture, built mechanically operated armillary spheres—they had already recorded sunspots, charted more than eleven thousand stars, observed Halley's comet. Centuries before Europe, the Chinese were to discover gunpowder and the use of coal, to invent paper and printing and porcelain, map grids, winnowing machines, and the humble wheelbarrow. Their treadle looms and spindles were to revolutionize textile making in Europe.

The construction of the Great Wall and its twenty-five thousand towers—"the longest cemetery in the world"—is believed to have cost a million lives, and set exacting standards for the ruthless exploitation of man in the mass thereafter. Half a million more died under whip and cangue in a single year when the six hundred mile-long Imperial Canal linking the Yangtse to the Yellow River was dug in the seventh century. However, grisly achievements like these were the stitching on the underside of the tapestry of a brilliant civilization that left the foreign traveler openmouthed. Marco Polo said of Kinsai—the former Song Dynasty capital at Hangzhou—"It is without doubt the finest and most splendid city in the world." A merchant of Venice with a sharper eye for the flesh than for the spirit of this sophisticated metropolis, he stood awestruck before its "stately palaces and mansions," its stone-paved highways, its great markets and public baths, and its abundance of unthinkable luxuries from iced soup to toilet paper. But Kinsai was also the repository of an uninterrupted culture that could be traced back to the ancient springs of Chinese civilization.

Like Greece, China was illumined half a millennium before Christ by an explosion of philosophical thought which inspired the finest scholars, administrators, poets, and painters down through the dynasties, and gave the government its comely form. For, unlike Europe, China was not misruled by brawling kings and beefy aristocrats; it was administered in accordance with Confucian teaching by sober scholars, who were selected by a rigorous system of written examination and then assigned to one or other of the boards or ministries that managed the affairs of empire. These were the "mandarins," the powerful civil servants of a China that even at the beginning of the Christian era extended from Korea to Vietnam, and with sixty million souls had a population greater than that of modern Britain. It followed that to these fastidious bureaucrats of the "Son of Heaven" who lived by the light of the one true Confucian culture, the benighted foreigner beyond the Great Wall was an "outer barbarian," an inferior being who must be kept firmly in his place.

Unhappily for China, the outer barbarian did not always see matters in the same way. In the fourth century the impudent Huns overran most of North China and burned down the capital at Loyang, and their parvenu empire was conquered by the Tibetans, who in turn gave way to the Tartars. At the end of the sixth century, China was reunited by the thrifty and prudent founder of the Sui Dynasty (after he had carved a path to the top by murdering his sovereign and fifty-nine princes). In the eleventh century, it was invaded by the Kitan, in the twelfth by the Kin, in the thirteenth by the Mongols, in the sixteenth by Japanese pirates who laid siege to Nanking; and in the seventeenth by the Manchus, whose Qing Dynasty endured until 1911.

However, none of these unmannerly intrusions shook the belief of the Chinese in their innate superiority, any more than a man feels spiritually degraded if he is bitten by a dog (or outpaced by a computer). The dog does not know that his victim is made in God's image, and the Chinese have, in any case, always succeeded in domesticating the brute.

The Tartars who flung the Tibetan usurpers out of North China were devoured and digested by a carnivorous Chinese culture until they not only adopted Chinese names, language, dress, and customs, but were rewarded by their ruler for marrying Chinese. Confucian society metabolized the alien Kitan and Kin and Manchu in the same way, absorbing them as the juices of a soft, ripe papaya will absorb a piece of tough, raw steak placed inside it. And it was a bad day for the Mongol hordes when their Khan was persuaded to tax the vanquished instead of butchering them, for within a century the sybaritic joys of refined Chinese civilization had so sapped their manhood that rebel armies led by a wandering beggar were able to chase them out of the Celestial Empire, and sack the remote capital of their transcontinental dominion at Karakorum.

But the Chinese had not reckoned with another predatory civilization whose men would match their pious arrogance and their blind belief in their own unique virtue, dismissing the Chinese disdainfully as "heathens" even as they themselves were disdainfully dismissed as "barbarians." The main confrontation between the empires of Confucius and Christ opened in 1517, when four Portuguese ships sailed up the Pearl River to Canton and set the tone for future cultural exchanges by succumbing almost immediately to a temptation to raid rather than trade, looting and killing indiscriminately.

In the century that followed, Dutch and British Protestants proved to a dismayed China that they could plunder and murder as callously as the most devout Catholics. Promise of profit thickens the skin wonderfully, however, and a thriving commerce developed in China's favor, until the ugly customers from the West discovered that they could balance their books better if they peddled opium to the natives instead of paying for their purchases of silk and tea, rhubarb and other oriental exotica in hard cash. The Chinese tried to stop the poisonous flow of "foreign mud" from Turkey and India, while the British and the lesser barbarians strove to prise more of China open to their traffic. The Opium War broke out, China lost, and the emperor was obliged to cede Hong Kong to Britain and let foreign traders settle and haggle freely in five coastal ports on the mainland.

The episode set a trend. By 1860 an Anglo-French expeditionary force under Lord Elgin had burned down the Summer Palace at Peking, and under the Treaty of Tianjin, China agreed to throw the Yangtse River open to European traders and allow missionaries into the interior. During the Boxer Rebellion in 1900, a second expeditionary force thrust its way into Peking to relieve the besieged Legation Quarter, another peace was signed, and from then on foreign governments acquired territorial concessions in Chinese "treaty ports," foreigners were tried in their own consular courts, foreign warships were free to sail in Chinese waters, foreign navies took over three Chinese harbors, foreign soldiers guarded foreign legations in the Chinese capital, and foreigners ran the Chinese customs and postal services.

Peking had already lost the penumbra of empire—great tracts of land in Central Asia and North Manchuria had fallen to the Russians, Formosa and Korea had gone to Japan, the Chinese tributary states in Southeast Asia to France and Britain. Meanwhile, metropolitan China itself was being "cut up like a melon" into rival spheres of foreign influence, with the British taking the Yangtse Valley, the French the southwest, the Germans the province of Shandong.

The dismemberment did not end with the turn of the century. Instead, rival powers began adding insult to injury by filching bits of China from each other, while ignoring the Chinese themselves. After their fleet was sunk at the battle of Tsushima in 1905, the Russians surrendered their rights and their railway in Manchuria to the Japanese, who were later to detach the entire territory from China and convert it into a puppet empire renamed "Manchukuo." Neither side troubled to consult the Manchu rulers of China itself, who were powerless onlookers. At the outbreak of World War One, the Japanese also occupied the German-leased territory of Qingdao and took over the German "sphere of influence" in Shandong. All that the dispossessed Chinese proprietors in Peking received were Tokyo's insolent "Twenty-one demands," which were designed to win for Japan license to loot most of the rest of China as well. In 1919 the Treaty of Versailles confirmed the Japanese in their inheritance of the defeated enemy's "sphere of influence," instead of restoring it to its rightful Chinese owners, who in their numbers and noble impotence seemed to have been mockingly symbolized by the pottery soldiers of Qin.

But this barefaced robbery by China's barbarian allies aroused a storm of student protest, and the Chinese delegation at Versailles was obliged to refuse to sign the treaty. A new phenomenon was creeping across the abused and humiliated "Middle Kingdom," a brushfire nationalism that consumed the minds of the young. It could be traced back to the uneasy awareness of thoughtful men in the nineteenth century that if something drastic were not done, China would be doomed. For if emperors could become senile, so could empires.

❀ *CHAPTER TWO* ❀

THE WEST had regarded Confucian China with wonder, and Voltaire had been moved to declare that its government was the "best the world had ever seen." But beneath the flattering makeup of legend lies the ugly skull of history, with its fraudulent grin. In 1598 the astounded Jesuit Father Matteo Ricci wrote of the magnificent two-hundred-year-old astronomical instruments he found in Nanking, "We certainly had never seen or read of anything in Europe like them"—only to learn that they were lying idle on a terrace because no Chinese knew how to use them anymore. A stultified China had turned backward and inward, seeking its inspiration in classical Confucian teaching, and insulating itself from the world beyond the Great Wall. The Empire that had seen no Dark Ages had seen no Renaissance either.

When the alien Manchus overran China in the seventeenth century, they showed even greater respect for the trappings and traditions of this archaic civilization (and its disconcertingly large population), and meticulously they upheld a Confucian philosophy that looked backward to a hypothetical "golden age" of the past for the secret of salvation, not forward to the future. In consequence, it remained archaic, so that in the early nineteen twenties a noted Chinese savant still felt obliged to write of the race whose genius had given us the two most dangerous weapons in history—the chemical explosion and the printed word—"China has had no science."

His lofty explanation was that, unlike lesser breeds, the Chinese sought wisdom, not mere knowledge and wealth. But in the nineteenth century there were already men who contemplated with sorrow and distaste the corrupt court, the medieval minds of the mandarins, and the whole crumbling curio shop of custom and precedent that the thieves from west and east were plundering.

The solution to China's problems seemed obvious enough—borrow from the West, as Japan was doing. But how could Chinese culture admit that it had anything to learn from foreign devils, and reconcile their heterodoxy with Confucian gospel? The conservative hierarchy begged the question by disdainfully ignoring the West and all its works, but would-be reformers came up with ingenious dodges for circumventing this difficulty, including specious claims that European science was worthy of study since its roots lay in "ancient Chinese mathematics."

Their movement captured the imagination of the young Manchu Emperor Guang Xu, who decreed that "there must be careful investigation of every branch of European learning, appropriate to existing needs," and for one hundred glorious days in 1898 he sent shock waves through China by pumping more than forty stimulating edicts into the expiring geriatric in an effort to restore the heartbeat. But this inauspicious temerity quickly drew frowns from the diehard Dowager Empress and outraged mandarins dependent on the status quo. The Empress reassumed the regency, and the over-eager monarch was isolated on a small island, to die mysteriously ten years later and just one day before the "Old Buddha" herself expired.

The Great Wall of tradition had been breached, however. Barbarian ideas were pouring into the Middle Kingdom in a confused mob, and the rearguard of its Manchu rulers had no alternative but to fight the reformers with reform, even if that meant sapping the Imperial structure as they did so. Revolutionary thought fed on the revolutionary changes the court reluctantly paid out like ransom money: modern schools in place of mandarinal examinations, modern laws, modern ministries, and, above all, modern "public discussion." By 1910 delegates from sixteen newly created provincial assemblies were converging on Peking to voice growing demands for a parliament, and it was promised for 1913. But in 1911 a spark of rebellion struck by mutinous soldiers in Wuhan started a conflagration which roared across an immense empire so riddled with dry rot that just eighty days later revolutionaries in Nanking could elect a certain Dr. Sun Yat-sen provisional President of the Republic of China. The ruined Manchus could only riposte by abdicating and proclaiming a "Republic of China" in Peking.

The long years of fumbling for a formula that would combine Chinese wisdom and Western knowledge without loss of face were over, it appeared. The theory that the secret of barbarian supremacy lay in the link between "science" and "democracy"—the system that gave the individual free rein to think for himself—was about to be put to the test. But the new China was setting out as two rival republics, not one. It was an ill-omened beginning for a fragile political concept bulging with notions so alien to Chinese thought that they might have been conceived on Mars.

"Democrazy," one Chinese wit called this strange principle of majority rule and mobocracy, whereby a country was constantly torn apart by rival groups peddling rival doctrines, and those who gained power perversely relinquished it at set intervals so that discord could be unending. For nearly three thousand years of recorded history, the Chinese had had no conception of nationalism, patriotism, or democracy as the West understands them. There was just no place for them in the scheme of things. China was the "Middle Kingdom," the center of the world; the emperor was the "Son of Heaven" and sole master of the earth. There were no independent "nations" to be patriotic against, for all other kings were his vassals. The humble among these barbarians who sent tribute were handsomely rewarded to encourage the habit, while the stiff-necked might be summoned to Canossa (provided they were not so powerful that they might embarrass everyone by refusing to come).

China was not so much a parcel of land as a spiritual realm, a Celestial Empire comparable to the concept of "Islam" or "Christendom," rather than "England" or "America." Men were loyal not to the soil of China but to their sovereign, the infallible pontiff who stood between them and Heaven. The will of the people was not consulted, for they had no separate will. In a Confucian society founded on the interlocking duties of brother to brother, son to father, pupil to teacher, and subject to Son of Heaven, the individual had no standing— as an individual. The empire was ordered by Confucian ritual and rules of conduct. Its scholar-mandarins were versed in the ancient Chinese Classics, and since that meant that they were educated in the perfect moral precepts of the past, they were above the law that they alone were qualified to administer. China was governed by a supreme autocrat and a privileged, indoctrinated elite in accordance with a single, sacrosanct ideology. Disputes might arise within the ruling monolith, but no outside dissent or rival doctrine could challenge it, for that would automatically be heresy, if not blasphemy, an affront to the Son of Heaven himself.

However, emperors were often fallible, mandarins were venal, and in an imperfect world benevolent Confucian teaching could be conveniently twisted to sanctify pernicious exercises in Legalism, a

Machiavellian philosophy of government based on a soulless system of prompt rewards and savage penalties, which had been the making of the First Emperor. If the mandarins were above the law, therefore, the millions often distrusted it as a weapon forged by the state, not to protect the individual, but to punish him. Laws were made harsh to persuade the people to keep clear of the courts, litigation was a dirty word; and prudent men settled their differences among themselves, according to custom and the moral code.

In the West, an honest man might reward a government's growing respect for his personal rights with a growing sense of responsibility towards society. In China, concern for society at the expense of the individual had precisely the opposite effect. The Chinese, to whom the apparatus of state meant the magistrate, the military, taxes, conscription, the corvée, and collective punishment, banded together in self-defense against it. Their loyalties rippled outward in fading rings from the family to the village, the clan, the guild, and the masonic brotherhood or secret society that was quite logically to degenerate into a protection racket. When Sun Yat-sen vainly tried to persuade his countrymen to switch their allegiance from their clans to the new concept of the nation, he was forced to conclude sadly that they were nothing but "a heap of sand."

With the law firmly fixed in his mind as a dangerous brute to be avoided, the Chinese might look with a kindly eye upon the outlaw as his enemy's enemy, and so his friend. Right and wrong were confused in evil times, for the "bandit" could too often be a victim of injustice driven into the greenwood by a rapacious Establishment, and the "hero" the contemptible rascal who had betrayed him. The most popular classical novel in Chinese literature is almost certainly *Water Margin*, the fourteenth-century blockbuster about China's Robin Hood and the antisocial antics of his 107 merry men in their mountain lair among the marshes of Shandong. But there was more to the mystique of the bandit than rebellion against society.

When a dynasty decayed and the emperors became puppets manipulated by greedy eunuchs and lying officials, the ordinary man could not look to his masters for redress, since most mandarins (like those of the Dowager Empress) had a vested interested in preserving the system, however rotten. The only course open to him, therefore, was armed insurrection. But the Chinese are patient people whose fury has a high flashpoint. In consequence, the history of China is not one of debate, reform, and gradual emancipation, but a repetitive tale of long periods of meretricious peace and mounting misery, which ended when the exhausted dynasty was obliterated in a sudden and bloody explosion of popular wrath instigated by a man of destiny (when it was not eclipsed by a foreign invader). The downfall of the emperor signified that he had lost the "Mandate of Heaven," and this passed to a new dynasty, which rose from the ashes of the old in a blaze of glory and good intentions, slowly declined, and was violently obliterated in its turn.

The vast, ragged armies of revolution were frequently aroused and mobilized by the militant chiefs of secret societies with strange devices and magic oaths, and joined by scholars in revolt against the conduct of the court, or provincial squires ruined by its depredations. But nine out of ten Chinese were peasants, and it was the wretched and abused peasantry who filled the ranks of the rebels. Just as the Chinese had looked up to the emperor and not the state, so they would look now to the charismatic leader of the uprising as the new focus for their loyalty, whether brigand, beggar, mutinous general, or mystic—the messiah with the latest panacea for all China's ills. If he lost, he would once more be a bandit, with or without a head. If he won, he might become first emperor of the next dynasty, and the cycle of totalitarian rule and terminal violence would begin again.

Democracy was outside the scope of the Chinese dream. One man, one vote? It would make no sense. A pig minder could rise to be prime minister in China by passing the imperial examinations, and a soldier's daughter become an empress; but although brains (and beauty) counted for more than blue blood, these admirable exercises in egalitarianism merely proved that men were not equal—"even the five fingers of the hand are of different length." Moreover, a Chinese was not an individual with his two feet planted squarely on the ground, but one link in a human pyramid of patronage and mutual protection that would at once collapse if everyone began posturing in the first person singular. There was no word for "freedom" in Chinese, any more than there was for "nation." Both had to be invented.

They were invented, however, and in his day Sun Yat-sen seemed the right man to make the successful cultural transplant they implied and ensure that it was not rejected, for he personified the synthetic Chinese of the future. Born to a farming family in the south, he was a champion of Confucian morality and the grid of loyalties that ordered Chinese society, giving every man his moral map reference. Yet he was also a Western-educated doctor who had been trained in Hawaii, a socialist, and a Christian. He visualized democracy cast in the Chinese idiom. His "Three Principles" embodied Western concepts—Nationalism and Democracy, as well as the "People's Livelihood"—but, like rebel leaders before him, he turned to the Chinese secret society for the musculature of revolution. He also planned to give the Chinese people three years of military dictatorship, followed by a further period on a gradually lengthening leash, before they would be cut loose to enjoy full political freedom.

But faced with two Chinese republics, one proclaimed in Nanking, the other in Peking, Sun Yat-sen was persuaded in 1912 to yield the presidency to the new "prime minister" in the northern capital for the sake of national unity. It was a fatal move. Yuan Shikai was an ambitious and devious soldier in the image of the Chinese warlords who had carved up the empire whenever the court was weak. He aped the democrat but put puppets in all positions of power, murdered the abler opposition leaders, bribed and bullied a pollarded parliament into confiding all power to his hands and making him president for life, and in 1915 coolly announced his reign title as the first emperor of a new dynasty. This superb piece of impudence had a logic of its own, for the Manchus had lost the Mandate of Heaven, and disoriented Chinese who knew nothing of republics were instinctively looking to Peking for a new ruler. But henchmen whom he had made military governors in the provinces now rounded on their master and declared their fiefs independent. Hoist by his own petard, Yuan became despondent, and in 1916 he died.

If the despot could fall captive to a pack of quarreling warlords, however, so could the democrat. The alien Chinese atmosphere in which Western concepts so quickly wilted was already taking its toll of Sun Yat-sen's ideals, for he had found them poor defense against the chicanery of Yuan Shikai. In 1917 Sun formed a military government in Canton with himself as its "generalissimo," and although the presence of 250 members of parliament ostensibly guaranteed that the democratic decencies were observed, the real power was wielded by the contending warlords of South China on whose volatile goodwill he depended. The vestigial organs of democracy in Peking and Canton struggled to survive, while for the next nine years China was churned up by the regional wars of these bemedaled bullies, who treated both with contempt. And not without reason. Political parties bought and sold votes and each other, provoking one bemused warlord to offer to pay the salaries of all the delegates in his provincial assembly if they would dissolve it and "stop squawking."

Like the shaven lawns of Oxford, it had taken the English parliamentary system centuries of growing and mowing to mature, but impatient Chinese, who saw material salvation in this wisdom of the West, had tried to raise instant democracy on a heap of sand. Their folly was later paralleled by those in an impatient West who saw spiritual salvation in the wisdom of the East, and tried to take short cuts to nirvana that led only to drug abuse, the phony cult, and the millionaire maharishi. But democracy, not the dharma, has been the main casualty in this farcical exchange.

The democratic powers themselves let it die. "The whites try to weaken the yellow race by attacking nationalism," Sun Yat-sen complained bitterly. He was right. While the Americans limited their support for him to words of sympathy, most Europeans looked at him askance as a man who put dangerous ideas into docile Chinese heads. If his movement did not simply fizzle out, it might one day forge a strong, united China far less complaisant towards their depredations than the impotent Manchus, the double-dealing Yuan Shikai, and the rat bag of rival warlords primarily interested in guns and gold who made sure that the country remained conveniently weak and divided.

Democracy having failed him dismally, Sun Yat-sen proceeded to reconstruct the movement with the help of Russian advisers dispatched to Canton by the Comintern, and by 1924 his Nationalist Party—the Kuomintang (KMT)—was a disciplined, authoritarian political organization with its own military academy. But it was not the only brotherhood that looked to Lenin's plausible agents for guidance. In July 1921 a dozen ill-assorted Chinese, who had felt their way through the fog of political uncertainty to find their own formula for a new China, met secretly in Shanghai to hold the inaugural congress of the Chinese Communist Party, and among them was an unwashed young militant with a thick Hunanese accent and a deceptively forthright manner called Mao Tsetung.

THE PATRIOT

*The Dragon appears in the field: It will be
advantageous to meet a great man.*
(THE FIRST HEXAGRAM OF THE
"I CHING": SECOND LINE)

❀ *CHAPTER* THREE ❀

H UNAN MEANS "south of the lake," and the valleys of this rich, rice-growing province of central China are watered by a scribble of rivers that snake their way north through the towering, matted mountains to an inland sea shaped like a recumbent dragon and more than 250 miles around—Lake Dongting. It has throughout history provided a dramatic setting for China's most hallowed institutions of violence—the bandits in its hills have been "as thick as the hairs on your head," and its villages have been plundered with depressing frequency by the armies of ambitious warlords or by peasant insurgents passing through to conquer the north from the south, or the south from the north. Dire circumstance and hard times have thrown up a sinewy, shrewd, boastful strain of bucolic Chinese, their vigor and vainglory fired by the chewing of red-hot chilies from childhood. Outstanding as brigand or soldier, the Hunanese has been called the "Prussian" of China, and brags that he is "not afraid of the Devil himself."

In the nineteenth century Shaoshan was just another Hunanese village, hardly distinguishable from all the others that straggled casually down the fertile valley of the Xiang River. But one of its tiled peasant houses was to become a national shrine. Mao Tsetung was born in a barely furnished room within its walled courtyard on 26 December 1893—the Year of the Serpent, according to the Chinese Zodiac, which meant that he would be cerebral yet intuitive, his sagacity laced with romanticism, a man quick to decide and stubborn once having decided.

"My father was a poor peasant, and while still young was obliged to join the army because of heavy debts," Mao told the American writer Edgar Snow. But he was far from feckless, and once back in Shaoshan started a small business as a middleman that soon enabled him to buy a hectare of land. Tightfisted like his neighbors, he sent

Mao Tsetung to primary school during the day to pick up enough learning to do his accounts for him, and then put him to work in the fields as soon as he came home. He was a man molded by harsh memories of famine and want, to whom waste, whether of time or tea leaves, was the ultimate sin. Food at home was adequate but no more. Life was frugal, softened for his sons only by their gentle, good-natured, illiterate mother.

Otherwise, Mao, the eldest of four children, was caught between an irascible taskmaster of a father at home and a severe disciplinarian of a teacher at school. Skirmishes were inevitable and began early. Mao, who despised the ceaseless parental money grubbing and had no stomach for shoveling manure, turned his learning to his own account. His wearisome lessons in Confucian morality gave him a skill in reading that he applied to less laudable works, enabling him to dream away hours in the dubious company of the bloodyminded outlaws in *Water Margin,* or the rival lords in *The Romance of the Three Kingdoms,* a rose-colored record of reprehensible stratagems employed in a sordid struggle for the mastery of China during the third century. These beguiling narratives that glorified rebellion and war were far more to his taste than the Confucian precepts he learned parrot-fashion from his strict tutor. But when his father caught him loafing and shouted that he was an idle layabout totally lacking in filial piety, young Mao would artfully quote the Confucian Classics to refute him.

He was learning his first lessons in strategy. At ten he ran away from school to escape one beating and stayed away from home for fear of another. But when he returned after three days, his chastened father and teacher behaved with unexpected mildness. "The result of my act of protest impressed me very much," Mao recalled. "It was a successful *strike.*" Three years later he threatened to drown himself when his infuriated parent chased him to the edge of a pond, and agreed to apologize for his behavior only after extracting a promise that he would not be beaten in the future. "I learned that when I defended my rights by open rebellion my father relented, but when I remained weak and submissive he only cursed and beat me more." He and his two brothers, his sister, and very often his mother would form a "united front" against the grasping bully who was head of the family, successfully isolating him. Here lay some of the seeds of Mao the man—not in some psychological revolt against authority born of his father's beatings, for all Chinese peasants beat their sons, but in the cold realization that it paid to rebel.

Mao had meanwhile picked up reformist tracts whose warnings that

China must modernize or perish struck an echo from a mind filled with gaudy tales of her grand past. Acutely aware that he could do nothing for his much abused country as long as he worked as an unpaid farmhand and bookkeeper for his father, he borrowed money to enable the skinflint to hire a laborer in his place, and enrolled in one of the modern primary schools which had opened nearby to teach "Western learning."

He was by now a lanky sixteen, big as a man, and he was greeted with disbelief and derision by piping fellow pupils to whom he was an overgrown lout, an ignorant laborer in "ragged coat and trousers" with the scrawl of a bumpkin, who solemnly took *Water Margin* and *The Three Kingdoms* for factual history. But he proved a voracious reader. To please his teachers and get ahead, he studied the Chinese Classics as well as "some history and geography," but outside the classroom he buried his nose in books that told him about China's frustrated modern reformers, about Napoleon, Wellington, Gladstone, Peter the Great, Washington and Lincoln, as well as the peasant founders of Chinese dynasties who had won their empires at the point of the sword. He had found a world of heroes.

Goaded beyond endurance, however, by supercilious children half his size who jeered at his naive reverence for legendary figures larger than life, he finally threw a chair at one of them. The fear and dislike he consequently inspired drove him into leaving when he was eighteen years old, and he made his way to the provincial capital of Changsha to enroll in a secondary school. Here, too, he was made to suffer, it seems—"I used to become enraged when I heard unpleasant things about myself," he said later. And he had a taste for violence that was matched by a growing racial chauvinism. As feeling against the decrepit Qing Dynasty in Peking mounted, he and a friend not only cut off their own pigtails (symbols of subservience to the foreign Manchu usurpers), but forcibly severed those of ten fainthearted fellow students who had failed to do so.

It was 1911, and the eve of the military revolt in Wuhan. But Mao was still a bewildered ignoramus who swallowed indiscriminately every book and paper he could lay his hands on, like a starving man let loose in a strange orchard of ideas. Sixteen before he first heard of America, he was eighteen before he heard of socialism or read his first newspaper, nineteen before he saw his first map of the world.

The political chaos in his groping mind reflected the political chaos in a groping China. From Wuhan an instant fuse of revolt ran to Changsha, where almost at once another insurrection exploded. Mao enlisted in the revolutionary army, and his cross-eyed view of society was illustrated by the way in which he spent his pay of seven dollars a month—two dollars on food, and the rest partly on newspapers and partly on water. For although other soldiers fetched their own water from outside the city, "I, being a student, could not condescend to carrying, and bought it from water-pedlars." He confused the old imperial reformers in Peking with the revolutionaries who were to proclaim a republic in Nanking, and when Sun Yat-sen yielded the presidency to the feudalistic Yuan Shikai in 1912, Mao thought the struggle was over and promptly resigned from the army.

His next moves were those of a blind man feeling his way towards a faint blur of light. First, he applied to enter a police college, but was almost at once deflected by an advertisement for a course in making soap that stressed its social benefits. Then he met a friend who urged him to take a three-year course in law, so he abandoned soap making. Hardly had he paid his registration fee to the law school, however, before he was persuaded instead to sign up for a commercial course by those who argued that since China was involved in an economic struggle for survival, she needed economists even more than police-men, lawyers, or soap makers. Once more, he duly paid his registration fee, but almost immediately switched to another commercial college which offered a wider syllabus—only discovering afterwards that most of the courses were in English, which he did not speak. Finally, he registered with a provincial middle school, but it proved unsatisfactory, and he quickly dropped out of it again.

At that point, he stopped paying registration fees, renounced all schools, colleges, and courses, and spent half a year at the Hunan Provincial Library, conscientiously reading his way through a "schedule of education" of his own devising. This included Adam Smith, Darwin, T. H. Huxley, John Stuart Mill, Rousseau, Spencer, Montesquieu, Greek mythology, the histories of (among others) Russia, America, England, France, and—as always—all the newspapers he could find. The blur was now a glimmer.

"For twenty-odd years I grew up eating honeydew, ignorant about everything," he once said. But in 1913 he entered the First Normal School, which trained primary school teachers, and he was to stay until 1918. He was still a "tall, clumsy, dirtily dressed young man whose shoes badly needed repairing," but the ruddy-complexioned bumpkin had gone. His face was large but pale, his hands soft and sensitive, and his eyes did not have "the sly, cunning look sometimes attributed to them," wrote his friend Siao Yu—who added slyly enough himself that

Mao's "good white teeth helped to make his smile quite charming, so that no one would imagine that he was not genuinely sincere."

It was not surprising if some sneered that he kept his tongue in his cheek, for the attentive, even humble manner that won him praise in class would give away from time to time to bold and provocative acts. He was nearly expelled for drafting a manifesto attacking the principal, and the college was searched by police after he had been reported for circulating subversive tracts. Moreover, the model student who piously damned money, sex, and laziness, and excelled at writing essays, would impudently draw an oval and call it *Egg* when faced with a compulsory still-life examination that bored him.

But then he was quick to rebel when affronted, for his hunger for knowledge had led him into an equivocal love-hate liaison. He was no longer an object of ridicule, but scars remained. While he might swallow insults and still court scholars in his single-minded determination to learn, it was for love of learning, not love of the learned. When Mao shrugged on his shabby tunic and bursting slippers, and grumbled loudly if obliged to wash his clothes, he sometimes seemed to be falling back deliberately on the familiar role of the malodorous peasant, rather than just being his slovenly self. "That's typical of the son of a rich father," he scoffed when he caught Siao Yu brushing his teeth after meals. Cleanliness might be next to godliness, but Mao was to be no friend of those on high.

He and Siao nevertheless set out together without a coin in their pockets to tramp through five counties, relying on the charity of farmers. "The peasants fed us and gave us a place to sleep. Wherever we went, we were kindly treated and welcomed," Mao remarked afterwards, not quite accurately. One senses behind this arduous journey an unspoken urge to know the people through the clear glass of penury, to sharpen the wits and harden the sinews in order to serve China better. He had been encouraged by his professor of philosophy, Yang Zhangzhi. Yang extolled the virtues of the simple "scientific" and "democratic" life as he had observed it in Britain, which involved not only mixing with the people, but practicing such Anglo-Saxon austerities as deep breathing, cold baths, missing breakfast, and brisk walks. Mao described how later he and his friends tramped up and down mountains in winter, sleeping in the open "when frost was already falling," and swimming "even in November in the cold rivers." These early triumphs of mind over matter engendered in him an enduring belief that, given the will, man in the mass could overcome all obstacles

—"climb a mountain of swords or cross a sea of fire," as the Chinese, much given to hyperbole, like to put it.

As an epidemic of radical thought began sweeping through the country in 1915, the first, stirring manifesto of a review to be known as *New Youth* called upon the young to rise up and "resolutely discard the old and the rotten," to renew China continually as the body renews its cells. Destiny was nudging Mao. He could not then know that he was reading a paraphrase of the fiercest of his future principles—the need for perpetual revolution—but he was deeply influenced by the progressive editor and the leading contributor of the magazine, with whom the liberal Professor Yang put him in touch. The mist was lifting, and the path narrowing, for these two men were to be the godfathers of the Chinese Communist Party.

❈ *CHAPTER* FOUR ❈

MAO WAS far from being red, however. He described his thinking at this time as "a curious mixture of liberalism, democratic reformism, and utopian socialism," and in 1918 he founded with others the New People's Study Society in order "to reform China and the world." He was not searching for a creed, but for a crowbar to prize his country free of foreign gyves—the wrong the English imperialists had done China was "even more atrocious" than that of the Japanese, he said, while America was "the most murderous of hangmen." He would judge any theory by one criterion only: its ability when put into practice to rescue the sick Chinese republic and its people from their sore plight.

At one point it occurred to him that the answer might lie not in the philosophical armory of the West, but in the traditional weapons of a China on which so many were turning their backs, and when appealed to by wrangling students, he told them to "imitate the heroes" of *Water Margin*. He did not know that with this offhand reference to the legendary band of rebels who defied corrupt government from their inaccessible mountain lair, robbing the rich and protecting the poor, he had solved half of the conundrum. Destiny was nudging him again.

Mao graduated from the Normal School at Changsha in 1918, and was at once caught up by a wave of enthusiasm for the work-study movement which was taking young Chinese radicals off to France. But although with others he made his way to Peking, in theory to learn some French before embarking for Europe, he decided against going himself. "I felt I did not know enough about my own country," he explained. He was poor at languages, and flinched from the idea of coming back as a "half-foreign" creature at whom his countrymen would look askance. The man whom some would later extol as the greatest living Communist was afraid of becoming an internationalist,

25

VISTA

and during his entire life would leave China only to pay two visits to Moscow. In consequence, China's most vitriolic critic of idle theory and most fervent advocate of practice was to know the world itself only on paper.

Professor Yang was now in Peking, and the impecunious twenty-five year-old Mao, shivering in the northern winter, was given a job as assistant librarian at the National University, where he was again humbled by the arrogance of intellectuals. "My office was so low that people avoided me . . . to most of them I did not exist. I tried to begin conversations with them on political and cultural subjects, but . . . they had no time to listen to an assistant librarian speaking a southern dialect." He was nevertheless moving in a widening circle of men and ideas at a time when the Russian Revolution was arousing excited speculation in a disoriented China that had not found its own way through the wood. He joined a Marxist Study Group, read the Russians, corresponded with anarchists—and fell in love with Professor Yang's daughter.

The terminal illness of his mother took him back to Hunan in 1919, and he was in Changsha when the Paris Peace Conference upheld Japan's claim to the former German "sphere of influence" in China. The explosion of wrathful student nationalism that this shameless exercise in international chicanery provoked—a nationalism learned, like so much else, from China's alien tormentors—was to be called the "May 4 Movement." Violence in Peking led to mass arrests, which in turn led to demonstrations, strikes, and boycotts throughout the country as merchants and workers were drawn into a tidal wave of agitation for drastic change.

Mao flung himself into the tumult in Changsha, petitioning the Sun Yat-sen government to throw out the tyrannical warlord who dominated Hunan, disseminating radical newspapers, and editing defiant and inflammatory reviews which were banned after he and his fellow militants led a general strike of students. Branded a radical, Mao retorted: "What is a radical? He is no more than a patriot who fights for the interests of his country and for liberation from despotic rule." For him, the two were the same. The practical end justified any theoretical means, but the means still remained to be found.

Changsha had become too hot to hold him, so he moved to Peking to continue his polemical assault on warlordism, and from there to Shanghai. An article he had published entitled "A Great Union of the Masses" in which he called for a broad, united front against oppression— "The triumph of the October revolution was the triumph of the unity of the Russian people"—had been widely read. His name was now known. In Peking and Shanghai he could talk at length with the two luminaries of *New Youth* whom he had so admired, Li Dazhao and Chen Duxiu, and read for the first time two Marxist works they put into his hands—the *Communist Manifesto* and Kautsky's *Class Struggle*.

He later said these works "deeply carved my mind, and built in me a faith in Marxism." But this looks suspiciously like rewritten history, an attempt by Mao to present himself as a budding theoretician in love with the doctrine. A friend of the translator said that in fact he had not really understood the *Manifesto*. He read only a fragment which had been translated into Chinese from a Japanese version, its alien abstractions twisted into the monosyllabic symbols of a culture that expressed even the simple concept of "length" in concrete terms as "long-short."

If Mao had not yet picked Marxism from the tossing sea of "isms" that was intellectual China, neither had his mentors. Li was still writing of the need to "remedy its defects," and Chen published a manifesto on "genuine democracy." Moreover, if Kautsky "deeply carved" Mao's mind, that merely proved that none of the three was aware that Lenin had denounced Kautsky as a renegade and that they were exclaiming over a work already on the Communist Index. It was hardly surprising. Few radical writings were translated into Chinese, and few Chinese radicals spoke a foreign language. None of them had read *Das Kapital*.

But even as Mao was struggling to scratch a living as a laundryman in Shanghai, while developing his plans for a comeback in Hunan, three instructors from the Comintern arrived in China. Headed by Grigorij Voitinsky, this team must have surveyed with some misgiving the Chinese ragbag of republicans, anarchists, socialists, and "a few prominent revolutionaries interested in Marxism" that confronted them. Lenin had laid down that the workers of the world should unite with the nationalists in Asia against the imperialist and capitalist enemy, however, and dainty exercises in doctrinal purity could come later.

The immediate business of the mission was to organize, to pull the heterogeneous nationalist movements in China together and hitch them to the geopolitical needs of its masters in Moscow. Its members talked the flexible tactics of revolution—how to create cells, marshal the millions, split the enemy, and assume dictatorship of the masses. If to a frustrated Sun Yat-sen their alternative seemed forged of steel beside the broken reed of democracy, for Mao it was what he had been looking for all along—the winning combination, "the best of weapons for liberating our nation," as he was to call Marxism-Leninism.

Mao returned to Hunan. His fortunes had changed. He had been offered a post as a teacher in the Normal School, and was later able to marry Yang Kaihui, the plain but clever daughter of his former professor. When under Comintern guidance, Li and Chen Duxiu put together the core of a Communist group in Peking and Shanghai, therefore, Mao was able to put together another in Changsha, supported by peripheral organisms designed to serve the cause of Marxism. By the end of the year he was mobilizing the workers in his spare time, and in May 1921 he traveled to Shanghai for the founding congress of the Chinese Communist Party.

The congress opened in an empty girls' school in the French Concession, but when the French police became too inquisitive, it was converted into a boating expedition. The political tastes of the conspiratorial picnickers ranged from democratic socialist to outright anarchist, yet they adopted an almost bombastically sectarian program that allowed for "no relations with other political parties." It may seem odd that Mao—described as "challenging everybody at meetings to the point of coming to blows" and "delighting in verbal traps"—was not listed among the dissenters who vainly argued in favor of collaboration with Sun Yat-sen (except in one doctored official biography riddled with tactful historical afterthoughts). After all, Mao had formed his first successful "united front" with his brothers and mother against his father when a child, and had not long before called for a "great union of the masses" against oppression.

But while he might spar to test the strength of his adversaries, it was often an act, and all the honest indignation carefully calculated. He would always pick his own ground and his own time for a real fight, and neither was propitious now—it would have been ironical, to say the least, if a party that boasted no more than seventy members in all China were to be split at its first congress by advocates of a united front. Unorthodox, resourceful, devious, Mao preferred ambush to confrontation, and whenever possible seized opportunity not by the throat, but by the scruff of the neck.

The Party needed men, and he went back to Hunan as provincial secretary to recruit members and to organize cells of students and workers. Exploiting a politically unexceptionable "mass education movement" launched by the Chinese YMCA with American money, he opened a branch in Changsha in which illiterate adults were taught to read. In place of the texts provided, however, the students were given others concocted by Mao, lamenting the evils of capitalism and the plight of the working poor.

This artful hoax held an implied rebuke for narrow sectarians who would not soil their hands by working with non-Marxists. The same was true of his success in wheedling a respectable study society directed by classical scholars into letting him use its premises for a "self-education college" disseminating Marxist ideas. Some have insisted that his motives were mixed, that the incongruous pursuit of ancient Chinese and modern radical philosophies side by side exposed the tough nationalist roots beneath Mao's flowering communism. But both were cases of "hanging out a lamb's head while selling dog-meat"—the characteristically culinary Chinese equivalent of putting a wolf into sheep's clothing.

Yet when two agitators were executed amid growing labor unrest, Mao earned himself a reputation for being imperturbable in a tight corner by confronting the military governor of Hunan in his office and coolly quoting British labor legislation to back up his contention that the government should keep its brutal hands off workers unless they broke the law. Taken aback, the warlord failed to have the temerarious troublemaker dispatched on the spot but later ordered his arrest. Flushed out of Changsha for a second time, Mao secretly handed over his responsibilities to comrades not yet proscribed and went to work at party headquarters in Shanghai.

The political pieces in the game were about to be shuffled. Michael Borodin, the latest Comintern adviser, had started upon his task of converting a "democratic" Kuomintang as loosely woven as cotton wool into a disciplined, close-knit Nationalist phalanx. The Communists were urged to join the organization as a "bloc within," a startled Sun Yat-sen finally agreed to accept them as "individuals," and the "individuals" then registered as members en masse.

Mao had already been elected to the Central Committee of the Communist Party, and in January 1924 he was made an alternate member of the Central Executive of the Kuomintang. Left-wing and Communist members now dominated the all-powerful political council of the KMT (which included Borodin himself), and when the Whampoa Military Academy opened a few months later, the Nationalist Chiang Kai-shek became its commandant, but the Communist Chou En-lai became its political director. The weasels were in the warren.

The sanguine, often ebullient Mao should have been elated. But the former library assistant and laundryman, the elementary schoolteacher who spoke only Chinese and had no degree, was looked down upon by KMT and Communist intellectuals alike. While Nationalists regarded him with suspicion, Communists accused him of being a lickspittle who kowtowed to the "bourgeois" Kuomintang, and as cracks and fissures quickly began to flaw the flimsy alliance, the recriminations from both sides became increasingly bitter. Unlike his more sectarian comrades, Mao believed in courting the KMT. For one thing, he was sold on "united-front" tactics. For another, the "bourgeois" KMT paid far more attention than did the proletarian Communists to the man, in his millions, in whom Mao himself was developing an unorthodox interest—the wretched, downtrodden, exploited, and abused Chinese peasant.

On a cool, clear day in Canton in November 1972 I was led by Communist cadres from one flagged courtyard to another, past long lines of enamel washbasins and bamboo bunks, neatly stacked rifles and drab uniforms and rope-soled sandals, into a small bare room with whitewashed walls. This contained little more than a wooden table, a bed of planks covered with a rush mat, two boxes of books, and a pile of dry, yellow newspapers. Forty-six years before, I was assured by a low-voiced official, Mao Tsetung had "brought the heavy boxes of books all the way from Hunan, hung on each end of a carrying-pole."

The room was a shrine, preserved for posterity and an endless flow of pilgrims. It was here that Mao had worked and slept as Principal of the Peasant Movement Training Institute of the Kuomintang in 1926. For he had gone to Hunan a sick and discouraged man two years before, only to come back to Canton with fire in his belly, thanks to the folly of a badly rattled British officer in Shanghai.

The officer lost his head on 30 May 1925 when faced with a column of demonstrators protesting the murder of a Chinese worker, and ordered the police of the International Settlement to open fire. Twelve students were shot dead and fifty wounded. More demonstrations led to more shooting, detonating a chain of strikes that reached Canton, where British and French police gunned down another fifty-two Chinese. A white-hot flame of xenophobic rage shot across China, and a total boycott of British Hong Kong was declared. For Mao, down among the tillers of Hunan's fertile soil, the heat of the hatred was a revelation. "Formerly I had not fully realised the degree of class struggle among the peasantry," he told Snow, "but after the May 30 incident and during the great wave of political activity which followed it, the Hunanese peasantry became very militant . . . in a few months we had formed more than twenty peasant unions, and had aroused the wrath of the landlords, who demanded my arrest."

In March 1926 he published an "Analysis of the Classes in Chinese

Society," in which he dutifully conceded that China's two million industrial workers should be the "leading force in the revolutionary movement," as Communist orthodoxy demanded, but noted in passing how few they were. He then went on to point out (with a careful lack of emphasis) that there were, on the other hand, 170 million peasants who did not own the land they tilled, including 60 million landless laborers who could be counted on to be "brave fighters" in a revolution —as could another 20 million *éléments déclassés* made up of "soldiers, bandits, robbers, beggars and whores."

Mao was moving out on to a creaking ideological limb. The party leader, Chen Duxiu, disdained the doltish peasantry and placed his faith wholeheartedly in urban revolution led by the industrial proletariat as the Russians preached it. But there was more to Mao's temerity than that. Sun Yat-sen had died. Chiang Kai-shek had assumed command in Canton, and was planning a "Northern Expedition" to roll up the more recalcitrant warlords opposing him, buy over the rest, take Peking, and unite China under Kuomintang rule. Mao was not only exhilarated by the revolutionary potential of the peasants, but saw it as a key to the success of this campaign and the future of the Communist-KMT alliance, both of which his patriotic instincts prompted him to support —at least for the time being. His reasoning was simple: The Nationalist armies would march north all the more swiftly and smoothly if the peasants were organized to rise against regional warlords whose troops barred the way, and if they were granted land confiscated from the rich, they could give the KMT more effective support.

In August 1926, accordingly, he slipped back into Hunan again to add fuel to peasant fury as the Nationalists overran the province. But in October, Stalin himself called for the fires of rural revolt to be damped down, and Chen Duxiu subsequently pulled Mao out of Hunan, "holding me responsible for certain happenings there, and violently opposing my ideas." Why? Because if the peasant movement had developed a "startling militancy," as Mao boasted, the Kuomintang were now duly startled. They had originally opened the training institute for agitators in Canton and incited peasant unrest because its immediate victims would be obstreperous southern warlords and their backers among local landowners. But now the jackboot was on the other foot.

As the Kuomintang marched further north, they found that the "local bullies and bad gentry" harried and beset by the enraged rustics Mao had helped to unleash were often relatives of officers in their own bourgeois ranks. Stalin, who was above all anxious to keep the KMT in hand, suddenly saw their fragile alliance with the Communists threatened by these bucolic assaults on Nationalist susceptibilities. And the alliance was already bursting at the seams. The Kuomintang had split into right and left wings, and as military commander in the field a fuming Chiang Kai-shek was finding himself called to order by a pack of KMT progressives in the government in Wuhan who had awarded the Communists two out of five new ministries, and were obviously not to be trusted beyond the range of a bolt-action rifle.

But this swing to the left only encouraged Mao to put the farmers first, and in March 1927 he presented a report to the Kuomintang on the rural tumult in Hunan that was suffused with revolutionary passion and almost breathless with enthusiasm. "The upsurge of the peasant movement is a colossal event," he wrote. "In a very short time, in China's central, southern and northern provinces, several hundred million peasants will rise like a mighty storm, like a hurricane, a force so swift and violent that no power, however great, will be able to hold it back. They will smash all the trammels that bind them and rush forward along the road to liberation. They will sweep all the imperialists, warlords, corrupt officials, local tyrants and evil gentry into their graves."

After the Kuomintang armies had passed through Hunan, he claimed, membership of the peasant associations had leaped from around four hundred thousand to two million, "and the masses directly under their leadership increased to ten million." Countless thousands were now "striking down the enemies who battened on their flesh," and there were violent revolts and serious disorders, Mao admitted. But, after all, "A revolution is not a dinner party . . . to put it bluntly, it is necessary to create terror . . . proper limits have to be exceeded in order to right a wrong."

The peasants had fined and humiliated their former masters, jailed them, banished them, and executed them publicly. They had frozen rents, slashed interest rates, stopped the sale of grain outside the province. They were vigorously attacking the "four thick ropes" that bound the Chinese people—the power of the state, the rule of the clan, superstition, and the subjection of women. They had set up schools and marketing cooperatives, and in many places all other authority had been erased and only their writ ran. The peasants were described as "the vanguard of the revolution," the leading role of the proletariat did not get a single mention, and even the Communists gave the report a tepid reception.

Mao next championed a tough draft regulation prescribing the death penalty for counterrevolutionaries, since "peaceful methods cannot suffice to overthrow the local bullies and bad gentry," and they must be liquidated "by direct action of the peasants themselves." He called for the confiscation of all land held not only by these sinners but by "corrupt officials, militarists, and all counterrevolutionary elements," and anyone owning more than four and a half acres of China. But the principle of "direct action" was thrown out, and the final resolution on land reform called for the stripping only of those unfortunates among the biggest landlords who had no relatives in the "revolutionary army" of the Kuomintang.

Bowing to authority, Mao reluctantly set out to curb the excesses of the vengeful peasantry in Hunan. His very single-mindedness of purpose prompted him to adjust subtly to the mood of the moment; he was more tongue than teeth, and only played the bully when the role required it. He had "a modest, restrained and profound glance, a pale and delicate skin, and in conversation a low but mild and persuasive voice," as one of the comrades recalled. He was to show that he could be "magnificent and imposing," but "among members of the revolutionary party, it was a kind of miracle if there was anyone who spoke with a soft voice. And Mao really spoke softly . . ."

He also had a flair for knowing when to get tough, however, and as soon as his Communist comrades rejected his proposals for rigorous land reform in April 1927, under the illusion that they could placate the Kuomintang, it was they who were caught blinking foolishly in the sudden, harsh light of reality. Having taken Shanghai nine days before, Chiang Kai-shek treacherously fell upon the Communists and armed militants who had led an uprising of workers within the city to coincide with his attack, and butchered about three hundred of them. Six days later he repudiated the left-wing Kuomintang government in Wuhan and set up his own rival regime in Nanking.

When well-wishers then tried to patch up the quarrel and reunite the two halves of the Nationalist movement, the Communists met the threat with a clumsy bid to gain complete control of the Wuhan faction in order to keep it out of the clutches of the Generalissimo. The disobliging response of the Wuhan KMT was not to swing left to meet the Communists halfway, but to swing right and purge their nest of these ideological cuckoos, and the "massacre" of comrades by troops of the right-wing Nationalists in Shanghai was now outclassed by an even bigger "massacre" of comrades by troops supporting the left-wing Nationalists in Wuhan.

The Party nevertheless continued to cling to the fraying cloak of the KMT connection, and plotted orthodox urban revolution in its name, beginning with an armed insurrection "under the Kuomintang flag" to seize the strategic city of Nanchang *pour encourager les autres*. The tactic did not work, however, for although the motley force hastily thrown together and pushed into action against the town in August 1927 managed to hold it for four days or so, few workers were inspired to rally to the "revolutionary committee" it set up, and Nationalist troops converging upon the scene obliged the insurgents to abandon it again and scatter southward.

Within a week, Chen Duxiu had been sacked from his post as Party secretary, a scapegoat for the bungling so far. But Mao was still a member of the Politburo, and he was now sent to Hunan with instructions to organize what became known as the "Autumn Harvest Uprising." For this ill-conceived escapade, he was told not to rely on any miscellaneous soldiery that he might scrape together. He was to fire the imagination of the revolutionary masses with a curtain raiser of political terrorism, killing off the biggest landlords and—once the mayhem gathered momentum—ruthlessly liquidating all bullies and "bad gentry" and government officials. That would ignite a self-generating rebellion of the masses, which would flare up first in the towns and thereafter consume the Hunanese countryside. But since all was to be perpetrated under the Kuomintang flag, Mao was not to form soviets, nor confiscate land from any but the richest landlords.

Mao objected that the discreditable Kuomintang flag should be discarded and *all* land confiscated immediately, misinterpreted his orders to mean that he could create soviets without delay, and recoiled with skeptical disgust from the questionable thesis—pulled out of thin air far from the scene—that political power could be generated by the spontaneous combustion of milling proletariat set aflame by an orgy of violence. He then put up a practical plan for attacking Changsha with four regiments of Kuomintang deserters and renegades, peasant volunteers, and militant miners, since the available spontaneous masses seemed somewhat thin on the ground. The Central Committee of the Party reproved him for his abysmal lack of faith and accused him of turning the revolution into a "military adventure." Mao solemnly protested that he, too, regarded his armed and organized regiments merely as "auxiliary forces"—and promptly sent the "auxiliary forces" into battle against the provincial capital.

After some initial success, one regiment was badly mauled, a second regiment made up of former KMT soldiers abruptly turned coat in the middle of the fray and struck a third in the back, and miserable failure was assured when not only did the workers in Changsha prudently decline to rise, but the apathetic peasantry treated his army as just another passing band of thieving soldiery. Mao's incandescent optimism had let him down. As one comrade put it disagreeably, "He promised a hundred thousand peasants . . . and in the end only five thousand turned out." After six days Mao called off the assault, withdrew with the survivors of two regiments, and when peremptorily told to return to the attack, either ignored or did not receive the order—he was never, in any case, a commander to throw good men after bad.

The Central Committee, grandly brushing aside the string of depressing fiascos that had constituted the "proletarian" revolution of 1927, began planning further insurrection in what was erroneously depicted as a favorable atmosphere of "permanent upsurge," and in doing so adopted Mao's proposals—heretical just yesterday—that the Kuomintang flag be abandoned and all land confiscated. But those ahead of their time inevitably suffer for it. Mao was branded a "military opportunist" whose aberrant notion of revolution was nothing more than a "rifle movement," and he was dropped from the Politburo.

Mao knew nothing of all this. Constantly harassed as he retreated southward from Changsha, the ragged remnant of his army dribbling deserters as he moved, he finally led the seven hundred-odd exhausted men who stayed with him across the border of Jiangxi province and up into the remote and inaccessible mountain keep known as Jinggangshan for the winter. He had taken his own advice to "imitate the heroes" of *Water Margin*. He had found his bandit lair.

THE BANDIT

All warfare is based on deception.
(SUNZI, FIFTH CENTURY B.C.)

❋ *CHAPTER* FIVE ❋

I T WAS OCTOBER 1927. The years of fatuity and failure had left the Communist Party in disarray and disintegrating, its numbers depleted by massacres and desertions, its leaders underground in Shanghai, its forces scattered untidily across the south in small patch pockets, living off the land among a largely indifferent peasantry. And the fatuity was to continue. On the sweeping assumption, firmly based on monumental ignorance, that "only the blind and faint-hearted" could doubt that the Chinese masses were moving towards a "new revolutionary upsurge," Communists armed with about two thousand rifles and a few grenades and machine guns were instructed by Moscow to plunge into another urban adventure, seize the city of Canton, and proclaim a "commune." Neither the KMT soldiery nor the workers in the town rallied to them, and in December they were annihilated in three days of fire and carnage during which the revolt was "drowned in blood."

Perched on his aerie on the mountainous border of Hunan and Jiangxi provinces and spared any part in this particular folly, Mao felt all the safer the following spring when Zhu De joined him with about four thousand men, even if only half of them were armed with a job lot of miscellaneous rifles. Zhu De was a peasant from Sichuan, a former secret society man and opium addict who nevertheless had graduated as an officer at Yunnan Military Academy and pursued a successful military career—fighting, plundering, judiciously changing sides, and rising to the rank of brigadier—before he threw it all up, went to Germany to study, and became a clandestine Communist. Enlisting for the Northern Expedition on his return to China, he had been a key figure inside the city of Nanchang during the abortive uprising in 1927, and he joined forces with Mao on Jinggangshan after extricating his troops and marching them through the southern provinces in search of a secure base, persistently harried by the Kuomintang. A bluff, resourceful, nimble-witted commander trusted by his men, he was affectionately nicknamed the "Cook" after he had escaped from the enemy by pretending to be one.

But the Party line, however thin, still stretched to the precipitous heights of Jinggangshan, and Mao complained some months afterwards that the Central Committee had "changed its mind three times within a few weeks in June and July." During that short period he was successively told that the "absolutely correct policy," which he should carry out "without the least hesitation," was to consolidate in the Loxiao Mountains of Jiangxi itself, to drive into south Hunan, and to set out for east Hunan. When he failed to obey these conflicting instructions for fear of violating at least two of them, a Party emissary from the affronted provincial committee in Hunan took over his post as secretary of the "Border Area" around Jinggangshan in July 1928, and promptly ordered an attack on Chenzhou in south Hunan.

Predictably, the attack failed, and the dangerously weakened Border Area would meanwhile have fallen to the Nationalists (who sensibly took advantage of this infantile move by invading it in strength) but for the obstinacy of a Communist rearguard of two hundred rifles, which fought back for twenty-five days in the face of discouraging odds, aided by such deceits as the lighting of firecrackers inside tin buckets which "exploded like machine-guns." Finally, a split in the ranks of the Kuomintang forced the enemy to withdraw. Returning from their costly foray in Hunan to restore the situation, Zhu De and Mao found that the shamefaced luminary who had dreamed up the operation in the first place was absent, retired sick.

Worse was to follow, for Li Lisan, the latest leader to fill the precarious post of Party secretary, was adamant in condemning as "peasant deviationism" any tendency to discount the militant urban worker as the "vanguard of the revolution" and to neglect the struggle for the cities—"the brains and heart of the ruling class." This stand ignored inconvenient statistics which showed that the number of industrial workers in clandestine left-wing unions throughout the whole of China was little more than thirty thousand, and that they contributed only 8 percent of the Party's membership. The statistics explained why Li Lisan had so far failed dismally to rouse the urban proletariat, but that did not deter him from conforming to fashionable ideology, and in June 1930 he ordered successive onslaughts against Changsha, Nanchang, and Wuhan.

Zhu De and Mao were to take Nanchang, while command of the assault on Changsha was given to an outstanding ex-Nationalist general called Peng Dehuai. Peng, a burly peasant who had run away from home to work as a cowherd and a coal miner, had risen to command a KMT brigade, but had turned his coat and joined Mao on Jinggang-shan with a thousand men after another abortive uprising in Hunan. He was nicknamed "Hades" because he was such a devil for duty, so it was said, that he had no time even to smile.

Peng burst his way into Changsha but within ten days was forced out again by the Nationalists, who grievously outgunned him, while Zhu De and Mao were beaten off with dismaying losses at Nanchang. In a desperate gamble to recover something from the wreckage, Li Lisan then ordered both columns to regroup and mount a joint attack on Changsha, but before that uneven struggle between the rifles of the Communists and the heavy artillery and bombers of the Kuomintang could end with the Reds being blown to rags, Mao persuaded his shaken comrades-in-arms to cut their already painful losses, defy the Central Committee, and withdraw. He was to learn later that his wife, who had been living under cover in Changsha, had been seized by the enemy and publicly executed outside the main city gate as a reprisal for the first attack.

Mao held more than his wife's death against Li Lisan, who derided his protracted guerrilla campaign in these forbidding hills of Jiangxi as "boxing tactics." But Li was not the only leader with whom Mao had crossed words. The three intellectuals who had in turn held the post of secretary of the Chinese Communist Party since 1921 had all gazed with a bilious eye on this rebel among rebels who exaggerated the potential of the peasant, the rural revolution, and the soldier, while paying no more than lip service (it was suspected) to the hallowed role of the proletariat, the insurrection in the city, and the purely imaginary "continuous upsurge" of the working masses. They might be on the same side, but their ideas only fitted where they touched, for the academic propositions of these earnest pundits were too often founded on what Mao in the field was quick to recognize as pipedreams. And each in turn was to be sacked as the scapegoat for the calamitous consequences in order to preserve the image of infallibility of the ludicrously ignorant oracle behind them all—Joseph Stalin.

From the outset, Stalin was more concerned about Russia than revolution, with the rider that the more revolutionary China could become—short of a steep descent into anarchy—the better it would be for Russia. When Comintern agents were dispatched to China to find suitable allies, therefore, they showed admirable impartiality by making contact not only with Sun Yat-sen and the left-wing editors of New Youth, but with the right-wing "republican" government in Peking, and the "feudal" warlords who still dominated much of the country. Stalin at first vetoed the Northern Expedition because by 1926 the Russians, anxious to stem the creeping influence of the incurably acquisitive Japanese, were courting the powerful military masters of Manchuria and North China who would not be amused by Chiang Kai-shek's advance into their fiefs. But Chiang forced his hand by temporarily arresting Communists in the Kuomintang and confining his Russian advisers to quarters. Obliged to sanction the Nationalist offensive, Stalin gave it his enthusiastic support once it gained momentum in order to prove that he had been behind it all along. Having flirted with the warlords at the expense of his Kuomintang protégés, he now championed the Kuomintang at the expense of the Communists.

These twists in policy designed to protect the interests of Mother Russia were justified by much plausible dialectical quibbling, for it could be argued that since China was feudal rather than capitalist, a bourgeois-democratic revolution must precede a socialist one, as doctrine laid down. Stalin was therefore putting his money on the Nationalists. But while his policies may have made sense in Moscow, it seemed to many in China that his priorities read from right to left, not left to right, leaving the Communists at the wrong end of the list.

When villagers ill-advisedly began seizing the property of Nationalist families, Stalin ruled that it should be the responsibility of the Kuomintang—not the Communists—to placate the people by meeting their minimal demands for land reform, since only the KMT could cope with China's "ocean of peasants." The Communists were merely to influence them. The implications of this arresting decision were not lost on men like Mao, who compared talking to the bourgeois KMT about land reform to "playing a lute to entertain a cow." The peasant revolution was to be cynically sacrificed on the altar of Russian policy—"socialism in one country" and the needs of "our regime, our state," as Stalin brazenly put it.

Even when Chiang finally ripped aside the veil of Stalin's sick fancies by slaughtering the Communist-led insurrectionists in Shanghai, and taught him an unforgettable lesson in the realities of China, the Russian continued to argue for a further five months in favor of collaboration with the left-wing of the KMT. He was not guided by the state of the game on the ground, but by his blind, egoistic urge to save his floundering prestige in Moscow in the face of opponents like Trotsky, who had angrily dismissed the rump Nationalist government in Wuhan as a "fiction." It was Stalin, therefore, who finally directed the Communists to seize control of it, get rid of its "unreliable generals," and form a new army of workers and peasants to support it.

He was under the absurdly mistaken impression that the left-wing KMT leaders would have no choice but to accept the change, believing them to be at the mercy of the revolutionary militants inside their organization and the revolutionary masses outside it. In reality, they were at the mercy of their own military, the "unreliable generals" who could muster seventy-five thousand trained troops in Wuhan against a rabble of radical amateurs with no more than two thousand rifles among them. He was right in one thing—the left-wing leaders of the Wuhan government had no choice. They closed ranks with the "unreliable generals" and cut their ties with the Communist Party, which quickly lost half of its members.

We have seen what then happened. Still obsessed with the need to prove himself right and in defiance of the grim facts, Stalin ordered the Party to exploit a purely illusory "upsurge" by mounting revolts in major cities—in one case, "even if it were certain to fail"—and so instigated the callous sacrifice of more than six thousand Chinese lives lost during the futile Canton Uprising of December 1927 (for which he afterwards blamed the Chinese). "The result of this lunacy," wrote a bitter Trotsky, "was the further defeat of the workers, the liquidation of the best revolutionaries, the disintegration of the Party, and demoralization in the workers' ranks."

In 1929 Stalin nevertheless decided that another "revolutionary high tide" was imminent, and in 1930 Moscow endorsed plans for more military assaults on cities, with urban workers playing their role as the vanguard of the revolution by simultaneously calling strikes within the walls. That senseless decision led to the foredoomed attacks ordered by Li Lisan that summer which could have cost Mao his footing in Jiangxi. Had the Russians been right about Mao, however, he could hardly have cared less. For with characteristic omniscience the Comintern had already published his obituary.

Mao was very much alive—if elusive. From time immemorial it had been the custom of the craftier mandarins and military governors in the more remote provinces of China to pay loud lip service to imperial edicts while quietly interpreting them to their own advantage, as the pious Scotsmen who so flagrantly promoted the opium trade with the Celestial Empire discovered just 150 years ago. In 1831 the Emperor, isolated in his far-off palace in the north, finally heard rumors of this unsavory traffic, and ordered it be stopped. The Viceroy of Canton promptly issued a public decree instructing Chinese merchants that they must "honestly exert their utmost efforts" to stamp out the commerce, adding the stern warning: "Let there not be the least trifling or carelessness, for if opium be again allowed to enter the interior it will involve them in serious criminality. *Oppose not*." But the Viceroy and the Admiral were elbow-deep in the drug traffic themselves. The Emperor's interdict merely enabled them to squeeze bigger bribes out of the vulnerable merchants, and the normal departure of the foreign opium clippers at the end of the shipping season enabled them to report that the barbarians had been chased off and would not dare to return. The smuggling, needless to say, continued unabated.

The separation of appearance from reality is second nature to the split-level mind of the Chinese, and Mao upheld this tradition in his mist-wreathed mountain retreat by echoing the orthodox cant propounded in far-off Moscow and Shanghai, while twisting his orders to suit himself. He was aided in this by differences that arose between the Comintern and Chinese Party leaders, which found him sometimes closer to one side, sometimes closer to the other, while progressively sifting out his correct course of action by treating both as Confucian "negative examples" that taught what not to do. He was further helped by poor communications between his Border Area and the Central Committee, which often left him obeying directives that had already been countermanded, and meant that any obnoxious instruction might invalidate itself if left for long enough in his nonexistent in-tray. And he doubtless recalled the dictum of Sunzi, the illustrious pre-Christian Chinese strategist: "A general in the field is not bound by the orders from his sovereign."

"Doubtless," because Mao may have seen himself as a righteous outlaw straight out of *Water Margin*, a copy of which he still carried, but he modeled his strategy on the guileful military lore set out in Sunzi's *Art of War*. Men of high morale are the key to victory, the antique Chinese Clausewitz teaches. They must not be squandered in profitless battles. The best general is one who will win a war without loosing an arrow, by undermining the discipline and the will of the enemy, spreading sedition, splitting his forces, sowing distrust between friend and friend, and goading one adversary into fighting another. If you must take the field, says Sunzi, remember that "all war is based on deception." When weak, pretend to be strong; when strong, pretend to be weak and so trick your opponent into making a rash attack. Use roundabout routes to take him unawares; offer him bait and await him in ambush; feign confusion, and then suddenly strike him hard.

Do not stubbornly confront an enemy who holds the high ground, or has the hills behind him, and do not follow if he pretends to flee. Choose your terrain, "fight downhill"—and only when certain of winning. If you outnumber him, hit him, if he outnumbers you, withdraw—"a small force is mere booty for a bigger one." Be flexible and elusive, fast on your feet, quick to jab and quick to duck. Avoid fortified towns and cities, and attack instead whatever is not heavily defended. He will have to disperse his forces to protect all possible targets, and "when he prepares everywhere, he will be weak everywhere." Then, "if I concentrate while he divides, I can use my entire strength to attack only a part of his, at a point of my choosing."

It was a guerrilla's bible, and Mao was quick to copy. "My strategy is one against ten, but my tactic is ten against one," he stressed. His military writings constantly paraphrase Sunzi, especially when he talks of intelligence, deception, flexibility, the dangers of imprudence, the need to win over the civil population, and the elementary mistake of hitting cities first. He already saw himself in a heroic light. When in Shanghai for the inaugural congress of the Party, a slightly inebriated Mao had agreed with a friend that in all Chinese history only two men had risen from nothing to become great—and then banged the table, upsetting the wine, to declaim boastfully: "I, Mao Tsetung, shall be the third." The second had been Sun Yat-sen, but the first had been a certain Liu Bang.

Liu Bang had started life two thousand years earlier as a peasant, a rough-tongued, boozing village headman who concealed a cunning and calculating brain behind much coarse humor. His humility, when humility was demanded, was matched only by his effrontery when effrontery paid, for he had the tongue-in-cheek qualities of the mime and the clown, and could switch on mercy or cruelty, menace or warmth, at will.

One day he was ordered to escort a gang of convicts condemned to forced labor to the work site of the First Emperor's tomb, but so many escaped on the way that he could confidently expect to be beheaded on arrival. He therefore took to the hills with ten of his charges to join the swelling ranks of outlaws in revolt against the Legalist tyranny of Qin. Untrained himself, he had a talent for manipulating men and attracting good soldiers to his side. And he listened to their advice. In consequence, just eight years after the Qin ruler died in 210 B.C., Liu Bang assumed the reign title of Han Gaozi—as the founding emperor of a Chinese dynasty that would endure for more than four hundred years.

The parallel could not now have escaped Mao. He had taken to the hills with a handful of rebels, he had the peasant background and play-actor qualities of the great emperor, and he, too, was to manipulate—yet depend upon—professional soldiers like Zhu De the Cook, "Hades" Peng Dehuai, and an outstanding graduate of Whampoa Military Academy who had assumed the soubriquet of "Tiger Cat"—Lin Biao. Chiang Kai-shek might be uniting China by force of arms, as Qin had done before him, but Mao Tsetung would liberate its people from the abuses of its new and ruthless master.

Jinggangshan was an almost impregnable fortress, a bleak anarchy of towering peaks shrouded in mist, their lower slopes a tangle of pine, bamboo, and creeper, haunted by wolves and bandits. Among these remote passes and palisades, Party orders to "proletarianize" the Communist movement must have made eerie reading. What Mao in fact did was to put *Water Margin* into modern dress and add 600 men and 120 rifles to his force by uniting his shivering, cotton-clad troops with those of two local outlaws. His faith in the human will convinced him that rascals like these—good examples of the *éléments déclassés* he had earlier estimated to number 20 million throughout China—could be molded into serviceable revolutionaries.

He set out to persuade the more distrustful villagers that his was not just another marauding bunch of bullies on its way to another battle, he enforced canons of conduct for the Red Army which were later codified as the "Three Rules of Discipline and Eight Points for Attention." These warned the troops to be courteous to the common people, to pay them for whatever they consumed, to give back anything they borrowed, and not to take from them so much as "a single needle or a piece of thread." The guerrilla army was like a fish, and the people were the water in which it must swim, he was to say ten years later.

To win over the poor peasants and wheedle recruits out of them, he at first ordered "complete confiscation and redistribution" of the land, but after many landlords had died of "direct action," he softened the rough and uncertain justice of his earlier seizures; by the spring of 1928 the Party was taking him to task for a reprehensible rightist tendency to be lenient, for letting rich peasants keep their fields, and for "not doing enough burning and killing."

For Mao was nothing if not inconsistent, and he was quick to learn that parceling out other men's acres among the landless was not always the best way to run a revolution. At times he needed the independent farmer on his side in the struggle to feed his half-starved troops. If he beggared the fellow, moreover, he might not only lose his support, but earn the contagious hostility of poorer peasants he was trying to please, to whom the victim was often a clansman before he was a class enemy.

On their return from their abortive thrust into south Hunan in July 1928, Mao reasserted his political authority over the Border Area, while Zhu De took command of the army. But in December, the Nationalists laid siege to the fortress with no fewer than eighteen regiments and finally knocked them off their perch. During the following year they were able to resettle in a bigger base further south, but they had been able to break clear of the Kuomintang only after a bitter and bloody struggle in which they lost half of their troops, and they were left with no more than three thousand men under arms.

Li Lisan chose this time to write complaining that the increasing power of the peasants in Mao's soviet was a threat to "proletarian hegemony," and condemning his policy of concentrating his forces in secure bases as theologically fallacious. Mao was told to adopt classical Marxist guerrilla tactics by dispersing the remnant of his army across the countryside in small bands of roving insurgents and agitators, whose task would be to inflame the peasant millions so that they would be ready to rise—but only, of course, when the industrial workers gave the signal.

Rejecting Li Lisan's horror of peasant power, an exasperated Mao retorted that the enemy would crush these wandering handfuls of homeless vagabonds piecemeal. For him, guerrillas without a base were like a man without a backside, who could never sit down and must collapse from exhaustion. It was only within a base area securely under their control that the Communists could systematically transform the political landscape—gaining the trust of the peasants with land reform, molding their minds, turning them into revolutionaries, and training them to be soldiers in a Red Army which could then move outwards, "spreading political power in a series of waves." In this way—as Sunzi had implied—the cities would ultimately be encircled by the countryside. Strong points most easily defended by the enemy, they would fall last.

Mao then proceeded to illustrate what he meant by expanding his new base until it covered nearly all of southern Jiangxi and was proclaimed the "Chinese Soviet Republic" with himself as Chairman. The fastidious Li Lisan continued to disagree sharply with his principles, however, and to view with disgust and some alarm a revolutionary movement whose spearhead seemed to be an armed riffraff of peasants and pig soldiers, bandits and beggars, and any other available *éléments déclassés*.

Mao himself later admitted that "there were still many bad tendencies in the Communist ranks"—too many of the troops had exaggerated ideas about democracy, and the "mentality of roving insurgents." At the end of 1929 he had called a conference at Gutian, where he contrived to put a noose around the amorphous army and draw it tight on an ideological slipknot. Amid much plain speaking on evils ranging from sloppy discipline to outright subversion, he emphasized that the cure for these ills lay in "rectification." The wrangling, democratic soldiers' "soviets" would give way to a system of political commissars and Party cells at all levels, and the commissars would share power equally with the military commanders. Political education would be given top priority. Mao's philsophy was taking shape—politics must rule all, for the secret of victory was not in machine guns, but in the minds of men.

Regular soldiers began to dress in a uniform and wear a red star as a cap badge, but there were no ranks, and analytical meetings were called before and after every action at which a unit commander might be criticized by his own troops. Matters improved, and by mid-1930 the Red Army had scored a series of local successes. These, however, only encouraged Li Lisan to order the assaults on major cities, which petered out when Mao persuaded his comrades to defy the Central Committee and call off their second suicidal bid to take Changsha.

To Mao, the issues must have seemed painfully clear. Not only was the Red Army in danger of being summarily butchered in a futile onslaught to conform with irrelevant dogma, but the Jiangxi base itself would again be thrown into hazard. And the Jiangxi base, the biggest of many isolated Red guerrilla strongholds that now mottled the map of China, was already in his eyes the cradle of a nationwide revolution. In a letter to Lin Biao he had quoted the old Chinese saying, "A single spark can start a prairie fire," and added jubilantly: "China is littered with dry faggots that will soon be aflame."

He had earlier allowed his native optimism to rush him into error when he proposed that the Red Army overrun all of Jiangxi and move into the two maritime provinces to the east, "with a time limit of one year for accomplishing this plan." The fact that he disposed of only 2,800 troops at the time did not make him think twice, apparently, and he would only concede later that the operation would take more than a year. But these instinctive flashes of now-is-the-hour impatience were matched by Mao's caution when "now" was obviously not the hour, and while this caution prompted him to defy the order to attack Chang-sha, more often than not it prompted him to comply—or seem to com-ply—with similar unpalatable instructions he received from those above him.

In consequence, academic students of the Chinese scene only add mud to already murky waters when they solemnly quote Mao on the vital role of the urban workers as the vanguard of the revolution, on the importance of the "struggle" in the cities, on the dangers of "sinking into guerrillaism," or on the wisdom of China's "true friend" Stalin. For these prevarications are then cited as proof that he was an orthodox Communist, fundamentally obedient to the message from Moscow, and not a rogue revolutionary with a "line" of his own for the liberation of China based on the peasant, the gun, and the lessons of a long history —suspicious of Russian motives and exasperated by the flatulent theoriz-ing of Marxist intellectuals.

This sophistry ignores the obvious. Like the opium-smuggling vice-roy faced with his emperor's interdict, Mao wanted only the freedom to say one thing, think another, and do a third if local conditions so dictated, and he was ready to endorse a silly theory on paper if he could flout it with sound practice on the ground. There was more to it than that, however. Sunzi had taught him not only how to fight a battle, but how to live a life, and Mao was a model of muscular flexi-bility who led a shifty, guerrilla existence, bending with the wind, backing down before the powerful, striking out against weakness. He ambushed men by leading them on until they betrayed themselves and then destroyed them; he placated the majority in order to concentrate a united front against one small handful of the enemy at a time ("my tactic is ten against one"); and he "dispersed" by dissembling when under fire himself.

Everything depended on timing. Mao the outlaw kowtowed to an order today that Mao the emperor would tear up tomorrow, rewriting history and compounding the contradictions that arise for anyone naive enough to take every word he said at more than face value. The leader who in 1936 spoke of his "complete agreement" with the policy of the Comintern in the twenties would maintain in 1962 that its members had "utterly failed to understand Chinese society, the Chinese nation, or the Chinese revolution." The Chinese judge a hero by his indis-pensable talent for tactical humility, the readiness to take a small loss today to make a great gain tomorrow—exemplified by the sagacious general Han Xin, who obediently groveled when waylaid by a gang of common bullies because he had better men to fight for bigger stakes.

The incident is still quoted as an object lesson more than two thousand years after it took place.

It was characteristic of Mao that he was as elusive in adversity as he was aggressive in success, when he would be carried forward by his own "revolutionary high tide," his belief in the power of the human will to work miracles. And this "guerrillaism" was to mean that once he saw in his mind's eye the socialist utopia of his dreams, he would not head straight for it, but tack towards it, taking a zigzag course that would in time bewilder nearly a billion Chinese.

CHAPTER SIX

Mao's guerrilla intuition, the instinct that tells when to fight and when to flee, was now to be put to the decisive test. By the end of 1930 he was rid of his pen-pushing adversary in Shanghai, for, like others before him, Li Lisan had paid the price of Stalin's delusions and been recalled to Russia in October to be arraigned for his errors. Ironically, these included the two abominable heresies he shared with Mao: his predilection for putting China before Moscow, and his impudent belief that he knew his country better than Stalin did. But Li still lingered in some men's minds, and two months later the Twentieth Red Army in southern Jiangxi rose in revolt against Mao after he had ordered the arrest of local Party leaders who had pushed the "Li Lisan line," branding them agents of a somewhat hypothetical "Anti-Bolshevik League" backed by the Kuomintang.

Mao might have fenced cautiously from a distance with Li Lisan when he was the chosen of the lord in Moscow, but Li was now a discredited scapegoat, it seemed, and Mao was not going to fight these rebel dogs with buttoned foils. He sent Peng Dehuai to suppress the revolt, and this so-called Futian Incident ended in a massacre in which up to three thousand officers and men were tortured and brutally exterminated. Mao had disposed of the enemy within and was now boss of the Party bureau in the Jiangxi Soviet, to which Moscow reluctantly gave its blessing.

If Li Lisan had paid the price of failure, however, Mao was to pay the price of success. While a mess of doctrinaire Party leaders had been wrangling over their own misconceptions in urban Shanghai, the soviets in the mountains had been flowering into pseudo-Marxist ministates that none could ignore. For the political pedant, the entire Communist phenomenon in China was assuming the hideous form of a doomed dinosaur, its peanut of a head and puny forearms in the cities surmounting a monstrous mail-clad body whose powerful hindquarters were activated by their own autonomous brain out in the provinces. To restore anatomical order and orthodoxy to this shambling ideological mutant, therefore, the Comintern sent out a new emissary named Pavel Mif, who had been teaching at the Sun Yat-sen University in Moscow and who brought with him his former Chinese students. There could hardly have been a more dramatic confrontation between practice and theory.

Mao, the battle-hardened peasant from Hunan, was now thirty-seven years old. He could look back on a long, perilous climb to the heights of the Jiangxi Soviet that had been all movement and military action. His flimsy claims to Marxist learning were uneasily founded on a few tormented Communist works teased into Chinese, and he was cutting a formula for a free China out of the hard rock of his experience—not of books, but of the sturdy peasant, the sweating soldier and the smoke of war, of thin cotton jackets and thinner gruel, poverty and danger. His desk was often a plank resting on a couple of stones, and "he had only the simplest belongings," his orderly was to recall—two blankets, one sheet, two uniforms, "a sweater, a patched umbrella, an enamel mug that served as his rice bowl." He was unwashed, earthy, careless of his clothes and coarse in his speech, the man on the ground with the hard-bitten veteran's contempt for the unmuddied and unbloodied, for the smart-aleck staff officers who knew it all from neat, chinagraphed maps of revolutionary doctrine back at headquarters.

Pavel Mif's young gentlemen from Moscow, sarcastically nicknamed the "Twenty-eight Bolsheviks," were nothing if not staff officers. Their two leading lights, Wang Ming and Bo Ku, were both only twenty-four years old, one the son of a wealthy landlord, the other of a magistrate. They had gone to Russia to study while still in their teens and knew nothing of practical politics or the Chinese peasant. But they had received the strictest possible upbringing in Marxist dogma, they had all the answers, and they could quote chapter and verse from the gospel with marvelous fluency.

Now according to holy writ the Communist Party acquired its mandate to rule solely because it was the party of the urban working class, and the urban working class were the leaders of the revolution. The peasants could only be regarded as bourgeois allies, and their movement was not to be fused or confused with the Party. "Only the industrial proletariat can liberate the toiling masses in the countryside," Lenin had laid down. That was the way it had happened in Russia, and so it was historically inevitable that that was the way it was going to happen everywhere else.

With a fine disregard for this doctrinaire rubbish, however, Mao had not only based revolution on the peasant; he had carved out soviets that were directed by a Communist Party and defended by a Red Army packed with these "bourgeois" yokels. The proletariat were nowhere, and this state of affairs appalled the orthodox. Not only was the Central Committee in Shanghai separated from what should be its proletarian base in the Jiangxi soviets, but the proletarian base did not exist—Chou En-lai revealed in 1930 that there were only two thousand workers in the entire Communist Party. And that meant that since a Communist Party's authority must be derived from the urban working class, the Chinese Party had no mandate to lead the revolution. Mao and his wretched peasants had undermined the entire structure.

Ordinary mortals blessed with a little common sense might simply have agreed that circumstances alter cases, but that was too much to ask of the rigid intellectual raised on Marx, and the Comintern now began to go through obscene dialectical contortions to prove that Communist canon could be reconciled with this Chinese anomaly, like a snake squirming around a stick.

As always with left-wing pedagogues, this involved much semantic finagling. Lenin himself had spoken of the peasants as "the rural proletariat," and the expression was used to prove that peasants were "proletariat," pure and simple. The trouble was, the peasant was not proletarian enough—he owned tools, if not land, and therefore could not qualify, for a proletarian by definition owns nothing but the sweat of his brow. It was also argued that the peasants were "proletariat" because they were organized into "labor unions," and in Russia the labor union was an exclusively proletarian organization; or because they participated in "soviets," and in Russia soviets were also exclusively proletarian; and, finally, Leninist logic was upended to prove that the proletariat *was* leading the revolution in China, since the Communist Party was directing it, and the Communist Party was the party of the urban working class. QED.

Innocent of all experience, their hands unroughened by rude practice, their mincing minds full of questionable dialectics and the will of Stalin, the Twenty-eight Bolsheviks took over the Party leadership early in 1931. Wang Ming became Party secretary, and in the autumn the Central Committee, hitherto a nagging, minatory voice heard only from a comfortable distance, decided to uproot itself from Shanghai and move in on Mao. The first to arrive was Chou En-lai, a senior member of the Politburo who could at once upstage him and a close supporter of the Twenty-eight.

On the face of it, that was not surprising. Chou was no peasant like Mao. He came of a genteel, intellectual Confucian family, whose men had been scholars and mandarins for generations. He had been educated at a westernized university, and, after being arrested in 1920 as an agitator in the May 4 Movement, was one of those who took the plunge into "internationalism" from which Mao had flinched—he set off under the work-study program for Paris, where he became a founder-member of the French branch of the Chinese Communist Party. He was a man of social graces, musical, fond of the theater, a fair linguist, even a good dancer. But beneath the smooth, cosmopolitan affability was a born actor, a fixer whose "five smiles"—carefully measured according to the status of the smilee—concealed the flexibility of a steel whip.

He had been behind the uprising of workers in Shanghai in 1927 and had barely escaped with his skin when Chiang Kai-shek's troops hunted down its leaders. But he was an adroit survivor, and although he had been obliged, somewhat humiliatingly, to confess to "rotten cowardly opportunism" in 1930, he had outlasted three successive Party secretaries, perhaps because his instinct told him to keep his head down and let others stretch their necks towards the summit. In due course that instinct was to serve Mao and Chou well. But that was not evident in 1931 when Chou, as director of the Military Affairs Department of the Central Committee, lost no time in joining the "Bolsheviks" in an assault on Mao's revolutionary idiosyncrasies.

Those idiosyncrasies had become more marked since the winter of 1930, for the success of the Jiangxi Soviet had knitted brows not only in Moscow, but Nanking, and Chiang Kai-shek had mounted the first of five "extermination campaigns" to destroy it. The Nationalists threw a hundred thousand troops into this struggle, whereas Zhu De disposed of only forty thousand. But the Cook led the Kuomintang a dance through the mountains, dispersing and then suddenly concentrating his very mobile army, always luring the frustrated enemy on, until he was able to catch five footsore KMT divisions almost literally napping after their exhausting peregrinations, and inflict a stinging defeat that cost them nine thousand men in captured alone. The drive petered out two weeks later.

The Nationalists opened a second campaign with 150,000 troops in May 1931. Again Zhu De enticed the enemy deep into the hills, the

Communist guerrillas melting away before strength and reappearing to strike out against the weaker units of warlords supporting the KMT, and when the enemy retired to draw breath six weeks later, the soviet had not shrunk but expanded, overflowing into Fujian province. Chiang Kai-shek was a plunger, however, and a month later he attacked with three hundred thousand men, this time outnumbering the forces of the peripatetic Zhu De by ten to one. Hard-pressed but using well-tried tactics, the Cook was still able to dodge the main weight of his massive opponent while hitting back viciously at isolated, bite-sized columns, so that when the third extermination campaign faltered in its turn, the Reds found that although they had lost another 10,000 men, they had captured enough arms and ammunition to make up their fighting strength within weeks.

Reprieve had come this time because Chiang was distracted by the ominous depredations of the Japanese in the north, who had seized Mukden and were laying their hands on much of Manchuria. But meanwhile the escalating Nationalist threat had justified Mao's unorthodox guerrilla principles beyond the field of battle. He had conceded that the Party must lead the revolution, but insisted that the struggle for survival on the ground was "exclusively military," that the Party and the masses must be "placed on a war footing." The soviet was a besieged camp. It had to smuggle in uniforms and blankets bought clandestinely from Kuomintang merchants if its defenders were not to freeze. It had to leave the rich peasants their fields so that they would raise all the crops they could plant (instead of burning their stocks and bolting for Nationalist territory) if they were not to starve.

This was too much for the purists, who put ideological righteousness before either guns or butter, and Chou En-lai fired the first round of a creeping barrage against Mao and his policies—his militarism, opportunism, pragmatism, and "general ideological poverty," his guerrilla tactics, his "capitulation" to the rich peasants. In November 1931 Mao was elected Chairman of the newly formed "Central Soviet Government" set up to administer all fifteen of the Red bases in China, but his position was already being undermined, for his opponents dominated the leadership of the Party. In August 1932 he was ejected from the Military Affairs Department, losing much of his control over the Red Army to Chou En-lai, and nine months later Chou edged him out of his key post as its political commissar.

How did that happen? By the winter of 1932 Wang Ming and other senior sophists among the Twenty-eight Bolsheviks had arrived in

Jiangxi prating of yet another "revolutionary upsurge" and of the need to expose Mao's apostasy, put the proletariat in the vanguard, and get back to the business of capturing big cities. They reasoned that the Red Army now disposed of up to two hundred thousand rifles, the time for will-of-the wisp guerrilla tactics and skulking behind one's own lines was over, and the moment for aggressive "positional warfare" had arrived.

Obediently, armies from two neighboring Red bases burst out of their borders and made advances spectacular enough to attract the baleful attention of Chiang Kai-shek and persuade him to pour half a million men into a fourth "extermination campaign." The Reds then found themselves pursued and scattered. When they ran like good guerrillas, they survived, but when they stood their ground and experimented with positional warfare, they were soundly thrashed, and one Red army lost twenty thousand of its eighty thousand men.

The "forward and offensive line" of Chou and the "Bolsheviks" was now the vogue, however. Mao's bag of military tricks belonged to yesterday, his critics sneered. His fluid policy of falling back before strength, of luring the enemy further into Red territory in order to surprise and smash him, simply meant that the enemy thrust his way deep into the soviet base, pillaging and killing and burning and convincing the aggrieved peasantry that the pusillanimous Communists were incapable of defending them. The Kuomintang must be stopped dead at the door.

In the Jiangxi Soviet the new strategy produced a draw at the end of the fourth "extermination campaign," but not before the Nationalists had been given a bloody nose. The one Red general who fought according to Mao's hit-and-run rules was damned as "flightist" and dismissed from his command, and a "political struggle" was then waged in which men who had backed Mao (like a certain Deng Xiaoping) were demoted, and Chou En-lai gained control of the Red Army.

Mao was meanwhile obliged to turn down a chance to collaborate with a Nationalist army which had mutinied against Chiang Kai-shek and set up a rival regime across the border in Fujian province. Mao was sorely tempted, but the "Bolshevik" faction in the Politburo denounced the "People's Revolutionary Government" of the rebels as a "bourgeois democratic" fraud, and the Comintern backed up this sectarian judgment by calling its offer of an alliance "a fresh swindle from the counter-revolutionary camp"—for reasons not far to seek. Stalin still regarded Chiang Kai-shek as the only man who could unite the Chinese against Japan in the higher interests of Soviet Russia, and he deplored all the strife that divided and weakened China. With the "Bolshevik" faction dancing to any tug on the twine from Moscow, the Reds of Jiangxi had the devil's advocate in their midst.

Always the political guerrilla, Mao virtuously echoed the Politburo's harsh denunciation of the Fujian renegades, and condemned those who had been loyal to his own fluid strategy during the fourth extermination campaign, ascribing the "victory" of the Communists to the "forward and offensive" policy of his opponents. But he would tell Edgar Snow three years after these events that their refusal to join hands in a united front with the rebels in Fujian, and the "adoption of the erroneous strategy of simple defence, abandoning our former tactics of maneuver," were fatal mistakes that had cost the Communists the Jiangxi Soviet.

For although the fourth extermination campaign had ended, it merged almost without a break into a fifth. And this time half a million Kuomintang troops began methodically hemming in the Jiangxi Soviet with a ring of blockhouses and concrete machine-gun posts connected by trenches and barbed wire, evacuating whole villages in order to create a dead and dominated no-man's-land through which no food, cloth, arms, or ammunition could pass. Once ready, the Nationalists closed in, slowly drawing the garrote tight on the two hundred thousand men of Zhu De's First Front Army, only half of whom were armed. Soon the Communists found themselves threatened with military and economic strangulation behind a shrinking perimeter within which they could both starve and be slaughtered.

Rejecting Mao's plan for a massive guerrilla diversion against the enemy's rear, the overconfident Central Committee again ordered the army forward to "halt the enemy at the gate" in a head-on confrontation with his tanks and artillery. At first the enemy was halted, but by April 1934 the Nationalists had broken in, and within five months they had overrun all but six of the seventy counties that had once comprised the Red base, leaving their catch no space in which to maneuver. At the end of October Moscow finally sent a radio message, urging the Communists to break out. But by then they had been gone a fortnight. The Long March had begun.

❀ *CHAPTER SEVEN* ❀

Moving only by night, a hundred thousand battle-weary soldiers, armed auxiliaries, Party cadres, women and children had assembled for the grim exodus, and as the First Front Army marched forward, it trailed in the dust behind it long straggling columns of mules and ponies and peasant carts carrying all that could be stripped from the dying Soviet Republic—rice, salt, gold, silver, office files and printing presses, factory lathes and sewing machines, as well as guns and ammunition.

To escape from its contracting prison, this shapeless multitude of shivering humanity and its meandering tail of bric-a-brac now had to break through four belts of blockhouses and barbed wire fast enough to reach the next one from the last before it could be reinforced. Yet, after much feinting and jinking, followed by bloody fighting at the barriers, the hammerhead of Zhu De's desperate army smashed a gap through each in turn, and the horde poured through. For the Reds were concentrated, whereas the Nationalists were dispersed, and "when the enemy prepares everywhere, he will be weak everywhere," Sunzi had written. Mao's ten-against-one tactic had paid off again.

Incessantly bombed and machine-gunned by Kuomintang warplanes by day, the Reds suffered up to thirty thousand casualties and lost much of their baggage train before they finally won clear. Where were they going? Their first object had been to break the Kuomintang grip. After that the general idea seemed to be to join up with the armies of two adjacent soviets which were also fighting their way out of encirclement by the Nationalists. They would then all move north together to take on the Japanese, whose troops had occupied Manchuria and seized Shanghai. But "if you mean, did we have any exact plans," Mao told Snow later, "the answer is we had none." They not only had no plans, they had no maps, and no acknowledged leader.

The intellectual fancies of the "Bolsheviks" and the conniving Chou En-lai had lost the Communists their great bastion in Jiangxi. Yet with Moscow behind them the "Bolsheviks" were still masters of the Politburo, and Chou En-lai was still boss of the entire Red Army. Mao, the man whose cunning and courage had built the bastion, was merely political commissar of the forces on the Long March, and nominal Chairman of a "Central Soviet Government" that governed only where it stopped to sleep.

That bald statement may ignore the mistakes of Mao, the generalship of Zhu De, the legitimate strictures of the Leninists, but the important point is that it was in this light that Mao saw matters. And understandably so. Before the Long March began, he had been progressively humiliated by his pettifogging opponents, dropped from the Politburo, excluded from Party meetings, denounced and dishonored, and finally put under house arrest fifty miles away from the capital of the Jiangxi Soviet at Ruijin. He set out on the Long March feeble and emaciated after a severe bout of malaria. His third wife,* who was pregnant, was dangerously wounded during a dive-bombing attack, her body riddled with splinters. Unable to walk, carried in a cart for the sick or strapped to a mule, she duly gave birth. But as the ordeal continued, she and Mao were forced to abandon their younger children to the care of peasants, and were never able to find them again.

Hotly pursued, the Communists soon discovered that their route to the nearest soviet was blocked by the Nationalists, and when they cut a way through the enemy after five days of costly fighting in which they lost nearly half their men, they found themselves facing yet another, larger Kuomintang army. It was at that dark moment that Mao was able to impose his superior strategic will on the dithering theorists ostensibly leading this forlorn expedition, after insisting that they must change their plan, avoid throwing themselves at an enemy opposing them in strength, and swerve instead through wild, sparsely defended country to the west where he was weaker.

The road to safety led the tattered and famished army along slippery mountain paths and up the faces of sheer cliffs into which steps no more than a foot wide had been hacked. And once these vertiginous obstacles had been traversed, there were foaming rivers to be crossed and more battles against a bigger enemy to be dodged or won by military sleight of hand that was often worthy of *The Three Kingdoms*. Men were not only lost in action; they sickened, starved, drowned, froze, faded away, and fell to their deaths. But the march was plagued

* See pp. 85–86.

by more than broken country, bombing and strafing, and the hovering divisions of the Kuomintang and their warlord allies.

Every tactical move the commanders made had to be sanctioned by bickering pedants in the political leadership who were ready to split ideological hairs even under the menace of a major attack, and whose niggling cost the Communists dear in dead. They were in a fretful frame of mind, for Mao's strategy of avoiding strength and hitting weakness drew the army into remote mountains where the available recruits were "bourgeois" peasants, and seemed to consign to a discarded past the forward policy of "seizing key cities," beloved of the "Bolsheviks." Moreover, as the Reds doggedly marched on from fight to fight, it became increasingly clear that while Chou En-lai and Bo Ku (now Party secretary) might wield authority on paper at the apex of their political card castle of squabbling committees and subcommittees, the real power lay with Mao and the generals who commanded the army on the ground. In the last analysis, it grew "out of the barrel of a gun."

In January 1935 the Communists took by stratagem the old town of Zunyi, some fifty miles from the border of the rich province of Sichuan, which was now threatened by ambulatory armies from three soviet bases abandoned during the fifth extermination campaign, each of which had embarked on its own "Long March." It was at this point that Mao, having moved from weakness to strength, and confident that he would be "fighting downhill," gave up his hit-and-run tactics and struck hard at his political adversaries.

An "enlarged" meeting of the Politburo was convened at his insistance in the narrow, upper room of a verandaed villa and attended after some demur by the Marxists from Moscow. And here Mao forced his opponents to eat crow, to accept fourteen resolutions that damned once and for all the policies of the "Bolsheviks" and their German Comintern adviser (Otto Braun) as "defeatist" and divorced from Chinese reality. The authors of the gross miscalculations that had sent them wandering into West China had also been guilty of "rightist opportunism," and Bo Ku in particular was singled out for a tongue-lashing for his blind obstinacy, for rejecting all criticism, and for abetting Chou En-lai in his "mistaken way of conducting war."

A head-on strategy based on the hollow principle of "not an inch of soviet territory to be lost" might be "politically correct" in theory, Mao said, but in practice the price paid had been the entire Jiangxi Soviet. Their exodus need never have happened. It had been a panicky, disorganized "house removal," and it had saddled them with an unwieldy baggage train of irrelevant civilian impedimenta that must be jettisoned. For the rest, the enemy was still strong, the Reds were still weak, and they must not indulge in "decisive" battles they could not be sure of winning. They must revert to Mao's guerrilla tactics, and must run away when the odds were against them in order to fight another day, for they were in for a "long, protracted war."

Bo Ku was dropped, but Chou En-lai, his nose for timing as keen as that of his future master, saved himself by adroitly switching to Mao's side in a dramatic volte-face, yielding to him his own position as Chairman of the Revolutionary Military Council. The post of Party secretary went to another "Bolshevik," but his power was nominal, for now Mao was also elected Chairman of the Politburo. For the first time the Chinese Communist party had chosen a boss without the blessing of Moscow—and Moscow continued to withhold blessing. The meeting over, Mao walked across to a nearby Catholic church in order to tell assembled senior officers of the First Front Army how things were going to be. From now on, the action would be decided by men of action.

His next move was to try and join forces with one of his most bitter rivals, Zhang Guotao, who had first met Mao when he performed his humble duties as assistant librarian in Peking and had been senior to him in the Party in the early days. Zhang had vehemently opposed the alliance of the Communists with the Nationalists and regarded Mao's enthusiasm for the peasant with suspicion and contempt. "The peasants take no interest in politics," he once wrote, "all they care about is having a true Son of Heaven to rule them and a peaceful, bumper year." He was to say much later of Mao himself, "He is a very practical man, and has never been bound by doctrine, principle, or ideal. Since he was young, he has studied and practised the rule of force, the art of seizing power, scheming and strategy, and he has been determined to achieve his ends by hook or crook."

When Mao was Chairman of the Central Soviet Government and political commissar of the First Front Army in Jiangxi, Zhang was Vice-Chairman and political commissar of the Fourth Front Army in the so-called Oyuwan Soviet to the north. Dislodged from its base during the fourth extermination campaign of the Kuomintang during 1933, the Fourth Front Army had made its way westward and set up a new soviet in Sichuan province, only to be chased out again. It was not until July 1935, after months of sinuous peregrination, that Mao finally met up with it at a place called Maogong.

It was a two-tier encounter, with the soldiers of the two raggle-taggle armies cheering and crying and yelling endless questions at one another simultaneously, while the leaders eyed each other carefully, taking each other's measure. Zhang had at his back some 50,000 rested veterans, Mao disposed of about 45,000 exhausted, lice-ridden troops in torn and patched uniforms, and almost at once the two fell out. Mao wanted them to march north to a Red base in Shaanxi province, from where they could later move against the Japanese. Zhang dismissed this plan out of hand as rash and impractical. Both men were making an unspoken bid for mastery of their combined armies. Mao prevailed, and they began to march north. Each kept command of his own column, however, and after a second acrimonious argument they split up again, Zhang trudging off westward with his troops to establish his own stronghold in the fastnesses of eastern Tibet, while Mao continued on the road to Shaanxi.

Several months later Zhang was finally persuaded to change his mind and make for the Shaanxi base, which Mao had already reached. But Zhang's army was neatly trapped by the Nationalists en route and almost wiped out. When he met Mao for the second time in 1936, therefore, it was Mao who disposed of a rested army, while a crestfallen Zhang arrived with barely 1,500 survivors.

Mao observed the precipitous fall in the fortunes of the Fourth Front Army without sorrow, for it simply meant that his archenemy had lost his rifles as well as his reputation. Now "ten against one," Mao set about annihilating the vulnerable Zhang, brutally stigmatizing him a "flight-ist," an opportunist, and a would-be warlord at a formal trial before the Central Committee of the Party. Zhang was obliged to make a public confession of his faults, and was then degraded and put under surveillance. In 1938 he fled to the Nationalists. He was to die in exile, in Canada.

Ruthless? "Revolution is not a dinner party," Mao had said. His second wife and his younger sister had been cold-bloodedly executed by the Nationalists,† one brother was killed fighting with the Red rearguard left behind in Jiangxi, the other was to be poisoned by a turncoat warlord, and his third wife had nearly died under the Nationalist dive bombers early in the Long March. He had lost his younger children, he had narrowly escaped capture and a bullet himself, and there was a fat price on his head. He had been vociferously censured by ignorant Marxist bigots, blinker-visioned quill pushers, and dialectical dandies from Moscow, dropped three times from the Central Committee of the Party although one of its founder members, and put under house arrest.

† See pp. 85–86.

To win and lose battles is a soldier's lot,
But it takes a brave man to bear insult and disgrace,

he was to write.

Sick at the outset, he had nevertheless made most of the Long March on foot, struggling on through a blood-and-iron nightmare of battles and bombing, sudden death and blinding fatigue, across an endless wilderness of fearsome Chinese geography, wearing his old eight-cornered cap and his fraying greatcoat. And the geography never relented, even if the enemy sometimes did. On the last leg of the trek the Reds had to cross the infamous Grasslands of Qinghai, a vast, dismal swamp some eight thousand feet up, wreathed in swirling mist, treeless and empty of wildlife. The queasy floor of this wasteland was carpeted with noisome black mud that sucked at the feet of the marchers until they broke out in loathsome sores, and invisibly pitted with treacherous quagmires that gulped down the unwary—Chou En-lai's wife sank up to her chest before being rescued. The wretched soldiery of the First Front Army took six days to stagger through this stinking morass, whipped by high winds and almost incessant rain, eating horses, boots, belts, fungus, and even poisonous weeds that made them vomit and sometimes killed them.

At the end of October 1935, some eight thousand of the original ninety thousand troops that had burst through the Kuomintang cordon in Jiangxi one year before arrived at the headquarters of the Red base in the northern province of Shaanxi. They had come six thousand hazardous miles, relentlessly pursued by the Kuomintang, and as remnants from the other southern soviets straggled in, the count showed that the entire Red Army, three hundred thousand strong a year before, numbered no more than thirty thousand men. Mao was by now forty-three, "a thin, stooping, gaunt, Lincolnesque figure," his hair grown long, his eyes large and searching, the skin stretched tight over his cheekbones. No, it had not been a dinner party. Nor was it to become one. But he had created a legend—a legend of indestructibility. And, as we have seen, Mao was a great believer in myths.

The soft, striated hills and cliffs of the loess soil that makes much of Shaanxi a moonscape of yellow dust are pitted with porous caves, and from being a tramp, Mao Tsetung now became a troglodyte. Settled and even secure after years of perilous wandering, he lived for a few months in one of these geological pigeonholes within the walls of an old frontier town, but was later able to move to another on the outskirts of Yanan which had three chambers with white plaster walls and brick floors, a few sticks of shaky furniture, and a small garden where he could grow tomatoes and tobacco.

He was a greedy reader and a glutton for work, forgetful of time—chain-smoking, perusing papers, writing, or talking endlessly to flagging listeners as the candles burned down through the night behind the padded cotton curtain that was the door of his dwelling. "He is plain-speaking and plain-living, and some people might think him rather coarse and vulgar," wrote Snow, a trifle prissily. He was all of that. He wore the shapeless gray cotton tunic and baggy trousers of a private in the Red Army, his possessions would hardly fill a soldier's pack, and if his teeth were black from smoking anything he could lay hands on during the Long March, his tongue was almost as foul. His thick hair was hippie-length, he "slouched when he walked, his shoulders bent, a peasant in his gait."

If he looked a slob, however, he was a smart slob, "seemingly relaxed to a point of carelessness" yet ever alert, who "had a way of gazing sidelong at you" to gauge the effect of what he was saying, and who combined "curious qualities of naivety with the most incisive wit and worldly sophistication." For one observer he might be a peasant, suck noisily at his cigarettes, search himself for lice, and casually take off his trousers when he felt hot. But for another he was a somewhat repellent aesthete with hands "as long and sensitive as a woman's," a high-pitched voice, a "feminine mouth."

He evidently cut no simple figure, but he needed all his peasant shrewdness now, for he was fighting a four-sided battle against the other three corners—the Japanese aggressor, the obsessively anti-Communist Chiang Kai-shek, and the bigoted minions of Stalin. Mao's survival depended on his ability to "conceive the campaign as a whole," which at that moment meant getting his priorities right. The correct course seemed to be to identify the Japanese firmly as the immediate enemy, and to unite against the hated "dwarves from the east" with the Nationalists, who could be knocked out at leisure once the Japanese had been eliminated. This strategy had two obvious advantages. The Communists could win over the masses by adopting a heroic stance against the foreign enemy, and ride to popularity on a rising wave of nationalistic fury. At the same time, it would deflect the firepower of the Kuomintang armies from the Reds to the alien invader, and, in the best traditions of *The Three Kingdoms*, Mao could then "sit on the mountain and watch the tigers fight."

In May 1936, accordingly, Mao sent telegrams to every possible ally, from Muslim minority to secret society, proposing a united front against Japan. He cajoled the triad leaders in the idiom of *Water Margin*, claiming that they had common aims—"You support striking the rich and helping the poor . . . you despise wealth and defend justice, and you gather together all the heroes and brave fellows in the world." At the same time, he called on Chiang Kai-shek to stop lashing out at the Reds and to join forces with them instead. A paper storm of open appeals followed this first gesture, its object to establish Mao as the zealous leader of a national crusade, to show up Chiang Kai-shek for a conniving traitor who preferred to set Chinese to kill Chinese, and to draw all decent men among the Nationalists away from the Generalissimo to defend the fatherland.

Chiang Kai-shek's answer was to order a Manchurian warlord called Zhang Xueliang and known as "The Young Marshal" to cross into Shaanxi and annihilate the garrulous Reds. It was a fateful mistake. The Young Marshal and his men wanted to fight the Japanese invaders of their homeland, not Mao, and were subtly subverted by emissaries from Chou En-lai. Instead of putting a lock on the Reds, they secretly allowed them to expand northward without fighting, cross the Yellow River, and make their headquarters in Yanan for a notional offensive against the Japanese. While Chiang had commanded that the beast be boxed in, the Manchurians had "let the tiger loose." Within a few months, a depleted Communist army that had been confined to four barren counties was in control of twenty-six. Chiang Kai-shek flew to Shaanxi to stop the spreading rot, and somewhat tactlessly announced yet another "extermination campaign," whereupon the exasperated Manchurians abducted him in what was known as the Xian Incident.

Not far from the tumulus that conceals the tomb of the First Emperor are the hot springs of Huaqing, an exquisite tapestry of terraced gardens and willow-fringed lakes and lacquered pavilions where one may soak in the steaming waters and peer into the two Spartan rooms in which Chiang Kai-shek was surprised in December 1936. The Generalissimo managed to flee while his bodyguards shot it out with his kidnappers, but was finally cornered in a nearby cavern, wearing his nightshirt but without his false teeth. His Manchurian captors quickly brought Chou En-lai into the negotiations with their chagrined hostage, and Chiang found himself buying his release—with a pledge to form an anti-Japanese front—from the persuasive Red mandarin whom he had narrowly failed to kill during the "Shanghai massacre" nine years earlier.

Once free, Chiang nevertheless continued to keep two hundred thousand regular troops on the border of the Shaanxi Soviet, even if in theory they were no longer blockading it. But the dialogue had been opened, and the Japanese now set about sustaining it. In July 1937 a minor clash between Chinese and Japanese troops already in North China provided Tokyo with a pretext for moving from nameless outrage to recognizable rape. By the end of the month, the Japanese army had marched into Peking and Tianjin, almost without firing a shot, and within fifteen months were to take all the main cities on the Chinese railway system down to the Yangtse River, including Shanghai, Nanking and Wuhan.

Faced with a full-scale foreign invasion, the Communists and the Kuomintang formally agreed in September 1937 to sink their differences and turn on their common enemy. At this point Mao appeared to make telling concessions to the KMT in the interests of forging a patriotic alliance. Apart from embodying hollow political pledges from both sides which were quickly to prove meaningless, their pact provided that the Shaanxi Soviet would be recognized as a "special region" under the KMT Government, and that the Red Army would be reorganized as the "Eighth Route Army" under the KMT high command.

But there was a catch. Mao refused to allow the Nationalists to plant KMT cadres in his revolutionary army, and kept it under the "absolute leadership" of the Communist Party to prosecute "independently and on our own initiative a guerrilla war in the mountain regions." How then would the distant Military Council of the Kuomintang exercise its authority? A year later Mao told the Central Committee that there were matters that "we should first turn into accomplished facts and only *then* inform the Kuomintang—such as expanding our army until it is more than two hundred thousand strong." And there were other things "which we shall for the moment do without asking for approval, since we do not believe the Kuomintang would consent to them at present."

Ignorance is bliss. The secret of harmonious cooperation within a united front lay in acquainting your partners only with decisions to which they could take no exception. Mao had drawn the deceitful guidelines for a strategy that would enable him to make maximum use of the alliance, yet stay free. He was convinced that the Kuomintang would in time disintegrate, torn apart by corruption and quarrels. He had never intended to feed himself to the brute, but to ride it, and once the ride was over, to consume the remains himself—"for when the fleet deer is caught," as the Chinese say, "the hounds are cooked."

While both were patriots, neither Chiang nor Mao proposed to goad the belligerent Japanese into so mangling his own army that it would later fall easy prey to the other. Each favored a live-and-let-fight policy that would leave his rival to face the enemy. "Trading space for time" and withdrawing before his swift advances, therefore, Chiang Kai-shek was soon holed up in Chungking, far to the west behind the Yangtse Gorges. His troops then held the Japanese to a standoff. To him, they were merely a "skin disease," whereas the Communists were heart trouble.

On his side, Mao refuted Nationalist sneers that he was solely concerned with dodging the enemy by throwing most of his army into the so-called "hundred regiments campaign" in 1940. But that was his only major military adventure against the Japanese, and his strategy was otherwise to ensure that the Red bases seeped across the absorbent map of peasant China like a stain on silk; he had already made it clear in 1937 that "conceiving the campaign as a whole" meant devoting only 10 percent of Communist energies to harassing the invader, 20 percent to "coping" with the Kuomintang, and the other 70 percent "to our own expansion."

He was not going to fritter his forces away. The army would "conserve its strength while destroying the enemy," in anticipation of the coming struggle with the Kuomintang for the mastery of China. Against the Japanese it would engage in a war of maneuver on a "shifting and indefinite" front, the regulars launching limited attacks against weakly defended targets while guerrillas sapped the strength and morale of the overstretched adversary by conducting a hit-and-run campaign in his rear. As existing Red areas crept forward on his front, partisans would establish new ones behind him, and the islands of territory he held would be slowly eaten away by a process of military metastasis.

The Communist armies grew rapidly. Mao was able to put nearly half a million men into the "hundred regiments campaign" and to double the number of his troops again in 1945. Some saw in this more evidence of a heretical tendency to turn the revolution into a "rifle movement," but Mao did not believe there was a purely military solution to anything. The role of the army was to destroy the enemy, but revolutionary war was "politics with bloodshed," guns were a means, not an end—"The Party must command the gun, and the gun must never be allowed to command the Party." "Conceiving the campaign as a whole" meant placing the ultimate stress where it belonged—on mobilizing and molding the peasant millions, the soil from which the soldier himself had sprung, and which he was in turn to liberate so that more peasant millions could be mobilized and molded.

Brazenly ignoring Kuomintang orders, the Communists filtered across the country, trickling into the gaps in the thin tracery of cities and roads and railways dominated by the Japanese to establish new Red bases. As the key to winning the revolutionary war lay in winning over the Chinese people first, regional troops were taught not only to treat the peasantry with respect, but to help them on the farm, educate them in the political facts of life (including the summary execution of traitors), organize them, and arm them. Mao had promised that the Party "desired" to safeguard the rights of all who opposed Japan, "including landlords, capitalists, peasants, workers," and that measures would be taken to "encourage private enterprise and protect private property." Once again he was calling for all hands on deck. The vile could be sorted out from the virtuous later, when the storm was over.

The Nationalists had renewed their blockade of the Shaanxi base in 1939,‡ and Mao was to remember how "we had almost no clothes, no cooking oil, no paper, no vegetables, no shoes for the soldiers or bedding for the civilians in winter." But common hardship and the need for self-reliance drew soldiers and civilians closer, despite the human element—the normal ration of thieves, cheats, and bullies among them—and Mao was not to forget that lesson either.

The base itself had grown to seven times its original size, but as they percolated down through the Japanese defenses, taking the line of least resistance, soldiers and cadres operating outside it were painting much more of North China red. By 1945 it was only one of nineteen bases, within whose borders ninety million people were administered by more than a million Party members and defended by almost a million troops. Mao had won his stake for a final gamble against the Kuomintang—in spite of Stalin and the "Bolsheviks."

‡ The official title was the Shaanxi-Gansu-Ningxia Border Region.

❋ CHAPTER EIGHT ❋

T HE RUSSIANS had stood by idly when the Japanese invaded Manchuria, they had subsequently negotiated the sale of their Chinese railway interests to the puppet government of "Manchukuo," and they had resumed diplomatic relations with the government of Chiang Kai-shek five years after he had massacred the Communists in Shanghai. With the same steadfast concern for Soviet interests that was to lead him into a pact with Nazi Germany in 1939, Stalin continued to insist that the Generalissimo, who had relentlessly pursued the Reds to Shaanxi after mounting five "extermination campaigns" against them, was the only possible leader of China and the one man with whom the Communists must join forces at all costs.

In October 1937, accordingly, a Russian aircraft flew for the first time to Yanan, bearing a few military comforts and one civilian discomfort for Mao in the shape of the senior "Bolshevik," Wang Ming, who had returned to Moscow in 1932. Wang Ming, armed with the seal of Stalin and the authority of a prestigious post in the Comintern, now delivered his edict: Within the united front, the Party should be completely subordinate to the Kuomintang, the army should be integrated into the Nationalist forces under the command of the Generalissimo, and the Communists should form a coalition government with Chiang Kai-shek and submit all their decisions to it for prior approval.

Mao was in what Sunzi called "death ground"—a back-to-the-wall situation into which a canny general might put his own troops, but never the enemy's, since they would then have no choice but to fight to the bitter end. For if the Communists were hog-tied and handed over to the KMT in this fashion, all would be lost. He therefore counterattacked fiercely, accusing Wang Ming of proposing "capitulation" instead of cooperation, and insisting that the Reds should never yield

69

their arms or their liberty of action to bourgeois bosses who might easily "vacillate or turn traitor."

Had Wang Ming won the day, Mao would never have retained for the Communists the key to their ultimate victory—the freedom to pursue "independently and on their own initiative a guerrilla war in the mountain regions" (and tell the Kuomintang only what Mao thought fit for their ears). The Chairman was obliged to make paper concessions to Chiang Kai-shek, but he kept that freedom and he could be satisfied. The Party censured Wang Ming for his "mistakes," and he lost his footing in the leadership. Tongue in cheek, Mao could afford to predict a "glorious future" for the Kuomintang and praise Stalin as a "true friend." Comintern strategy had been finessed. He had got what he wanted.

It had not been easy. Wang Ming had come from his master in Moscow with specific instructions to help Mao—that stumbling semi-literate from the ideological sticks—to construe his Marx correctly. Yet Mao was to emerge victor on the dangerous battlefield of doctrine also, to be confirmed as Chairman and hailed as the supreme architect of the winning philosophy—the "mass line."

The Red Army School in Yanan was a colony of caves carved out of the friable loess in which rough-hewn rocks served as the desks and stools, but it grew into an "Anti-Japanese University" filled with eager, questioning students to whom Mao delivered the lectures that provided the grist for his first published philosophical works. These were to be derided by his supercilious detractors as poor, plagiarized stuff, full of loopholes that showed him to be no abstract thinker. But that was where his strength lay. A man of action and a half-baked Marxist sycophantically lauded by others as a theorist, he was unfettered by scholarly doctrine, and his theories were all about action.

"All genuine knowledge originates in direct experience," said Mao in *On Practice*. Practice alone was the touchstone of truth. "If you want to know the taste of a pear, you must change the pear by eating it yourself." To know war, you must fight a war, he added, coming nearer to the knuckle of his argument. The "most ridiculous person in the world" was the know-all who picked up a smattering of second-hand knowledge and at once set himself up as an authority—Mao was later to compare him with a "blind man groping for fish." And not much better were the "Leftists" who let their fantasies outstrip fact, straining to "realise in the present an ideal that can only be realised in the future." Small wonder that the critics panned him, for he was striking back at the intellectual snobs and smart-aleck Marxists from

Moscow who had so consistently made his life a misery with their visions of a proletarian cloud-cuckoo-land. But in his attack on Wang Ming at a full session of the Central Committee in October 1938 he went further.

The theory of Marxism was international, but its practice must assume national shape, he emphasized. For the Chinese, "any talk about Marxism in isolation from China's characteristics is merely Marxism in the abstract, in a vacuum." The Party faced the urgent problem of sinifying Marxism, giving it a Chinese face that matched Chinese reality. This meant that "foreign stereotypes" must be abolished and "dogmatism must be laid to rest," to be replaced by a "fresh, lively Chinese style and spirit." Marxism had no intrinsic "mythical value," but was simply "extremely useful," as he put it, and diligent analysts would later discover that nearly 50 percent of the quotations in his *Selected Works* were from traditional Chinese writings and only 4 percent from Marx and Engels. But while he saw China's past as a "precious legacy" that could act as a guide to China's present, he was up against a Party wall of incomprehension from those who were "proud, instead of ashamed, of knowing nothing or very little of their own history."

The stiff-necked and the idolaters were going to have to learn or leave, however. In 1942 Mao launched a "rectification" campaign to rid the Party of the sick contagion of "foreign formalism" spread by Wang Ming and the "Bolsheviks." He attacked all that these political poseurs stood for—narrow book learning, vapid jargon, "theory for theory's sake," the servile swallowing of foreign ideas "raw and whole." They were subjected to self-criticism, "struggled against" at mass meetings, and purged.

Mao had already transcribed Marxist revolution into the Chinese mode by basing it on the peasant instead of the urban proletariat, and in 1940 he published *On New Democracy*, in which he applied abstract Marxist theory to concrete Chinese conditions by predicating a long interregnum before a feudal China could go socialist. During this period of "New Democracy," even the big businessmen of the national bourgeoisie would be magnanimously accepted as junior partners in an alliance with the working masses, and private enterprise would flourish as a junior partner of the public sector.

To Stalin, that was rank heresy. Orthodoxy demanded a bourgeois revolution (under the leadership of Chiang Kai-shek) as the forerunner of the socialist revolution, yet Mao was skipping a phase to include the bourgeoisie in the socialist revolution itself. But for Mao this was not a question of theory. His object was to persuade the Chinese that now was the time for all good men to come to the aid of the Party. New Democracy was another page of his blueprint for a specifically Chinese revolution for which Marxism-Leninism was merely the chop of authority, the scripture to be quoted to justify both means and ends.

Mao's entire philosophy was based on the belief that the secret of reshaping society lay in reshaping the individual; that if landlords repented and redeemed themselves by laboring in the fields, even their damning "class status" could eventually be changed. But to become one of the masses, he told intellectuals in 1942, "you must be determined to undergo a long and even painful process of remolding." When he had attended bourgeois schools where no self-respecting student would dream of carrying his own bag, he himself had felt that only intellectuals were clean and manual labor was dirty. But he had come to see that it was the scholars who were dirty, whereas the workers and peasants were "cleaner than both the bourgeois and the petty-bourgeois intellectuals, even though their hands are soiled and their feet smeared with cowdung."

There was nothing abstract about this speech, for he was addressing the famous Yanan Forum on Art and Literature, and to a man who believed in "cultural revolution" as much as he believed in armed insurrection, in the power of the word to recast the minds of the many, his hearers were formidable potential allies. Art and literature, he told them, were political weapons that must serve the revolution by "uniting and educating the people." China's authors must drive home lessons about the glory of labor and the evils of bourgeois indolence and rapacity, and for this they must leave their intellectual aeries and get down among the masses, "go into the heat of the struggle, go to the only source, the broadest and richest source" of raw material. There were too many who still carried "the muck of the exploiting classes in their heads," he concluded.

They did not all like to be told that they should write Socialist kitchen-sink, churn out popular literature in the service of the Party, abandon their standards of style, their freedom of subject, their right to create as their imagination prompted, so that they would "fit into the revolutionary machine as component parts." Once more Mao found himself challenged by the aesthete and abstractionist. But he also had his staunch supporters, and foremost among them was his latest wife, whom he had renamed "River Green"—Jiang Qing.

Jiang Qing had been born in about 1914 to an impecunious Shandong carpenter who beat his wife mercilessly, until one day she fled with her small daughter strapped to her back and went to work as a servant.

Friends and relatives helped the growing girl pay her way through school, and she eventually joined a government-sponsored dance and drama college. By the mid-thirties she was acting in modern plays and mediocre films in Shanghai.

In 1937, after an abandoned marriage to a left-wing critic and a dead-end liaison with a director, the future Dragon Lady of China arrived in Yanan, and it was here that Mao first saw her, ready with a dozen earnest questions, when he lectured to the makeshift Academy of Arts. The large brilliant eyes shone with equivocal fire, and a quick wide smile illumined with a hint of sensuality a face that was provocative rather than merely pretty. They were the features of a second-rate actress afflicted with an inaccessible itch to make the big time, and her small, lithe figure, driven by the dynamo of her ambition, quickly caught the eye of the Chairman. Fifty and rapidly infatuated, Mao packed his third wife off to Moscow for mental treatment, and half-cajoled, half-bludgeoned a reluctant Central Committee into giving him freedom to put his pregnant mistress in her place.

For Jiang Qing, it was a sweet-sour triumph. They married in the face of heavy disapproval from Party veterans and their well-worn wives, who had made the grueling Long March beside their husbands and knew they showed it. She was cold-shouldered, despised as a scheming lightweight out of her league, branded as bogus behind her back, and the strictures passed on her were to persuade Mao to bow to Party prejudice and keep her out of the political limelight for the next twenty years. A vindictive leading lady deprived of her entrance and barracked while still offstage, she soon had a long list of scores to settle, and she would one day be called "the most evil woman in the world." Mao had brought a time bomb into the Party. But it already had a built-in time bomb in the thickening figure of Mao himself.

He was no longer just "comrade," but the "Chairman" whose priceless contribution to posterity had been to wed the "universal truth of Marxism with the specific practice of the Chinese revolution," trimming alien theory to fit the pattern of China's past culture and present needs. He had been called "our brilliant great leader, our teacher and saviour"; by 1944 that unctuous hymn of homage, "The East is Red," was filling the air, and his retouched portraits were everywhere. His published works were being energetically circulated among Party cadres (not without a vigorous push from the Chairman) to be marked, learned, and inwardly digested. These included a panegyric in the form of a Party resolution lavishing praise on his leadership which he had unblushingly composed himself.

"Maotsetungism" had arrived, and Mao was now larger than life. In 1940 Liu Shaoqi—future Vice-Chairman and First Secretary of the Party—declaimed, "Only the Thought of Mao Tsetung can inspire us to go forward from victory to victory." Five years later Liu was holding aloft the same "Thought" as a torch that would inspire not only the Chinese, but those struggling to free themselves from bondage everywhere, "for the emancipation of the peoples of all countries in general, and of the peoples of the East in particular." The Russians were far from happy. First, Mao had told Snow somewhat tartly in 1936, "We are certainly not fighting for an emancipated China in order to turn the country over to Moscow." Then he had torn the emissaries of the Comintern apart for preaching hypothetical poppycock, as a preliminary to sinifying the faith itself. And now, with makeshift Marxism as his message, he was seeking to eclipse Stalin as a universal messiah who would be the true preceptor of do-it-yourself revolution throughout the underdog world.

Much time is wasted in arid argument about his nature by opinionated men whom Mao himself would have ridiculed. Was he a dedicated believer who underneath it all venerated the Moderator in Moscow, however fallible he might be? Or a patriotic maverick who thoroughly distrusted him? In fact, Mao was like an ambitious Puritan who finds that intelligent *interpretation* of the Christian ethic—to be frugal, thrifty, hardworking, continent—is the secret of material success, and then parades his profits as proof of his piety, fervently praising God for the gift of Mammon, until it is hard to separate creed from credit rating. But it was not the original text as quoted by Stalin that ensured the success. It was the "interpretation"—the free translation into Chinese by Mao.

While Stalin may have resented the blasphemous pretensions of Mao, Mao regarded the sins and follies of Stalin with a certain detachment. The Chinese can turn on temperament as if from a tap and manufacture mock melodrama to suit all occasions. But this talent for histrionics (not to say hysteria at times) springs from the need to show the "face" of appropriate emotion where none in reality is felt—to weep noisily at funerals, laugh at the singularly unfunny, pour curses on an enemy from a cornucopia of simulated rage, bubbling with exotic epithets and accusations. They can never be judged by their words, only by their deeds. For behind all the sound and fury is an emotionless, almost clinical recognition that people must pursue their destinies—in Peking Opera, the general with the red face is brave, the mandarin with the white nose is treacherous, and this is preordained by the paint. Men's actions are dictated by their blood, environment and professional instincts. The carriage maker wants his clients rich, the coffin maker wants them dead, said the great Legalist philosopher Han Feizi. Policy is a matter of profit, not passion. Mao would no more expect Stalin to further the interests of China against those of Russia (as he saw them), and therefore to favor the Communist Party against the Kuomintang, than he would expect to "get ivory from a dog's mouth."

For Mao, the dedicated schemer whose first object was to make himself master of a strong and independent China, the diminutive despot sitting at the apex of the Soviet hierarchy and pursuing his policy of "socialism in one country" was in many ways himself in a Russian mirror. Mao would learn all that he could from Stalin (without swallowing it "raw and whole"), praise him, defer to him, and bow to his superior wisdom, while ignoring his advice, outwitting him, and upstaging him by turns. Emotion was irrelevant, as it was irrelevant when Mao liquidated those who stood implacably in the way of revolution. He did not cut them down with hatred in his heart. Their elimination was business, not pleasure; surgery, not savagery. He was, to his credit, a cold-blooded killer.

Stalin remained faithful to his role, Mao to his. Under cover of their anti-Japanese alliance, the Reds and the Kuomintang skirmished with each other in both North and South China, until in January 1941 the Nationalists cast aside all pretense of bonhomie and deceitfully attacked the rearguard of the Communist New Fourth Army, killing or capturing 9,000 men, including the commander and his deputy. But Moscow continued to describe Chiang Kai-shek as the leader of China and "the symbol of Chinese unity." Stalin looked with displeasure on the emergence of an independent Communist movement with ideas of its own. He wanted it tucked firmly under the arm of the Kuomintang. And in this he saw jaundiced eye to jaundiced eye with the Americans.

The united front still existed as a "front," since the Chinese—in their time-honored fashion—were still talking even while they were fighting each other. By 1944, however, they seemed to have reached the breaking point, and Washington decided to step in and try to hold them to their alliance against the common Japanese enemy. The Communists and the Americans had their first serious taste of each other's ways in November, when the U.S. Ambassador to Chungking, General Patrick H. Hurley, flew into Yanan unannounced, wearing a fedora and a fancy bow tie. His meeting with Mao was marked by much metaphorical backslapping, but their blithe assumption that they understood each other (although Mao knew virtually no English, and Hurley could not even pronounce Chinese names properly) quickly led to ludicrous misunderstandings.

With disastrous speed, they worked out a proposal for a coalition government between the Communists and the Kuomintang, Mao signed it, and Hurley witnessed it. But it was rejected by Chiang Kai-shek in Chungking as a device to enable Mao to usurp power from him, whereupon Mao accused Hurley of dishonoring his own signature. Chiang then put forward an equally unacceptable counter-proposal, under which the Communist forces would have been swallowed without trace by the Nationalist army. This was simply ignored. Meanwhile, Mao, perhaps under the bizarre impression that he had opened formal relations with the United States when he sent Roosevelt a congratulatory telegram on his re-election, followed up with a message to Washington suggesting that he pay an immediate visit to the White House for an "exploratory conference." The message was never even acknowledged.

Like Stalin, Roosevelt was putting his money on Chiang, not Mao, and by July the disgruntled Chairman was protesting a trifle inaccurately, "Since I have been able to fight Japan with a few rusty rifles, I can fight the Americans too." Official Communist history was to dismiss Hurley as an "untrustworthy American envoy" who "tore up the agreement bearing his signature," but when the atom bombs dropped on Hiroshima and Nagasaki in August 1945 cut the war off in mid-sentence, the Americans continued their forlorn search for an equation that would reconcile the two sides. Just eighteen days after Japan surrendered, Mao therefore found himself boarding an aircraft for the first time in his life, in order to fly to Chungking for a meeting with Chiang Kai-shek.

Number Thirteen Red Crag Village outside Chungking is a pleasing three-story villa, perched on a stony bluff of clay, in which Chou En-lai lived for much of the time during the war against Japan. It was there that he performed, with a smooth aplomb that concealed the iron hand of the dedicated conspirator, the taxing role of Communist anchorman within the enemy camp, his mandate—and his life—resting on the fiction of a united front as diaphanous as the Emperor's new clothes. The sparsely furnished house, with its polished wooden floors and staircases and whitewashed walls, has the innocent air of an overgrown cottage, but it is equipped with an ingenious priest hole and a secret exit, and the windows with their tranquil view over the valley are heavily barred. Upstairs is another shrine, a simply appointed bedroom with a desk, a bookcase and rattan chairs whose principal embellishments are an antique American wireless set and a faded portrait of the Chairman in a pith helmet. Mao Tsetung slept here.

An elaborate Chinese charade followed Mao's arrival in Chungking. Chiang threw a banquet for him, entertained him for two days at his summer villa, and put a car at his disposal. At the end of five weeks Mao was proposing the toast "Long Live Chairman Chiang" at a lavish Kuomintang reception, and two days later they signed an agreement solemnly pledging themselves to "cooperate in peace to build a new China." Meanwhile KMT cameras and machine guns ringed Number Thirteen, Chou En-lai tasted Mao's drinks in case they were poisoned (or to keep him sober), and the night the agreement was signed, Mao's car was bombed as he sat watching opera with the Generalissimo. The high-flown phraseology of the agreement itself concealed a nonevent, settling nothing and leading nowhere. Chiang had ordered his subordinate generals to mount four major operations against the Reds even as he was haggling with Mao.

General George Marshall, who arrived in November as the special envoy of President Truman to mediate in place of Patrick Hurley, persuaded the two parties to try and work out a second agreement under which they would keep their armies apart—"I can only trust that its pages will not be soiled by a small group of irreconcilables," he wrote, hoping without much hope for a lasting peace. Two months later it was already clear that the two leaders themselves were filibustering, and negotiations staggered on for a few weeks, only to collapse in mid-April when in their turn the Communists mounted an offensive against the KMT in Manchuria. Marshall revived the talks in May, but a truce reached in June fell apart in July, and a cease-fire declared in November disintegrated before the month was out. He left China at the beginning of 1947, and although the Kuomintang and the Communists were to continue to talk while fighting until 1949, the talk was just talk, but the fighting was fighting.

Mao, ignorant of American ignorance, had failed to understand American good intentions, and depicted the "so-called mediation" of Washington's envoys as a "smoke screen for strengthening Chiang Kai-shek and suppressing the democratic forces in China." But he could not be blamed. U.S. Marines were already landing on the northeast coast of China a week before he left Chungking, and the Americans were to compromise their role as peacemakers by transporting half a million Nationalist troops to the north to hold the Communists in check. Trapped in an alien environment and underestimating the Communists, they had not realized that this was to be war to the knife. Mao had.

The armies of both sides had begun dragging their toes across the start line as early as the spring of 1945, cautiously moving into the gaps left by depleted Japanese garrisons as they slowly withdrew, and the Japanese surrender was the signal for a race for strategic assets in ground, guns, men, and material for which the prize was to be all China. By April 1946 the Communists, fighting few formal battles but mounting punishing raids that wrecked KMT communications, were masters of most of Manchuria. Three months later, the preliminary scramble for positions over, Chiang Kai-shek mounted a general counteroffensive and China—free from the depredations of the foreign barbarian for the first time in three centuries—was plunged into a final bloody struggle for domination between Chinese and Chinese.

Mao remained buoyant. The Reds only had "millet plus rifles," but they would prove more than a match for the warplanes and tanks of "U.S. Imperialism and the Chinese reactionaries." He was fifty-three now but looked thirty, a man "with the long streaming blue-black hair, the round silver-rimmed spectacles, the fine cheekbones, the pursed, almost feminine lips, and the air of a college professor," according to his biographer, Robert Payne. His incurable optimism was not immediately justified. After a year of untidy, frustrating battles and grinding sieges, the hard-pressed Communists had been thrown out of much of the territory they had snatched when the war ended. By the autumn of 1947 Mao's bold gamble had failed—and he had been bombed out of Yanan itself.

But as a good Chinese gambler Mao could not have lived with himself had he failed to make the bid. He might have lost a kitty, but he still had his stake—the formidable Communist armies in the field. "If we preserve men instead of territory," he said when a commander objected to leaving Yanan without firing a shot, "we shall ultimately preserve both men and territory. But if we try to preserve territory instead of men, in the end we shall lose both." The PLA—the "People's Liberation Army," as it was now called—must once again conserve its strength, and its orders were to confine itself to limited attacks and harassing wear-and-tear operations that would keep the enemy on the run.

Fortune had turned back the clock in more senses than one, for thirteen years after he had trudged out of his Jiangxi stronghold in 1934, Mao was setting out from Yanan on a second Long March. Once more he was to lose a son who would never be heard of again, to wrangle endlessly with cautious comrades who challenged his elastic guerrilla tactics, to struggle through the mountains strafed by Nationalist planes and relentlessly pursued by Nationalist troops. Within a month the frugal Yanan fare of millet laced with swede and cabbage and shy slivers of meat had shrunk to an unappetizing porridge of "flour and elm seeds." As the Communists moved on, marching by night from camp to camp, fatigue and hunger scored lines in his face while stripping his body of middle-aged spread. At times both Mao and Chou En-lai were too weak to walk and were carried on stretchers, the Chairman's uniform in tatters, the socks of the Chief Political Commissar of the People's Liberation Army showing through the broken soles of his shoes.

But when the Nationalists came uncomfortably close, Mao told his nervous companions not to worry. "Today the world is not theirs; it is ours," he assured them with little apparent justification. He wanted his adversaries on his heels, in fact, for he was once again luring them on. His own tortuous progress and the hit-and-run tactics of "Hades" Peng Dehuai in Shaanxi were opening gambits in a masterly game that would end with Chiang Kai-shek cornered in Taiwan. For while a huge Kuomintang army was successfully drawn into playing tag with its elusive Communist quarry in that inhospitable region, two powerful Red armies moved down behind it to seize the strategic mountain ranges to the southeast. The effect of this ploy was to cut off and neutralize four hundred thousand Nationalist troops milling around Mao to the northwest and simultaneously pose a dire Communist threat to the Central Plain of China.

This Central Plain, which stretches south from the Yellow River to the Yangtse, has been regarded as the key to the military conquest of China since the days of Confucius (as Mao well knew), and it was menaced by three Red armies. Chiang's predictable reflex, therefore, was to divert to its defense reinforcements that would otherwise have gone north to Manchuria, where the mobile tactics of the Communists under Lin Biao had already forced half a million hard-pressed Nationalists to fall back on the towns. But Mao had finessed him. His immediate objective was not the Central Plains. It was Manchuria, where the Reds were now free to tighten their grip on the freezing countryside and then close in on the isolated KMT garrisons, one at a time. The moment for positional warfare had finally arrived, but it would be fought in accordance with Mao's old guerrilla principle of "ten against one."

By November Chiang Kai-shek had lost Manchuria, the Communists had gained a great industrial base on the Russian frontier, and Lin Biao could deploy up to eight hundred thousand men against the KMT to his south. The time had come to overrun the Central Plain, where the PLA had been playing hide-and-seek with the frustrated Nationalists while Manchuria crumbled, and in a brilliant campaign that lasted sixty-five days and cost Chiang Kai-shek another half a million of his best men, two Red armies not only routed the Kuomintang, but broke their heart. The Central Plain had lived up to its reputation. Within four days of this decisive victory, the KMT surrendered Peking, and two hundred thousand more of the enemy fell into Communist hands.

With the north conquered, Mao found himself on the banks of his Chinese Rubicon—the 3,600-mile-long Yangtse that cuts the Middle Kingdom in two from Tibet to the Yellow Sea. When Caesar crossed the little river above Rimini he flouted the laws of Rome, but Mao would be flouting the will of the Kremlin. Stalin had earlier told him categorically that "the uprising in China had no prospects," and when it was dramatically demonstrated to him that the uprising did indeed have prospects, his reaction was to urge Mao to be content with half a loaf and to limit his ambition to forming a "people's republic" north of the Yangtse. He should leave the land to the south of it to the Nationalists and so avoid provoking the warmongering American imperialists.

The Soviet Union had continued to be dependably disloyal. In 1941 Stalin had signed a pact with the victorious Japanese (embracing their foreign minister as a "fellow Asiatic") which recognized the "territorial integrity" of Outer Mongolia and Manchukuo—the two puppet states they had respectively scooped out of a mutilated China. Four years later the Russians, having declared war on their defeated Japanese fellow Asiatics and marched into "Manchukuo," signed a treaty of alliance with Chiang Kai-shek under which they promised to return the pilfered territory only to the Kuomintang government.

The Russians' behavior in Manchuria nevertheless remained equivocal. They forestalled the PLA by occupying the towns themselves. They then dismantled all the industrial equipment and machinery that could be carried away and shipped it back to the Soviet Union in purloined rolling stock, extracting nearly a billion dollars' worth of booty. But although they subsequently handed over some of the denuded cities to the Kuomintang before they withdrew, as they had promised, they turned others over to the PLA—or at least left the KMT and the Communists to fight over them, having first supplied the Reds with arms.

But which Reds? A possible explanation for these dubious maneuvers was that Stalin was planning to set up a puppet state on the Sino-Soviet border under a Chinese more to his liking than Mao. This was a general named Gao Gang, who now emerged as the Communist boss of Manchuria, and who was soon to head a delegation from the "Manchurian People's Democratic Government" to Moscow to sign a separate trade agreement with the Soviet Union.

By that time, however, Mao had already ignored Stalin's advice and crossed his Rubicon. In April 1949 the 2nd and 3rd Field Armies of the PLA forced their way over the Yangtse along a three-hundred-mile front and quickly took Chiang Kai-shek's latest capital at Nanking. While the British, American, and other diplomatic missions remained in the city to await the Communists, the Soviet Embassy decamped with the fleeing Kuomintang. But the Red armies swept south so fast that by October they had taken the southern port of Canton and flung the KMT off the mainland and onto Taiwan, a hundred miles across the water. China had been "liberated," and Stalin was obliged to concede victory.

On 1 October 1949 Mao Tsetung stood on the high rostrum of the Tiananmen, the Gate of Heavenly Peace in Peking, and proclaimed the People's Republic of China to the world as the packed square below roared out its paeans of praise. It was a moment of unearthly, intoxicating triumph for Mao the patriot and soldier, the poet and romantic. Like Liu Bang, the village headman with the "air of a dragon" who had founded the glorious Han dynasty more than two thousand years before him, he had taken to the rain-soaked hills with a handful of wretched fugitives, and from this threadbare beginning had woven for himself a legendary destiny that had made him master of an immense empire, the biggest nation on earth. And he had achieved this in the face of all the hazards that man and nature and the yo-yo of fate could devise, earning the ecstatic eulogies of all as a "genius such as never before appeared in Chinese history, most perfect representative of the Chinese, and leader of the people of the world." The bandit had become king. In a poem that contemptuously disparages the lords of the past from the First Emperor to Genghis Khan, Mao himself had concluded:

> All have gone.
> When counting great men,
> Look only at today.

"The Chinese people have stood up," he now declared proudly. It naturally did not occur to him that possibly the best thing for the Chinese people would be if at that precise moment he himself stood down.

THE EMPEROR

"I won the Empire on horseback!" said the Emperor.
"Why should I bother with the Classics?"

"You may have won it on horseback," replied the scholar Lu,
"but can you rule it on horseback?"

(RECORDS OF THE GRAND HISTORIAN

ON THE EMPEROR HAN GAOZI, 202–195 B.C.)

❀ CHAPTER NINE ❀

MEN REACT differently to power and glory. The megalomaniac First Emperor built himself a maze of 270 palaces and pavilions, and the filthy beggar who freed China from the Mongol Khans to become the first emperor of the Ming Dynasty tyrannized a court of ruinous magnificence. But when Liu Bang was transformed into the emperor Han Gaozi, he cursed his architects for running up something far too fancy for his rude village tastes while the country lay in ruins, for he knew the value of the common touch. So did Mao. Last of a long line of distinguished conquerors, he moved into a villa of faded elegance in the ornamental park of the Forbidden City in Peking that had served as the ruler's private library, but this "Study of Chrysanthemum Fragrance" was little more than a lodge in the grounds of the stupendous imperial palace and, like it, in poor repair.

Here, it is said, he lived as simply as before, rising late after working through the night until dawn, lighting one cigarette from the stub of another, padding about his study in black cotton shoes, wolfing whatever plain fare was put before him or forgetting to eat entirely. For the millions he was the same scruffy, unsanitized Mao, a warm, burly figure with the accent of a Hunanese peasant, his mouth as full of homely advice and even homelier scatalogical obscenities as a tailor's with pins— human, sentimental, his eyes moistening "when speaking of dead comrades, or recalling incidents in his youth," or at the mention of his martyred first love, Yang Kaihui, more than twenty years after she died.

But at once the crystal begins to cloud. Chinese weep easily when the script demands, so that it is difficult to distinguish sincerity from stage directions—even for the actor. At the age of thirteen Mao had primly rejected the nineteen-year-old girl his father had foisted on him as his first wife, but more than sorrow could moisten his eye. Much has been made of his devotion to his second wife, but after he had sent her to live in Changsha with their children, he took as his lover on Jinggang-shan a petite eighteen-year-old revolutionary named He Zizhen, and the public beheading of Yang Kaihui in 1930 was later laid at his door by those who claimed that his shameful neglect had left her a hostage in the hands of the enemy.

He Zizhen became his third wife and bore him five children, including those who were abandoned during the Long March and never seen again—"counterrevolutionaries," he called them facetiously, because they got in the way. But once they were settled in the honeycombed hillsides of Yanan, his eyes and feet began to roam again. When Jiang Qing appeared, Mao announced that he was going to part with the sick companion who had shared with him the hazards and hardships of the Long March, dismissed the objections of Party dogmatists as "feudalistic," and took the new favorite into his cave.

This ruthless desertion of a loyal wife for a well-turned newcomer, who becomes another loyal wife to be deserted for another well-turned newcomer—so sordid in others, so romantic in ourselves—may have the usual sordid, romantic explanation. But his women and children—left behind and lost, missing, killed in action—like his crumpled clothes and casual habits, belong to the careless side of Mao, victims of a half-felt, half-feigned indifference. He was a dreamer who modeled himself on the Chinese hero—rough and ready of tongue and manner, a wily fighter and a valiant poet, the verse he dashed off in his spiky lopsided hand overblown with hyperbole. And the Chinese hero must be allowed to take love lightly, for if it looms too large in life, he loses his martial luster. For Liu Bei, the paladin in *The Three Kingdoms* so admired by Mao, destiny demanded that he leave his wives and baby son behind when fleeing from the enemy, so that he could escape more easily to rally his forces. They, too, were "counterrevolutionary" encumbrances in that moment of peril. When one of his commanders then risked his life to rescue the child, Liu Bei impatiently threw the brat aside, exclaiming, "To preserve that suckling I nearly lost a great general." He was not being a heartless father; he was simply playing his appointed role and preserving his image.

Visitors to Yanan found Mao benign, calm, kind, sincere, aloof, inscrutable, sly, sinister by turns. Some saw in him the bucolic first emperor of the Han Dynasty, who returned to his home village to dance happily and a trifle unsteadily among the farmers, but for others he seemed to be following the chilling Legalist counsel on the "way of the ruler" that had inspired the first Qin emperor: to be enigmatic, removed, unfathomable, unpredictable, withdrawn—lonely. Agnes Smedley of the *Manchester Guardian* wrote of a "tall, forbidding figure" who was respected rather than loved and whose "spirit dwelt within itself, isolating him." She had put her finger on the right key.

Mao saw himself as a man of destiny, and he was isolated by a single-mindedness that could be served by a multiplicity of moods. The single-mindedness itself was characteristic of the Chinese, who concentrates on one thing, one ambition, one enemy at a time. Mao concentrated on becoming the savior—and master—of China. Behind all the bravado in his uneven verse there was an unwavering vision, and since all who did not share it were by definition myopic—doomed tomorrow however dangerous today—his policy was to "despise the enemy's strategy, while respecting his tactics." His steadfastness of purpose gave him the power to analyze clearly, endowed his oratory with disarming if spurious candor and lucidity, and enabled him to react quickly, decisively, and courageously, whether he was funking a frontal attack on a town or cold-bloodedly ordering the execution of "counterrevolutionary" comrades.

For the vision called for action, and Mao was not just a dreamer, but a more formidable animal—the dreamer-schemer who is contemptuous of both the weightless theories of the academic and the soulless devices of the pragmatist. A man must first gain experience from his senses, build a theory on that experience, and then test the theory by putting it into practice, he said. If he felt rain wet on his hands, he implied, he might reason that it would quench his thirst, but he must prove it by drinking it. There must be none of the guesswork for which the Chinese had a weakness—the wisdom of the Taoist alchemists who conjured up such scientific gems as the belief that starlings turned into mussels in winter. Life was real, and he had no time for "bourgeois" abstracts like love, freedom, truth. Communism was not love. It was "a hammer for destroying the enemy."

Mao not only modified Marxism-Leninism to meet Chinese specifications in order to foment a peasant revolution, but he took whatever he could use from the traditional Chinese philosophies Communism was to eclipse, and from Western societies that he might otherwise disparage as bourgeois and barbarian. The Chinese must sift the good from both foreign cultures and Chinese history, he insisted, from those distant in space and distant in time. He had "hated Confucius from the age of eight," but if he sinified Marxism by passing it through a yellow filter, he Marxified Confucianism by passing it through a red filter, extracting from the Sage whom he otherwise condemned quotations with which he would refute fellow Marxists as he had refuted his father when it suited him. The result of all this magpie Maoism was not another impractical blueprint for socialism, but a model of cultural cannibalization that worked.

The cannibalization involved more than Communism and Confucius. Mao believed that hardship tempered the will, and physical adversity yielded spiritual riches. Confucius had compiled the *Spring and Autumn Annals* while "in dire straits," and other great Chinese of the past had produced their best ideas and finest work when jailed, exiled, blinded, or mutilated—"sages who were experiencing anger and frustration." But the human will was not an iron pick, nor was destiny inanimate rock. Man could not simply hack his future out of the future with it. For the world was made up of "contradictions," of an unending struggle between opposites which ensured that nothing stayed put. Without constant transformation, life itself would never have evolved, and perennial unity would be a "pool of stagnant water." The momentum of the universe depended on the interaction of complementary yet conflicting forces like light and darkness that inexorably turned old harmony into new discord, and from old discord produced a new harmony. Mao was Marxifying Taoism this time, his cosmos of contradiction and struggle matching Taoist belief in a universe undergoing unending change through the interplay of yin and yang.

Do not strive against a formless fate, said the Taoists, but move with it. Mao was not a man to bludgeon his way towards his objective in the spirit of Balaclava, for destiny itself was to be "despised strategically but respected tactically." "Straw sandals have no pattern," he once remarked, "they shape themselves in the making." He was accused of being a cautious slyboots and a devious opportunist who cynically made use of others. And so he was. To beguile bourgeois allies or the Kuomintang or Stalin, Mao would quote fulsomely from Confucius, call himself the "younger brother" of Chang Kai-shek, welcome a contentious Wang Ming from Moscow as "heaven-sent"—and give them all the scaly side of his tongue the next day. Lin Biao was later reported to have written of Mao, "Today he uses sweet words and honeyed talk to those whom he entices, and tomorrow he puts them to death for fabricated crimes." Mao welcomed this encomium as a testimonial to his revolutionary spirit and had the document circulated within the Party.

He agreed with Machiavelli that if a man assumed the mantle of a responsible leader, he must "not flinch from vices which are necessary for safeguarding the state," as the Florentine put it. Was there need to inflame the hesitant peasants against the landlord class in liberated areas, once the Reds were winning? Then the mob must see blood. The pack was accordingly let loose on the fattened fox, and Mao noted with satisfaction after its violent dismemberment that the "political consciousness" of the masses had been raised considerably "through the struggle to settle accounts" with the rich and the rotten. But it was purely a matter of expediency. He did not have Stalin's cultivated taste for towers of skulls. "It isn't good to kill people," he said. "We should arrest and execute as few as possible." If you frightened them too much, they would conspire against you, instead of speaking openly and revealing the heresy in their hearts.

Mao's dedicated perfidy raised no eyebrows in China, for it was born of Chinese instincts that spring from the deep soil of the Chinese past—patience, caution, fortitude, a single-minded determination to survive and succeed. If history makes man, man makes history; the "contradiction" that gives the Chinese story its repetitive yin-yang pattern of prudent acquiescence punctuated by sudden revolt is mirrored in the workaday behavior of many Chinese. And although he once described Taoism as "twaddle," Mao was one of them.

When the Taoist sages urge man not to strive against nature, they are not telling him to be idle, but to so time his acts that they flow with the cosmos, as the surfer catches and rides the wave. Masterly inactivity is balanced by masterly action, the effortless move—synchronized with the rhythm of all things—that meets the minimum resistance. It is seen in the deft sweep of the brush on treacherously porous silk that marks the gifted Chinese painter, and in the yielding pivot of the black belt who uses his opponent's own momentum to bring him down. The keys to this "nonaction" are timing and total self-confidence, and Mao was made in the tradition of the Chinese bravo who will dismiss obstacles with a boastful metaphor and gamble all on the turn of a card, once intuition tells him that the psychological moment has arrived when the spontaneous stroke will beat the system.

When does it arrive? Taoism teaches that everything becomes its opposite when it reaches its peak—the darkest hour is before the dawn—and so "haste is transformed into deliberation, and deliberation into haste," as Mao himself added. Did Brutus say there is a tide in the affairs of men, which, taken at the flood, leads on to fortune? For Mao, the prophet of the "revolutionary high tide," Shakespeare never penned a truer word.

At that almost mystical moment, boldness is all and indecision fatal. In 1927 Mao threw himself into the "Autumn Harvest Uprising," convinced that the banks of peasant patience were ready to burst and "raging torrents" of popular fury would roar irresistibly across Hunan, tumbling the wreckage of feudal society before them. And after conserving his army and carefully placating the rich during three years of civil war, he ordered the Reds in 1948 to cast aside all "fear of U.S. imperialism, fear of carrying the battle into the Kuomintang areas, fear of distributing the land of the landlords, and fear of confiscating the capital of bureaucrats." The time had come for yin to give way to yang. And he was right—as he was right to overrun all China while the going was good, ignoring Stalin's specious advice to stop at the Yangtse. Revolution and war had their own wavelike rhythm, Mao believed, and this reinforced his faith in flexible guerrilla principles.

Like the rifled barrel of the gun from which political power grew, his tactics were therefore as tortuous as his strategy was straight. But what had been the alternative during these formative years? He could have bowed to the "Bolsheviks" with their diplomas in dialectics from Moscow, their barren theories spinning in a vacuum of inexperience, their lofty assumption that they had a god-given mandate to use half a billion Chinese as laboratory rats for lethal experiments in applied dogma. No one hearing the doctrinaire cant uttered in institutions of higher learning by callow armchair radicals in the West could fail to sympathize with Mao when he rejected their theses. Their empty pretensions were, as always, an intolerable affront to the intelligence.

Had he listened to them he would have had to accept a suicidal strategy based on going baldheaded for cities full of mythical revolutionary proletarians, as advocated by Stalin—Stalin, who was quite ready to see Chinese Reds massacred if it furthered Muscovite diplomacy, and who, "when our revolution succeeded, said it was a fake," as Mao was to tell the Central Committee one day.

Stalinist orthodoxy ignored the sheer lack of means of the Communists in China, a lack of means that was to be the core of Mao's own philosophy. Their poverty in weapons with which to fight fixed battles for towns was complemented by their poverty in urban workers ready to rise and join them. Making a virtue out of a necessity, therefore, Mao converted this hole in Russian reasoning into the hub on which to turn a peculiarly Chinese revolution, whose precepts—or prejudices—radiated from the center like the spokes of a wheel. From it he derived the principles of peasant revolution, his insistence on the vital importance of self-reliance, the doctrine that dedicated man in the mass was more than a match for modern weapons and even the megaton (the atom was a "paper tiger"), the conviction that a revolutionary army operating with the support of a trained militia and a mighty "sea" of loyal

Chinese was invincible, since in war "people, not things, are decisive."

Lack of means also dictated a long drawn-out strategy, a protracted struggle in which the weak became strong by capturing weapons and men and converting them to their own use, absorbing lesser adversaries and setting them against the main opponent—"capitalize on contradictions to win over the majority, and crush your enemies separately," he urged. And he practiced what he preached. He beggared the landlords while "protecting" the rich peasant, attacked the big monopolists while "protecting" lesser merchants, and promised even the national bourgeoisie an honorable if ephemeral role in his "New Democracy." He joined forces with the Kuomintang against the Japanese, and when the Japanese were knocked out, turned on the Kuomintang and knocked them out too, and by these devices took the rungs of the ladder, one by one, to the top.

But the success of his manipulations depended on a climate of danger and discord. "The soaring dragon rides the winds and mounts the mists," says a famous ancient commentary, "but if the clouds scatter and the mists dissolve, he will lose the power on which he ascended." The hero must catch the turbulent updraft if he is to "trail in the vault of Heaven," for it is war that gives the warrior his chance, not peace. The Japanese invasion had distracted Chiang Kai-shek from his chosen task of pounding his fellow Chinese to dust, while enabling Mao to rally the people to his side by riding the wind of anti-Japanese hatred that blew across the land.

In tranquil times men and loyalties went soft, and the thin shell of solidarity could crack under the slightest pressure. It was struggle and suffering that had prompted the Reds and the masses to close ranks, and bound impossible allies together in a common cause. Communism had come out of chaos, order out of disorder, in accordance with the theory of contradictions, the law of the unity of opposites, and the "twaddle" about yin and yang. "The revolutionary situation is excellent" was the catch phrase Mao used to describe the satisfying prevalence of strife, schism, violence, riot, and uproar throughout the world at any given moment—the "great disorder under heaven" of the ancients.

These, then, were the ingredients of blood and background, books read and lessons learned from brutal experience that made up the sum of Mao Tsetung as he stood on the Gate of Heavenly Peace on that famous day in October 1949. The very name of the monument might seem auspicious, for beyond the delirious sea of Chinese below lay a vast, incoherent China ravaged by half a century of conflict. But there was cruel irony here. If the splendid and unique gate was dedicated to the ideal of a timeless peace in which the shattered state could be restored, the splendid and unique liberator atop it was dedicated to unending revolution, contradiction, and struggle. Only through these could he realize his dream of an egalitarian utopia in a world in which unity must lead to disunity, balance to imbalance, "sudden change" was "absolute and permanent," and timeless peace would be no more than "a pool of stagnant water." The day had arrived when China needed mandarins—and it was stuck with a messiah.

❀ *CHAPTER TEN* ❀

I N 1945 Britons over twenty-one exercised their peculiar democratic rights by pulling the power from under Winston Churchill, the one man to whom so many owed so much, on the principle that the rigors of the immediate past and the rewards of the immediate future called for different qualities of leadership. But the Chinese (who regarded the British election results as beyond belief) had no such option, and, like an old soldier who sees in the disciplines of military life the cure for the messy civilian aftermath, Mao Tsetung now set about applying the rules of the "people's war" to the people's peace. War is always simpler than peace, however. Men whose "revolutionary consciousness" had been easily aroused to fight Japanese and flog landlords did not share Mao's vision when it came to building socialism. They were (as he was to say) "poor and blank," like a virgin sheet of paper on which beautiful things could be written or drawn, and so to "enable the masses to know their own interests," they would have to be told what they wanted.

Mao was following in the footsteps of Confucius, who had inspired a social system ordered by moral education rather than a legal code, a system that had known no lawyers or politicians or loyal opposition, but only a ruler and his mandarins and the illiterate "poor and blank" millions. Law was only for criminals and traitors (anyone who argued back). Confucius had given the Chinese morality; Mao would give them ideology. They would be programmed until his signals evoked the right revolutionary reflexes. His purpose was to destroy the old society and put his dream in its place, and the key to success lay in transforming their thinking until they had a single socialist mind.

This would not be achieved by browbeating ("in the end the strictness of my father defeated him—I learned to hate him"), but through the "mass line," whose operating principle was "democratic centralism." "Centralism" meant that Peking would lay down a policy on paper, and "democratic" meant that the Chinese millions would be instructed in it and their reactions on the ground reported back to the capital. Peking would then "summarize experience" from all over the country, and from that synthesize a final program that was now, in theory, the incontrovertible "will of the people." Lenin had worked this shuttle between the higher and lower echelons of the Party; Mao extended it to the masses. However, the purpose was not to consult the wishes of the people in order to grant the people their wishes, but in order to impose on them the wishes of Mao with the least possible friction, in the best tradition of the well-timed master stroke that meets no resistance because it goes with the grain.

The machine that transmitted the political "line" and registered the feedback was the Party. Communism had replaced Confucianism as the single sacred doctrine of the state, the Party cadres had replaced the mandarins, and Mao the emperor. A new monolith had supplanted the old, but the shape of the step pyramid was familiar, and at its apex was the figure of the teacher-ruler, the philosopher-king to whom the Chinese had given their loyalty and looked for instruction for two thousand years.

That did not mean that harmony reigned, however, for Mao believed in equality for "people," not the equality of man. Only the working poor were "people." The rest were nonpersons, and to give them the same rights would be to renounce the motive force of the revolution itself—class struggle. Any tactical alliance with rich peasants and the bourgeoisie was like the tactical alliance Mao had made with the villainous pair of bandits on Jinggangshan—not wedded bliss, but a honeymoon of convenience. Even when the last landlord and the last capitalist had been eliminated, said Mao, there would be further contradictions in society, for killing a bourgeois did not kill bourgeois thought.

Class war would therefore go on forever. If it ceased, and "landlords, rich peasants, counterrevolutionaries, bad elements, and ogres of all kinds were allowed to crawl out," it would not be long before "a counterrevolution on a national scale inevitably occurred," and the Party became "revisionist or fascist." There could be no lasting unity, for "one must always split into two" as new contradictions arose. But this was a cleansing process, a progressive shedding of the old and rotten, a continual refining of the strain. It called for frank confrontation and open conflict where ideas clashed—"Even violent struggle is good," Mao was to say twenty years later, "for once contradictions are exposed, they are easily resolved." He had a healthy fear of the hidden canker, and in the back of his mind was the memory of those long centuries of pent-up resentment that had always ended in a murderous explosion of mass fury. The people must be coaxed into airing their views and arguing the toss, for in that way dangerous dissent would be dissipated and the compression lost through leakage.

Criticism and self-criticism revealed men's mistaken reasoning, and in open dialectical debate they could be shown the error of their ways (since it was axiomatic that the Chairman's Thought must win any argument, there was no question of changing Mao's mind, but merely of "educating" theirs). Only a "handful" of unregenerate blasphemers—always estimated at 5 percent of the population—need be struck down. For all others the principle to be observed was that of "treating the illness to save the patient." The contrite could be absolved of their sins and welcomed into the fold. Nonpersons could become "people," as a heathen could become a Christian, an infidel a Muslim, or an "outer barbarian" a civilized Confucian—by conversion. And the conversion could be conferred from on high, or come from within. A bourgeois or a rich peasant became "people" when Mao needed him, or when he shed his "class nature" by repenting of his faults and redeeming himself through honest toil.

All this leniency was designed to ensure that at any given moment the largest possible number of Chinese would be behind Mao. However, the logic that evoked clemency also evoked callousness. Mao's single-minded devotion to revolution might persuade him to rally enemies to his flag, but it also persuaded him to destroy friends. For he saw men not as men, but as walking ideas, right and wrong, to be broken or restored to favor dispassionately according to whether their thoughts conflicted or blended with his own. He was like a gardener in a Taoist cosmos of interminable change—weeding, pollarding, trimming, and training, since no condition or shape was ever final. As "one class is uprooted, another emerges," he said. Socialism would give way to Communism, Communism would go through "many revolutions," and then it, too, would give way to something else. The struggle against capitalism alone might last for "several centuries."

It is odd that Mao should have talked of a time span at all, for revolving history seemed to warn China's would-be saviors that she was trapped in a never-ending contradiction between dream and decadence. As we have seen, a visionary hero might lead a rebellion against a dynasty long gone rotten in the hands of a venal, self-perpetuating bureaucracy, and found a line of his own. But with the advent of peace, power would once again devolve upon the professional administrators, scholarly mandarins raised on Confucian doctrine and reeking of "book perfume" who would become the new entrenched Establishment. And since time corrupts all things, this bureaucracy would degenerate in its turn, clinging to position and privilege and resisting change until the dynasty was violently demolished and the cycle began again.

Mao the Chinese even more than Mao the Marxist-Leninist felt the hazards of history in his bones. The Party cadres would be the mandarins now. They, too, could freeze into a rigid elite, a new "ruling class" seduced by the "sugar-coated bullets" of bourgeois life, lording it over the masses and thus losing touch with them. Mao's answer to this danger was to keep the revolution moving toward the ultimate socialist utopia with an endless series of violent jolts, never allowing the masses and the cadres to regain their balance for more than the brief breathing space needed to consolidate the last advance before provoking the next upheaval (the idea of "complete consolidation" made Mao "feel uncomfortable.") China was to be subjected to "perpetual revolution," and equilibrium would never be more than a hiatus between two disequilibriums.

Faithful to the guerrilla principle that had worked before and must work again, Mao would bypass the Party in order to keep in direct touch with the spring of power and the source of his mandate, putting his message over to the millions through a string of popular slogans and mass campaigns designed to purge the Chinese people of old customs and bourgeois habits, to persuade them to love the army, or hate America, or reform their thoughts, confess their sins, pool their farm tools, or kill flies. They were to be subjected to an unending process of kneading and shaping and "rectification" under a new system of "education"—whose immediate basic requirement was a new system of education.

Some students of Mao have protested that he was essentially modest because he shrugged off the extravagant titles that were heaped upon him, saying that he wanted to be known only as a teacher. But that is an absurd misreading of the man. The Chinese venerate two archetypes, the teacher and the emperor, and to be philosopher-king was to have the best of both worlds—what was a "Great Helmsman" beside that? Mao was a dominie by training and didactic by instinct, and he now had the biggest captive audience in the world. But it was a mixed audience. The overwhelming majority of the peasants and the proletariat were wonderfully ignorant, even illiterate, an instrument waiting to be played. The intellectual, however, was the "stinking ninth" —the lowest of the low. He was an intractable, distrustful creature, his heart hardened by bourgeois books, and his head so filled with conceits that there was often no place to put the truth; a pretentious snob who despised the unwashed and disdained the unqualified, clutching to himself the fetishes of his academic learning.

Mao distrusted that learning. "We shouldn't study too many books," he said. "Not even books on Marxism. A dozen should be enough. If we read too many, we will become doctrinaire or revisionist." In all history, Mao claimed, no scholar had been outstanding, the best poets had not taken the imperial examinations, the best emperors had been semiliterate. New schools of thought were always started by young people whose minds were not blocked by the accumulated silt of scholarship. "Confucius started at the age of twenty-three, and how much learning did Jesus have? Sakyamuni founded Buddhism at the age of nineteen." The same was true of Sun Yat-sen, Karl Marx, Maksim Gorki, Benjamin Franklin.

But China still needed her intellectuals, and the root of the matter, therefore, was that education itself must be revolutionized. The Chinese had suffered long enough under a stultifying system whereby students chanted meaningless lessons by rote and were judged solely by their ability to write classical essays and pass examinations, a system dominated by arrogant teachers of dead dogma who could not even recognize the "five grains" on which all China fed. The classrooms were filled with the sons of landlords, moreover, while the poor were left to their illiteracy.

Mao wanted "proletarianized" schools whose pupils would be drawn from the families of peasants and workers, and whose object would be to train not rulers but "revolutionary successors." All study would be geared to practical work in the world outside the classroom. There would be an "exchange of experiences" between school, farm, and factory, and a curriculum in the idiom of Marx but with the accent on technology, so that the young would become both "red" and "expert." Since the class struggle was perennial, the main purpose of education must be to teach men to substitute ideological for material values, to put socialism before self. Like artists and writers, academics must reform themselves by going down among the masses to learn "proletarian wisdom" and the facts of life at mud level. The imagined superiority of the mental worker was a pernicious myth that must now be exploded.

But the peasant, the worker, and the soldier would also learn from the professor, the doctor, and the writer, and the cross-pollination continue until all Chinese humanity merged into a single hybrid—the "new Communist man." A proletarian projection of the Confucian ideal, the all-round gentleman who was scholar, general, poet, and artist, he would be at once farmer-worker-teacher-soldier-cadre, a cog in a classless, self-sufficient, egalitarian utopia in which every man would be Everyman; science and technology and all the arts of war and peace would be the prerogative of the masses, not of a privileged elite of professional experts.

Poverty of means had produced a "people's army" on the principle that, if suitably molded, the masses beat the machine, and the same logic that put mind before matter would now dictate that farming should be collectivized before it was mechanized, politics should come before productivity, socialism before modernization, in a new China in which men were to be conditioned by Mao's Thought to work solely for the community.

Mao had a vision of the People's Republic as a honeycomb of self-reliant collectives defended by their own peasant militia and enjoying "an appropriate degree of power," so that theory in Peking would be tempered by the reality in the provinces. His aim was to coax the Chinese into undergoing spiritual death and transfiguration, into switching their loyalty from the clan to the commune, from one human pyramid of mutual aid and protection to another. However, since all the selflessness would demand a "high level of ideological consciousness" that could not be injected into men overnight, he slyly appealed to the less laudable side of human nature by arguing that the collective would automatically bring great material rewards that could not be won by other means—since the means did not exist. Only the men.

But although Mao seemed to be practicing what he preached when he tested his theories on the sounding board of half a billion compatriots, he also laid down that since "failure is the mother of success," failures must be repeated until the "anticipated results can be achieved." And that "anticipated" meant that any revolutionary change he inspired must be pushed through until it was proved to be correct. If a piece of the action refused to fit into the objective Chinese puzzle on the ground, the timing or the tactics must be wrong and should be trimmed. It could not be discarded, for by definition the principle was right, and therefore a tactical retreat could only be followed by another advance. Mao was thus coming perilously close to emulating the blindness of the "Bolsheviks" from Moscow who had tried to hammer a Russian proletarian revolution into the jigsaw of peasant China.

Naturally. For the passionate antidogmatist had by now accumulated his own dogma, the calcified mental detritus of twenty-two years of conflict. But the guerrilla strategy that had won the war would lose the peace. He was to plunge the people to whose rescue he had devoted his life into the deep end of an economic and cultural revolution that would leave them still gasping for breath and struggling to survive when he died twenty-seven years later. His dream was to be their nightmare. For the sum of his astonishing qualities as thinker, soldier, patriot, visionary, flexible tactician in politics and war, was the seeming infallibility that had confounded false friends and true enemies alike, and transformed him from the bandit on Jinggangshan into the emperor in Peking. And nothing is more corrupting than to be constantly proved right.

❀ *CHAPTER ELEVEN* ❀

Aᴿᴛᴇʀ ᴛᴡᴇɴᴛʏ-ᴛᴡᴏ exhausting years of incessant war and want, Mao Tsetung had arrived only at the beginning of his monstrous self-imposed task—to restore sanity to a country of 550 million souls that had suffered half a century of gang rape. The tired band of aging generals and political commissars who had inherited the land could not pause for breath. Their immediate concern was to pump life into the shriveled economy and ensure that people had enough to eat. And for this they had to rebuild from the wreckage—the dazed, half-demolished cities, the broken dams and crumbling dykes that promised dearth and disaster; and the scorched earth where nothing grew.

But that was only the basic problem. They also had to impose a whole new political and economic system on a subcontinent they had overrun so fast that it was still rotten with rebels ranging from big business and the bourgeoisie in the towns to the "bandits" in the hills. They had scotched the snake, not killed it. They had yet to deal with the inaccessible Chiang Kai-shek, plotting his "return" with his rump government and more than half a million troops in Taiwan, with more than a million Kuomintang guerrillas still on the mainland, and with nearly two million more Nationalists of dubious loyalty who had rallied or surrendered to the Red armies.

Undaunted, Mao nevertheless planned to invade Taiwan in 1950 and to bring once more within the sacred borders of China another territory filched from her by the thievish outer barbarian—Tibet. Tibet was laboriously retrieved, but instead of recovering Taiwan, the PLA was drawn into a profitless war in Korea with promises of Russian arms and aircraft. By the end of 1950, Chinese troops were taking terrible punishment from modern firepower for which the "people's war" had not prepared them, amid a "sea" of not-so-friendly Koreans and on a narrow, conventional front that allowed for no fancy footwork in the guerrilla tradition. Human-wave tactics won ground only temporarily, and when in May 1951 "Hades" Peng Dehuai launched a desperate saturation attack with twenty-one divisions against the UN lines, he lost more than a hundred thousand men in five days. It was a lesson he was not to forget—just as Mao was not to forget the staggering bill the fight promoters in Moscow presented to him for the guns and planes they had given him to do their fighting for them.

The Russians? In December 1949 Mao had flown to Moscow to meet Stalin, but only after nine weeks of tedious talks accompanied by wooden smiles on both sides had he managed to extract from the Kremlin a miserly annual credit of U.S. $60 million, to be doled out to China for the next five years in exchange for painful territorial concessions ("It was like taking meat from the mouth of a tiger," Mao said later). In the ensuing months some 3,000 Russian military advisers arrived in China to modernize the army, however, and in 1953 an agreement was reached whereby the Soviet Union would provide the money, the machines, and the technology for 141 major construction projects, so that the People's Republic could copy the Russian model and develop a socialist economy based on a big heavy industry.

Mao might have felt uneasy, but he was not selling China—he was putting her in pawn to be redeemed later. Beggarmen can't be choosers, and in this case nor could the motley club of ex-tinkers, tailors, soldiers, failures, cowherds, carpenters, miners, and thieves who had set out to transform their penniless country into a paradise. They needed not only the Russians, but all the home-grown professional talent they could mobilize—not only the peasants and workers, but the intellectuals and administrators, the industrialists and the businessmen. Accordingly, once it was evident that he was to be the heir to all China, Mao clarified his earlier essay on "New Democracy" in a paper entitled "On the People's Democratic Dictatorship."

This beguilingly straightforward document laid down that China would heel-and-toe the Russian chalk line, basing the future Chinese socialist society on the proletariat, and would "lean to one side" by allying herself with the Soviet Union, since the Chinese revolution could not survive in a hostile world without "international friends." However, the proletariat would lead a united front of "the people," which *at the present stage* would include not only the peasants but the petty bourgeois and the national bourgeoisie.

Mao meant every word in 1949, and took back every one within seven years, when this-is-now had become that-was-then, and zig had given way to zag in accordance with the iron law of contradictions.

But meanwhile the united front was a convincing enough octopus, its huge, voracious, all-seeing Communist head served by eight tentacular "democratic" parties of non-Communists that could more easily reach out to elements of society distrustful of the Reds—like the former KMT, the minority peoples, the intellectuals, the national bourgeoisie— and draw them into the fold.

The master of a trading house in Canton or the managing director of a textile mill in Shanghai now found himself working under new and curious conditions. Since China was to enjoy full employment, no workers could be sacked. Wages bore no relation to output, output (regulated by state quotas) bore no relation to sales, sales no relation to profit, but local bureaucrats fixed the prices of raw materials and finished products so that the difference between outlay and income was just enough to give the boss a living. Mao had declared with disconcerting candor that when the time came to nationalize the enterprises of such people, "We shall carry out the work of educating and remolding them a stage further." He had correctly calculated that businessmen would be blind to the hazards of tomorrow if they smelled interim dividends today. And he needed them.

Land reform in the countryside was correspondingly lenient, designed to win friends and influence the "people." At the outset the poor peasants were promised fields to till, title deeds, and "protection of their right to ownership," and only the big landlords lost their properties. Mao was bent on eliminating the classes one by one, and it was a time to box clever, to spare the highly productive rich peasant and keep the misplaced confidence of the bourgeoisie until their "revolutionary usefulness" was exhausted. "We must not make too many enemies," he said.

However, "political consciousness" was raised, as Mao had remarked, when peasants saw blood. The Land Reform Law of 1950 provided not only for the confiscation of land, therefore, but for a "struggle against landlords," and Mao announced that while there must be no indiscriminate killing, more than a mere handful of these wealthy miscreants must be executed in order to show the peasants that they were now the bosses. The masses themselves would not like it "if we did not kill some tyrants in a revolution of six hundred million people," he added in 1956.

But in China men bowed low in the street when the most commonplace imperial edict was carried past on the back of a palace mandarin. The Chairman's decrees were sacred commandments, and all over the country they were seized upon by lesser cadres eager to outdo each other and display their revolutionary zeal among the masses (if only for fear of being charged with dawdling). His slogans were therefore like matches struck in a gas-filled room. Yet time and again he would strike the match, tempted perhaps by the sheer power of his words, and "let there be light" would be converted not into a brilliant glow, but a blinding explosion.

Mao might protest, "People's heads are not like leeks; once you cut them off, they do not grow again," but in 1950 he was no longer on the ground. He could not see that it was impossible for cadres to "shout slogans to intensify the mounting anger" of a mob until it was yelling "kill, kill"—and then persuade it to disperse quietly after some landlord had merely been dressed down and stripped of all the land he could not work himself.

According to Mao's definition, there were nearly 35 million "landlords" in China (peasants who owned slightly more land than had his own father). Of these, 20 million were publicly arraigned by people's tribunals and summarily dispossessed before crowds of jeering peasants, and between two and three million were taken away and shot, sometimes in batches. By the end of 1952, land reform had been completed. The landlord class had been "isolated" from the majority and duly liquidated, and the astonished poor and hitherto landless peasants found themselves owners of anything up to half an acre each.

Solutions forever father problems, and it soon emerged that many of the new owners of these plots lacked the tools to cultivate them, that the diligent outstripped the lazy, and therefore more "rich peasants" arose to buy up the land again and employ the feckless as hired help. However, Mao himself was to prove that St. Matthew's "from him that hath not shall be taken away even that which he hath" was no contradiction in terms after all, but a viable proposition.

Seasonal cooperation was customary among Chinese farmers, and in consequence the peasants were not unduly alarmed when cadres began to encourage them to form first casual, and then permanent "mutual aid teams" of up to ten households which worked together all the year around, gradually accumulating a common stock of animals and farming implements that none of them personally owned. In 1953, however, they were led a stage further up the lower slopes to Utopia when they were coerced into pooling not only their labor but most of the land they had been given. In principle the land still belonged to the individual farmer, but it was now on permanent loan to a "cooperative," which paid him a form of rent for his field and wages for the work he did.

In 1954 the emphasis shifted again, and "advanced cooperatives" were put together in which the peasant was not paid for his land but only for his toil as a member of a permanent "production team." Except for his invisible share in the cooperative, he was now collective labor. His personal holding was reduced to a "private plot" a few yards square, covering not more than one-twentieth of his original property and just big enough to raise a row or two of leeks and a few chickens. And dazed as he was by this sleight of hand, he was to discover that while Mao the Great Savior might have emancipated him, Mao the Grand Illusionist was not through with him yet.

The state had proved an Indian giver, and by 1956 the landless were to be virtually landless again. Their title deeds would have promised them no legal protection against their losses in any case, for in the tradition of Imperial China, the law was the scourge of the state, not the last resort of the citizen. Of old, it had been the servant of morality; now it was to be the servant of Maoism, and for nearly thirty years it would not even be codified. "It is impossible to speak of justice in isolation from Party principles," as one Communist authority put it in 1951. "Whatever agrees with Party principles is just; whatever disagrees with Party principles is unjust." It was for the law to uphold the Party, not the Party the law, whether those at the apex had decided landlords were to be shot, rich peasants spared, or poor peasants stripped. The "bourgeois legal concept" of a judiciary above the interests of Party and state was anathema. The main purpose of justice was to further the revolution.

Party directives, not laws, told cadres how to conduct themselves, and in 1950 these called for the "resolute suppression" of all counter-revolutionaries and "major vicious elements." By mid-1951 the first mass trials were safely under way, and a massacre followed. Mao himself put the total number of counterrevolutionaries and other class enemies slaughtered throughout the country at a modest eight hundred thousand, but in the same year the official press claimed that "over one million armed bandits" had been exterminated. In 1953 Chou En-lai said the figure for all categories had reached two million, and later hinted that it had doubled again.

If those beyond the proletarian pale were to be sorely chastised, the "people" themselves were not to be spared. At the end of 1951 Mao called on all political cadres to "wave banners and beat drums, to launch a mighty and irresistible struggle against corruption, waste and bureaucracy" in Party and administration. As in the days of the blood-thirsty Empress Wu more than twelve hundred years before, boxes were set up in every city into which anonymous informants could slip a tip against any benighted jack-in-office who had fallen victim to the lure of bourgeois "sugar-coated bullets." Voices were raised violently at open tribunals, one official in every twenty found himself under fire, Party members were forced to make public confessions and purged, sometimes flung into prison, even shot.

This "three-antis" campaign melted into a "five-antis" campaign against "bribery, tax evasion, fraud, theft of state property, and divulging economic secrets," which was directed against the bourgeois businessmen, the industrialists and traders who had so far survived as "people." Denunciations poured in as enthusiastic cadres abandoned their other duties in their eagerness to incriminate commercial delinquents of dubious class origin. Mass meetings of workers were organized to tear the mask from the unacceptable if familiar face of the capitalist boss who paid them, and to "expose the crimes of the bourgeoisie." Private companies were expropriated, or their owners confronted with colossal fines calculated to bankrupt them, so that the state could rescue them with loans that would thereafter keep them on the end of its financial puppet strings. Some 350,000 businessmen were found guilty in the course of a "struggle" that took millions of their employees from their work, and several thousand among the ruined jumped off the nearest roof.

Mao, it seemed, was giving the mob bread and circuses. But in May 1952 the pressure gave way to leniency, as, in accordance with the timeworn tactic of the inquisitor, the arc lights and the cosh give way to the soft voice and the proffered cigarette. In both the "three-antis" and "five-antis" campaigns, Mao's object was not to annihilate, but to cleanse the ranks, punish the stubborn, and chasten the rest—to "kill the chicken to teach the monkey," as the Chinese say. Counterrevolutionaries may have been massacred, but these other transgressors were merely being "educated." They were not incorrigible enemies, but experts, wanted, *people*.

Obdurate intellectuals had meanwhile been subjected to a "thought-reform" campaign, after two years on a regime of Marxist literature and manual labor had failed to root out their "feudalistic, imperialistic, and other mistaken concepts." But since they, too, had skills China needed, the hectoring of diehards at mass criticism sessions alternated with the quiet study of Mao Tsetung's latest Thought (an expurgated edition trimmed of earlier ideological howlers and tailored for the fifties). The object was to persuade writers and artists and teachers—disoriented and even panicking as their traditional culture vanished—to make Maoism their polestar for the future.

Even at the other end of the sorry scale of recalcitrants due for retribution or recasting, counterrevolutionaries condemned to the firing squad might be given a "temporary reprieve" since, in a sense, they also were needed. The Mongol Khans had learned that it paid them better to tax the vanquished Chinese than to exterminate them, for most men are worth more alive than dead, and the Communists now learned that the damned could serve socialism better as forced labor than as fertilizer. Those ready to work should therefore be spared, said Mao, "so that rubbish can be transformed into something useful." By recycling the wretches, moreover, the state would be extending a compassionate hand to class enemies, since "forced labor would compel them to change themselves and so become new men." The compulsory work camp was to develop into a vast and highly profitable reservoir of cheap labor dedicated to the redemption of the wicked—landlord, capitalist, counterrevolutionary, bourgeois—into which the security services poured millions for the good of their souls and the reconstruction of China. But few were seen again.

The wicked could also save themselves by putting the finger on their fellow trespassers—"redeeming guilt with merit"—and since the children of class enemies were themselves class enemies unto the second and even the third generation, they were encouraged to wash themselves free of all stain by denouncing their parents. "Everyone must understand," said one official publication, "that it is glorious to induce your own relatives to confess, or to report them; it is only shameful to shield them."

Mao was trying to transform a semifeudal society imbued with Confucian concepts, which (according to one Legalist critic) would prompt a magistrate in ancient times to hear a civic-minded son accuse his father of theft, and then execute the son for filial impiety, not the father for stealing a sheep. To encourage a child to squeal on his parents was to strike at the foundations of the ancient, worm-eaten structure within which father and family came first and the state nowhere, just as bunching households in cooperatives was to break up the home as well as build a socialist economy. The links of the old chains had to be snapped, and the "feudal system" of arranged marriages officially gave way to "free choice" under a new law. The family was an outdated "production unit." It had no place in a collective society and would ultimately be abolished, Mao had said.

What applied to business applied to love. Private "bourgeois" love must be subordinated to the public sector—love of country, the masses, hard work, science, and state property. And men could demonstrate this public love by responding with unflagging alacrity to the slogans and campaigns that were carrying them forward to the farther shore. The "patriotic health campaign" mobilized them to kill off all dogs, rats, flies, and other pests in the country; the dogs were duly slaughtered, citizens were given quotas for killing rats, and even ministers could be seen lashing out with fly swatters in their well-appointed sanctums to meet their norm of fifty dead a day. The campaign to "Resist American Aggression and Aid Korea" extracted enough money in "voluntary" contributions from the masses to pay for "3,349.7 fighter planes." A campaign to purge the trade unions of misguided officials who pandered to the workers instead of boosting production was followed by a campaign against "slack labor discipline," while down in the country drives were launched against everything from illiteracy to drought and dirty habits.

But many among the Chinese were exhausted by all the mammoth meetings and "spontaneous" parades and "voluntary" chores, and resented being drained of their penny savings and stripped of their promised land in a Promised Land. Fearful of further strictures, they nevertheless became listless or quietly rebellious, and soon peasants were pulling out of the cooperatives, neglecting crops, slaughtering pigs for cash, drifting to the towns. Battered by repeated blows—the liquidation of landlords and counterrevolutionaries, the mass hunt for bourgeois sinners in the cities—the economy developed a pronounced limp.

The blame fell on the cadres, and not without reason. The sanctimonious zealots among them could turn an inch of Mao's Thought into an ell of arbitrary action, but they were often outdone by other mandarins of less impeccable record who had earlier been chastised for right-wing deviations, and who overcorrected by becoming loud-mouthed leftists. Both groups now stood accused of "commandism" and "bureaucraticism," for instead of wheedling the peasants into giving up their tools, their livestock, and their land for their own good, they had bullied and blackmailed them, "advancing blindly" and using "crude methods" like fining reluctant farmers on the spot, or threatening to brand them "capitalist" if they did not comply. They had also forced peasants to dig useless wells or to uproot growing plants, beaten up those unable to repay loans, and driven many to suicide.

Yet Peking forced the pace again at the end of 1953 by issuing a directive on the "transition to socialism" which so spurred on the cadres that in the following year they hastily threw together nearly ten times the number of cooperatives they had been ordered to form. The reaction was disastrous. Within five months 364,000 malcontents—mainly among the peasantry—had been tried for "economic sabotage," and there was an urgent call for more scapegoats for the increasingly sullen mood of the masses, the winded economy, the need to impose rice rationing, and the "blind flow of peasants to the cities."

In mid-1955, accordingly, it was officially explained that slippery counterrevolutionaries who had escaped earlier purges had exploited "tensions" and the "tight food situation" in the countryside in order to foment unrest and disrupt the cooperatives. A campaign mounted against the sinister figure of Hu Feng, an author accused of plotting with reactionaries and renegades inside and outside the Party, widened into a witch-hunt for "alien class elements," during which nearly two million cadres were grilled, and a hundred thousand unmasked as "rightists" were consigned to forced-labor camps.

Everything is a matter of perspective. It may seem to those living in more placid political climes that during the six years from 1949–1955 a destructive revolutionary tidal wave had swept over China, drowning millions, carrying away the moldering structures of the past, and leaving a stark new landscape in its wake for the numbed survivors. But an impatient Mao may well have seen it as a wearisome period of consolidation. The first five-year plan had been officially launched only in 1953, and its targets had almost at once been cut back by 30 percent "for lack of raw materials and trained labor." Much of China's business remained in the hands of the bourgeoisie, and the preamble to the constitution formally adopted in September 1954 promised only "gradual" socialization. Mao himself had felt obliged to declare that it would require "fifty years or ten five-year plans" to transform a rustic China into a modern industrial giant.

He was by now sixty-one, however, and appeared at times to be losing momentum. The Dalai Lama, who had talked to him a few months before, remarked, "He did not look healthy, and was always panting and breathing heavily . . . he was slow in his movements, and slower still in his speech; he was sparing of words and spoke in short sentences, each full of meaning and usually clear and precise; and he smoked incessantly. . . ." The cuffs of his shirt were torn, and his shoes looked as if they had never been polished. The sick consequences of his exercises in crash collectivization had meanwhile strengthened the hand of a go-slow group within the Party that had already taken steps not only to cut the pace of the revolution on the land, but even to put it into reverse, so that by 1955 some 200,000 cooperatives had actually been disbanded. Could their words continue to carry weight?

Some would argue that it would be quite wrong to assume that Mao was master of China and solely responsible for her destiny, and, ritualistically speaking, they would be right. He was accountable to the Central Committee of the Party and required its seal on his schemes, and now the constitution stipulated that all decisions that affected the state must in turn be ratified by the National People's Congress. The NPC was the highest instance of the legislature, "the supreme organ of state power," and had "the final decision on all important matters affecting the life of the nation"—including the national economic plan.

But there is no need to refute that argument here, for events were to speak for themselves.

❉ *CHAPTER TWELVE* ❉

J ULY 1955. The Hall of Magnanimity in the Forbidden City was a forest of black paper fans stirred as if by a stiff breeze, for it was well over a hundred in the shade, and beyond the high vermilion walls Peking shimmered in the heat haze. But the fans were agitated by the hands of some two thousand delegates to the National People's Congress who had assembled from all over China. The "supreme organ of state power" had been convened to ratify the final draft of the first five-year plan. Caution had prevailed, and the plan, which was approved unanimously, included a severely modified program for collectivization whereby even by 1957 only one peasant in three would have been coerced into joining a cooperative. "They're having to slow down, and even disband a lot of them," a colleague beside me murmured as I scribbled away. Too many cadres had kicked rather than coaxed the peasants into cooperatives, and the peasants were kicking back. China had 600 million mouths to feed, yet the output of grain was falling because the state was taking most of it and paying a poor price.

The fans vanished and there was a febrile outburst of clapping as Premier Chou En-lai appeared on the rostrum, solemn and self-possessed in a neat blue Mao suit, to deliver the closing address. "*Qinaide tongzhimen* . . . Dear comrades . . ." "Where's Mao?" I asked. The other shrugged.

Mao was not there because he was bypassing the National People's Congress, the Government, the Politburo and the Central Committee, and telling the masses through a meeting of regional party cadres that these august bodies were behaving like a bunch of twittering old biddies. "Throughout the Chinese countryside a new upsurge in the socialist movement can be seen," he said, "yet some of our comrades are tottering along like a woman with bound feet, constantly complaining that others are going too fast. . . . This is not the right way at all.

It won't do!" He then called for the number of cooperatives to be doubled—thirty million farming families should be collectivized by 1958, he insisted, and all of China's peasants drafted into advanced cooperatives by 1960. The recalcitrant leadership in Peking had been sidestepped, the "supreme body" flouted. Mao had lost patience and given the revolution another brutal thrust forward. The emperor's edict had gone out, and, like the mandarins before them, the local cadres made doubly sure that they were seen to "tremble and obey."

Thirty million families by 1958? The Central Committee belatedly endorsed Mao's new timetable after a suspiciously prolonged session in October, whereupon the unrepentant Chairman foisted a further cut in the deadline onto the provincial yes-man of the Party at the end of the year. Within three months more than 90 percent of all peasant China had been "cooperativized," and the entire crash program was completed by 1957, three years ahead of his original estimate. Half a billion peasants had been ripped out of their semifeudal existence and stamped into a new experimental design for living.

Meanwhile not only were small shopkeepers and craftsmen jostled into urban cooperatives, but bourgeois private enterprise tolerated under the "people's democratic dictatorship" now fell under the axe and was "transformed." Mao let the already harassed businessmen know what was in the wind, and after they had bowed to the inevitable and fallen over themselves asking to be nationalized—some within as short a time as five years—he relieved them of their assets within a fortnight. It was like getting a cat to eat chili, Mao is supposed to have said. "Rub the chili into the cat's ass, and when it begins to burn, the cat will lick it off, and be glad you let it." The 760,000 former capitalists were for the most part retained as salaried managers of their own businesses and compensated for their losses with a payment of fixed interest for the next seven years.

Out of a boundless optimism born of his instinct that a "socialist upsurge" had arrived, Mao wrote of the "transformation" with the same disdain for pusillanimous understatement that he had shown when describing the revolutionary mood in Hunan thirty years before. It was a "raging tidal wave sweeping away all demons and monsters," and by the end of the third five-year plan in 1967 the grain yield would have multiplied two and a half times to reach nearly 450 million tons, cotton output would be four times the 1956 figure, steel output six times.

Time would blow away this grandiloquent froth, leaving the flat beer of truth (the grain yield in 1967 was only fractionally higher than it had been twelve years before). But Mao had hurled China into her first "little leap forward" to attain these impossible targets, whipping up the millions with the slogan, "More, faster, better, more economically"—and once again the economy threatened to fall apart like a figure in a fun-fair mirror, as bottlenecks and blind boosting of unwanted industrial output dislocated supply and demand. In the countryside, the already twice-told tale was repeated. Cadres confiscated property out of hand, pressed peasants willy-nilly into cooperatives, ordered them to plant the wrong crops, or drafted them into huge labor gangs to build irrigation works. In revenge, more peasants took off for swollen cities already plagued with unemployment, while many of those who remained behind killed off even their draft animals, sold the meat on the black market for ready cash, and conspired to hide their grain—in some areas holding back one-third of the harvest.

In September 1956 the Eighth Party Congress found itself trying to repair the damage done by Mao's bid to force through a program that the Central Committee had been obliged to endorse "enthusiastically" just eleven months before. Swerving to the right, the Party set out to soothe the ruffled peasant, cutting back the size of the cooperative and the authority of the cadre, giving greater freedom to the small production team and even to be individual household again, and allowing farmers to cultivate more land for their own profit and sell some of their produce on free markets. The latest battle for socialism had again shown up the multitudinous shortcomings of the ten million officials recruited into the hierarchy, and by November the Chairman had made it clear that since his timing of the "socialist upsurge" had been faultless, the "work style" of the cadres had been responsible for the friction and the failures. They must therefore be "rectified" again.

Rectification was urgent because Nikita Khrushchev, addressing the Twentieth Congress of the Soviet Communist Party in Moscow, had damned Stalin for a murderous bungler whose ruthless minions had inflicted a reign of terror on the Russian people and whose "personality cult" was an abomination. The towering figure whom Mao had mourned dry-eyed and dry-voiced in 1953 as "the greatest genius of the present age" and a benefactor noted for "his ardent love for the Chinese people" had been flung abruptly onto the rubbish tip of history as a sadistic despot better dead.

Never had possible comparisons been more odious. The shock of Stalin's desecration stiffened Mao's resolve to keep close to the masses, to make it plain through repeated sifting and correction of the erring

Chinese bureaucracy that he was not in the same category as the Russian despot. When a high-voltage charge of liberalism then ran through the Communist world, detonating the Hungarian "counterrevolution," it further stimulated his own urge to take the lid off dissent in China and to dissipate the contradictions between Party and people through open argument. Stalin's error had been to "alienate himself from the masses" by solving those contradictions "from above"—usually with a bullet in the back of the head. Mao would not make the same mistake.

It was therefore not only the bewildered Chinese peasants who were now to be reprieved, but their traditional partners in revolt, the disgruntled scholars. The intellectual was continuing to prove a problem child. In 1956 it was said in Peking that only four out of every ten educated Chinese supported the system, one actively hated it, and there was a dangerous tendency for the rest simply to opt out of it. Moreover, those professional men who were ready to work for a socialist China favored the Russian model for reconstruction, which was based on heavy industry and a modern urbanized society that would need their know-how.

Once again they had fallen out of step with the Chairman. In 1949 Mao had himself spoken of the "shift to the cities," of the need for the Chinese to follow the one shining example they had before them—the Soviet Union. But that was then. When he went cap in hand to Moscow at the end of the same year, he found that he was able to squeeze a meager loan out of Stalin only by making expensive concessions, which included recognizing the "independence" of former Chinese territory that had become a Russian puppet state—Outer Mongolia. And Peking had since been compelled to prevent Stalin's marionette Gao Gang from turning Manchuria into an "independent kingdom" by excommunicating him, once the old tyrant himself was secure in his tomb.

The new Russian leaders had proved less predatory and increased their economic aid to China, and when Nikita Khrushchev visited Mao in 1954, they kissed and embraced like old lovers. But despite several thick coats of synthetic camaraderie, both men were cool and wary underneath. Mao offered Khrushchev a thousand divisions to crush America; Khrushchev told Mao that a few American nuclear missiles would convert his divisions into dust, and asked instead for a million Chinese workers to cut timber in Siberia. Mao riposted by tartly warning Khrushchev not to look upon China as a source of cheap labor. "He really knew how to put us down," the Russian remarked later.

To Mao, the successors of Stalin were pygmies who played with such pernicious concepts as "peaceful coexistence" with the American imperialists, yet who were not prepared to treat the Chinese as equals. By 1956 the time had come for China to start cutting herself free of Soviet apron strings. She must draw on Soviet achievements, but not on Soviet backwardness—"Some people are so undiscriminating that they say a Russian fart is fragrant. . . . The Russians themselves say it stinks," he said in one of his habitual references to sins of emission.

In April, two months after Khrushchev had torn the death mask from Stalin, Mao delivered a pivotal address to the Politburo on the "Ten Major Relationships." In this speech, he contended that aping the Muscovites and putting a "lopsided stress" on heavy industry had paradoxically slowed down its development. How? Light industry had been left lagging behind and investment in agriculture neglected. Now the peasants not only fed the country but provided the raw material for light industry, and profits from the sale of light industrial goods generated the capital needed for reconstruction. "So if you have a genuine and strong desire to develop heavy industry," he reasoned, springing an ambush on those who had, "you will place importance on agriculture and light industry." The Chinese must not fall into the error of the Russians, who had squeezed the peasants too hard—"You want the hen to lay more eggs, yet you don't feed it," he complained. "What kind of logic is that?"

He was inverting Soviet priorities and spelling out an equation for self-reliance. But to become self-reliant, China would need her skilled minds more than ever. Peking would have to defuse the discontent of the intellectuals and persuade the professionals outside the Party to "shift their position of neutrality to one of alliance with us," as the *People's Daily* put it. In May, accordingly, Mao borrowed a classical phrase—"Let a hundred flowers bloom, let a hundred schools of thought contend"—to encourage critics of the system to emerge into the sunlight of a new intellectual freedom, and to open a frank dialogue with the Party.

The re-edited version of what he said stipulated that the dialogue must be kept within the context of the "transformation to socialism" under Communist leadership. That should have been obvious in the first place, however. It would be as absurd to expect the Chinese Politburo to tolerate any talk of abandoning communism in favor of parliamentary democracy as it would be to ask the Pope to sanction polygamy. But otherwise Mao was determined to "liberate" the ideas of the non-Party intellectuals and to coax them into exposing the frailties of the bureaucracy, which would then be duly rectified. Only four months after the Eighth Party Congress which had carried out the autopsy on his last ill-fated leap, the Chairman was on the rebound. The old smash-it-and-see glint was back in his eye, and he was showing symptoms that by now were becoming distressingly familiar to those around him.

In January 1957 an irrepressible Mao told a conference of Party secretaries that they should not be afraid of discord, but ready for it. A "big disturbance" might flare up, but "our country will emerge all the stronger once the boil bursts." Candid exchanges between Party and people would ensure that cadres did not "cut themselves off from the masses," as they had in Hungary. They were already asking for trouble. They were going soft, falling to the "sugar-coated bullets" of bourgeois temptation, obsessed with personal fame and gain and promotion. There were "instances where a cadre could not be satisfied with a rise of one grade, even a rise of two grades left him weeping in bed, and perhaps only a three-grade promotion would get him out of it," Mao remarked sardonically.

His belief in the cleansing powers of confrontation was beginning to come through again, loud and clear. Speaking in February on "The correct handling of contradictions," he stressed that "contradictions among the people" were healthy, for they saved the revolution from stagnation, "pushing society forward." Just as religion could not be abolished by administrative decree, so "the only way to settle ideological questions among the people is by the method of discussion, criticism, persuasion, and education, not by the method of repression or coercion."

But he was using "the method of coercion" even as he spoke. He was talking directly to an audience of nearly two thousand leading citizens made up of Communist cadres and non-Communist intellectuals, deliberately pushing the two groups into a nationwide wrangle without first asking for the approval of the Central Committee. He was again outflanking the hierarchs of the Politburo, many of whom recoiled with alarm from the idea of inciting neutral intellectuals to criticize the Party, pitting the outsiders against the insiders. After much internal rumbling the divided leadership nevertheless launched the rectification campaign in April, directing it against "three evils" among the cadres—"bureaucratism, subjectivism, sectarianism": that is, against the despotic petty bureaucrats, the dogmatists, and the pharisaical bullies who treated all non-Communists as canon-fodder. Mao saw the campaign as a "movement of ideological education" to be carried out "as gently as the breeze or mild rain." But that was not to be.

Cautious and suspicious at the outset, intellectuals were teased or intimidated into tossing discretion aside and "criticizing boldly." A bourgeois friend of mine in South China was ordered to write posters reviling local bureaucrats—"life's garbage," as one author had unkindly called them—and was given a severe dressing down for prudently contenting himself with a few niggling parochial protests. "We don't want yes-men," he was told curtly. "You will write three hundred serious complaints against Party cadres within the next week." He was convinced that in its early stages the object of the operation was not to trick malcontents into betraying themselves, but to clear the air between the long-suffering public and the Marxist martinets Peking had imposed upon it. But although all censure might at first have been "voluntary" rather than voluntary, the Chinese, thus encouraged, slowly responded with a swelling thundercloud of damning obloquy that burst in a roaring tempest of malediction, as pent-up resentment against the Party and all its works was finally "liberated."

On 25 May Mao warned the country, "All words and actions that deviate from socialism are completely wrong." But he was shouting into the rising wind. By the end of the month men were on their feet protesting that the Party "stood on the backs of the masses"; its cadres were rotten with ulterior aims and selfish motives, but while their faults showed up at street level, "the recklessness starts in Peking." The status of Marxism-Leninism as the guiding ideology of China should be "abolished," one professor told an academic forum bluntly. It was neither the repository of universal truth, nor the answer to all problems; it made men doctrinaire and led them into inadmissible error.

The ground rules were forgotten. "Nothing can be wider than the gap between the Party and the masses," cried one intrepid lecturer in physics. "The Party has made mistakes and the leaders should submit themselves for punishment." If they did not reform, they were doomed: "The masses will kill the Communists and overthrow you . . . the downfall of the Communist Party does not mean the downfall of China." It was putrid with sectarians and malefactors, an economist told another forum in June. The masses had deserted it, and it would soon collapse. "Might overcomes right, and it is possible to mount machine guns to deal with trouble. But what if the machine guns are turned around for action?"

Not to be outdone, the students of Peking University demanded general elections and an end to the absolute leadership of the Communists, for as things stood the National People's Congress was nothing but a "mud idol," and the "destiny of six hundred million is dictated by the pens of six men" who "take arbitrary action and issue reckless orders." Mao—the supreme advocate of putting all theory to the test of practice—was to be accused of being "hot-tempered" and "impetuous," and of imposing dogmatic decisions without first studying the facts.

The intellectuals of China were sick of being put through ideological hoops. New, inflammatory magazines proliferated, and the blasphemies multiplied with the posters—"Down with Mao," "Bring back the Kuomintang." There were protest demonstrations, strikes, and scattered outbreaks of violence in which Party offices were ransacked and cadres beaten up. The "Hundred Flowers" campaign had produced a bumper crop of "poisonous weeds," and telegrams from uneasy comrades urging that rectification be canceled "flew like snowflakes."

Mao raised a wet finger to the wind, and on 8 June the *People's Daily* signaled a hairpin turn ahead by describing the ubiquitous critics of the Party as insidious "rightist elements" who were using the pretext of rectification to "clamor openly for an end to the great cause of socialism, and drag history backward to bourgeois dictatorship." A shocked Politburo promptly converted a movement that had been launched to rectify the "commandism" of the bloated bureaucracy into a drive to smother dissent outside it. The belated pretense that it had been a trap from the outset, specifically designed to lure all these "demons and devils, ghosts and monsters" into giving their nefarious game away, failed to disguise the monumental blunder the Chairman had made in allowing the Party to be publicly pilloried from end to end of China.

By July an intensive "struggle" was being waged against all transgressors, abject confessions were being torn from thousands of battered and chastened intellectuals not only outside but inside the Party, and these disclosures of the danger within enabled Mao to ram home a demand for further rectification of "rightists" in the Communist ranks who questioned his tactics. In addition to 400,000 intellectuals (according to Mao), 810,000 cadres were sent "down to the country" to improve their minds through manual labor. Pitched out of their homes and offices, they were put to work in the fields or on land-reclamation sites, where many found themselves interminably carting away stones and dirt like the Foolish Old Man in Mao's favorite Taoist fable who set out to remove two mountains by hand to improve the view. Some remained "ill at ease in their minds," reported the *People's Daily* with masterly restraint, but an idyllic picture was painted of those on the farm "who used to cover their noses with handkerchieves when passing a dunghill but now scramble to carry baskets loaded with excrement." There were nevertherless rumors of rebellion and even official accounts of men being executed for "armed uprising," but this unrest provided an added pretext for converting rectification of the Party into rectification of the whole country—a "great mass debate" that would afford Mao limitless opportunities for reconditioning the millions for the classless society to come. He had turned blunder into bonus, and he continued to inspire all, it was said, with "boundless socialist fervor."

CHAPTER THIRTEEN

BOUNDLESS SOCIALIST FERVOR" was not unconfined within the Politburo, where Mao's grasshopper tactics shocked the economic ants among his colleagues, and the dire consequences of his rash experiments in instant collectivization evoked undisguised dismay. At the Eighth Party Congress, therefore, he had found himself facing the more pragmatic mandarins for what was to become an elliptical struggle between them to preserve Party unity at each other's expense. And first among these mandarins was a slender stick of a man in a patched cotton tunic and cloth worker's cap that almost put Mao's own proletarian inelegance to shame—Liu Shaoqi.

Like Mao, Liu was the son of a Hunanese peasant, and both spoke Chinese with the muddy accent of their province. But there similarity ended. The corpulent Mao, no longer Lincolnesque, was normally bursting with vigorous, orotund speech and gaudy fancies, a fat man full of artful words and glances; the desiccated Liu with his dry, direct gaze was the master of scholarly dialectical discourse, of monotonous marathons of words as gray as the hair on his head. Mao was the vulgar peasant revolutionary, the impatient patriot and dreamer who had stayed behind in China to stumble alone through the alien thickets of Marx. Liu was a Moscow-trained theoretician and a professional *apparatchik*, the author of the cadre's handbook, *How to Be a Good Communist*. He had fought a clandestine urban revolution under an alias, rousing miners, organizing underground unions, industrial strikes, and general unrest behind the enemy lines in Shanghai and Canton, and the hostile cities had left their mark on him; he was soft-voiced, colorless, laundered, married to a beautiful acolyte from a wealthy, bourgeois family.

As Vice-Chairman and First Secretary of the Party, Liu had endorsed the report of Chou En-lai which stressed that China should not be thrust into economic adventures she could not afford; he called for a sane approach to development, as even-paced as his own dull delivery, and specifically denounced the "leftist deviation" of placing too much emphasis on class struggle. A self-effacing Mao hardly opened his mouth when his colleagues adopted a rational second five-year plan devoid of "leaps" and poked furtively at the soft clay at the foot of his image. It was true that Liu Shaoqi had gone through the motions of praising him for "steadfastly upholding the Party's principles of democracy and collective leadership," but Mao had a sharp eye for gift-wrapped brickbats.

He was under no illusions. Khrushchev had given the "moderates" in the Party a golden opportunity to pin their Gulliver down. He had smashed the monstrous idol of Stalin and his "cult of the personality," and now Mao could be cut to life size on the pretext that he was being saved from a similar fate. Liu's god was the Party, not Mao, and Mao had known his views since Liu had told a meeting that for anyone to claim to be an infallible leader was like "pushing leeks up a pig's snout to make it look like an elephant." Any man who thought himself "number one in the world," refused to accept criticism, and expected only to be praised and flattered, "helped the enemy to endanger the life of the Party."

The forthright "Hades" Peng Dehuai—he had been known to burst in on Mao while he was sleeping to tell him he was wrong—now proposed that all mention of the "Thought" of Mao Tsetung should be dropped from the new Party constitution, and Liu endorsed the change. The Party Secretariat was reorganized so that it would work independently of Mao, and was confided to the care of the short, sharp, piledriver of a man who presented the constitution *sans* Mao, speaking up firmly in favor of collective leadership and pointedly stressing that Khrushchev's condemnation of the personality cult was of vital significance to *all* Communist parties.

Like Chou En-lai, Deng Xiaoping came of bourgeois, even mandarin stock, and they had both cut their ideological teeth on the Chinese Communist movement in Paris. But while Chou was from a corner of Zhejiang renowned for a wine as smooth as sherry, Deng was from the rich and restless province of Sichuan, famous for its fiery liquor, its hot dishes, and its high-tempered revolutionaries. He had made the Long March, and later played a vital role in the "liberation" as the chief political commissar of the 2nd Field Army, which crossed the Rubicon for Mao after the Reds had reached the north bank of the Yangtse River in 1949.

Unlike the urbane Chou, he was an abrasive, hardheaded organization man, an elitist who believed in being "expert" before "red," in trained management, central planning, and the need to build a sound technological and industrial runway for China's takeoff into socialism. This was the veteran who now took over the day-to-day running of the Party from Mao. The Chairman had ostensibly been rescued from his own "cult." The go-slow group and their attendant technocrats had caught him at low tide.

Yet the Party had meekly—if tardily—sanctioned the objectionable faits accomplis that Mao had sprung on it—the decision to double the cooperatives in 1955, the "rectification" campaign, the blooming of a hundred flowers that in 1957 turned out to be poisonous weeds. At the Eighth Party Congress in 1956, Liu Shaoqi had tried to undercut Mao's enthusiasm for relentless class war by contending that the struggle between the proletariat and the bourgeoisie had been all but resolved already. But after Mao took him rudely to task for his complacency, Liu made a precise 180-degree turn and by 1957 was shamelessly echoing the messiah himself, insisting that it was in fact the "major contradiction" facing them all on the road to socialism, as if he had never said anything else. No one raised an eyebrow. Why? Paradoxically, Mao's flagrant miscalculation in launching the runaway Hundred Flowers campaign had proved him right—the struggle was not over. But that was not all.

The dragon can be tamed until you can ride on its back, the Legalists said of the Chinese ruler, but touch the scales at its throat and you die. For the Chinese Communists, as for the imperial mandarins before them, there was only one true political system, and Mao was at its apex. Anyone who challenged him head-on before the masses was inviting annihilation, since the antonym for "emperor" was "bandit." Their strategy, therefore, was to yield to the restive Chairman the easier to ride him, persuading him in private to modify his precipitate flight to socialism if possible, and reining him in only after he had obviously erred (as they did in 1956). Their atavistic instinct told them they must reason with him within a united empire, not defy him publicly and divide it. Liu could protest, but Mao had the final say. The object was consensus, not conflict. There must be no visible breach.

But that meant that the Politburo was perpetuating the old Chinese pattern of long periods of ostensible harmony that would end only in open rebellion when the situation had so degenerated that the "contradictions" had become insufferable. All that ensued, therefore, was not simply a madness of Mao's making, but a covenant of folly between Mao and the mandarins who echoed him, who might question his wis-

dom within the Party but would loudly uphold the fiction outside that
he was a unique genius and could do no wrong. This conspiracy to
defraud the public blew more hot air into the Chairman's inflated ego,
and reduced the gullible masses to blind faith in his magic (thus putting
the ultimate weapon in his hand). It also prompted witless foreign
sinologues to quote every slavish encomium uttered by his opponents
as further proof that all was for the best in the best of all possible
Chinas (as Voltaire himself had suggested in another age), on the
fatuous premise that it must be true, it was all on the record.

Communist principle was thus molding a despot in the tradition of
imperial China. The Chinese had regarded the founding emperor of a
new dynasty as a father who would bequeath to them an entire realm
as his legacy. His loyal followers hesitated to gainsay him, and would
bear with his worst faults and his "tyrannical spirit," since they would
forever be in his debt. When Mao was transmuted from bandit into
emperor in 1949, therefore, he shrugged on China as a garment that he
now owned and could dispose of as he willed, like all who had come
before him. He used Marxism as emperors had used Confucianism—as a
respectable cloak for the exercise of personal power; he was a law unto
himself, his wilfulness fed by a romantic's egoistic disdain for the rules
that showed up even in his unorthodox poetry. Like the heroes of *The
Three Kingdoms* and *Water Margin*, he would bind men to him by
showing a calculated clemency when they were weak and vulnerable—
"sending charcoal when it snowed." But he did not forget that while
Liu Bang the contender for China had cherished his able lieutenants,
he had found it expedient to rid himself ruthlessly of the "meritorious
dogs" once they had won him the empire, lest the ambitious among
them exploit their prestige and popularity in order to dislodge him
in turn.

It may be objected that this hardly sounds like the same "dragon"
who allowed others to override him, clip his wings, even erase his
"Thought" at the Eighth Party Congress. But of course it is. He had
been caught in the down draft created by the failure of his "little leap"
and Stalin's fall from grace. The role of the Chinese ruler is to fade
from the scene when plans go awry, and leave it to his mandarins to
assume responsibility for picking up the pieces. He is only to the fore
when things go right. The guerrilla in Mao prompted him to make a
tactical retreat, and the Taoist in him told him that the time for the
magisterial counterstroke had not yet come. Since he had the last word,
he would get his way later—and sure enough, within five months he
was dragging the Party backwards into the rectification campaign.

If Sunzi's *Art of War* had taught Mao sly, flexible tactics, Sima Guang's *General Mirror* had armed him with all the political ruses and wily diplomacy to be found in more than 1,300 years of Chinese history. "Reading historical novels only makes you dream," Professor Yang is said to have told him, recommending that he study this eleventh-century masterpiece. "Reading real history can make the dream come true." He was to be proved right. The *General Mirror* runs to 294 chapters, but Mao—whose sketchier acquaintance with Marxist literature has been noted—appears to have memorized every trick in this monumental work.

It was not to be wondered at that he showed a superior talent for the "techniques" of power first laid down by the Machiavellis of China in the fourth century before Christ. He built contradictions into government and Party, choosing this man as the antithesis of that, until he was sure that he could drive a wedge between his lieutenants at any time if they showed signs of ganging up on him, since there would always be one group to support him against the attacks of another. And if his colleagues proved too obstructive, his commanding position on the high ground as charismatic father of the revolution enabled him to go directly to the masses themselves. The sycophantic echoes of his own much-publicized slogans, bouncing back to Peking from the provinces through Party channels, would give him a popular mandate to do what he wanted.

If the Party then opposed him, it would be the Party that was isolating itself from the people. Once he had leaked his latest personal whim to the lower echelons, therefore, the higher could not flout it. They had been skillfully bracketed, and if Mao would not retract, the Politburo would be compelled to endorse his "line"—even if it made their flesh crawl. "Democratic" centralism thus strengthened his autocracy, and the options open to his adversaries were either to ride his latest mass campaign in order to deflect it from its course, or to incite those involved in it to discredit it by being destructively overzealous—both hazardous stratagems known as "waving the red flag to defeat the red flag." Mao was playing without scruple on the paramount need to preserve Party solidarity, and one senses the contempt he sometimes felt for his critics in one of his later poems:

> In a minuscule world
> Flies dash themselves against the wall
> Buzzing
> Sometimes shrill
> Sometimes whining.

The flies could hardly be blamed if they did whine. China's intellectuals had lurched from the Hu Feng purge to the disarming liberalism of the Hundred Flowers campaign and back to a repressive antirightist drive within two years; the ill-prepared cadres had been plunged into a helter-skelter program for collectivizing the peasants, and then rectified for being overhasty; the peasants had been given land, had lost it again, had been cooperativized, decooperativized, and cooperativized once more; and the young people in the country had been prompted by all the asset stripping on the farm to flock to the bulging cities, only to be thrown out of the cities and herded back to the country again. The People's Republic seemed to be advancing on Utopia with the exhausting sinuosity of a sidewinder.

The mandarins around Mao had no quarrel with the goal, only with the pace at which he wished to rush it. Their differences were nevertheless to lead to the polarization of the Politburo, and the emergence of "two lines" so mutually hostile in the Chairman's eyes that one would be upheld as "proletarian and revolutionary," while the other would be damned black as "bourgeois and reactionary."

To Mao, the schism must have seemed maddeningly familiar. Five months after he had proposed in his paper on the "Ten Major Relationships" that agriculture should come before heavy industry, the Party had adopted a second five-year plan that provided for steel production to be tripled and pushed farming into the background again. Agriculture could not be collectivized until it was mechanized, Liu Shaoqi had argued, because the peasants would not fall into line until they were confronted with machines they could work profitably only as a team, and heavy industry must first supply those machines. Like the deformed yet recognizable shadow of the Twenty-eight Bolsheviks, pontificating fallaciously on the incontrovertible virtues of urban revolution *à la russe*, the go-slow group in the Party were still preaching the doctrine of urban reconstruction *à la russe*—a doctrine that would make China dependent on Moscow indefinitely.

For the moment Mao had allowed the moderates to prevail, but he had taught the disbelieving dogmatists of the thirties the winning virtues of a peasant revolution that relied on man in the mass, not mechanical aids, and he was now ready to repeat the lesson. The rectification and antirightist movements had justified the banishment of a million bureaucratic Party cadres and reactionary intellectuals to the countryside for "re-education." The cross-fertilization of the Chinese people that was to produce the new communist man could be said to have begun. Mao was ready for the next masterstroke.

THE GREAT
LEAP FORWARD

Seeing men all behaving like drunkards,
How can I alone remain sober?
(WANG CHI, CIRCA 700 A.D.)

❊ *CHAPTER* FOURTEEN ❊

Arriving in Peking in 1958 after an absence of nearly three years, I had no means of guessing from my first view of the city that beyond its towering gates the whole country was in the grip of a peculiarly Chinese mania, for if to Sunzi all war was based on deception, to the Communists so was all peace. The same sun blazed down oppressively on the same vermilion walls, but China had meanwhile doffed one mask to assume another—different, but equally misleading. In July 1955 Peking was swarming with blue-clad neuters, the women hardly distinguishable to a Western eye from the men. Purposeful and expressionless, they appeared to have been reduced to anonymous units, the moving parts of a single piece of socialist clockwork. They had not been, of course. Socialism was no more than knee high. Private business still flourished, men ran their own shops, independent farmers tilled their own land, and some agricultural cooperatives were actually being disbanded.

But since then the streets had burst into color, into recognizably human life. In the summer of 1958 the women grew their hair long or sported permanent waves; they wore Western frocks, flower-patterned Chinese cheongsams, shorts, jeans, and blouses, all of them made from a multitude of distressingly gay materials. Some even used lipstick. China was making scented fabrics, perfumed earrings, sixty brands of cigarettes and two hundred kinds of liquor copied from all over the world, so that bars could serve the unwary foreigner ersatz replicas of everything from a Manhattan to a Singapore sling. In Shanghai, roof-garden restaurants threw dances, idle crowds watched baseball, thronged amusement parks. But although this painstaking frivolity inspired by the decadent West might dazzle the poor purblind alien, it had nothing much to do with reality.

Behind all the scene shifting, the significant changes had been in just the opposite direction, and I encountered my first when I called on an official I had known at the Foreign Ministry in Peking, to find that his wife was doing his job. "He's been sent down to the country, to work," she explained, blank-faced. "You are not likely to see him. He won't be back for three years." Others were not to be so lucky. A student told me that half of his schoolmates had been uprooted from their homes in the capital and dispatched to distant parts of China to labor on farms or in forests. They were not coming back at all.

Xiafang—the "down-to-the-country" drive—had hit more than "rightists" and "rectified" cadres. All officials under fifty of both sexes were encouraged to "volunteer" to be "transferred downwards" for at least one year, so that they could learn about life from the peasant by plowing and sowing, carrying manure and cleaning pigsties. As for intellectuals, "They will achieve nothing if they fail to integrate themselves with the workers and peasants," Mao had declared earlier, and authors in particular were being urged to go through the purifying sheep-dip of sharing their days with the toiling masses.

As many as three million students had already been packed off to the country as part of a Maoist revolution that was shifting the emphasis in learning to "politics and productive labor." Paperwork was to be complemented by practice—"All schools must set up factories and farms," said the *Red Flag*, China's leading theoretical journal, "and all factories and farms must set up schools." Graduates who had dreamed of sheltered "bourgeois careers" would be tempered in the rough school of life, to emerge both "red" and "expert"; only a minority moved up the scholastic ladder without budging from their hometowns. Meanwhile, an explosion of part-work—part-study schools in the villages of China offered a little learning to children of illiterates who had never seen a blackboard before, and in this way the sons of the yokels on the ground and the pampered migrants from the cities—farmers, students, cadres, and intellectuals alike—were eventually to be fused into a single breed of "cultured peasants."

But to gaze out of a carriage window at the grotesque cliffs and crevasses of pockmarked loess, the desolate moon country of Chinese cave dwellers that flanked the iron road through Shaanxi to Xian in 1958, was to wonder how Mao—who knew it so well—could possibly base his egalitarian dreamland on this idyll. "All up and about at five-thirty A.M.," say my scribbled notes. "Teams of small children working in the valleys. Tumbledown mud houses. Haggard old men in rags. Bony beasts. Doors leading only to caves. No lights after dark."

Xinli Advanced Cooperative in Sichuan province was not like that—

not the unsightly dust of centuries that the Chinese could not sweep under the rug, but a showplace on the approved visiting list for foreigners. Yet while the piggeries and cowsheds were as absurdly clinical as a Swiss dairy farm in a milk chocolate commercial, the same small tumbledown homesteads with crumbling walls and gaping roofs dotted the emerald-green fields. When I looked more closely, however, I saw that they were not just neglected. They had been abandoned.

"Where does everyone live?" I asked the teak-faced cadre beside me. He turned and pointed silently. In the middle distance there rose a grim, gray barrack of a building like a penitentiary on a moor. It was a communal dormitory with one central kitchen and dining hall, built to house and feed a hundred families that had been moved out of their cottages and each allocated two diminutive earth-floored rooms within it. It was to be one of many, as the last vestigial stake of the peasant was taken from him all over China, and he became a paid laborer in a "people's commune."

The cadre did not reveal this to me, but I could hardly complain, for I was in exalted company. Mao had not yet submitted to the Politburo his plans to push China one stage further towards total collectivization, but had once more waylaid it with a fait accompli. Touring the country in April 1958, he had quietly encouraged the "spontaneous" formation of these human anthills in which ultimately no one was to own anything because everyone would own everything, and the first was put together that same month. Yet when the Party Congress met in May, they were not even mentioned, and it was not until nine days after my visit to Xinli Cooperative in August that the Politburo was convened to "discuss the question of people's communes."

Eleven more days were to pass before Party leaders gave formal consent to their creation, in spite of claims that they would be fulfilling the "great aspirations" of 500 million peasants. But by then neither the Party leaders nor the peasants had much choice, for between 170 million (official figures) and 350 million (unofficial figures) had realized their "great aspirations" willy-nilly and were already commune members. It only remained to reorganize the rest, and that was achieved in the following two months. Within a single year 750,000 farming cooperatives had been merged to form 26,500 people's communes nearly thirty times their size, in which the peasant shared his illustory collective wealth with up to 50,000 of his fellows.

Mao was turning dream into reality. The commune was not just an agricultural syndicate. It was a self-contained conglomerate of farms, fisheries, and factories with its own schools, hospitals, and defense corps, within which the peasant, the worker, the teacher, the student, and the militiaman were to be ground evenly into peasant-worker-teacher-student-soldier. Its members were represented by a rubber-stamp congress, but it was administered by a local government committee dominated by Party cadres who ran everything, selling all its produce, buying all its needs, and managing all its money.

The Chairman could line up persuasive arguments for creating the communes. The cities were so packed with people that it had become almost impossible to keep them in simple wants, yet an emaciated agriculture was expected not only to feed and clothe the towns, but to pay for industrial development. At the same time Peking's control over the country was too rigid. The provinces should be given more freedom to use their initiative, and should pass on that freedom to lower echelons —"The counties and districts and townships should not be put in a straightjacket," he had said two years before.

Mao conjured up a vision of a balanced, decentralized China, reassembled in a harmonious pattern of self-reliant cells, and as rational as a chessboard. Within the cells all boundaries would be erased, so that farming could be mechanized, women could be released from family chores for collective labor, men could be mobilized for work on major public projects, and the surfeit of unemployed humanity in the over-crowded cities could be absorbed and digested under the *xiafang* system. Small local factories would make the machines needed for mechanization and (he later suggested) light arms for the militia.

Between Peking above and the humble production team below, the people's commune would become the standard subdivision of an egalitarian society; the capital-and-province, town-and-country "contradictions" would go, and a new, uniform social and economic grid of these "production-administration units" would be stamped on the republic in place of the untidy and uneconomical mosaic of the old society. China was to be containerized.

For Mao there was more to it, of course—the union of mental and manual labor, and the emergence of the compleat Communist who could "use a pen to write articles, a hoe to weed, a gun to fight, and a platform to make political propaganda," jack of all trades but master of only one Thought. There were communes in the cities, often organized around some giant industrial complex, but they were poor, half-hearted imitations of the real thing down in the country, where at one stroke private possessions were sometimes reduced to little more than a man stood up in. The peasant no longer owned a private plot, a pig, a donkey, or a tool bigger than a spade. The commune took everything, including his house if he had one.

The pittance he had earned from his allotment had gone, and he was paid for his work with a mixture of rice coupons, free canteen meals, simple daily necessities (if available), and a fixed wage that might be worth no more than half of the total, or even a tenth—some communes supplied not only free food but free clothing, housing, education, cinema seats, and haircuts in lieu of cash. Just as the boundary markings between fields were removed and the verges plowed up for planting, so were the social boundaries flattened and the landscape of life itself changed, as the entire community was reorganized for a purely collective existence and the last pathetic signs of individual "bourgeois" ownership were obliterated.

In the more advanced communes the family was simply dismembered. Children under four went into nurseries, and by the time they were seven they would be boarded out in one of China's nine million primary schools to learn to eat, work, and sleep collectively. Old people were moved into "homes of happiness," where they fed poultry, wove baskets, or mended clothes. Husband and wife ate in a mess hall. The food was meager and coarse—rice, millet buns, sweet potatoes—and the "mess hall" itself might be an open space outside a primitive communal kitchen, without tables or benches. *China Youth Daily* published a sad little poem from a peasant on this controversial subject that ran:

> At the sound of the cease-work bell
> We enter the mess hall to eat.
> Taking one mouthful of rice,
> We find sand between our teeth;
> Helping ourselves to vegetable,
> We find grass stalks in it.
> We lay down our chopsticks,
> And go to work again.

Since isolated families wasted precious working time walking to and from the distant mess hall, the gap was plugged by tearing down their scattered crofts and moving them into communal "habitation centers" like the one at Xinli. These were built around the canteen, whose collective urns and caldrons had often been cast from the melted-down cooking pots of individual households (remolding was not confined to man). With no need to cook or care for young or old, one wife could now look after four living units, liberating three married women for collective labor, so that in time nearly 50 percent of the manual work force was female. "Women hold up half of Heaven," the ancients had said. Mao had given the old saw an extra twist, but few in the new paradise savored the irony.

Freeing women for hard work was an end in itself, but it was also a pretext for replacing the family with the fellowship of the labor shift. The old Confucian obligations between father and son, brother and brother, were to give way to a man's obligation to his mates in the collective and, beyond that, to the Party. China had seemingly beaten the Russians to communism by taking a shortcut.

No pastoral idyll awaited the intellectual "transferred downward" from city to people's commune, however. Told that the Party committee of her university had magnanimously "decided to let teaching staff go to the countryside to undergo thought reform by eating, living, and laboring with the peasants," a schoolmistress suspected of "rightism" (since she bore the telltale puncture marks of a Western education) was promptly constrained to "volunteer" in order to improve her image. Parted from her four-year-old son, she found herself living in a mud hut of two tiny, candlelit rooms and sharing the brick bed that filled one of them with a peasant woman and her son, as well as six of her colleagues. The floor was of earth, the room airless, the peasants were filthy, and when she produced her one bar of soap it was denounced as a "bourgeois luxury." The squalor was "part of our ideological toughening process," she said afterwards—she could hardly complain, since of course Mao himself would not have minded it.

On their first morning the teachers were squadded, given long-handled shovels, taken out to the fields, and ordered to dig furrows one meter deep. They started this back-breaking toil of "plowing" without plows at six-thirty, stopped briefly for maize gruel two hours later, and worked on until noon, when they were given a bowl of soup and a maize cake, which they ate squatting where they were. After that they put in another five hours of spadework from two until seven, with nothing to sustain them but a single gourd of water. But they were not through yet. During the whole of the first month they would take their frugal supper in the fields—the flyblown food was always the same, a few simple variations on maize, cabbage, and broad beans—and continue digging from eight until one or two in the morning by the light of smoking carbide lamps, often shoveling by touch.

At weekly meetings the sick and exhausted teachers had to find ways of standing up and making the right ritualistic noises—"I thank the Party for giving me the opportunity . . . my impression of the village is that things here are much better than I expected." Lies inevitably failed them, and nobody believed a word anybody said, but that was irrelevant. There were numerous "ideological tests"—to drink from a cup that a lousy, dirt-encrusted peasant had just used, to accept with gratitude a stinking quilt black with grease. The schoolmistress was to do a stint carrying manure in one hundred pound baskets down steep hillsides, and another beating human excrement into a smooth paste for use as fertilizer. But to wash something, or to flinch from a meal of maize cake and salted roots crawling with worms in a "mess hall," was to be damned for a bourgeois backslider.

Dysentery, and a kidney damaged by overwork as a beast of burden, finally won her a reprieve—though not before her Party secretary had given her the benefit of his displeasure for falling ill. Pandering to one's health was "typical of a capitalist intellectual," he declared. But for the moment the fight was over.

The word is not ill chosen. Mao, the master strategist whose military prowess had won him his empire "on horseback," who had proved that his principle of a "people's war" fought by the millions was the sure formula for victory, was going to prove it again. The commune was to become an army camp in which the bewildered peasants were rudely shaken out of their idle civilian routine. Formed into platoons, companies, battalions, and regiments, they were roused by the bugle or the sound of whistles before dawn, and marched off to the fields in work squads, cigarettes extinguished, spades at the slope, banners waving bravely in the wind, singing revolutionary songs. They did not simply go to work—plowing, sowing, reaping, struggling with the seasons and the elements; they "made war on Heaven." They did not tackle urgent farming tasks, they "stormed the fortresses of nature"; their fatiguing stints of distasteful labor after dark were "night actions" to be fought in "combat style," and they were warned to "observe military discipline," to "behave like soldiers," to "act as if in battle." The fields were not just fields; they were "the front."

The slogan "every man a soldier," which justified all the dragooning, was the master key to Mao's dreams. It covered everything from communal living to the mobilization of the masses, from the imposition of strict discipline on the entire Chinese people to the regimentation of most of them in the militia—the human "sea" in which any imprudent invader would be drowned. "Worker-peasant-soldier" embraced more than farm and factory hand; in many provinces cadres and workers on the roads and railways, in finance offices and trade bureaus, tax departments and statistical divisions, were also formed into army corps and reclassified "commanders" and "fighters."

The new dual-purpose units of Chinese humanity were to be production brigades in peace, militia battalions in war, ready to drop the pen or the plow for the sword when the first blow was struck. An average people's commune might boast fifteen battalions, and the number of nominal militia in all China was soon estimated at between 200 and 250 million—nominal, because although a small minority were earmarked to handle more sophisticated arms and equipment, only one man in ten might be issued a rifle, and one in forty be properly trained to use it.

China was not at war with the imperialists, however, but with China, and the immediate effect of all the militarization was to make it easier to mobilize shock troops to fill some breach or break through some bottleneck in the economy. Setting up their tactical "fighting headquarters" and working day and night without cease, conscript armies of workers threw themselves into gigantic farming and water-conservancy programs on a scale hallowed by the feats of the despots who had built the Great Wall and the Imperial Canal. On one project in Shandong alone fifteen million people were mobilized to plow up thirteen million acres of land. The Chinese were exhorted to toil like "ants removing a mountain," and the huge black-clad columns I watched building one reservoir looked like nothing else as they tore the scenery up by hand, one shallow basketload of dirt after another, until it was utterly transformed as far as the eye could see.

These monstrous labor gangs often marched great distances to the site of their corvée, where they might live for months under campaign conditions, building their own camps and toiling twenty-four hours a day on a two-shift schedule right through the winter by the light of anything from arc lights to candles. They had to bring their own baskets for carrying soil and their own spades and shovels, they were given two meals of plain rice a day, and paid nothing. A typical *xiafang* student working on a reservoir said, "We were not treated like laborers, but like the inmates of a concentration camp . . . the atmosphere of the place was very frightening." Miracles were bought with the common coin of misery, and much was achieved. "We have a new theory of evolution," a cadre explained to me in Xian. "You believe God made man, but in fact man developed through labor. It wasn't your God, it was work." One thing was obvious: You could not believe in both deities simultaneously.

Those who take his Utopia at face value could argue that many aspects of the people's communes would have earned the blessing of the saintly Sir Thomas More. The Utopians wore the same plain clothes all the time, a household was made up of not less than ten people (not more than sixteen), and when a city became too crowded, the overflow was obliged to *xiafang* to a backward area. In the towns a bugle was blown to announce meals, and thirty households assembled to eat in a communal dining room under a district boss (to eat at home was bad form), while the under-fives were fed in nurseries. All internal movement within the country required a permit, and people usually traveled together on a group passport. There were no private meeting places, as "everyone had his eye on you," and since there was a free exchange of surpluses between towns, the whole island was "like one big household." Gold was disdained and work exalted.

But "Utopia" means Noplace, just as "Erehwon" is Nowhere in a looking glass, and More was not only fantasizing but pulling our legs, like the rest of the utopia-mongers. It is not surprising, therefore, that while the ideal Chinese Noplace might have been clearly marked on the map in Mao's mind, it was difficult to see it on the ground.

The drafting of 100 million peasants for work on water-conservancy projects alone drained indispensable labor from the farming communes; the large peasant "battalions" proved less efficient in the fields than had family teams with pride and profit to lure them on; and breaking down boundaries had not opened up the land to mechanization, for no machine had yet been invented that could cope with the idiosyncrasies of the flooded paddyfield. The communes were sternly criticized for wasting labor and material, for in a new society ruthlessly streamlined for production, output was "very unstable" and "registering little or no increase."

The depersonalized peasant had been deprived of his land, and compelled to exchange family life for a communal existence under autocratic officials who, according to the official press, simplified their methods of work on the principle that "to organize along military lines just meant giving orders." Many tried to put Mao's concepts into practice by stamping all inequalities flat and paying everyone the same without regard for performance, so that the industrious found themselves financing the loafers. The familiar Chinese pattern of the patient peasant goaded into belated revolt—now threatening to become as repetitive after nine years of communism as it had been during the past nine centuries of empire—surfaced again. The rustic beneficiaries of Mao's ideological bounty once more dodged collective work with the guile of their kind, slaughtered cattle, robbed silos, poisoned fish ponds and even, on occasion, the food of their cadres. Students sent down to the country were openly antagonistic, regarding an agricultural career as a degrading loss of face. "Instead of showing respect for manual workers, they despise them. This is a feudalistic, aristocratic, and bourgeois point of view," the press complained. Nobody wanted to be equal.

As usual, the human factor had let the social planners down, and the planners now launched a series of campaigns to educate the malcontents. Too many were under the unfortunate impression that they worked for the state, and were therefore clamoring for more money and better conditions. But when they were told that they themselves were the masters of their communes, they became all the more exigent, for China had unwisely boasted that grain output had doubled between 1957 and 1958, and they found it difficult to understand why, as the bosses, they should be on such short rations.

It had meanwhile been impressed upon cadres that they should "let politics take command of everything," and many had then assumed that business methods could be forgotten. Some commune accountants dispensed with bookkeeping altogether, records of income and expenditure were found to be inaccurate or entirely missing, and the explanation was advanced that as all money now belonged to the state anyway, there was no point in keeping track of its movements. Administrators accustomed to rigid control from above failed to grasp the principles of financial autonomy, and cadres spent commune reserves without thought for the morrow. Conversely, leading officials of some communes concluded that as they were self-sufficient units, there was no need for the state at all, and hoarded grain that should have been surrendered to it. "People are simply becoming stupid with overwork," a foreign Communist living in Peking told me. Why?

Mao may have shuffled and then redealt China into 26,500 people's communes, each of them potentially strong in all four suits—farming, industry, culture, defense—but matters did not stop there. For this bold and sweeping redistribution was related to a daring gamble to lift China right out of the orthodox Russian pattern for reconstruction, and in one jump put her ahead of Britain as a modern, industrial state—the "Great Leap Forward."

The original economic plan for 1958 was comfortingly pedestrian—grain output was to increase by less than 6 percent, steel by less than two million tons. But in January of that year an exalted Mao riding the crest of one of his own waves decided that the Chinese were now being "swept by a burning tide," and once their energy was harnessed, they would catch up with Britain within fifteen years. "We shall produce forty million tons of steel a year," he announced, "against just over five million tons today." His twelve-year agricultural plan would be completed in eight years, some said five, even three.

In March the masses were told that "miraculous surprises" were in store, and seemingly impossible "advanced targets" would be reached as men "put politics in command" and begged to take on more work for less money. Doing everything "faster, better, more economically," they were going to smash the industrial sound barrier and convert their backward republic into a modern, affluent colossus in one breathtaking burst of human energy—"hard work for three years, happiness for a thousand."

The tactics were familiar: During the spring a peripatetic Mao first passed his chiliastic message of national salvation to the masses in the provinces, and only in May did a Party congress formally launch the Great Leap Forward in the name of the Chairman, after he had regaled delegates with imaginative and invigorating statistics. Steel production was to be doubled—"With eleven million tons next year, and seventeen million tons the year after that, we shall shake the world." Had he calculated it would take China fifteen years to accomplish the miracle ahead? He now spoke of producing those 40 million tons of steel in five years, overtaking Britain in seven, America in the remaining eight.

Three months later the Party also sanctioned the rejigging of China into people's communes, which were not only to double grain production, but to set up their own "backyard" steel furnaces to boost national output and enhance their own self-sufficiency. Communism was around the corner, and in October the *People's Daily* proclaimed exultantly: "Today, in the era of Mao Tsetung, Heaven is here on earth." For the masses, the Millennium had arrived; for Mao, the Day of Judgment.

✸ *CHAPTER* FIFTEEN ✸

C HAIRMAN MAO SAYS . . ." There is an old-fashioned children's game in which everyone must follow their leader and obey his orders (however preposterous they may be), provided he prefaces them with the words, "O'Grady says"—but ignore him if he does not. Like men hearing a call to arms, peasants abandoned their fields, textile workers their spindles, and students their classrooms to devote themselves to building furnaces and turning out backyard steel, as Mao had commanded. Echoing his exhortations to "go all out and aim high," to "concentrate twenty years in a single day," the Chinese hurled themselves pell-mell into the greatest uncoordinated do-it-yourself drive in history, and by October 1958 they had constructed seven hundred thousand "small iron foundries" employing one man in every ten in the entire country.

Wuhan medical college was closed down completely for the campaign, one student recounted later. "Everyone took part, even the doctors and nurses from the college hospital. We built over twenty native-style furnaces in the college grounds." They had to fetch the cement, stones, bricks, iron bars, and pottery clay from places ten miles and more away, and they had nothing to carry even the earth in—"We used to tie up the ends of trousers, fill them with clay, and sling them over our shoulders, like sacks." They made very little steel— "just a few pounds a day"—but no one cared about the amount. The main thing was to respond to the Party's appeal and to learn what the life of a laborer was like. Medicine could wait.

Not all were so modest. Mao's vainglorious arithmetic had blown sober facts and figures up into thin-skinned fantasy, cadres all over China rose to the challenge, and, as the statistics soared skyward, their reports of improbable local gains began to trouble those afraid of heights. Hebei province alone claimed that during one twenty-four hour period in October its backyard Bethlehems had produced as much iron as the entire industry of the United States. Other regions were making "high-grade carbon steel," and Henan boasted that every county in the province had a ball-bearing factory "up to Swedish standards." The 102 counties of Shaanxi were each building 10,000 small plants, and a thousand more were opening in the province every day, the director of planning told me in Xian.

Genuinely exhilarated (when not prudently stage-drunk), the Chinese strove to push their production graphs ever higher, each man eager to be seen to be out in front. The Swiss manager of an aluminum factory in Shanghai to whom I talked had been astounded to see his workers make the incredible jump in output impatient officials had demanded from above—"It could only happen in China." But quality, by definition outnumbered, too often loses to quantity, and this was to prove true not only of aluminum, but literature. Authors answered the call for "more, faster, better" by churning out half a dozen worthless potboilers in the time it would have taken to write a serious book, and the one million poems extolling Mao and the communes composed by peasants in accordance with the egalitarian "every-man-a-Shakespeare" principle were to be mercilessly dissected by the profane.

The story was everywhere the same, for the same principle applied: Mao had condemned the "vulgar theory of balance," disequilibrium was normal, and where one branch of the economy fell behind another, it must always be adjusted "upwards." The speed of the convoy had become the speed of the fastest ship. In every factory I visited the cadres were stampeding the workers into setting themselves higher targets which were always "subject to further revision," their voices nagging away at one's sanity with hallucinatory figures and forecasts, like the whispers of a mad tipster.

The Tianjin Steel Works and the Xian Agricultural Machinery Plant were to double their production during 1958, the Xian Condenser Factory to multiply output by five. "Our timetable for overtaking the British originally covered two years," a trade union cadre yelled at me above the clamor of the Shanghai Diesel Factory, "but then we got together with the workers and cut it to one year, and since then we've reduced it to six months." I looked him in the eye, but he did not blink. Instead, he coolly told me that the plant had manufactured 1,400 diesels during 1957, but at a series of meetings the elated workers had agreed to raise the target for 1958 first to 2,800, then to 4,200, and finally to 5,600 engines. "And next year?" I asked, even more coolly. Unabashed, he gave me the Chinese equivalent of a shrug. "Who knows?"

The Shanghai Chemical Industry Factory was not to be outdone. After five conferences, the workers had fixed the 1958 target at five times the value of the output for the previous year, and instead of introducing eight new products, as originally planned, they were making 130 (sic). At the Wuhan Iron and Steel Complex a second furnace scheduled to be built by the middle of 1959 was already working because (and I could have joined in the chorus) "after a series of meetings" the workers had agreed to move the date for completion forward to December, then October, then September, and finally August. And as with the diesel engines and steel furnaces, so with condoms. "In 1956 we sold six and a half million sheaths, most of them foreign," a gentle old lady in the Ministry of Health told me in Peking, "but this year we shall be putting out twenty-four million." And next year? The Chinese shrug.

All industry had become a crash operation, and one emerged from the crash—as from all crashes—dazed, if not stunned, pinching oneself to make sure one was alive and awake. But the countryside offered no relief. On a fine summer evening in West China a cadre pointed to a pastoral scene of peasant women tearing up clumps of grass and clearing weed from a pond, their conical hats bobbing and dipping in the fading light. "Number Two Production Team," he said. "They're collecting green manure. We use everything we can lay our hands on for fertilizer. This year we are spreading about three tons per acre, but to reach our new production targets we reckon to put down up to four hundred or even five hundred tons per acre next year." Between a hundred and two hundred times the weight? I broke the awkward silence by asking another question, only to be plunged deeper into the morass of my own mistrust. "This year wheat output will reach eighteen hundred pounds per acre, but next year it will be twenty-five thousand pounds per acre—thirteen times as much," he replied, rattling out figures with the flat certitude of a computer. "The first rice crop this year yielded thirty-six hundred pounds per acre, but the second will yield nearly twenty thousand pounds." And after that? Another Chinese shrug.

How could this miracle be achieved? By plowing furrows at least a meter deep, piling on the fertilizer, using more and better seeds and planting them closer together—"so that in some places ten shoots will grow where only one grew before." Fretful questioning of the pundits in Peking evoked a further string of escalating zeroes that clicked upward as inevitably as the score on a pinball machine. During the first six months of the year, grain output had risen by nearly 70 percent, the early rice crop was double that of 1957, and the wheat crop had been heavier than that of the United States. And small wonder if, as the jubilant cadres claimed, the peasants were harvesting up to twenty-two tons of wheat per acre, and thirty tons of rice (not to mention raising three-ton pigs). But these figures in a dreamscape were nearly ten times life size. Where had they come from?

In January 1958 Mao had inspired a working program for the Great Leap which stipulated that farms all over the country should cultivate "experimental plots," and ministerial experts explained that in consequence every cooperative had marked out one of these agricultural test beds which might cover no more than a quarter of an acre, but would be run like an intensive-care unit. It was here that "ten shoots might grow where only one grew before," and record yields were made public so that farm officials throughout China might learn just what could be done if you really tried.

Mao had pushed millions of cadres all over the country into a stupendous rat race. Since all imbalance was to be adjusted upwards, the statistics from a pampered plot of prime soil producing the maximum possible yield under optimum conditions contained an unspoken message for men who had been ordered to "go all out and aim high." Yet its spectacular output bore no more relation to what might be achieved over a million indifferent acres in another part of the republic—even if the labor, the irrigation, and the sheer weight of seeds and fertilizer necessary were available—than a hothouse bears to Cold Comfort Farm. Some responsible officials in Peking were careful to point this out, but they would then quote the record figures for a larger "model" area—a particularly lush spread of five hundred acres, for example—which cadres in the field still felt they had no choice but to try and top, irrespective of local conditions.

Or at least appear to do so. For where they found themselves trapped between hypothetical targets they could not reach, and their fear of being stigmatized as go-slow reactionaries if they fell short, they frequently fudged. And where they did not fudge themselves, the local statistical office fudged for them, "adjusting" their findings "upward" so that they conformed with the quotas required, and confirmed the wisdom of Mao. Statistics had become political. As a leading government specialist later explained in Peking, the proper purpose of his department was to "fully utilize statistical data to reflect great success."

This only thickened the fog. The mandarins were once more reporting back to the capital what the emperor wanted to hear—especially in industry, where the more honest plant managers might add no more than an imaginary 30 percent to their true output, but the less scrupulous would solve their production problems by simply doubling or even trebling it on paper (according to one Chinese statistician who survived the ordeal). A spiral of phony figures as substantial as smoke thus rose heavenward as the returns from factory and field outbid each other, prompting a gratified Peking to call yet again for "more, faster, better"; and when Mao in consequence declared that the agricultural yield had not only doubled in 1958, but would double again in 1959, all China responded with more of the same. No one could hold back, for as the Tang Dynasty poem has it, "Seeing men all behaving like drunkards, how can I alone remain sober?" By the time Mao realized he had been inspired by nothing more than his own echo, it was too late.

Yet beneath all the statistical smoke, there was fire. The Chinese were unquestionably turning out "more, faster" in many fields and factories. But it was here that the collective delirium was paradoxically doing the most damage. If leap-happy workers at the Shanghai Chemical Industry Factory were persuaded at five successive meetings to fix the 1958 target at five times the value of the output for the previous year, they were still only juggling with disposable strings of digits. But when you caught them achieving it by speeding up the rotation of a colander so that it turned out first four, then eight, then sixteen, then eighteen meters of PVC a minute, you found yourself backing away from the whole madly spinning enigma.

It was the same in every shop. The reactor that normally produced a batch of Bakelite in seven hours was now doing the job in three because the temperature had been raised twenty degrees, while next door three rolls of plastic and four of insulating cloth were being force-fed into machines made to take only one. And it was the same with the men. "Some are working seven days a week on three shifts a day around the clock," a proud cadre told me, "and, of course, making far more than before."

He was not talking about money. In a fever to treble production, iron workers in Chungking were contriving to get ninety tons of steel from a furnace with a capacity of only fifty. In Wuhan they had progressively increased the temperature in the furnaces from 1,100 to 1,513 to 1,789 degrees in order to tap pig iron ever more frequently. But the last straw is not always a figment of the camel's imagination. "Ours is the only chemical factory of its kind," one Cantonese manager told me, "and the boiler is seventy years old. But one day a Party official arrived and told me to increase the pressure in the boiler from a hundred to a hundred and fifty pounds per square inch so that the reactor process could be completed nine times a day instead of six. When I told him he was turning it into a bomb, he accused me of being a bourgeois reactionary. So what could I do?" He gave me a slight, I-told-you-so smile. "Great Leap? The connecting pipe burst when the pressure reached a hundred and twenty pounds, and we were out of production for a week while repairs were made."

Mao had rewritten the timetable, the gauges were rising, and many had their fingers to their ears. As the overworked machines fell apart, so did the overworked men, and the steam seeped out of the Great Leap Forward. Exhausted workers slept at their benches, ignored by bleary-eyed cadres. In the diplomatic ghetto in Peking, yawning laborers put up jerry-built blocks of flats for foreigners in which the ceiling plaster fell almost as soon as it was dry, lift elevator-shafts were out of true, floors sagged, and the first shower brought the first damp. During marathon trade negotiations, dog-tired Chinese officials repeated themselves mindlessly to aliens itching for contracts. In the communes, peasants dazed after working sixteen hours on a crash program and a crash diet suffered terrible burns when they carelessly slopped molten fire onto the floor from backyard furnaces.

The skeletal road-and-rail network collapsed under the strain, for the map of China was now stippled with a great rash of hungry "small ironworks" and local manufacturing plants that had to be fed continuously with coal and coke and ore from mines and minipits and junk piles elsewhere. "Coal and iron cannot walk by themselves," Mao recognized somewhat belatedly in 1959. "They need vehicles to transport them. This I did not foresee." Meanwhile steel output might soar on paper, but the steel was too often pig iron of poor quality, fit for the scrap heap rather than the smithy—three million tons of it "failed to meet the requirements of industry."

There was no single set of blueprints for constructing the best furnace, and the backyard system was proving the enemy of standardization. Urged to become self-reliant by building up their own local plants, the communes copied haphazardly from each other, or simply tried to make everything they needed in their own way. In one car-repair shop I was able to watch a gang of metalworkers and mechanics laboriously putting together by hand a bus of their own design, in another a travesty of a Land Rover, in a third a gimcrack combine-harvester. Man-hours and money were no object, and by the end of

1958 Chinese genius had produced 50 different kinds of car and 173 different types of tractor—most of them one-off originals or one-off copies. Dispersal had proved uneconomical.

So had the combination of deep plowing, crash fertilization, close planting, and book cooking in the countryside, for it was easier to "emulate" a car built in Coventry or Detroit than an "experimental plot" in the next province. Deep plowing—carried ever deeper to outdo the neighbors—drained off water tables and left the fields crumbling; overworked land eroded as surely as overworked men and machines; seeds that sprouted splendidly in one soil shriveled in the furrows of another; and a record tonnage of fertilizer fed into the land proved it could kill as surely as a surfeit of lampreys. The Chairman had won an illusory victory, for although it was announced that China had produced a staggering 375 million tons of grain in 1958, within a year a recount would cut the figure to 250 million, and this in turn was to be dismissed as a gross fabrication. The Great Leap Forward had proved a "paper tiger."

Caught once again in a down draft, Mao beat a tactical retreat before moderates mobilized by Chou En-lai, and when it met at Wuhan in December 1958 the Central Committee was able to call for the "consolidation" of the communes. After a face-saving gloss about the achievements of the past year, the Party resolution discouraged the forging of more urban communes, frowned on the egalitarian system whereby the same free supplies were doled out to the diligent and the downright lazy, and stressed that workers and peasants should in future be paid "to each according to his labor."

For the starry-eyed observers who had protested that all the ugly tales about drudgery down in the country were the inventions of diseased minds, the resolution unconsciously offered enlightenment: It restored to the peasants their right to pursue "domestic sidelines," and promised that henceforth their property would remain their own, "including houses, clothing, bedding, and furniture." They would also be allowed to keep "the odd trees around their houses, small tools, animals, and poultry" and even their own private cooking pots, for not only would "the cohabitation of men and women and the aged and young of each family" be permitted in deserving cases, but "certain commune members may cook at home."

The building of unisex dormitories was to come to a halt. Twenty years were no longer to be "concentrated in a single day," and it was recognized that the transition to communism was "a rather long and complicated process"—the word "gradual" appeared in the text more than one hundred times. Mao's latest mess was being "tidied up," and at the end of the conference Mao himself yielded his post as head of state to Liu Shaoqi.

But twenty-three years would pass before he would be publicly reproached for being "smug about successes and impatient for quick results," and although he was to complain that he had been treated like a "dead ancestor," he did not subsequently behave like one. He had conceded to his peers at Wuhan that his final target of thirty million tons of steel for 1959—a sixfold increase over 1957—had perhaps been impracticable after all. But only two months later he was again talking directly to provincial secretaries in his role of Party Chairman, and airily dismissing the recent cutbacks imposed by the Central Committee as merely a temporary device to let the people "relax a little" in readiness for the exertions ahead, as "most likely there will be a Great Leap Forward every year." By "consolidating," Mao implied, the Party was simply gathering China together for the next jump.

Unrepentant, he confessed that "economic work" was like a "child playing with fire," but he did not admit that in inciting the masses to make a Great Leap Forward he had been like a man playing with water. But the sad truth was that he had allowed 650 million fellow-Chinese to beguile him with a treacherous reflection of his own vision that had only to be touched to dissolve.

❀ *CHAPTER SIXTEEN* ❀

Passing a peking market in his curtained limousine one day, Chairman Mao reputedly objected to the long lines of housewives he saw waiting to buy food. "There should be no need for this," he said. It was enough. The fault was rectified forthwith—not by ending the shortages that caused the queueing, but simply by abolishing queues, so that during the Great Leap Forward there was much jostling around the vegetable stalls, but cadres could truthfully tell foreign visitors, "There is no queueing in China."

This was the land not only of the hysterical legend that an entire court had admired an emperor's nonexistent new clothes, but of the historical record that an entire court had admired an emperor's non-existent new horse. To test his hold over the intimidated palace and the weakling who had succeeded the First Emperor in 210 B.C., the all-powerful Chief Eunuch presented his master with a deer, saying it was a horse. The court dutifully admired this make-believe steed, and when the emperor himself protested that it was a deer, the Grand Astrologer warned him sternly against entertaining dangerous delusions.

In China individual "face" becomes collective facade, a conspiracy to preserve the appearance of the decencies, especially when the decencies are not being preserved. The masses were not peremptorily ordered to stop queueing and start crowding. They were merely encouraged to argue themselves into a "spontaneous" decision to do so, just as the peasants had come to a "spontaneous" decision to form people's communes. The secret of the system was simple. It dignified the victim by giving him the initiative of a "volunteer." The private industrialist who had been systematically taxed out of business "made a gift of his enterprise to the people." The dispossessed shopkeeper was entitled to a percentage of future profits but "voluntarily contributed it to the

146

nation." The householder whose property was confiscated was offered reasonable compensation but "waived his right to it in the public interest." And "consultation of the masses" clothed the naked dictates of the emperor in the see-through "will of the people."

The traditional readiness of the Chinese to blend in with the crowd and murmur "rhubarb" with the rest was enhanced, moreover, by the discouraging examples of what happened to heretics. Unwritten clauses in the constitution provided in effect for coercion of the people, by the people, for the people, and the "mass line" applied to police work as to all else, so that everyone was obliged to inform on everyone in a democratic manner. It was therefore safer to conform, to join the highly competitive witch-hunts and emulation drives and sycophantic choruses, and the conspiracy thus became a monstrous charade.

"When we were called out for mass criticism against some poor wretch accused of being bourgeois," a Shanghai cadre was to tell me long afterwards, "we had nothing in our hearts. We probably didn't know whether he was good or bad. But we had to jam a dunce's cap on his head and parade him through the streets and yell imprecations at him, a whole mob of us, on pain of falling under suspicion ourselves. And he had to put a good face on it, because he knew we were all acting, just as he was acting when he confessed all his imaginary sins and wrote his self-criticisms, and anyway next time it would be somebody else's turn. We had completely lost faith in the Party. We just did what we were told. Or pretended to." He paused and hesitated. "But, you see, if by chance we were told to really tear him apart, to demand that he be consigned to a labor reform camp for life, or even shot, it would happen. He would be executed to satisfy the will of the masses, meaning us. And the terrible thing would be that all the time we would just have been acting."

This was the formal farce in which a schoolteacher sent down to the farm to stir human excrement into a smooth paste would say, "I thank the Party for giving me the opportunity to understand the ways of living of our peasants," a Party cadre would berate her for being a "capitalist" because she finally fell sick, and both would really be concerned only with remembering their lines. While for the detestable minority of class enemies retribution might be ruthless and even terminal, for the majority of the "people" whom Mao wished to remake in his own image there was always recourse to well-rehearsed mummery. A "sincere" self-criticism could earn a disgraced cadre a reprieve from political purgatory, but few "sincere" self-criticisms were sincere. Mao wanted to remold the Chinese, and the Chinese were therefore going through the motions of being remolded. The facade was like a paper window, as thin as it was opaque.

Mao was not the only Chinese with a sense of timing. In May 1958, despite his private doubts, Liu Shaoqi officially endorsed the Great Leap Forward in the air-castle rhetoric of the Chairman, citing the usual exuberant production statistics, hypocritically chiding those who had damned the "little leap" of 1956 as a "reckless advance," and deriding all rejection of imbalance as "giving up food for fear of choking." At that stage Liu had to content himself with interlarding his pharisaical cant with a warning to the Party against "wild flights of fancy" and attempting the impossible, along with a few references to future difficulties and the evils of "blind development."

The Chairman himself had shown he knew his countrymen well enough to fear they might produce snowballing statistics instead of a solid core of achievement—"If everyone is trying to surpass everyone else, the country may be thrown into confusion," he had warned in March. If things were rushed and targets unrealistic, "the work will be crude, and the masses will be overly tense . . . We must get rid of empty reports and foolish boasting."

But if Liu's ostensible enthusiasm for the Great Leap Forward in May was diluted with a thin infusion of caution, Mao's ostensible caution in March had been laced with a stiff shot of gung ho: "We should do our work boldly and joyfully, not hesitantly and coldly," he had urged twice within minutes, and later: "We should not fear disorder . . . to say that mistakes can all be avoided is an anti-Marxist proposition."

His recognition of the risk China would run makes all the more dubious his decision to take it, but he was trapped by the contradiction in his own makeup—between the canny guerrilla whose touchstone was practice, and the romantic dreamer with the blood of a nation of gamblers in his veins. He was the victim of an irrational optimism who did not heed his own warnings against free-style figuring. In the mid-fifties he had prophesied that by 1967 China would produce 430 million tons of grain, up to 20 million tons of steel, 6 million tons of cotton, and 183,000 tractors. (The true figures were to be 230 million tons of grain, 12 million tons of steel, less than 2 million tons of cotton, and only 24,000 tractors.) But it was correct, he said in 1958, to "crave greatness and success, to be impatient for quick results, to despise the past and put blind faith in the future."

Mao's irreverent dismissal of all obstacles and enemies was reflected in a book published in Peking called *Stories of Not Fearing Ghosts*. This slim anthology of classical, often comic tales emphasized the wounding disdain of the Chinese hero for supernatural horror. In it, ghosts were maltreated and humiliated in every conceivable way—sold, eaten, upbraided for not being human, ridiculed for their ugly faces, haunted back, and frightened to death. "There is nothing to be feared in the world," declared one character aptly. "Only man is timid."

The book was hailed by the official press as a "great necessity." Imperialism, reactionaries, revisionism, landlords and bad bourgeois elements, Marshal Tito, flood, fire, drought and a deviationist climate were all "so many demons, ghosts and evil spirits opposing socialist construction," and to stamp them out was therefore "the serious fighting task of every revolutionary." The message for the Chinese millions was that if the most hideous and terrifying problem—animal, mineral, or vegetable—were outfaced, it would disappear.

The spirit that to dare all was to win all was intoxicating, not only to a leader who saw the nation as "swept by a burning tide" or "rising like a tornado or tempest," but to equally imprecise compatriots who were ready to boast that they would "climb a mountain of swords" for him, or "concentrate twenty years in a single day." There was thus more to the mass mimicry of the Chairman than an animal urge for protective coloring. For as in Mao himself, caution and bravado, measured speech and the dream of the masterstroke tend to interact in the minds of many Chinese, the one compressing the other like the spring of a gun until it suddenly expands and day-to-day docility gives way to armed revolt, "consolidation" to a great leap forward. But now the opposites truly complemented each other, for while prudence dictated that the Chinese echo Mao, what they were echoing were slogans inviting them to imprudence, couched in the heroic idiom of war.

The Chinese are a nation of echoes, imbued after two thousand years and more of Confucian veneration for precedent with an instinct to conform, to emulate, and to find inspiration in neat quotations, whether antique aphorisms or modern catch phrases. The love of encapsulated wisdom is reflected in a written language that expresses abstractions in concrete metaphor—"security" is a drawing of one woman under a roof, "contradiction" a combination of a spear and a shield—and so emulation is matched by extrapolation, a tendency to derive a general principle from a single vivid illustration. And if the metaphorical nature of the language inclines the Chinese towards misleading exaggeration, its concrete nature makes him take things literally. In consequence, when in 1950 Mao declared that about 8 percent of all Chinese were landlords to be "struggled against," a local cadre would convert the rough national estimate into a precise parochial quota, and make sure that in his district eight men out of every hundred were denounced as class enemies and duly dispossessed.

These were the people on whom Mao called in 1958 for a Great Leap Forward, for "hard work for three years" that would bring happiness for a thousand, for everything to be done "better, faster, more economically," for all imbalances to be adjusted "upwards," and for experimental plots to be cultivated as pacemakers for people's communes all over China to emulate. And the results were predictable.

Fired by hyperbole and heady ideas, the more revolutionary Chinese of 1958 were a combustible mixture, high on heroics, addicted to dreams and dramas larger than life. And if for the militant the evocative battle cries of the Chairman were sacred law, for the faithless they were passwords to survival. Throughout China, therefore, all men whatever their secret thoughts would chant aloud the strip language of the slogan just as all men—good or bored—mutter the same orisons in church. The Chinese felt at ease when they could make mechanical responses, and this was a charade that left little room for common sense or questioning. Their single-mindedness, moreover, could make the zealous—and the prudent—among them slaves to one overriding purpose, which they would pursue obsessively and beyond reason, blind to all else.

The logic that encouraged farmers to abandon their fields to the weeds while they rushed off to turn out bathtub pig iron may suggest a mental hiccup, "But what is one to say of the modern metallurgical works that stopped production for three months to make backyard steel?" asked a Swiss economist who was with me in China at the time. One might ask the same question of the commune cadres who decimated the chicken population in order to pluck the feathers for forge fans. Or of the officials who melted down heating stoves for the iron, forgetting that in winter people have to keep warm, so that, among other things, the iron would be needed to make heating stoves again. Or of the geniuses who plowed up rich cattle pasture in order to emulate a record rice-growing "experimental plot" in another province.

Production, it often seemed, was being mindlessly sacrificed on the altar of production—but sometimes it was destruction. The formation of the first people's commune coincided with a campaign to kill all the sparrows in China, as these unremarkable creatures (code-named "grain-destroying sparrows" for the purpose of the operation) had been listed among the four pests whose extermination Mao had personally urged upon his fellow Chinese, a process which he said would be an ideological experience calling for "free airing of views, great debates, and big character posters."

It called for more than that, however, since the sparrows were not to be massacred by a small professional elite, but by the masses themselves. All over China millions of people dropped their spades, switched off their lathes, abandoned their office desks and their schoolrooms, and stormed out to do battle with the birds. Their weapons were pots and pans, bits of iron, cheap tin trays, and everything else that would make a loud clanging noise, and they banged these together so that the ear-shattering charivari kept the twittering malefactors in the air until they fell to the ground exhausted and could be killed in comfort.

"The entire city was mobilized for the antisparrow campaign," a factory official from Wuhan told me afterwards. "We 'volunteers' would go up on the roof, hammering on anything we could lay our hands on and yelling our heads off. Everyone was out—workers, kids (they loved it), office cadres, shopkeepers, housewives. The schools closed down, and production was cut by about half for a whole week. Well, there were literally millions of us, so of course we got a certain number of sparrows, but a lot flew off to the countryside. Not enough, though, it seems. Because the next crop was half-destroyed by the pests the sparrows normally ate. So they took us off birds, and in 1959 it was bedbugs."

Pitched, meanwhile, into a contest of statistical one-upmanship whose goals automatically receded whenever it seemed they might by some miracle be reached, frustrated cadres were projecting a mirage of the miracle. And the mirage was sustained not only by falsified production figures, but by much crafty semantical scene painting, whereby not only did conscripted workers become "volunteers" who had "spontaneously" voted to toil in the muckyard, but compost heaps became "fertilizer plants," radio sets became "broadcast-receiving stations," water mills became "hydroelectric stations," pig iron became "carbon steel," and a man picking up ferrous metal in a field with a magnet was called an "industrial element." This was all quite normal to the Chinese, who in their day had called the entrance to the torture house of the secret police "The Gate of Beautiful Vistas," and a dish of boiled humanity "two-legged mutton." Confucius had vainly called for the "rectification of names" 2,500 years before. The weakness for self-delusion was of long standing.

Literary purists who deplore the use of quotation marks to distinguish fake from genuine have not had to cope with this looking-glass land of the two-legged "industrial element," nor face the truth that the only succinct way in which to distinguish between those who gave their loyalty and those who paid lip service to Mao is to describe them as Maoists and "Maoists."

Behind this rough-and-ready division there were, of course, more than 600 million variations on the theme, but since all wore the same mask and bowed to the same gods, all were capable of the same irrational behavior, and it was impossible to know whether they believed in it or not. Despite falling output, one commune went on growing cotton unprofitably for twenty years after Mao had personally inspected its fields, because no one dared to suggest switching to another crop for fear of being charged with "disloyalty to the leader." Another wasted 16,000 workdays vainly trying to emulate the Foolish Old Man in the fable by flattening a mountain by hand in the hope of acquiring an extra acre or two to farm.

Meanwhile the infallible leader who preached practice had failed to practice what he preached. Mao himself had not taken the mountain apart stone by stone, but had committed the greater folly of trying to blow it up overnight. He had been driven by his impatience to outstrip the ideological gnomes in the Kremlin, and he was to claim that the Great Leap Forward had successfully put an end to "blind faith" in the Soviet model for socialist construction. But he had left economic rubble in its place. For when he trusted his instinct that a "revolutionary upsurge" had arrived, he forgot that it was he himself who had made the waves.

He might also have been misled by his sublime or ridiculous faith in the will of the masses. The man who believed it was "all in the mind" knew the mind of the Chinese better than any other. Yet he had speculated with it, exploiting weaknesses, gambling on strengths. A playactor from a nation of playactors, he could not have been fooled by the charade but chose to fool himself. He must have known that if he shouted "Great Leap Forward," China might try to jump out of her skin but would be more likely to put on an elaborate show of doing so. The obverse side of the proposition that if you disbelieve in ghosts they will disappear is that if you believe in the mirage it will become the miracle—and Mao desperately wanted to believe that the Great Leap Forward was indeed a great leap forward.

Guilt was shared, however. Mao could not evade responsibility for the mess that was China, any more than God can evade responsibility for the mess that is man. On the other hand, although the Chairman imposed the mistakes—"O'Grady says"—the mandarins and the masses acquiesced in them. Deng Xiaoping had abetted him by dutifully under-lining the "very pressing" need for more urban communes, Liu Shaoqi had launched the Great Leap, and the gang of 650 million had then gone to work on the script, compounding Mao's errors in order to prove him unerring. They had chosen calculated dissimulation rather than open dissent, and in consequence they had got the Mao they deserved, for each had distorted the other, and it was now difficult to say who had been remolding whom. They were all Chinese, trapped in a Chinese comedy of manners.

Mao, who knew the conventions, could hardly be forgiven his myopia—or for turning a blind eye. It did not take a genius to write in 1958, "After learning how workers had decided arbitrarily to double, treble, even quadruple the original figures for current production which had been, after all, soberly worked out by their own experts in the first place, I could only reflect how appropriate it was that the most famous dish in China should be called *canard de Pékin*." In fact, I wrote it myself.

For the foreigner, the Chinese facade started with the "cheese" syndrome. The first glossy magazine a visitor picked up after crossing the border into China would be filled with photographs of happy children —or peasants, workers, soldiers, wrinkled geriatrics, disabled veterans, even hospital patients awaiting major surgery—all of them showing their teeth in an eternal land of smiles and sunshine. He would then be led down an insulated rat run that would take him between invisible walls to selected farms, factories, and shipyards, clinics and kinder-gartens, museums and monuments passed fit for international consump-tion. In cities like Peking and Shanghai he would be free to wander at his leisure, but leisure was scarce, for his program was packed with action by professionals who knew that the foreign devil finds mischief for idle hands, especially if he is an inquisitive newspaperman.

Since crime had officially vanished from China, he could not throw away a pair of old socks in Peking without having them returned to him in Wuhan. Since China officially tolerated religion, he would be greeted in scheduled temples by smiling monks who would tell him how awful life had been for priests and pagodas before the atheists took over. Since the bourgeoisie were being magnanimously allowed to take part in the building of the new China, he would be driven to the sumptuous mansion of a tame Shanghai textile tycoon who would assure him almost with tears in his eyes how much happier he was now than he had been in the bad old days when he was making millions.

But even the veteran of a dozen tours remained unaware of the care and attention to stagecraft that went into the illusion. "When your Prime Minister Clement Attlee visited Canton in 1954, not only were the fronts of all the buildings he would pass freshly painted for the occasion, but people who worked or lived along the route were rehearsed in their roles for three months before he came," one of the extras told me afterwards. "Even an old chap who sold cigarettes from a pitch outside our office—one stick at a time—was given ten lessons in what to say if by chance the foreigners stopped and asked him something. It was standard procedure."

It was the fault of the foreigner if he deceived himself. The Chinese doubtless hoped that he would extrapolate in his turn, and take the "models" he was shown to be typical of all China, but they would regard him with contempt if he did. And there was no reason why he should, because the system was far from foolproof: invisible walls do not hide, and information, like water, can percolate down to the senses through the narrowest of cracks. Yet he did deceive himself—when he was naive enough, arrogant enough, or eager enough to find nothing wrong. That meant that although on occasion he might be a diplomat or journalist with partisan views, he was usually an academic or some other visiting "intellectual."

One French professor described the mass labor projects he had seen as a manifestation of the "*active* and *voluntary participation* of the majority*," his impression being that the Party had succeeded "in marrying its authority to the peasant's consent." Another declared that economic growth during the Great Leap Forward implied "great clearness of thought, a lucid vision . . . shared by the masses." What he had observed had been "a real technical revolution coming from the masses themselves." The distinguished author Sir Herbert Read, who visited China in 1959, wrote of the people's commune: "It does not matter what the system is called . . . *what counts more than statistics is the happiness and contentment of the peasants.*"

The eminent sinologist Dr. Joseph Needham praised the emancipation of women that allowed them to follow "careers" on the farm or the railway, in the factory or in intellectual work. Referring to the drudgery of the housewife in the peasant home of the past, he asserted that the cooperatives, the communal canteen, and the public bath "seem more like heaven on earth to millions." The free mess halls were "a matter of pride in China today, not of compulsion or regimentation." For the writer Felix Greene, who quotes these gentlemen with approval, the cost in misery paid by the Chinese for their collective achievements was a "tired cliché."*

As fellow travelers had done in the grisly heyday of Stalin's Russia, so intellectuals from abroad clamored to get in on the act in Mao's China, propping up the facade by taking official show-and-tell for truth. But although many got things so gratifyingly wrong, Mao must have wished they had been right. Had the sunrise over China been real rather than academic, he might have been more justified during the single year of 1958 in matching a bold and revolutionary domestic program with an equally bold and revolutionary foreign policy. For while the first would indeed sentence the Chinese to "three years of hard work," the second would threaten to postpone "happiness for a thousand" by plunging them into a dangerous confrontation with both nuclear superpowers simultaneously.

* These quotations are taken from Felix Greene's book *A Curtain of Ignorance.* The italics are his.

THE FACADE CRACKS

When the Ruler loses his godlike qualities, tigers
prowl behind him.
(THE "HAN FEIZI" THIRD CENTURY B.C.)

❀ *CHAPTER* SEVENTEEN ❀

URING THE LONG, dry summer a million cicadas in the old Legation Quarter of Peking would suddenly begin to trill in unison, as if at a hidden signal, and then just as suddenly stop, leaving a heavy silence. But the day after my arrival in 1958, this shrill whirring-by-numbers went unheard. The Chinese themselves had taken over.

They packed the avenue outside the British Embassy, a wall-to-wall mob of strident workers and cadres and students that moved slowly through it in massive shifts day and night for nearly forty-eight hours without a break as new contingents arrived to replace the old. And for this spontaneous demonstration against perfidious Albion, the 250,000-odd extras had been liberally supplied with red banners and paper pennants, makeshift latrines and watermelon stalls had been set up, raucous loudspeakers in the dusty trees blared endless imprecations, government cine-cameras recorded the proceedings, and at night powerful arc lights were focused on the gateway of the famous compound.

The high wall was already papered from end to end with "big character posters" execrating the warmongering Anglo-American imperialists for their despicable act of aggression in sending troops into Jordan and Lebanon in order to foment a crisis in the Middle East, and within two days one hundred million people all over the country would down tools to hold immense protest rallies. "The Chinese people are very angry with you over Jordan," I was warned by a frigid female official who threatened to cancel my visa.

Were they? The great red double doors of the embassy were kept open during the entire performance, and two members of the staff stood just inside them, facing the mob and ready to receive petitions. Cadres eager to instill some hatred into this hot, tired, cheerful, and inquisitive cross section of the enraged Chinese people would wave their fists and bellow insults at the imperturbable barbarians, and the crowd would virtuously chant the responses: "Down with the British government. Get out of Jordan." Hemmed in and questioned by a handful of youthful zealots as I pushed my way towards this litany through an amalgam of Chinese, I was nevertheless released with embarrassed smiles as soon as I asked if anyone could tell me where Jordan was. In front of me, a venerable delegate of the indignant masses handed in a written protest at the gate, shouting some carefully memorized contumely or other, but when the British second secretary who took it from him then stuck out his hand, the old man solemnly shook it (to be whisked around the corner by outraged cadres for immediate re-education).

The Chinese servants of the mission balked when called upon to join the masses in the mudslinging against their "red-haired" masters, but trooped out philosophically to curse the chargé d'affaires in feeble accents after he had personally told them to do so, and then trooped back in again to apologize and get on with their chores. Walking out of the embassy again that night into the glare of the arc lights and the anonymous roar in the darkness beyond, I had to step over a squirming "John Bull" who was just being bayoneted by a ferocious "Arab" in a dramatic sketch performed to howls of approval from the onlookers— who then made way for me to pass through them without demur. On the next day the charade ended, and the cicadas were back.

In 1967 a similar mob would burn down the British chancery and beat up members of the staff, but this time the script called only for sound and fury. The Anglo-Saxons had been given a ritual warning. And perhaps not just the Anglo-Saxons.

Ten days later Nikita Khrushchev flew into Peking for secret talks with Mao. He had failed miserably to stop the British and Americans from putting troops into Jordan and Lebanon, and his muted reaction had been to propose a summit meeting of Security Council members. In Mao's book, the Russians were running true to their old form. It was inadmissible that Moscow should hold truck with the American imperialists who still supported the bandit Chiang Kai-shek in Taiwan, and after a few days of ill-tempered horse-trading, Khrushchev bowed to the objections of the disgusted Chinese, and dropped the suggestion. Instead, he recommended that the UN General Assembly debate the tension in the Arab world, but when that threatened to take the edge off the crisis, the frustrated Chinese provoked another within forty-eight hours by bombarding the Nationalists on the fortified offshore island of Quemoy. A belligerent Mao was going to teach fainthearts that the only thing the imperialists understood was a hard smack on the nose, and the reluctant Russians thus found themselves in danger of being dragged willy-nilly straight from the brink of one war to the brink of another.

Mao's minimum objective was to show the Kuomintang their own vulnerability, that the Chinese Communists could punish their enemy any time he became too obstreperous with a limited but devastating in-and-out operation that would leave him permanently uneasy in the future—as they were to do again when they invaded India briefly in 1962, and Vietnam in 1979. Moreover, tension had to be maintained if the millions were to take the strain of the Great Leap Forward, and a foreign threat could concentrate the mind wonderfully—as Mencius had said, "The absence of an external enemy will lead to the ruin of the state."

The external enemy was unnervingly on cue. As PLA artillery pulverized Quemoy, the Americans poured men, ships, and jets into the arena; the U.S. Navy escorted Nationalist convoys, the U.S. Air Force flew shotgun beside Nationalist transports making air drops over the beleagured island, and American Sidewinder missiles fitted to Nationalist fighters blew the Communist air force out of the sky over the Straits of Taiwan. On the other hand, Khrushchev warned Washington that "an attack on the People's Republic of China . . . is an attack on the Soviet Union" only after the danger had passed, and Moscow did not supply the Communists with the air-to-air missiles that might have matched the Sidewinders and given their jets a fighting chance.

The Chinese could be excused for feeling trapped between two evils. Stalin's successors might have increased Soviet economic aid to Peking, but in the best traditions of the loan shark, the more they gave the deeper they drove China into debt and the more China became dependent upon them. Even where their views appeared to coincide during the first half of the fifties, appearances were sometimes deceptive. The Chinese had conformed with the peaceable foreign policy of "international cooperation" with bourgeois governments laid down by the Kremlin. But they had adroitly translated it into a purely tactical offensive to re-establish their traditional influence over Asia, offering plausible pledges of friendship to non-Communist states while exploiting the prestige of Peking (as their ancestors had done in times of weakness, when words had to make do for weapons). Moreover, the master builder of this spiritual dominion was not Mao, the advocate of the "omnipotence of revolutionary war." It was Chou En-lai.

Chou was not only premier and foreign minister of China. He was yin to Mao's yang, mandarin to Mao's messiah, and where Mao awed,

Chou soothed—polished, courteous, comforting in his readiness to agree to disagree, exuding understanding with masterly guile, skillfully vague without being glib. Put together, the two revolutionaries were like the reversible cloak of a quick-change artist, one man for all seasons. In 1954 Chou signed a treaty incorporating the "five principles of peaceful coexistence" with Pandit Nehru, the bourgeois Indian leader whose overthrow Mao had specifically urged just five years before. The following year his practiced urbanity stole the show at the Bandung Conference, where twenty-nine nations promised to cooperate with one another "on the basis of mutual interest and respect for national sovereignty." Neutral states welcomed these conciliatory gestures on the part of China with nervous relief, Chinese goods and aid and propaganda poured into uncommitted Asia, and Peking's reputation soared as Asian dignitaries flocked to the People's Republic to see at first hand how the Communists solved the familiar problems of the backward.

But sweetness and light are both of ephemeral texture. In 1956 Khrushchev declared that peaceful coexistence between the Communists and even the Western imperialists was now desirable, for war was no longer inevitable. The enemy could be beaten at his own game on his own ground—not the battlefield, but the polling booth and the marketplace. A year later the leaders of twelve socialist states who had convened to celebrate the fortieth anniversary of the Bolshevik Revolution stamped their official approval on this squalid heresy, making it international Communist policy. Mao himself felt constrained to sign their infamous declaration, but not before he had made his inner thoughts plain.

"The east wind prevails over the west," he told the assembled comrades. The Communists were on top, and they should confront the enemy, not compromise with him. A Chinese memorandum stressed that peaceful coexistence must be looked upon as no more than a tactic to fuddle the imperialist adversary. It must not be regarded as strategy. War, on the other hand, would have "no other result than the end of the world capitalist system." Even a nuclear holocaust held no terrors for Mao, it seemed. "If the worse came to the worst and half of mankind died," he had assured Nehru, "the other half would remain, imperialism would be razed to the ground, and the whole world would become socialist."

Behind all the Russian reasoning and the Chinese death-or-glory histrionics loomed one immutable truth—China and the Soviet Union were incongruous partners separated by a political generation gap that was more likely to be closed by a spark than a smile. The Soviet Union was now forty. It was one of the only two superpowers, it had arrived, it belonged to all the best clubs, and it even threatened to grow old gracefully. It was less concerned with the niceties of ideological revolution than with the hideous problems it shared with the United States—the sophisticated mathematics of the balance of power, and the appalling responsibility in the years to come for preserving the peace of the world (and the world in one piece) with one finger on the button of a nuclear arsenal that could blow it to bits. It did not want to see the Red dawn that might follow an atomic Armageddon. Its pedestrian ambition was to achieve global dominion for socialism in a manner suitable to the day—a slow but inexorable middle-aged spread of political influence and economic power.

By contrast, China was lean and hungry and had a long way to go, a slighted and resentful giant struggling for recognition, excluded from the United Nations and subjected to the intolerable affronts of lesser states. And then there was Mao—round-shouldered now in his buttoned-up uniform, his bushy blue-black hair receding with his past, gesticulating as dramatically as ever with his long fingers as he made his points in pungent prose and a low, telling voice. For the old revolutionary whose victory had been born of bloodshed and disorder, the tactician who joined one enemy only in order to lick another, the Russian thesis was anathema.

"Peaceful coexistence" with the American arch-imperialists could logically only be excused if it were an act of pure chicanery, or sanctioned by the presence of an even greater adversary. Revolution could not be turned into a glorified takeover bid, and to urge that the Communists try to seize power by parliamentary means was to "throw away" Lenin—the man who had first preached that war was inevitable. Mao's world was one of discord and contradiction, of demons to be wrestled and bogies—real or stuffed—with which to frighten Chinese weary of the struggle for Utopia. "The imperialists will never lay down their cleavers," he would say; the Americans had "a deep-seated hatred for the Chinese people" and were trying to put a stranglehold on them.

Insular prejudice heavy with a sense of history distorted Mao's judgment, so that when the British recognized the People's Republic in 1950, the Communists allowed them to open an office in Peking, but refused to exchange ambassadors and sent no reciprocal mission to London. The cunning and insatiable English who had flogged opium to the Chinese, sacked and burned the Summer Palace, wrenched Hong Kong from China, and lorded it over much of the land were to be humbled in their turn. To this end Peking was apparently ready to throw away a unique chance to set up a listening post in London, to recruit a revolutionary fifth column from among anticolonial overseas Chinese through consulates in Malaya and other British dependencies in Asia, and to drive a wedge between the obnoxious Anglo-Saxons (since Britain recognized Peking while the United States recognized Taipei).

But although poetic justice (so dear to the Chinese) might dictate that Britain be treated with measured disdain, Mao was not to write off the United States, for he was absorbed by the strategies of big powers, and may well have looked on the drama of his day as a revival of *The Three Kingdoms* in modern dress. China's past was at his shoulder, reminding him that in a three-sided struggle for supremacy the state that was courted by its two rivals held the balance between them, that the one they ganged up on was doomed, and that safety lay in keeping Washington and Moscow apart, "setting barbarian to fight barbarian" so that it would be China that eventually emerged the sole victor.

Behind all the revolutionary belligerence lay an obsession with the tactics of the power game, and where the Russians saw the outline of a ménage à trois, Mao now saw the outline of an eternal triangle, with China at the apex. While the Chinese might raise their hands in protest at any perfidious Soviet proposal for peaceful coexistence, therefore, they were themselves ready to open low-level talks with the Americans in Warsaw in the hope of cajoling Washington into switching diplomatic recognition from Taipei to Peking. This dialogue led nowhere, however, and by 1958 it was China that was in danger of becoming odd man out.

Remarking the mole on Mao's chin, a soothsayer had prophesied with the confidence of his kind, "You will not travel far from your native place." Nor did he. In consequence he saw the whole world through a mental fish-eye lens as a globular magnification of the China he had liberated. Its capitalists were like the bloated *taipans* of Shanghai, where a starving coolie could fall dead in the street without meriting a passing glance; its landlords were usurious slave drivers, its factories stinking sweatshops, its bourgeois governments as greedy and venal as the Kuomintang. London was the London of Karl Marx—and so of Dickens, Fagin, Bill Sykes, Oliver Twist. The man who hammered away at the importance of judging all things by the detail on the ground, not the doctrine on paper, was well read and sometimes surprisingly well informed—but too often he himself mistook for reality the images the written word had painted on his mind.

With the same genius for generalizing that afflicted so many of his countrymen, Mao stuck labels on men and institutions that forever fixed their condition and conduct. Workers in the West were "totally impoverished." The higher standards of living of the more fortunate were ascribed to their ruthless exploitation of colonized peoples (Mao had to be assured that the affluent Scandinavians had no possessions in Africa, having confused them with the Belgians). "British socialists" were "imperialist" and would "never let India free," Ramsay MacDonald was a "traitor" because he had not formed a "government of workers" when the Labour Party came to power, and his successor Clement Attlee would be quizzed in Peking as to why he, too, had failed to rid himself of the bourgeoisie when he became prime minister. All social-democrats were opportunists, said Mao, and all democratic governments despotic. Neville Chamberlain was worse than Adolph Hitler.

If China was the model for Mao's distorted vision of the world, however, it was a China in which his guerrilla strategy, his "mass line," his faith in man over the machine and in perpetual revolution, had all been proved correct. He therefore believed that what had worked for the millions inside China would work for the billions outside, whose behavior would be predetermined by their "class nature" and the misleading labels he gummed on them.

To his mind the Chinese experience had vividly exposed, once and for all, the grim hazards of coexistence with the enemy. Stalin had chosen Chiang Kai-shek as the supreme architect of a bourgeois revolution, the Communists had then played handmaiden to the Nationalists within the Kuomintang, and they had been massacred for their pains at Shanghai. Victory had become conceivable only after Mao had led his residual rabble up Jinggangshan to give the Reds the final argument for the first time—their own independent army. The lesson was obvious. Marxist movements must always have a fighting force at their disposal —"Without the people's army, the people have nothing." To back a purely bourgeois revolution was to flirt with disaster.

Yet Khrushchev had aped Stalin by bolstering an untrustworthy nationalist leader like Nehru at the expense of the Indian Communists, just as Stalin had bolstered the disreputable Chiang Kai-shek at the expense of the Chinese Communists—and, like Stalin, Khrushchev had deliberately undermined the proletarian revolution by discouraging them from organizing their own "armed struggle." Mao had seen it all before, knew all the lines, and he therefore tried to impose his gospel on all others.

In consequence, he judged states solely by their behavior towards China, for he was ready to coexist with bourgeois governments only on China's terms, the lion lying down with the lamb as long as it remained a lamb. Those that did not conform had to be corrected, and if they offended, Peking was quick to chastise them—the Indians when they objected to Chinese troops crossing their disputed border, the Indonesians when they had the temerity to discriminate against immigrant Chinese traders, the Japanese over a minor matter of face.

The countries of Asia began to revise their first impressions. Scratch the new China and the old China appeared, the overpowering presence that had always been too close for comfort. Neighboring states were alarmed and repelled by this imperious bully that so ruthlessly suppressed revolt in Tibet, blared insults at India, violated frontiers at will and expected the victims to condone the aggression in the interests of peaceful coexistence, a China touchy, arrogant, and bellicose behind her Communist blinkers. Instead of being lured to the left, they recoiled to the right. The honeymoon was over.

Inevitably. External loyalties did not exist for Mao. They had no more relevance for him than they would have had for a Chinese emperor on the Dragon Throne who saw the highly inaccurate geopolitical map of his day as a patchwork of barbaric vassals. Mao was Chinese par excellence, and it was as natural for him to dream anachronistically of China as the Celestial Middle Kingdom, center of the world and repository of the one true civilization, as it was for Winston Churchill to dream anachronistically of empire even as the British supernvoa fell in upon itself in a galactic gravitational collapse.

"Patriotism and internationalism are not at all in conflict," Mao declared, and of course they were not. They were inextricably intertwined. For China could only regain the illusion of being the heart of the universe once the world was transformed by bloody revolution in the manner of Mao Tsetung. His eyes were fixed on the point at which the traditional concept of China as mistress of the world, the cosmic unity expounded by all Chinese philosophy, and the Communist theory of international revolution intersected to prove that peace depended on oneness, and oneness on the elimination of all opposition.

In 1957 Mao urged all fraternal Communist states to share out their wealth among themselves like good egalitarians, so that all "people" would have the same. Since he was master of more "people" than the rest of the bloc could muster among them, China would have been the strongest of them all had they complied. And that was always the object of the operation, whether he was demanding "equality" in policy making (to shield the Soviet Union from any temptation to impose "selfish" decisions on its partners), or exhorting all nations to outlaw nuclear war (since the feebler the weapons they fought with, the more man in the mass would count). Mao was out to stamp the world Chinese.

On the other hand he was hypersensitive about China's own sovereignty, and when Khrushchev tried to talk him into agreeing to set up a joint Sino-Soviet naval command that would give Russian submarines the use of bases in China, Mao is reported to have told him curtly to keep out—"We have had the British and other foreigners on our territory for years, and we are not going to let anyone use our land for their own purposes again." Later he was to accuse the double-faced Russian of plotting to gain control of the Chinese coastline in order to blockade it. Khrushchev was meanwhile exasperated by what he regarded as Mao's harebrained schemes for "liberating" China from dependence on the Russians and winning the race to create a totally Communist society. In consequence, he angered Mao by jeering at the Great Leap Forward and the people's communes, and by describing the Chairman as a victim of "muddled thinking," the collapse of whose absurd experiments could only discredit communism throughout the world.

He was also making the Chinese glance neurotically over their shoulders by challenging their territorial imperative. Moscow was directing an energetic diplomacy towards bourgeois states on the periphery of China, and in 1959 granted massive credits to New Delhi. Almost at once, the armed revolt in Tibet and the flight of the Dalai Lama precipitated a violent border dispute between China and India, but the Russians adopted a strictly neutral stand, wringing their hands in sorrow over this breach of the peace rather than springing to the support of their Chinese comrades—"Khrushchev backed Nehru in attacking us," was to be Mao's indignant reading. Six months later Khrushchev twisted the knife in the wound by visiting India (and Afghanistan and Burma and Indonesia) and extending another credit to Nehru's government that was more than twice the size of all he had granted the previous year.

The Soviet leader was rapidly losing patience. He had not forgotten how Mao had described with such sweet reason in Moscow the idyllic results of a catastrophic nuclear holocaust—"On the debris of imperialism, the victorious people would very swiftly create a civilization thousands of times higher than the capitalist system, and a truly beautiful future for themselves." The gloomy soul of the Russian did not respond, it seems, to the misplaced efforts of the ever optimistic Chinese to make everyone look on the bright side. "Only people blinded by their craving to have nuclear weapons in their own home could fail to see that such rantings are a fraud," Moscow was to comment. Mao was irresponsible and belligerent and not fit to be trusted with a sample atom bomb, and in 1959 the Soviet Union therefore tore up the two-year-old Sino-Soviet agreement on New Technology for National Defense under which he was to have been given one.

Three months later Khrushchev flew to the United States to confer with President Eisenhower, and had the gall to go on to Peking, where he informed the flint-faced Chinese that war with the imperialists was no longer an option anyway. By January 1960 he was talking of total disarmament and proposing to cut the Soviet army by more than a million men. He then upbraided the Chinese for clinging to the outworn Leninist doctrine that armed conflict was inevitable, and told an international Communist conference in Bucharest, "Anyone who thinks communism can be advanced by war belongs in a lunatic asylum."

The Chinese retorted with some asperity that "all attempts to carve up Lenin's teachings must be utterly smashed," and denounced the belief of the Russians in the possibility of "peaceful competition" with the wild bunch to their west as nothing but a dangerous delusion. In the course of more fighting behind the arras, Khrushchev damned Mao for a dogmatist, and the Chinese damned Khrushchev for a despot who opposed revolution in his shameless anxiety to prove the inevitability of peace.

Mao could show his own gun-shy mandarins that he was scoring points. He was winning the sympathy of "some comrades" in Eastern Europe and splintering Communist movements elsewhere. When delegates from eighty-one parties convened in Moscow towards the end of 1960, it took them two weeks to agree upon a final statement of such felicitous ambiguity that the Russians could claim it was a blueprint for détente, and the Chinese a blueprint for struggle. While the Soviet Union remained the symbolic leader of the Communist camp—a post Mao would not try to abolish since he planned to occupy it himself—it was no longer the sole prophet of Marxism-Leninism. As Mao saw it, Moscow had lost the Mandate of Heaven. Both sides claimed that socialist solidarity and their "indestructible friendship" had been preserved, but from that moment on their fraternal relations were to resemble those of Cain and Abel.

Khrushchev had already decided that Soviet aid could no longer act as a brake on the headstrong Mao, and the number of Russian experts in China had been quietly whittled down. Then, in mid-July 1960, Moscow ordered all the remaining Soviet advisers to return at once to the U.S.S.R. They were to be out of China by the end of August, and they had no choice but to stop work, roll up their plans, and go. The Chinese were left without blueprints to build as best they could the factories, the dams, and the bridges the Russians had abandoned. The setback they suffered may be measured by the fact that by 1957 the plants and mines constructed and equipped by the Soviet Union in China were producing more than half of the country's entire output of steel and coal, although only one project had been completed for every five or more planned. The Russian decision to "scrap hundreds of agreements and contracts and to discontinue supplies . . . inflicted incalculable difficulties and losses on China's economy, national defense, and scientific research," the Chinese were later to confess.

Mandarins of less exalted spirit, if of a more mathematical turn of mind than Mao, now read the balance sheet of the previous years without pleasure. Prima-donna policies, a waspish intolerance of contradiction, and the itch of an aging messiah to remold the millions at home and the map outside had lost China the golden chance Chou En-lai had created at Bandung to win over the Third World. They had deprived China of Soviet nuclear know-how and of massive Soviet technological aid, and sabotaged the third five-year plan which with Russian assistance could have given the People's Republic the self-sufficiency Mao craved by 1967. And they had isolated China in the triangular power struggle, simultaneously making distrustful enemies of the United States and the Soviet Union, and possibly driving them together. After the bedlam of the Great Leap Forward, the Chinese were alone, facing three years of famine and want.

But Mao saw things in his own light. It was dangerous to depend on others, better to be strong and free and suffering—"deprivation, austerity, and struggle make for self-reliance; obsession with comfort makes men decadent and spiritually barren," he said. The Americans had "dropped a rock on their own foot" when they ringed China with embargoes and made her shift for herself, and the Russians had obligingly compelled the Chinese to become totally independent when they treacherously withdrew their aid and their advisers. They also "forced us to take our own road" in nuclear science by brazenly breaking their word and refusing to give Peking the bomb, the Chairman was to point out much later. In consequence, China had put together her first nuclear device in record time, and thereafter was able to "produce a hydrogen bomb in only two years and eight months . . . faster than that of America, Britain, and France." He was to write a poem comparing Soviet attempts to subdue the will of the Chinese to "mayfly shaking a tree."

Mao was making a virtue out of something he himself had first made a necessity, and waving a practiced hand over the accumulating debris to create the illusion that it had been spread there to pave the way to the promised land. But it was already clear by 1959 that his impatience had burned a hole in his infallibility, and nowhere was this felt more deeply than in the institution that had put him where he was—the People's Liberation Army.

❧ *CHAPTER EIGHTEEN* ❧

M AO HAD LAID DOWN that "politics must command the gun" from whose barrel all power grew, and to him an indoctrinated army raised in the pure tradition of "people's war" was the core of the revolution. But all who emerge from the ideological incubator bounded by the sealed frontiers of a socialist state face certain hazards when they are exposed to the free polluted air outside. And for the PLA, Korea proved no exception to this rule.

Its generals were not seduced by the bourgeois way of life or the dubious democratic processes so vigorously abused in Seoul, for they saw nothing of those. But their faith in Mao's doctrine that militants by the million beat modern weaponry was shattered in 1951, both by the murderous firepower of the enemy that massacred their ill-armed troops and by the way the odds evened up once Moscow had supplied them with the means to fight back. Like men clad in shot silk, senior commanders ostensibly loyal to the Chairman's guerrilla strategy in China stood revealed in the light of Korea as fervent advocates of a sophisticated conventional army equipped by the Russians, in which professional competence would come before politics, and marksmanship before Marxmanship. There was sedition in the ranks.

In the first half of the nineteen fifties the entire Party network within the PLA frayed, and political commissars were told to take orders from the commanders of their units because "military matters" now came first. The PLA was reorganized on Soviet lines. Officers were granted privileges and wore badges of rank, rustic egalitarian traditions were forgotten, and the Chinese army began changing into one of those time-serving, grumbling, scrimshanking bodies of professionals that have been winning and losing wars stoically since Sargon conquered Syria nearly five thousand years ago.

Nothing stayed put in Mao's China, however. By 1957 the inspired press was accusing military units of "mechanically copying the experiences of foreign countries," and Marxmanship was restored as obligatory moral weapon training in an army whose dedication to Mao's Thought was described as its "spiritual atom bomb." Ten thousand officers were sent off to Manchuria for indoctrination, and orders were issued that senior commanders were to be given a five-year course in dialectical materialism and Party organization. All ranks were earnestly abjured to "check and overcome the corrosion of bourgeois life-styles." Instead, they were to display "the agility of live tigers and dragons," and to make this easier for them, the baggage train was eliminated—wives and children were packed off to their villages, where their husbands could visit them once a year. Officers were meanwhile directed to spend one month in the ranks, "eating, sleeping, working, drilling, and playing together" with their comrades.

Although the hand of Mao Tsetung himself could be seen in the return to the practices of the past, not all commanders responded with enthusiasm. The rift had been widening between the blood-and-iron veterans, who were more comfortable with rifle-and-millet revolution than with jet-age war, and the "professionals" who were furtively fighting for a modern army. But with the creation of the people's communes, the Chairman twisted China into a social form that preserved and even caricatured the anachronisms the "professionals" wanted to shed, turning old virtues into new vices.

Within the communes, the "every-man-a-soldier" drive revived the moribund militia and the concept of "people's war"; whole regiments and even divisions of the regular army were deployed for mass construction projects instead of military maneuvers, and the commanders of others were swept "down to the country" to organize the new labor armies of peasants dispatched by the million to build canals and reservoirs, to tame rivers or crash-plow virgin land; meanwhile for the soldier back in his barracks, the slogan "politics in command" called for more precious training time to be spent on ideological study.

For many generals the Great Leap Forward was therefore a great leap backward, and perhaps no one personified resistance to it better than the Defense Minister, "Hades" Peng Dehuai. The brawny cowherd from Mao's own province of Hunan had come almost as far as Mao had himself since they both rebelled against their fathers, and much of the time they had been too close for comfort. Unlike Mao, Peng was a peasant among peasants yet a professional, always at his ease with troops yet a stickler for duty and discipline who won ready affection and respect—"he would even shove his hand inside a sentry's shoe to see whether or not his feet were warm," one veteran recalled. If Mao was the guerrilla who knew how to run, Peng was the soldier who knew how to stand:

> Who dares to hold his halberd at rest, his horse stock-still?
> Only my great general Peng.

Mao composed these lines when "Hades" was responsible for the defense of Yanan, and they could hardly flatter a fighter more, for they implied a comparison with the unflinching hero in *The Three Kingdoms* who became the Chinese god of war. But Mao was not fond of other gods, and both Peng and Zhu De were rivals for the hearts and minds of the men from the day the two experienced commanders arrived to reinforce him on Jinggangshan. Through the smog of real and rewritten history, moreover, there emerges Mao's suspicion that "Hades" always favored conventional war over guerilla strategy, the "Li Li-san line" of going for town rather than country. He was later to be accused of flouting the Chairman's tenets and mounting costly and abortive operations against the Kuomintang in 1936, against the Japanese in 1940, and against the Americans in Korea in 1951. There was also a suggestion of sexual jealousy, even of a brief clash in Yanan over the authoress Ding Ling between a misty-eyed Mao and this hard, ugly, crop-haired soldier who had for women the magnetic quality of iron.

What is certain is that Mao needed and used that iron before he finally flung it on the scrap heap. In 1935 he confided to Peng Dehuai the vital task of defending the Shaanxi Border Region. "Hades" expanded it to the frontiers of Russia and Mongolia, and in 1948 his command was reorganized as the 1st Field Army—one of the four major fighting formations pitted against the Kuomintang for the final showdown. Three years later he took over the Chinese troops in Korea from Lin Biao—and learned all he needed to know about the importance of weaponry as against the human wave and the human will. Among the men he lost was a son of Mao. The Chairman had sent him as his unnamed successor to acquire the cachet of Korea, to see war for himself —and to report back to his father. Peng had treated him simply as a soldier, and regarded his death as an equally simple sacrifice. Mao was bitterly angry.

But the star of "Hades" was not to fall yet. After the Liberation, Mao had set out to muzzle most of the "meritorious dogs" who had brought him to power by putting them into peaceful occupations, much as the famous founder of the Song Dynasty had done a thousand years before. The marshals of China who so inconveniently commanded the loyalty of millions of armed men found themselves deskbound in departments dealing with foreign affairs, scientific research, even sports. But they could not all surrender their pistols for pens. In 1954 Peng Dehuai became Minister of Defense, and it was during his first three years in the post that political study and the peasant militia were pushed aside where possible, so that China's professional soldiers could be trained in the modern military tactics and technology they would need to win a war in these exacting times.

When the Party leadership convened at Wuhan at the end of December 1958 to assess the damage done during the past year, moreover, Peng was prominent among those who taxed Mao with simultaneously provoking the Americans and the Russians, and inflicting on the country the twin hardships of the people's communes and the Great Leap Forward. But he did more than that—he stuck a fist through the Chinese screen of simulated harmony behind which the Party wrangled. A peasant outraged by what was being done to peasants, he went down among them, touring three provinces and publicly lamenting their sorry condition. "What was the revolution for?" he demanded fiercely of cowed Party officials in Shandong. "Why did we fight for so long? It was to give the people enough to eat. And now you ask them to *love hunger?* What kind of revolution is that? Shame! Shame!" Blunt, stubborn, honest as an average day, he could not contain himself. Everything they had fought for had been ruined. Something drastic would have to be done. And it was.

In August 1959 the Central Committee met at Lushan, among the peaks of Jiangxi province, and "Hades" read out a hard-hitting memorandum that was later denounced as a "fierce onslaught" on the Chairman and the Party line. Capital construction during the Great Leap Forward had been "hasty and excessive," he said, and money had too often been poured into irrelevant instead of into vital projects. A people that had been getting more than a pound of rice a day since 1933 had seen their ration cut to just over three-quarters of a pound in 1956, and to only half a pound in 1958, and if this continued there would be food riots. How had it come about? "Extreme left-wing tendencies" had developed, and Mao's call to "surpass Britain" had incited overeager cadres to commit excesses that had "alienated the masses." Reports of "incredible miracles" had persuaded men that the food problem had been solved and all could now concentrate on programs like the "seriously superficial" plan for iron and steel production.

"Some comrades" had become "giddy with apparent success" and fallen victim to "petty-bourgeois fanaticism," but Mao's slogan "Put politics in command" was "no substitute for economic principles, still less for concrete measures," declared Peng, who reputedly went on to electrify his audience by describing the Great Leap Forward as "a rush of blood to the head," a "high fever of unrealism" that prompted "blunder after blunder." Mao, he implied, had "turned a blind eye and a deaf ear" to failure. If the Chinese had not been so good-natured, "it might have been necessary to call in Soviet troops."

This was not the whining of scholars or the callow bombast of protesting students, nor even the measured censure of men like Liu Shaoqi or Chou En-lai heard in the privacy of the Politburo. It was an open denunciation of the appalling wrong that Mao had done by flinging nearly 700 million Chinese into a chaotic economic "battle" without plans, without maps, without precise operation orders or adequate weapons or training, with nothing to ensure victory, in fact, beyond heady war cries and gaudy banners. In a protracted Party debate, a solid block of support emerged for Peng Dehuai, who had called for a penetrating reappraisal of policy. The moment of truth had arrived for the Chairman, and he was to show his mettle as a guerilla with an outstanding demonstration of single-minded duplicity, during which he led the comrades through a meandering argument slippery with guile that brought them back to his side.*

Mao firmly disclaimed responsibility for the communes. He had not "invented" them; he had merely proposed them. It was the people themselves who had seized on the idea, and what came from the people was of course sacrosanct—"we must not pour cold water on this kind of *broad mass movement*," he said, straight-faced. It was the beginning of a new charade. The fiction was to be maintained that the Chinese were still free to make a choice, to blow out a spark Mao himself had struck instead of hysterically fanning it into a prairie fire, and they were therefore responsible for the choice they had made.

And if the echo from the masses absolved him, he insinuated slyly, so did the echo from the Party pundits around him. The miscalculations made during the Great Leap Forward could hardly be his fault—"I am a complete outsider when it comes to economic construction, and I understand nothing about industrial planning," he protested, metaphorically spreading his hands. Who was responsible for the backyard furnaces? Mao the ignoramus had checked the feasibility of producing nearly eleven million tons of steel with the specialists, and "everyone

* For the sake of simplicity, I have taken a shortcut by including here one or two related remarks Mao made in a second speech delivered the following month.

said it could be done . . . we could raise the quality, reduce cost, lower the sulphur content, produce really good iron."

The economy had been thrown off balance? It was because the planning experts had apparently done away with all planning; they had neglected to come up with proper estimates or point out how much coal, iron, and transport was going to be needed. Nobody "uttered a murmur" during all the preliminary conferences, he was to complain, it was only when the cracks appeared that the cat-calling began. In short, the Chairman was responsible, but the others were to blame. Once again he was bringing down the enemy with his own momentum, deftly turning all the Chinese yes-manship he had extracted from them back on the Party and the people.

Moreover, even if 70 percent of the communes fell apart, he went on, 30 percent would remain, and a partial victory was still a step forward to the ultimate Communist society. Marx himself had declared that the Paris Commune of 1870 would be justified if it lasted only three months. Arousing the revolutionary spirit of the masses while learning from mistakes was an advance in itself. Consequently success was not to be measured by immediate economic results, he argued, leading his hearers gently into their next ambush. Yet as soon as there was not enough pork, there were waverers ready to shout, "You have done things badly," and when there was a shortage of umbrellas in Zhejiang province, they even called it "petit-bourgeois fanaticism," he went on, flinging Peng Dehuai's insult back in his face. These fainthearts were nothing less than corrupt "bourgeois elements," for when they constantly drew attention to failure instead of to success, they shook the faith of the masses and threw the revolution itself into jeopardy.

The message was clear. Honest fellows closed ranks and preserved the unity of the Party when things went wrong, balancing spiritual gain against material loss, a future perfect against a past imperfect. In other words, the bigger the mess, the more they must all back Mao. To make a loud fuss about the shortages and privations he had caused by tinkering with an economy he did not understand was now revealed as right-wing heresy. "If we do ten things, and nine are bad, and they are all published in the press, then we will certainly perish," he said. In such circumstances he would "go to the countryside to lead the peasants to overthrow the government," and if the Liberation Army did not follow him, he would "organize another Liberation Army."

And having "fixed" his adversaries as a matador fixes his bull in the arena, Mao concluded by making an appeal in familiar functional idiom for the catharsis that dispels explosive secretions of dissent—"Comrades, you must all analyze your responsibility. If you have to shit, shit! If you have to fart, fart! You will feel much better for it."

Peng Dehuai had had the temerity to challenge Mao, but the substance of that sin cast an even more hideous shadow. He had attacked Mao's misguided meddling with China's economy, but he was also a fierce opponent of the principle of "people's war," and in both of these blasphemies he saw eye to eye with a far greater heretic—Nikita Khrushchev. "Hades" wanted China to have a modern defense with a nuclear kick to it, and he needed Russian help to get it. Khrushchev was ready to provide, if Peking toed the Kremlin's line on peaceful coexistence.

Against that background, the chronology of events for the year 1959 looked damning for Peng. He had set out on a protracted goodwill tour of the Warsaw Pact powers in April; he met Khrushchev in Tirana in May and in Moscow in early June; the Russians went back on their pledge to give the Chinese nuclear know-how in July; and in August Peng dropped his own bombshell on the Lushan conference.

Suspicion led to allegation, and allegation to a wild sea of charges. Peng was said to have told Khrushchev just what he thought of Mao's policies, and to have given him a letter denouncing in unseemly detail the people's communes and the Great Leap Forward. The Russian had then withheld the atom bomb from Mao, but had promised Peng that if matters fell out right, the Soviet Union would supply the Chinese with all they needed to update their antiquated weaponry. Armed with this, Peng was to persuade the Politburo to jettison Mao and make it up with Moscow.

A dangerous conspiracy between "revisionists" at home and abroad had been exposed, it appeared, and thereafter the convenient axiom that critics of Mao must be creatures of the Kremlin was to serve the Chairman well (and to poison Peking's relations with the Soviet Union to the end of his life). The Party had been infiltrated by opportunist troublemakers, he told a meeting of the Military Affairs Commission. For the fourth time it had been misled by purveyors of a false "line"—Li Li-san, Wang Ming, Gao Gang, and now Peng Dehuai (four men whose common fault was their closeness to the Russians). Peng had hatched a plot to split the leadership at a time when it needed the unity that only

iron discipline could guarantee. And worse. It was "absolutely imper-
missible to go behind the back of the fatherland to collude with a
foreign country," Mao said.

But he was "beating a dog that was already in the water." When at
Lushan he threatened to "organize another Liberation Army" if the
soldiers did not follow him, the generals present rose to protest their
loyalty to Mao, and the intimidated gathering he had just chastised for
pandering to his ignorance swung over to his side again, indignantly
rejecting the memorandum of the man who had voiced for so many
their own unspoken thoughts. The Party resolution blackguarded Peng
as the leader of an "anti-Party clique" who had been intriguing against
the Chairman for the past thirty years, and whose nefarious activities
were "fraught with danger for the future of the Party and the Army."
The Wuhan conference had exonerated Mao by blaming "alien class
enemies" for the muddle and misery in the communes, and the Lushan
conference blamed "right opportunists" for the fatuities of the Great
Leap Forward. Mao called for a new "struggle" within the Party, and
a rectification campaign to "smash all right opportunists" was launched.

Dismissed from office, his reputation in stage rags, Peng Dehuai was
to wander in the political wilderness for the rest of his life. His backers
among the top brass in Peking were also sacked, but all kept their
positions in the Party. True to his tendency to treat men leniently as
malleable thoughts rather than unredeemable thinkers (especially when
they were as popular as Peng Dehuai), Mao accepted a somewhat
perfunctory self-criticism from "Hades," even remarking that if he
changed his ideas he would "instantly become a Buddha."

Things could never be the same again, however. Even Zhu De had
wavered when Peng challenged the Chairman's "general line," and
although the Party had upheld him in the end, Mao felt loose boards
under his feet. He had kept his mandate but lost much of his mystique.
Obstinate and combative, "Hades" continued to bombard the Party
with memoranda on the need for a drastic change of policy, and so
became a symbol of sanity for those who put rice before revolution.
But Mao's drive to "scatter" these "antileftists" made sanity a sin again,
the decisions taken earlier to modify the madness of 1958 were therefore
often shelved by the timid, and the rural revolution rolled on under the
momentum of the Great Leap Forward.

The Lushan communiqué had nevertheless admitted that the gigantic
jump in grain output claimed for that first year had been an optical
illusion, and now flood and drought joined folly to send a sick China
into a long economic decline. By 1962 the production figures for grain

and cotton had fallen below the 1957 tidemark, and steel output was down to eight million tons from eleven million in 1958. Big public construction projects had been abandoned, and even national showpieces like the major steel, motor, and tractor plants were working at little more than 30 percent of their scheduled capacity. China was unloading silver and gold reserves, and buying grain from abroad. The second five-year plan had quietly died.

"Three bitter years" dragged by as famine crept across whole provinces. In the crowded cities people were eating as little as five or six ounces of rice a day, and drawing a ration of four ounces of sugar and perhaps half a liter of cooking oil a month. Market stalls were often empty of the most common vegetables, and families went for weeks without even seeing a piece of meat. Items like wood, paper, or soap would simply disappear from the shops, the cloth allowance was cut to less than three feet a year at one point, and—yes—in Canton umbrellas were restricted to one a household.

Dropsy, beriberi, and tuberculosis were taking a heavy toll, and when urban workers drifted down to the communes in search of more food, they would sometimes cross with peasants from the communes drifting to the provincial towns to escape hunger on the land. First priority was given to farming, millions were conscripted for a "new high-tide agricultural drive," and all available hands were dispatched to the fields to bail China out. Thousands of regular troops and militia were deployed in the mountains to shoot game for the national larder, and detachments of workers spread out in search of wild plants that might make up for the acute shortage of cotton in the textile mills.

The entire population was told to cultivate common chlorella, officially described as a unicellular hydrophyte with a phenomenal yield of albumin, fats, carbohydrates, and vitamins which multiplied so fast that "thirty crops a year may be expected." It was nourishing pig swill and poultry feed, but now the Chinese set out to grow mountains of this pondweed to make bread, pastry, sauces for the table, even to replace powdered milk for babies. They were already consuming wild herbs and tree bark and cotton-seed cakes intended for animals, and according to one official report, the peasants were eating worse than their own dogs had in the past—"people are too hungry to work and pigs are too hungry to stand up."

But for the Chairman, who saw China's history through a prism of prejudice, the hideous calamities of a feudal yesterday put the privations of the present in perspective. The masses were enjoined to console themselves by remembering the "bitterness of the past" in order to realize how lucky they were now. The measure of their hardships was in fact the measure of their happiness, they were told. They were as fat as they were thin. This was the reasoning that enabled Mao to speak scornfully of those who fussed about shortages of "vegetables, pork, grain in some regions, even umbrellas." Twenty years later an economist in Peking would reveal that in the year 1960 alone, the population of China *fell* by eleven million.

There were no official statistics for misery and mortality at the time, but the horsemen of the Chinese apocalypse were not ghosts that Mao could stare out of existence, and by 1962 the moderates—Liu Shaoqi, Deng Xiaoping, Chou En-lai—had met the crisis by dismantling the gimcrack internal structure of his egalitarian utopia, while reverently preserving the shell intact. The backyard furnaces were forgotten, industrial workers were paid piece rates or a fixed wage boosted by a bonus system, and the number of people's communes had meanwhile trebled because they had been cut to one-third of their former size.

The new commune was little more than a formal frame for a system within which the small production team of perhaps twenty families ordered the work and managed the money. Peasants could cultivate marginal land and their own private plots, raise their own pigs and poultry and sell them in the local free market, go in for sidelines, and keep much of the cash they made. Egalitarian "free supplies" for all gave way to payment to "each according to his work." China was back to the village collective, and politics had lost command; there was a pause in the class struggle, a breathing space before the next dialectic leap, and a slight but unmistakable smell of capitalism in the air. Mischievous writers had begun pulling the threads from the fraying fabric of Mao's dreams, and a pernicious play was put on in Peking called *Hai Rui Dismissed from Office*.

Hai Rui was about an upright mandarin of the Ming Dynasty who protected the poor peasantry from the abuses of greedy local gentry with influence at court, and who was in consequence summarily sacked on the orders of the Emperor. Mao, with his keen eye for an historical allegory, must have been quick to see the connection—especially when the sixteenth-century stage peasants asked for their confiscated lands to be returned to them, and begged to be rid of the rascals who had persecuted them. The parallel was too obvious. The land had been taken from the peasants when the cooperatives and the people's communes were formed, and the rascals were the overweening Party cadres who had treated them like cattle. Although the play had been written before the Lushan meeting, Hai Rui was now identified with Peng Dehuai, champion of the downtrodden tiller of the soil, and the Emperor who so unjustly dismissed him was Mao.

This theatrical slap in the face was the work of no ordinary scribbler, but of Wu Han, vice-mayor of Peking and a man associated in Mao's mind with the "revisionist" clique of bound-feet Marxists who constantly threatened his revolution with the death of a thousand "buts"— pragmatic mandarins, "professional" soldiers, and precious scholars whose petty minds could never encompass the vision of a messiah. Party unity was evaporating, and with it the mist of make-believe that had concealed the cracks in the monolith. The "lines" were being drawn for an ideological war to the knife. *Hai Rui Dismissed from Office* was to prove a curtain raiser to chaos.

❀ CHAPTER NINETEEN ❀

Since all belonged to the same faith, the Maoists struggled to preserve the reality of the people's communes and the Great Leap Forward, while the "Maoists" conformed by preserving the titles—in whose sacred name they could then commit with impunity the acts of ideological vandalism necessary to dismantling them. In mid-1961, accordingly, Liu Shaoqi spoke with bogus enthusiasm of the "superiority" of the "people's communes" and claimed that China had made "big leaps forward for three consecutive years." But this show of ecumenical solidarity was part of the illusion and purely tactical. The messiah was up against the golden calf of pragmatism, and a few months later Liu methodically took him to task for his "revolutionary optimism" in a long, cold, and damning assessment of the consequences of his works, delivered before seven thousand senior Party cadres.

Mao had said that the situation was "favorable," Liu remarked, but he could only have been referring to the political situation, since "one can hardly describe the economic situation as favorable, in fact it is most unfavorable . . . our economy is on the brink of collapse." The Great Leap Forward itself had been too precipitate, and "our losses in manpower, fertile soil, and natural resources have been so heavy that it will take seven to eight years to put matters straight." Thanks to all the mistakes that had been made, the masses had "starved for two years," and while three parts of the catastrophe could be blamed on nature, seven parts must be blamed on the stupidity of man.

The comrades must be allowed to speak up, Liu maintained, even if they criticized the "Three Red Banners" of Mao Tsetung (the General Line, the Great Leap Forward, and the People's Communes). Peng Dehuai's memorandum to the Chairman at Lushan had quoted facts and "matched the truth"; those who had been "mercilessly attacked" simply for agreeing with him should therefore be brought back from political purgatory and the "verdicts" on them "reversed." Eight months later, Peng Dehuai himself asked to be reinstated, submitting to the Tenth Plenum of the Central Committee an eighty-thousand-word report on the errors of Mao and the evils of the immediate past, and both Liu Shaoqi and Deng Xiaoping supported his appeal. But Mao turned it down, for the gloves were already off.

Sticking verbal pins through an unlabeled image of the Chairman, Liu had scathingly denounced "left opportunists . . . these almost hysterical people according to whom any peace in the Party is intolerable— even peace based on complete unanimity"; and in a new edition of his book *How to Be a Good Communist,* he wrote of "dogmatists" who in the past "had the impudence to require Party members to venerate them as Marx and Lenin," and who had "issued orders to the Party like patriarchs, tried to lecture to the Party, abused everything in the Party, and wilfully attacked and punished Party members."

The moderates were attacking downhill. In 1959 Utopia had proved unapproachable, the wings of the Chinese Icarus who had flown too close too fast had melted, and the mandarins had been called in to pick up the remains. Mao was obliged to watch the groundlings around him put his revolution into reverse yet again, for the modern history of China was becoming as mindlessly repetitive as a recurring decimal. With the Russians gone and the economy paraplegic, the country's Communist leaders once more needed not only the goodwill of the peasant, but the bourgeois brains of the Chinese intellectual—the "expert" from the professional elite rather than the "red" all-rounder.

In 1961 Chen Yi, Foreign Minister and former commander of the 3rd Field Army, told students bluntly that it was wrong for them to waste too much time swotting politics and shoveling manure, because their technical education would suffer—"who would want to fly with a politically pure but incompetent pilot?" he asked. Experts could best show their "redness" simply by being expert. This was not easy for Mao to take from the bald and adipose marshal, a *bon viveur* of mandarin stock who had studied in France and displayed a regrettable bourgeois fondness for dancing and food and well-cut uniforms. But Chen Yi's comment was apt, for it was discovered that in their anxiety to make men socialist and shield them from obnoxious foreign influences, the Chinese were well on their way to raising a generation of ignoramuses capable only of mouthing ideological platitudes.

The "Hundred Flowers" movement was revived among savants, but while non-Communist intellectuals were not to be bitten twice and poured no new torrent of abuse upon the Party, something far more sinister occurred—from high up in the ranks of the hierarchy itself a stream of oblique criticism was aimed at the anonymous shadow of the Chairman. Regular newspaper columns and essays written by members of the Peking Committee or the Propaganda Department of the Party decried the cretinous optimism that had inspired the Great Leap Forward, the evils of forced labor, the lunacy of unnamed men who antagonized both America and Russia because they were too ignorant of the first, and too conceited to learn from the second. *Hai Rui Dismissed from Office* was only the first of a series of historical allegories and other allusions to the sufferings of the peasants, the crimes of bureaucrats, and the follies of heedless monarchs and self-appointed seers who arrogated to themselves the divine right of being right.

In *Hai Rui Upbraids the Emperor*, the mandarin rebuked the ruler with the words, "All officials know that you have become so obsessed with doctrine that you are out of your wits." A seemingly innocent article on amnesia noted that those suffering from this disconcerting ailment failed to keep their promises, and that it led to irrational outbursts of rage and finally to madness. Half-seen barbs skillfully stippled a pointillist portrait of an unnamed egoist on the verge of senility who was concerned only with imposing his will on others, a high-handed and intolerant bigot bemused by empty flattery who heard and saw nothing of the Chinese masses, ignored their wishes, rejected their counsel, and shrugged off their cries for help.

At a literary forum held in August 1962 under the aegis of the Propaganda Department, the presiding bureaucrats urged authors to stop writing idealized rubbish about cardboard socialist heroes with cardboard socialist sentiments, and to depict the misery of the millions, to show the real horror as it was happening to real people trapped in a society that treated a harmless human desire for peace and plenty as damnable heresy. The bureaucrats were the same men who had championed the camp and kitsch of "socialist realism" in the past, and they would never have turned their coats without powerful backing from above. The mandarins at the apex of the party had pulled the country through the "three bitter years" into which the Chairman had incontinently plunged it, and with China taking the first hesitant steps on the road to recovery, they evidently believed the moment had arrived for them to turn to the offensive.

Mao's revolution was in danger of stalling, for malicious circumstances had once more dictated that China would be saved not by "more, faster, better" socialism, but by a lapse into capitalism. The masses, no longer limited to two bowls of watery rice a day, knew it only too well. Given the scent of personal profit again, the peasants were devoting their energies to their private plots and to haggling over the price of their pigs and chickens in the local free market, but skulking when summoned to take part in communal labor. They had lost their confidence in the ability of the collective to cushion them against catastrophe, and in consequence the communes were rotten with "spontaneous capitalist tendencies" and a reprehensible apathy towards selfless toil. Men peddled rather than plowed and displayed in general a lamentable tendency to revert to type—to spend too much money on food and clothes and weddings and funerals, to consult fortune-tellers, push children into profitable marriages, speculate, and dodge taxes.

But the first sign that the Chinese were putting on weight predictably prompted Mao to prescribe another diet of dialectics. One can only gain experience through practice, he had reminded the conference of seven thousand cadres in January 1962, and the recent hardships and defeats the Chinese had suffered were therefore merely stepping-stones to "final victory." The reactionaries were forever planning a comeback, however, and in a socialist society "new bourgeois elements" could still be thrown up. "*Never forget class war*," he urged in a dramatic appeal to the Tenth Plenum of the Central Committee in September. It was the signal for a counterattack from the left, and the Plenum bowed to his will. A "socialist education movement" was to be launched to "break the circle of spontaneous capitalism." This was later to merge with a "four cleanups" campaign to curb the abuses of officials who hoarded grain, fiddled accounts, conspired with the peasants to cheat the state, or simply cheated the peasants. Blame for the wrongs of the past was again pushed on to the cadres in the communes, where as many as seven out of ten were sacked and replaced with men whose sole qualification for the job was often a retentive memory for the Thought of Mao.

The Chinese were to be remolded once more and the selfish peasants harried into returning to the collective fields to hoe to the "line." The "Maoists" having spurred them on to produce more by whetting their appetite with the prospect of personal gain, the Maoists employed ingenious devices to make it turn to ashes in the mouth. "Class war" was artificially resuscitated in an almost landless society, and accusatory fingers pointed at farmers who had made a success of their private plots—they were now potential "new bourgeois elements," suspected of vile ambitions to "speculate and wreck markets, amass large profits, and live parasitic lives." A "patriotic grain" campaign simultaneously shamed the peasants into selling even their surplus produce to the state at the state's prices, instead of flogging it for what it would fetch in the local free market. Led on by some well-primed shill who would publicly offer to cut his own rations to the bone in order to deliver up every last cabbage "not needed for his own consumption," they had no choice but to respond with spurious cries of enthusiasm.

Teams of cadres meanwhile fanned out across the country, delving into the communes, dismissing delinquent officials, and "mobilizing the masses" to study the Thought of Mao. "Memory meetings" were organized at which old men reminisced about the horrors of life before the Liberation, and this lugubrious oral history was laboriously collated for the future edification of the millions. Peripatetic cultural groups raised the "class consciousness" of villagers by acting improving plays. *Xiafang* was now a "glorious duty," and by 1965 forty million migrants in all had "volunteered" for it.

But one year before that Party leaders were already admitting (with varying degrees of secret satisfaction) that Mao's message was falling on deafened ears. Peasants had been known to stone the improving plays, and blasphemous youths to jeer at the bitter memories of the old, while an apathetic majority mechanically repeated the stale revolutionary slogans. Many cadres were chary of reproving idle workers who had been encouraged to denounce them, and many others stopped reading books for fear that the "fragrant flower" they devoured today might be blacklisted as a "poisonous weed" tomorrow. Art students in at least one university neglected to wash in case they were charged with showing a bourgeois preoccupation with hygiene, and the day would soon come when factory hands would go absent so that they could not be accused of putting productivity before politics. In self-defense, China was falling back on the "nonaction" of the Taoists. Everyone was primarily concerned with keeping out of trouble.

It was in this discouraging atmosphere that Mao issued his decree, "Learn from Dazhai." Dazhai was a working model of the Chairman's Utopia, a production brigade in Shanxi province whose members had proudly turned their backs on material rewards, and asked for their private plots to be taken away so that they could devote all their time to collective labor. At Dazhai, it was said, all men "put politics in command" and collectivization before mechanization; "revolutionary will" replaced rustic resignation in the face of a malevolent nature; the peasants were "educated" to give their services selflessly to the community and "never forgot class struggle"; the cadres labored in the fields beside the peasants; the old were paid for light work as much as the young were paid for heavy; and grain, fruit, and vegetables were distributed to each according to his need.

This was the self-reliant, egalitarian paragon all China was told to emulate. In 1980, when Mao was gone, the "verdict" on Dazhai would be "reversed" and the whole operation exposed as a "put-up job," a model of nothing but fraud and waste. That in its turn may be an exaggeration, for where truth is what the Party thinks, and the Party is split into two lines, there is no single truth. The real significance of Dazhai, however, was that the closer it came to the dream of Mao, the farther it was from the desire of men.

"Try to think like one of us," the Chinese cadre in Peking sighed when I naively objected to some distasteful aspect of the people's communes. "Political study means endless debates—and we love talking. Self-criticism was imposed on us by Confucius, and confession by our ancient system of justice. We have no tradition of privacy, we enjoy a hubbub around us and are easy converts to communal living. And since when have the Chinese objected to hard work?"

He was echoing Mao, and since Mao did "think like a Chinese" himself, how could he have gone wrong? When talking to the seven thousand cadres, he had admitted that it might take from fifty to a hundred years to "build a great and mighty socialist economy," as if he and China had all the time in the world. But that was only one side of Mao; his belief that all was in a constant state of flux, which gave him his elongated sense of perspective, also gave him an itch for change. Nor was that all. There were moments when the tired septuagenarian showed through, and it became increasingly evident that age was adding to impatience.

Revolution was the proper occupation of the masses, Mao believed, for only through perpetual revolution could he realize his vision of an egalitarian collective society. And that was because whenever the ideological pressure slackened, the Chinese slid back into their bad old bourgeois habits. But while he recognized this as a recurring sickness to which man was heir, he refused to treat it as terminal. It did not seem to occur to him that in trying to transform the Chinese into egalitarian angels, he might simply be promoting them to the level of their incompetence, in accordance with the Peter Principle. He was forever pushing them upwards, only to see them roll back again, but the significance of this did not appear to trouble him—that the terrible futility of the ordeal of Sisyphus lay not in the stone, but in the law of gravity; and that the terrible futility of his own ordeal might lie in the nature of man, in the sad truth that perpetual revolution was necessary precisely because his prescription for the happiness and salvation of the Chinese people was to make them do what they did not want to do.

At his word, a purely illusory China came into being through the press, a China in which happiness was emulating the submissive ox, asking for no rest and no reward, abandoning the "bourgeois" concept of human love, eating pondweed, and curing serious diseases not with medicine but with doses of Maoist zeal (consumptives were advised to try "fresh air, calisthenics, and revolutionary optimism"). The worker did not like leisure—he found it dull, for tranquillity and ease "can only make one feel disgusted," and contentment lay in constant struggle. There was no such thing as homesickness, and young people were delighted to be sent to the other end of the country to join the front line of production—"energetic as tigers, pushing carts with loads of more than one thousand pounds, pouring sweat." They desired nothing, for family and possessions were the enemies of happiness and freedom. Work was joy, struggle was serenity, the ideal life had been defined.

Few wanted to make the supreme sacrifice and live it, however. The Chinese viewed Mao's Utopia with much the same misgiving that assails the Christian promised a heaven of harps, pink clouds, nightshirts, and endless choral singing. The militant peasants who had made his revolution had not mobbed their landlords and joined his armies to become landless labor in a people's commune, and as soon as the reins slackened, they reverted to their sock-under-the-mattress mentality, dissolving from a monstrous regiment of automatons into an amorphous rabble of energetic, calculating Chinese—Sun Yat-sen's "heap of sand." The aims of Mao and the masses were now diametrically opposed. The more stable the economy, the more the people wanted the good things of life, but the more he wanted another great leap forward; the more they asked to be left in peace, the more he saw its dangers, as the apathy and corruption and incompetence unmasked in one campaign cried out for another, and the gradual hardening of the Party into an ossified bureaucracy threatened China with a new mandarinate for a master.

His answer was bigger and better doses of class struggle. But when the doses produced distressing economic side effects, the moderates stepped in to prescribe their toxic antidote, "putting profits in command," and this in turn goaded Mao to further "revolutionary" action to neutralize the poison. In consequence China became like a man dizzy from popping pep-up pills and tranquilizers.

In June 1958, for example, peasant families in one area were still allowed to possess small plots of land for raising vegetables, fruit, and poultry. In October 1958 the plots were confiscated and became the property of the newly formed communes. The following April the peasants were given back their plots, together with little red cards which read: "This private plot belongs to your family permanently, and crops grown on it shall be disposed by your alone." Within four months the plots were again taken away from the farmers and used for growing food to supply communal mess halls. By December 1960, however, it was realized that nothing at all was being cultivated on many of them, and they were redistributed to their owners—with more little red cards saying that they belonged to the lucky recipients "permanently."

By 1964 the demoralized, suspicious, and bewildered masses had seen class struggle come and go, and contradictory slogans slide in and out of fashion as fall followed leap. Intellectuals had been courted and castigated and courted again. Students had shuttled between town and country, never sure when classes began again whether this time the accent would be on academic learning or political study and more manual labor. Meanwhile married people all over the country were in danger of being caught out by shifts in the population policy, as fanfares for the Maoist "mass line" in man power alternated with pragmatic family-planning campaigns. For what started out as a politically immaculate conception for some happy couple might end nine months later with a bourgeois-reactionary birth. Everyone knew that if by chance he did get jam today, it would be gruel tomorrow.

Mao believed in the gruel of life. "Your father was dauntless and resolute in the face of the enemy," he told his nephew in the contemptuous voice of war bores the world over expounding on the horrors of peace. "You grew up eating honey . . . you have never suffered; how could you be a leftist?" Suffering and simplicity *comme à la guerre* were the secrets of the good revolutionary life. In 1964 he remarked with a certain relish, "If the atom bomb should explode, we would simply find ourselves back in Yanan," and went on to recall how in his hardy youth he had lived on eight dollars a month "and got along without worrying about clothing, food, or lodging."

Paradoxically, Mao was behaving like Imperial China, arrogant and hidebound behind an inadequate Great Wall of tradition and prejudice. He harked back to his own "good old days," as the Confucians had harked back to the golden age of the ancient sages, and in the same way attempted to meet the challenges of the present with the precepts of the past. Harassed by younger nations technically attuned to a scientific era, nineteenth-century China had fallen victim to its own anachronisms. Unable to bridge the gap between the guerrilla tradition and the day of the computer, Mao, too, clung to the outdated tenets of his own golden age in the wilderness, not realizing that he was committing the same fatal error as the "feudal" society he had destroyed.

This irony left the Chairman mired in contradictions. The wavelike rhythm of war in which troops fought, rested, and then rose to fight again merely dislocated the economy and mystified the masses when applied to the arts of peace. Man's attachment to Mammon made nonsense of Mao's optimistic conviction that revolution and growth would reinforce each other, the revolution inspiring the Chinese to work, the growth inspiring them to make more revolution. The men with the expertise needed to transform China into a modern socialist state were by definition professionals from an entrenched elite who looked askance at political upheaval, while the zealous revolutionaries who really believed "politics commands all" were for the most part naive and unqualified idealists who were bound to bungle things. Similarly, Mao's egalitarian aims might require that the poorest peasants inherit the earth by taking over in the countryside, but the poor peasants were too often poor because they were ignorant, lazy, or stupid. The more productive and capable farmers were naturally to be found among those who were also more enterprising and affluent, and therefore politically dubious.

Meanwhile the "mass line" designed to propel China forward in science and technology threatened to put her into reverse as these disciplines were taken out of the hands of trained specialists and confided to the millions. While scientists passed much of their time at political-study meetings or laboring on the farm, peasants and workers were encouraged to spend it perfecting their own "practical" innovations, having been assured that nothing was technically beyond them provided they adopted a "socialist approach" and avoided the sin of "bookism"—that is, superstitiously accepting as truth everything written in established scientific works.

The consequences were not always happy. One worker, for example, tinkered away for weeks on end at expensive equipment, watched by exasperated cadres too afraid of being accused of "bookism" to intervene, until finally an American-trained aerodynamics expert was called in to tell the enthusiastic amateur that he was wasting his time. Not even a "socialist approach" and the Thought of Mao could make perpetual motion possible.

❧ CHAPTER TWENTY ❧

THE MORE MAO HAMMERED his doctrine into the masses, the more he evoked a wooden response instead of the "lively style of debate" he had earlier encouraged. The lean Mao of Yanan—cautious, patient, flawless in his flexibility and a devil for the facts—had once derided dogma with one of his vivid excremental quips by saying, "Even cow dung is more useful as a panacea," for in those days he saw it clearly as the bullshit that baffles brains. But the questioning Cassius had become a stout, graying, bowed, and often brooding Caesar whose own dogma could not be denied.

He and he alone knew what was good for China, however bad it seemed. The worm of righteousness had eaten into his soul, and he was prepared to take his country on a pilgrim's progress to perdition. He might have to cut corners on the way, moreover, for Sunzi could teach him no footwork to dodge the passage of time, and with the passage of time his power was waning. Despite all his violent shaking, the Party and administration were slowly solidifying against him—and his mass line.

The signals were unmistakable. Mao wanted to see the peasants raise their own "political consciousness" during the socialist education movement by coming forward to confront venal cadres publicly, as they had confronted their landlords during Land Reform. The moderates interpreted the movement otherwise, however. Their "model" was not Dazhai but a production brigade at a certain Peach Blossom Village, where an investigating team of Party officials "dispatched from Peking and personally led by the wife of Liu Shaoqi had taken pains not to arouse the mob against the local cadres, but to purge those found wanting themselves. This was not a revolution from below, but a rectification raid from above, and the lesson was clear. The hierarchy was to be judged by the hierarchy, not the hoi polloi. Once again, the mandarins were undermining a mass campaign of Mao while covering the sound of their sapping with noisy protestations of support for it— "waving the red flag to defeat the red flag"—and would not attack it frontally until it had already crumbled.

Mao's answer to growing defiance within the Party was predictable. He would isolate it by turning back to the elements that had made up his victorious "people's army"—the people and the army. Frustrated by the disputatious hierarchs, he would go down to the millions among whom their voices sang small, but his charismatic image loomed large. Mao could talk to the Chinese as no mandarin could, writing what he wanted on the "blank sheet" of their ignorance and illiteracy and their urge to follow a leader, using the bucolic idiom and homespun obscenities they understood, acting the familiar role of the rough-edged rogue-hero they all admired.

More grumbling within the Politburo was therefore matched by more glorification of the Chairman outside, for the greater the ostensible infallibility of Mao, the greater the fault of his carping critics. His Thought was the embodiment of pure and absolute truth, and the young were exhorted to use it to transform themselves into "rustless screws" of the revolution. Others saw it as a "sharp weapon," and this martial metaphor was perhaps more significant, for it was adopted at a military conference chaired by Lin Biao, the marshal Mao had chosen to succeed the disgraced "Hades" Peng Dehuai as Minister of Defense.

Lin Biao—the "Tiger Cat"—was the son of a Hubei factory owner who had been "ruined by rapacious landlords," the apocrypha ran. He went straight from school to the Whampoa Military Academy in Canton and was commissioned as one of its most brilliant students before he was twenty years old. He fought in the Nanchang uprising, and after joining Mao in the mountains of Jiangxi, commanded the vanguard on the Long March. He made his name when he gave the Japanese a bloody nose by ambushing an entire brigade in 1937, almost before the declaration of war was dry. Eleven years later he took the last Kuomintang stronghold in Manchuria and marched his 4th Field Army six hundred miles to the outskirts of Peking in little more than two weeks, persuading its incredulous Nationalist defenders to give up quietly. He then struck down the length of China without much resistance until his troops reached the Gulf of Tonking in the far south.

On paper, he was another Patton. His 4th Field Army held for the Chinese all the glamor of Montgomery's Eighth Army in wartime Britain. It was also a focus for furtive professional backbiting, however, for Lin Biao's spectacular advance south against the Kuomintang had been made possible only by the hard slogging of the 2nd and 3rd Field Armies in the Central Plain, and their bold forcing of the Yangtse. Significantly, three of the four principal actors in those pivotal exploits had been Liu Shaoqi, Deng Xiaoping, and Chen Yi—the mandarins who now believed in "experts" more than "reds."

Moreover, although time might have worn away the rough edges of truth, leaving the fiction to emerge, Lin Biao was not cast in the mold of the conventional hero. Standing beside the rotund Mao at public rallies, he cut a small, seedy figure, his thin wedge of face distinguished only by its brushlike, faintly quizzical eyebrows. His oratory was excruciating—a shrill, halting delivery in a thick provincial accent—but once off the rostrum, he was a soft, persuasive talker with a disarmingly modest manner. He was no pundit with a political mind of his own, but a soldier who led a Spartan life and held the loyalty of his men. He must have seemed just the instrument Mao needed to rout the jealous "professionals" in the PLA who spurned "people's war" and were clamoring for a streamlined army in a dangerously imperfect world.

On his side Lin Biao, aware that he was a political lightweight, saw that he could only outstrip the competition by staying in the slipstream of Mao, and he quickly confirmed the Chairman's good opinion of him by sycophantically echoing his master. The early writings of Mao were first widely distributed in Manchuria, where his obsequious acolyte was in command, and when in 1960 another volume of Mao's *Selected Works* came out, Lin Biao tripped over his own overstretched similes in his eagerness to fawn—"Like a beacon, this brilliant thesis of Comrade Mao Tsetung illuminated the road of our advance . . . so that"—two pages further on—"at times when the sky was overcast, we were able to see that the darkness would soon end and the light of dawn showed ahead." Five years later he was to take Mao's "brilliant thesis" that guerrilla movements should first capture the countryside and then surround the cities, and give it the status of a blueprint for world revolution. In his much-publicized essay of September 1965, "Long Live the Victory of the People's War," he predicted that the have-not "country" continents would eventually surround the "city" states of capitalist Europe and America.

From the outset, he shifted the emphasis in military thinking back to Mao's concept of "people's war," and used the "sharp weapon" of Mao's Thought to convert the PLA into a sharp weapon for the Chairman—and himself. The Party's grip on the army tightened, and all units were ordered to train in "fighting at two hundred meters" and hand-to-hand combat, in ambushes and night operations more suited to the guerrilla tactics of a "people's army" than a jet-age defense. Plans were laid for an "intensive, repeated, and widespread" campaign to promote the "serious study of Mao Tsetung's works." Army ranks were abolished, the militia was expanded, the uncooperative "professional" chief of staff (Luo Ruiqing) was fired, and the "Little Red Book" of potted quotations from Mao began to circulate within the PLA. With Lin's help, Mao was creating a power base that would out-Party the Party—and command the gun.

"The whole country must learn from the PLA" was already the slogan of the day, for the disciplined army was to be the demonstration team of the undisciplined masses. PLA propaganda groups were sent into civilian offices at all levels to bring the good word to the godless, and civilian cadres were attached to PLA units for political training. In accordance with Mao's express wish, "political departments" like those in the army were created in government ministries, in financial and commercial bureaus, in trade and transport offices, while "political instructors" filtered down to factories and farms, mines and oil fields, armed with the Thought of the Chairman. Mao and Lin Biao were bypassing the bureaucracy and setting up their own circuits.

Mao had not forgotten that victory depended on the pen as well as the sword, however, and he had meanwhile launched another offensive on the cultural front. But he once suggested that the Chinese were bad judges of character ("rather inept at singling out certain people"), and he was to discover that if he had made a dangerous mistake in choosing Lin Biao as his commander in one sector, he had made an even bigger one when choosing his commander in the other—his scheming and sharp-tongued consort, Jiang Qing.

By 1962 the frustrated actress who was the wife of Chairman Mao had been resting between parts for more than twenty years, for the role of First Lady did not give her a line to say. She seems to have spent the long hiatus metaphorically darning Mao's socks, while holding an ephemeral post on the fringes of the world of art. But if she had been domesticated, she had not been tamed, and when the appearance of *Hai Rui Dismissed from Office* in 1961 gave her her big chance, her subsequent portrayal of ruthless feminine ambition was to be favorably compared by her enemies with the performances of the more memorable empresses in China's bloodcurdling history.

Whereas Mao saw art as an ideological weapon in the service of socialism, his opponents were turning the weapon against him by arguing loudly that art should be in the service of art. In his eyes, the "revisionists" were perverting the means to mold the masses, and as the insidious assaults on him multiplied, he accused his tormentors of using literature "to carry out anti-Party activities." His answer was to develop a two-pronged counterattack: Lin Biao began to convert the army into a cultural workshop, and Jiang Qing was given the task of "rectifying" the theater which had offered the Chairman so brazen a political challenge.

She went to work with a will that was to prove the bane of Chinese showbiz. Perceptive, quick-witted, and seemingly indefatigable, she first riffled through one thousand Peking operas being played throughout the country, to find them a mess of ghosts and gods, generals and concubines, feudal sentiment and bourgeois sentimentality. "On the stages of a socialist society we are still acting works about emperors and aristocrats," she sneered, and began pulling out these "poisonous weeds" and replacing them with Marxist morality plays. A tireless meddler with a maddening passion for ideological detail, she was to have pitched the whole rich repertoire of traditional Chinese drama into the trash basket by 1964, and substituted a frugal fare of seven "revolutionary" operas and ballets that creaked under the weight of improving Maoist messages about collectivization and class war.

That year provided what were by now the familiar conditions for a "cultural" offensive by Mao against the nefarious forces of human nature, for China was once more a gaunt convalescent on the road to recovery after one bout of straight socialism, and therefore to his mind ready for another. A new pantheon of proletarian heroes and moral pacemakers appeared in the press, including a young man who vowed to be a night-soil collector all his life ("glorious labor that constitutes one of the 360 traditional trades of China"), and a road mender who declined to change his work shift on his wedding day (since uxorious distractions should not take precedence over collective labor).

The criteria were laid down for all forms of art, from music to *maquillage*. "Blind adoration" of bourgeois composers was severely condemned, and students were taken to task for dangerous imperialist reflexes, like weeping at the sad bits in Tchaikovsky's Sixth Symphony. *Rigoletto* was "full of ideological poison and decadence, depravity, licentiousness and shamelessness," while at the other end of the scale pop music and "capitalist dancing" were scandalously devoid of class struggle.

Journalists were warned to avoid the "bourgeois luxury of independent thinking," and told that if at all times they reflected the Thought of Mao they could not possibly go wrong, for then even a mistake would not be a mistake. Not only men but motifs were quizzed suspiciously by Maoists who saw a bourgeois under every bed. Potters who painted traditional designs on their bowls and vases were accused of "propagating capitalist ideas and feudal superstitions," and cowed into replacing them with strings of graceful Chinese characters reading "Confess and Win Leniency," or "Recalcitrance Earns Severe Punishment."

The humbler arts were not forgotten. Handkerchiefs appeared embroidered with slogans like "Exert the Utmost Effort: Strive Upstream," and the birds and flowers that normally decorated fancy Chinese stationery gave way to gear wheels, tractors, even entire industrial complexes. Editorials hit out at drainpipe trousers, pointed shoes, and fancy hairdos because they reflected "the corruption, degeneration, and ugliness of Western civilization." Dressmakers were praised for "upholding fine socialist practice" by refusing to make extravagant clothes, and restaurants too prone to put bourgeois portions into the bowls of the proletariat were reminded that it was "more important to serve politics than food."

Or entertainment. In the days of feudal oppression, an itinerant storyteller might delight a crowd of Chinese layabouts for the umpteenth time with the oft-told tale of Madame White Snake, or some swashbuckling episode from *Water Margin*. But that was a "bitter memory" of the past. Now, special teams of spare-time narrators for whom "politics is the first concern" would preach street-corner Marxism to tired bystanders on summer evenings, or regale them with enlightening anecdotes about early Communist heroes.

The educative process started almost at birth. In the best families the first words tiny tots were taught to say were "Chairman Mao," and as "Mama" went out of ideological fashion, so did Mama herself. Parental love was merely a form of private ownership, children were warned. Capitalism began at home. The young were being trained to live collectively again, and there was a heavy demand for exciting yet instructive books for them with titles like *The Crimes Committed by the Living King of Hell* (eleven stories of rapacious rent collectors) and *Behind the Smiling Face of the Capitalist* (real-life experiences of a brutal mutton-restaurant proprietor). But the cultural assault ran foul of the truism that children tend to be more inspired by gangsters than good guys. Teachers complained, for example, that a B-movie called

The Knife Thrower about a poor wretch who was saved by kind Communists from his wicked capitalist exploiters left no Marxist message on the tender minds of their charges; their only reaction was to round up children even smaller than themselves and start throwing knives at them.

The exuberant young were artlessly reflecting the attitudes of their elders, who at times showed their distaste for the results of Jiang Qing's crusade to replace the romantic rubbish of the past with model revolutionary plays by stoning the actors, but more often simply stayed away on the night. Faced with empty houses, theatrical companies then tried to please the people instead of the Chairman's wife by putting the old, colorful legends back in their repertoires. That was not to be tolerated, however, and they were promptly rebuked for "giving the audience what they wanted." It was not that Madame Mao was against a blending of past and present, but when she tried to "weed through the old to let the new emerge," she ran up against an insoluble contradiction. It might be possible for a modern drama like *The Heroic Drought Fighters*, or even an operetta like *Grandma Sees Six Different Machines*, to possess a certain artistic integrity. But to take the grand idiom of traditional Peking Opera with all its pageantry and elegance —the stylized gestures of a concubine picking up a nonexistent flower, or of a plumed general striding downstage—and then try to transpose it to an ideological cliff-hanger called *A Bucket of Manure* was inevitably to kill both.

By 1964 her strenuous artistic efforts to "raise class and socialist consciousness and stir up proletarian revolutionary feelings" had encountered stiff resistance, and when she dragged the prestigious Number One Peking Opera Company into performing the first of her experimental revolutionary plays in the capital itself, she could only explain her temerity by demanding, "If you don't go into the tiger's lair, how can you get the cub?" She had not asked for formal permission from the Peking Party Committee, for it was dominated by a clique of case-hardened senior cadres who put every possible obstacle in her path, tying up companies and theaters, encouraging bitchy backbiting and passive sabotage on- and offstage, and raising last-minute technical difficulties at every turn. Peng Zhen, boss of the Committee, described her revolutionary plays as still at the point where they "wore bottomless baby's rompers" and "sucked their thumbs," while another member remarked sarcastically that they were about as stimulating as "plain boiled water."

When the Chairman obliquely warned the intransigent against behaving "like high and mighty bureaucrats" who were in danger of "sliding down to the brink of revisionism," the Peking Propaganda Bureau obediently started a rectification campaign. But within four months this had shrunk to an anemic debate on the arts, and six months later it was dead. There was an acrid smell of revolt in the air. Some even believed the old guerrilla was finished. But in August 1965 a proud and bitter Mao, stiff and slow in his walk, told André Malraux ominously, "I am alone with the masses—waiting." He then left Peking for his favorite retreat at Hangzhou, taking with him his wife and his secretary and speech writer, Chen Boda. He was drawing back to strike again. Hangzhou was not far from Shanghai—the spiritual home of a heterogeneous quartet who would one day be widely known as "The Gang of Four."

CULTURAL REVOLUTION

*I would rather betray the whole world than
let the world betray me.*
(CAO CAO, THE ROMANCE OF THE
THREE KINGDOMS)

❈ *CHAPTER* TWENTY-ONE ❈

You must redress the injustices done to the people. Only with the return of their land can they live in peace. HAI RUI

I
N NOVEMBER 1965 the leading Party newspaper in Shanghai published a stinging attack on *Hai Rui Dismissed from Office* by a master of the universal art of venomous literary criticism, who damned it categorically as a "poisonous weed." Did it plead for the "return of land" to the peasants? Then it echoed the "demons and ghosts" who "clamored for private farming" and "wanted to demolish the people's communes and restore the criminal rule of the landlords and rich peasants." Did it plead for "the redressing of injustices"? Then it spoke for "the imperialists, landlords, rich peasants, counterrèvolutionaries, undesirable characters, and rightists . . . who felt that it had been wrong to overthrow them and vociferously clamored for redress." The two themes, therefore, "formed the focal point of bourgeois opposition to the dictatorship of the proletariat and the socialist revolutionary struggle."

Yao Wenyuan, the writer of this pithy diatribe, was the son of a Shanghai author but a second-rate performer himself whose frustrated yearning for literary fame was to take him perilously high. Short, heavily built, moon-faced, he was afflicted with a shy, uncouth manner and a mistaken impression as to where he was going. "Balzac made himself as renowned with his pen as did Napoleon with his sword," he said once. He was defining his personal dream. But he was cursed with little creative talent. In consequence, he gained a name as a critic bent on cutting his way to the top by blackguarding better writers. Seizing the opportunities offered by successive political purges of "antirightist" literary figures in the nineteen fifties, he developed into a spiteful and self-righteous Maoist whose cold-blooded casuistry and cruel way with words could quickly condemn the purveyors of "poisonous weeds" to labor reform in distant and insalubrious regions.

Yao's persistent scalp hunting brought him to the side of Jiang Qing, to whom he toadied shamelessly. He helped her to revise her revolutionary operas, she helped him to revise his explosive attack on *Hai Rui* and its author Wu Han, and both were helped by their *tertium quid*—a long-faced, myopic cadre in his mid-fifties named Zhang Chunqiao.

Zhang surfaced in 1950 as a radical writer and former guerrilla, and rose steadily through posts in Party and press in the sprawling municipality of Shanghai, until by 1962 he was the ultimate arbiter of its literature and arts, education, and ideology. He had long since proved his loyalty to Mao's revolutionary line, for he had unmasked and purged cultural heretics during the antirightist campaign of 1957, having recruited Yao Wenyuan as his hatchet man. But his big chance came when Peking disdained Jiang Qing's "model" operas, and she brought them to Shanghai. Zhang gave her the cultural keys of the city, and her controversial efforts were successfully staged after the usual exhaustive nit-picking—between them they revised one work twelve times. He was no zealot at heart, however. He was an astute politician but a shallow Marxist, a tactical trimmer who mistakenly put his money on Mao and was to end by losing everyone else's trust in his anxiety not to lose his own shirt.

This was the dubious trio, quickly nicknamed "The Shanghai Mafia," that Mao was to pit against the established order of the People's Republic he had worked all his life to create. Yao Wenyuan's attack on *Hai Rui* was the signal for the biggest exercise in political evisceration of the Chairman's career, the "Great Proletarian Cultural Revolution," and while Yao's ostensible target was the author of the offending play, Mao was already looking beyond him. His object was to force the man behind Wu Han to take a stand, having first made sure that he would catch him with his feet crossed.

Once again the Chairman was to show himself a master of tactical legerdemain in the best traditions of Jinggangshan. Peng Zhen, Secretary of the Peking Committee and mayor of the city, was a ranking member of the Politburo, a muscular sexagenarian with an easy, confident style who, as cultural chief of the Party, was now the immediate patron and protector of the unholy nest of revisionist writers like Wu Han who held office under him. Yet when a special Group of Five was formed to direct a "cultural revolution" against this "black gang" of reactionary scabs, Mao allowed Peng Zhen himself to become head of it. It was not a grotesque mistake. Faced with the distasteful task of having to bite his own tail, Peng Zhen was evidently expected to take the teeth out of the movement and save his friends by converting the Maoist campaign into a hollow "Maoist" one, whereupon his turpitude would be revealed. Mao was leaving the thief to mind the store in order to catch him in the act, and Sunzi would have approved.

Peng Zhen justified the strategy. In February 1966 he produced an evasive report in the name of the Group of Five which pleaded for the cultural revolution to be limited to "gradual reform" and peaceful debate. The comrades "should not attack each other," but confine themselves to "scholarly criticism," it insisted—"we must not behave like scholar tyrants who are always acting arbitrarily and trying to overwhelm people with their power." The Chairman was struggling to cast out the devil he saw threatening the very soul of socialist China, and Peng Zhen was trying to trick everyone into thinking this vital conflict could be solved with tea and seminars. He stood condemned by his own words. Mao had caught him in the open.

The Maoists rejected Peng Zhen's report, and on 16 May 1966 the Central Committee put out a circular that the Party, the government, and the army were all infiltrated by a "bunch of counterrevolutionary revisionists." The Chairman was opening a general offensive against his enemies. The Group of Five and (shortly afterwards) the Peking Committee itself were both dissolved, and a new "Cultural Revolution Group" was formed with Chen Boda as nominal chief but the real power in the hands of his deputy—Jiang Qing. By early June Mao himself was back in Peking and in command of the situation again.

How had he done it? All of his innate contempt for democracy when democracy ran counter to his dreams informed the moves that had taken him from withdrawal in weakness to ambush in strength. In the intervening months, he and Lin Biao had energetically canvassed support in the provinces, the obstructive chief of staff had been sacked, and the "Tiger Cat" had switched troops he could trust from Manchuria to the capital. The Chairman had then confronted power on paper with power on the ground. But he had been careful to violate constitutional practice strictly within the framework of the constitution. He had not drawn a gun. He had merely allowed his adversaries to see his shoulder holster, as he had when he confronted the "Twenty-eight Bolsheviks" at Zunyi in 1935, during the Long March. He had then summoned a lopsided Party meeting at Hangzhou packed with his own supporters, which in the name of the Central Committee imposed a minority decision on the majority—the absent moderates.

In the past Mao had isolated powerful class enemies by picking them off, one by one, from right to left, and now he was upending that horizontal tactic, working from the bottom to the top of the pack instead. The attack on Wu Han had been a prelude to the dismissal of Peng Zhen, and the eclipse of Peng Zhen was to be the prelude to the downfall of President Liu and his sawn-off shotgun of a partner, Secretary-General Deng Xiaoping.

As always, the Chairman chose his terrain with care. Nine days after the rigged meeting at Hangzhou had dealt a foul blow to the "independent kingdom" of his enemies in Peking, a small group of persons at Peking University put up the first of millions of "big character posters" that were to provide a lurid running commentary on the coming tumult. The poster accused the president of the university of deceitfully whittling down the cultural revolution against the "sinister black gang" to a common-room wrangle, as Peng had advised. Within days Mao had given it his personal benediction, for it boldly challenged those in high places, and it echoed the spirit of his own call for an "attack on all fronts" against the bourgeois-ridden hierarchy. The spark struck, the prairie took fire. Just one week later it was reported that Peking University was papered with more than a hundred thousand posters—and counter-posters, for sympathizers of the well-dug-in academic staff were fighting a bitter rearguard action amid mounting disorder and sporadic violence, as discipline collapsed and teaching periods disappeared without trace beneath the fumes of rowdy political meetings.

The offending chancellor was dismissed for bourgeois transgressions that were to be laid at the door of innumerable college and school principals all over the country within the next two months—they had neglected politics and the Thought of Mao; they had promoted revisionist professors, and reverted to traditional book learning and the old scholastic curriculum; they had thrown out the proletarian concept of work-study, and cut manual labor to a month a year; and they had "put marks in command," showing an iniquitous preference for "gifted" students while spurning duffers—even when the duffers were the sons and daughters of workers and peasants.

Loud cries for radical change arose from the campuses of China, and in mid-June it was announced that the schools would close for six months so that a new system of education could be worked out. Their classes canceled, students could now devote themselves seriously to the tasks of pasting up posters and printing incendiary handbills, to arguing and brawling and "dragging out" their terrified teachers for mass confrontations. The formless, dissolving political picture with its theme of growing disorder had the feel of Mao's invisible hand, and behind it was a strategy designed to kill five birds with one stone.

It has been remarked that Mao had a healthy, outdoor distrust of formal learning, for it was divorced from both practice and class struggle, and therefore suspect. There was far too much studying going on, he had said in 1964. The period of schooling should be reduced and the syllabus "chopped in half." "Do not run along behind the teachers and be fettered by them," he cautioned his nephew. "Class struggle is your most important subject . . . if you don't know about class struggle, how can you be regarded as a university graduate?"

He encouraged his niece to rebel against overwork ("just stay away and tell the others that you want to disrupt the school system"), and advised his own child to go down to the country and tell the poor peasants, "Papa says that after studying a few years we become more and more stupid. Please be my teachers. I want to learn from you." A new trace was now to be laid over the old school grid. Entrance examinations would be scrapped, and students would be chosen for their proletarian background and political purity rather than their scholastic performance. There would be less academic study and more ideology and manual labor again. And more *xiafang*.

Mao was troubled by the abyss that had opened up between the cadres and the millions, and his so-called "May 7 Directive" ensured that city bureaucrats also served their term of political study and pig minding among the peasantry. But he was even more troubled by the generation gap that had opened up between the veterans of the revolution and the pliable young, who must somehow be saved from the corrupting power of peace. For if class struggle was to be perpetual, there must always be worthy successors to perpetuate it.

A campaign was therefore mounted to train "heirs of the revolution," and this reflected the growing sense of despair and the shadow of betrayal that dogged the old messiah. He was now seventy-two, and few of those around him were much younger. When he died, he could be succeeded by a shuffling line of short-lived Communist popes presiding over a people's republic eroded by bourgeois instincts and "poisoned by Khrushchev's revisionism." The Party was shot through with "false Marxist-Leninists," the press warned, and beyond them was a new generation that might well abandon the revolution altogether and settle for a welfare state and pork twice a week.

"The young must be put to the test," Mao had told Malraux in 1965. The human clay could be hardened in the kilns of the communes and class war, but there was a more drastic alternative—the "Great Proletarian Cultural Revolution," a gigantic auto-da-fé in whose flames China would eventually be purified and his five aims achieved: the transformation of teaching, the purging of the Party and state, the overthrow of the reactionaries, the salvation of youth, and the forging of dedicated successors.

Mao had lit the fuse in the schools, convinced that once they were fired with a proper spirit of rebellion, the volatile young would detonate the inert mass of peasants and workers in their turn, and the entire revisionist structure would be blown apart. For the yin of youth was matched by the yang. The immature creature who crept around today behaving like a backsliding bourgeois slob could be magically transmuted tomorrow into the stuff of martyrs, filled with a selfless urge to do good, to live rough, to give all and take nothing. China was brimming with the spirit and energy of raw young people who could be as ready to serve as they were to sulk. All that was needed was to throw the switch. And Mao had his finger on it.

When the President of Peking University was sacked, and the Party sent in its first "work team" to direct the cultural revolution on the campus, Mao left Peking again and did not return for fifty days. Once more Sunzi would have approved, for he was luring Liu Shaoqi into the open as he had lured Peng Zhen before him. The task of the work teams was ostensibly to "hold high the banner of Mao Tsetung's Thought" in colleges, factories, and offices by explaining the heinous crimes of the "black gang," firing impenitent addicts of the bourgeois revisionist line, and re-educating minor offenders. But again Mao had left the thief to mind the store. With the Chairman out of the way, Liu and Deng Xiaoping were free to send in men of their own pragmatic persuasion who would not openly defy the latest Thought of Mao, but distort it in order to deflate the rebels and protect their own academic allies.

Madame Liu took a work team into Qinghua University just as she had earlier taken a group of cadres into Peace Blossom Village; once more revolution from below became rectification from above, and the wrong heads fell rapidly into a widespread net. "They did not point the spearhead of the struggle at the handful of power holders or the reactionary academic authorities, but at the revolutionary students," Jiang Qing was to protest vehemently, and as the vicious spiral of shouting matches, trumped-up charges, forced self-criticism, and furtive political persecution mounted, so did popular opposition to the "white terror" of the revisionists. A climate of fear and hostility had been successfully created in which tough, proletarian teenagers could be discreetly encouraged to form semiclandestine cells for militant action in the future. These were to be the "little generals" of the Cultural Revolution—the Red Guards.

Mao returned to Peking in mid-July, and on 1 August 1966 presided over a plenary session of the Central Committee of the Party called to give formal consent to the rebellion that was going to shatter it. One week later the plenum duly approved a sixteen-point charter for the "Great Proletarian Cultural Revolution," whose declared object was "to struggle against and overthrow those persons in authority who have wormed their way into the Party and are taking the capitalist road," whose executors would be "the masses of workers, peasants, soldiers, revolutionary intellectuals, and revolutionary cadres," and whose path-finders would be the revolutionary young. The watchword was, "Put daring above everything, and boldly arouse the masses; do not be afraid of disorders." The strategy as always would be to unite the great majority of Chinese and "concentrate all forces to strike at the handful," while "upholding the banner of Mao Tsetung's Thought" and "putting politics in command." The immediate targets were the "four olds"—the "old ideas, culture, customs, and habits of the exploiting classes" that the bourgeois reactionaries employed to "corrupt the masses."

The revolutionaries were enjoined to make a careful distinction between the real monsters and the merely mistaken, and to use the power of debate when solving contradictions among the "people," not coercion or force. But while Mao may have wanted to keep the whole ungovernable juggernaut under fingertip control—or at least appear to do so—he was still quoted in the directive as saying that the revolution could not be "refined, gentle, temperate, courteous, restrained or magnanimous." The "revisionist" work teams were denounced and disbanded, and the Red Guards given their head. "You say it is right to rebel against reactionaries," Mao wrote to one group, "I enthusiastically support you." On 5 August he put up a big character poster of his own entitled "Bombard the Headquarters," attacking "leading comrades" who during his fifty-day absence had "enforced a bourgeois dictatorship . . . juggled black and white, encircled and suppressed revolutionaries, and imposed a white terror."

Thirteen days later he mounted the rostrum of the Gate of Heavenly Peace in Peking to survey a sea incarnadine of waving flags and banners below him and take the march-past of a million Red Guards. He was wearing one of their armbands, dressed in military uniform, and flanked by his "close comrade-in-arms" Lin Biao, now sole Vice-Chairman of the Party and his chosen successor. "We must strike down, smash, and utterly expose the counterrevolutionary revisionists, the bourgeois rightists, and the reactionary bourgeois academics," the marshal shrieked hoarsely at this intimidating if untidy Chinese Nuremberg. His was the main speech on that memorable day, but Jiang Qing would open the second Red Guard rally at the end of the same month, when another horde of half a million delirious young militants would pour into the great square.

The lineup on the Gate of Heavenly Peace reflected changes in China that acted like a sudden ecological imbalance, producing strange hybrids and freakish phenomena on the upper slopes of power—a Party with two quarreling heads; a President of the People's Republic (Liu Shaoqi) who had slipped to seventh place in the hierarchy, while as chief of the Cultural Revolution Group a back-room nonentity (Chen Boda) climbed above him to fifth; an incongruous symbiosis between pen and sword that would shortly make Jiang Qing "Adviser on Cultural Work" to the army, and the army the main repository of Chinese art and literature (in Mao's England the Royal Ballet would have been taken over by the Ministry of Defense at this point); and beyond this a flattening of the features of the political landscape into a "mass line" subject to no law, as all constitutional activity stopped dead, and neither the Party Congress nor parliament was convened to ratify the arbitrary decisions taken by China's egalitarian autocrats.

Below, meanwhile, was a seething ocean of teenagers hopped up on endless ideological talk and the exhortations of their leaders to "dare to rebel," to "root out" the customs and culture of the past, to "strike down" the unholy anti-Mao, whether revisionist hierarch or bourgeois academic, and to "smash the old world to bits." The army had brought them before Mao from the four corners of the republic—the vanguard of another ten million to come—and Mao sent them out again, liberated from their classes, to ride the overloaded railways and "make revolution" throughout the country—excited, exalted, quixotic, idealistic, rebellious, vengeful, vicious, iconoclastic, callow. The Chairman had thrown the switch, and China exploded.

❀ CHAPTER TWENTY-TWO ❀

A FLICKERING SEQUENCE taken from some old black-and-white news-reel will suddenly shock into life the dullest TV documentary of man's past misdeeds by putting the drama into the present tense again, and in the same way yellowed press cuttings of the period may jerk the reader back to a reality now sixteen years away. In August 1966 I wrote for *The Observer*:*

Like a middle-aged man afflicted with mumps, the 17-year-old People's Republic of China is in the grip of an infantile revolutionary fever that normally hits new nations when they are less than 12 months old. Highly organised from behind, blessed in the editorial columns of the *People's Daily*, the mobilised young of Peking are out painting the town red.

From 12 to 20 years old, these new "Red Guards" are swarming through the capital bent on destroying every vestige of foreign, bourgeois and revisionist influence, from the very name of Peking itself to its last line of decrepit taxicabs. Demanding that the city, now plastered with posters and cluttered with portraits of Mao Tsetung, should henceforth be called "Dong Fang Hong"—"The East Is Red"—the Red Guards have started by renaming the thoroughfares. The Square of Heavenly Peace (Heaven is bourgeois and so is peace) has become "East Wind Square."

Gangs from a widespread and militant movement which seemed to spring into being only last week are rampaging across the city. Students have partly wrecked the Sacré Coeur school operated by foreign nuns, smashing a statue of the Virgin, sticking up a poster depicting the Pope concealing armed Americans, and a notice

* For the sake of clarity, all names in these extracts from my earlier articles have been transposed into *pinyin*.

reading: "Foreign devils, you are dogs and bastards, and your dirty work is unmasked."

The lunatic fringe want all books that do not reflect Mao's Thought to be burned, traffic lights to be changed because it is inadmissible that "red" should mean "stop." The youth of Peking, setting an example that is being quickly followed in Shanghai, Canton and the rest of the country, are out to strip China down to her bare, comfortless chassis in a burst of xenophobic and revolutionary frenzy whose meticulously organised spontaneity must be regarded as highly suspect. The police do not intervene when the boys and girls turn out in predatory bands forty strong, the press does not report their acts of vandalism and intimidation . . .

Kids in khaki uniforms and red armbands had taken over the capital and "declared war on the world." They were ransacking shops and houses for anything "bourgeois" they could find, haphazardly smashing or seizing priceless porcelain and cheap capitalist kitsch, ancient Chinese carvings and modern foreign prints, scrolls and dolls, jewelry and jazz records. Tombs and temples were desecrated, stone inscriptions and antique sacrificial vessels attacked with heavy hammers, holy images flung on bonfires. Within weeks the zealots and the hooligans were out of hand, each in his own way—cracking the fingers of a talented pianist because he played Chopin, pitilessly breaking both legs of an author, and locking a leading playwright in a filthy shed, to be let out solely to clean public latrines.

"He was so brutally beaten that it was beyond imagination," the wife of Lao She was to say afterwards of the well-loved author of *Rickshaw Boy*. The Red Guards had burned his books, forced him to crawl on the ground barking like a dog while they hit him with heavy clubs, and then shut him in a chicken coop and ordered him to recant. "Blood was dripping from his face . . . there was not one inch of his body that was not black and blue." He committed suicide to escape his youthful persecutors (or was murdered). Before the autumn was out, Lin Biao was metaphorically flapping his hands at the havoc. "Carry out the struggles by reasoning, not coercion and force," he cried. *"Don't hit people."* Leaflets were already being distributed, vainly forbidding the vandals to sack the homes of revolutionary leaders, "investigate" Party or government offices, or keep the valuables and the rubbish they confiscated in the name of the Chairman.

Red Guards were everywhere, often fervent and dedicated "pilgrims of Mao" who trekked across the country in pious imitation of the Long March. Their breviary was the Little Red Book of his *Quotations*, and their holy lands were the mountain fortresses in which he had set up his guerrilla bases. The passion of the great proletarian cultural revival touched all. Passengers flying from Peking to Canton were handed texts of Maoist anthems, and the whole aircraft would start singing the Old Hundred of the revolution, "The East Is Red." Before international ping-pong matches, Chinese players stood in reverent silence while extracts were read from the Chairman's writings, and men cried that his words were more precious than food. Within two years the presses would have turned out 740 million copies of the Little Red Book, 150 million sets of his *Selected Works*, 96 million copies of his *Poems*, and the country would be flooded with pictures and busts and buttons and badges bearing his hallowed features.

Once more the Chinese had thrown themselves into the ideological rat race, and their addiction to the reductio ad absurdum and sensitivity to symbols were to prompt mindless acts of persecution on the crumbling edge of insanity. A mother was hauled before a "struggle meeting" because her five-year-old child tied a Mao badge on a pet cat. An elderly worker was charged with "suspicion of intent to murder" and branded an "active counterrevolutionary" for putting his hands around the neck of a bust of Mao while cleaning it. Safety regulations were denounced as "bourgeois," for they were "not in keeping with Mao Tsetung's Thought" but the work of those who "frantically" spread the "revisionist philosophy of survival." Foolhardy workers who got themselves killed while demonstrating their readiness to dare and die in the Maoist manner were posthumously loaded with praise, even when they had only been trying to rescue a bucket from the bottom of a well.

There were no typical Red Guards, for they came by the million, and they were united only by their creed (when it did not divide them), yet the Chairman himself addressed only a few well-worn Maoisms to them—"You must let politics take command, go to the masses, be with the masses." He then dropped from view, leaving Jiang Qing as the interpreter of his will during the crucial months that followed the last Red Guard rally in November 1966—and virtual mistress of a huge, ungovernable army made up of an entire generation of Chinese youth.

Intoxicated by her role in this gigantic spectacular with its cast of millions, a slim, often deceptively soft-voiced mob orator in a trim army uniform who could "twist an audience around her finger until it was incandescent," Madame Mao now moved downstage, ready to whip her "little red devils" into bloody-minded fury. At times she would argue cogently and compellingly, but at others fire them with crude flattery that inflated their collective ego—"Chairman Mao is leaving China to you," she told them. "You will govern China." When obliged to preach moderation as near-anarchy spread, she would adopt an ironical tone that belied her ostensible appeal for an end to violence, and then suddenly conclude by shrewishly inciting her inflammable audience to further mayhem against the "black dogs" or "rotten eggs and slippery backsliders" who were their common enemy.

The ever-willing Red Guards were goaded into driving out the old cadres entrenched in Party and administration, into seizing weapons from the army, and in December 1966 into turning their talents to the task of humiliating Jiang Qing's hated rival, the American-born wife of Liu Shaoqi. Madame Liu was subjected to a mass "examination," and a few months later pushed in front of a mob more than 200,000 strong, dressed in a bourgeois cheongsam, spiked heels, and a necklace of painted ping-pong balls. But she was far from being the only prominent personality to be "dragged out" by the vindictive school-boys of Peking, who would not hesitate to kick a hero of the revolution through the streets with a shameful placard around his neck, while they swore at him vilely for his past services to Mao and motherland.

But volubility is no measure of victory, and the onslaught of the militant Maoists on the hydra-headed Party bureaucracy met with fierce resistance. Faced with a mounting campaign of mudslinging and catcalling, and finally the invasion of their offices by yelling Red Guards, the defenders were compelled to shape their strategy to confound an enemy to whom the sacred mandate of Mao had given immunity. Their answer was to fight Mao with Mao.

Beleaguered Party committees throughout the provinces organized their own "Red Guards" of local students and workers, and heads were broken and blood was spilled as "Maoist" met Maoist in mirrorlike confrontations, in which right reflected left and wrong was therefore indistinguishable from right. By the end of 1966 the ability of the "bourgeois reactionary" revisionists to strike back had reduced the Cultural Revolution to a massive exercise in isometrics, bringing the entire struggle to a strenuous standstill. The Red Guards had failed, and the stubborn stonewalling of the adversary was to compel left-wing editorialists (who had earlier described Mao's opponents as "a handful of leaders taking the capitalist road") to speak of the life-and-death struggle of "the revolutionary minority against the reactionary majority." The damned now outnumbered the blessed, it appeared. But that proposition flatly contradicted page 255 of the Little Red Book all the Red Guards were waving: "The individual is subordinate to the organization; the minority is subordinate to the majority." The last pretense that Mao was acting with the full approval of the Central Committee had been abandoned, and only one law remained: *Vox Mao vox populi vox Dei.*

It had become evident that more people must be drawn into the maelstrom of antirevisionist fury. In December 1966, accordingly, the Cultural Revolution was carried to the shop floor and the farmyard, workers and peasants were organized into militant groups of "revolutionary rebels," and at the turn of the year the *People's Daily* called on all Chinese to "seize power from below." They were to take as their inspiration the Paris Commune proclaimed in 1871, when the French workers had overthrown the old order in a pointless cataclysm that left the masses the bosses of the city for seventy-two chaotic days. The significance of the Commune was that it had had no other master but the mob, for all men were paid the same, and all officials were hired and fired by popular demand so that they could never develop into a self-perpetuating elite. The Chairman's latest maneuver in the fight for an egalitarian China was becoming clear, it seemed.

Shanghai responded at the beginning of 1967 with the "January Revolution," a Maoist coup initially directed against revisionist cadres who were manipulating workers with material rewards instead of Mao's words, and workers who had committed the sin of striking for more pay instead of for more politics. Denouncing this "evil wind of economism" behind which could be seen the sinister hand of Liu Shaoqi, Red Guards and "revolutionary rebels" took over the city's main newspapers and opened a ferocious verbal assault on the municipal government and Party committees. The masses rallied to their support, the local bureaucrats were booted out of office, and one month later the leaders of the revolution proclaimed the "Shanghai Commune."

It was a moment of triumph for the Shanghai Mafia. The chairman of the Commune was Zhang Chunqiao, the vice-chairman Yao Wenyuan. Yao had become Mao's polemical hit man and master of propaganda, turning his talent for tirade against one senior Party leader after another, and now he had his reward. But there was another name to add to the short list of heroes—that of an obscure security guard at Number Seventeen Cotton Mill in Shanghai. Wang Hongwen was a tall, self-assured, articulate, and photogenic fellow who had shown an unexpected talent for organizing his comrades, and having first roused the workers at his own plant against the "capitalist-roaders" who managed it, he had moved on to mobilize two million more behind Zhang Chunqiao. That in itself guaranteed him a future of meretricious promise, and he was to make up the number in the unsavory partnership later to be known as the "Gang of Four."

The omens, deceitful as ever, appeared good. Zhang Chunqiao hailed the Shanghai Commune as a "great victory for the Thought of Mao," and sent the Chairman a telegram of homage servilely addressed to "The Red Sun in our Hearts." He and Yao had every reason to expect an enthusiastic reply. Mao had cited the example of the Paris Commune in his original sixteen-point charter for the Cultural Revolution, he had urged the masses to seize power from below, and he had warmly welcomed the capture of the Shanghai press by the rebels. "Internal rebellions are fine," he had said a few days afterwards. "This is a great revolution . . . the upsurge of revolutionary power in Shanghai has brought hope to the whole country."

But whereas the abortive Paris Commune had survived for seventy-two days, the Shanghai Commune was to last only seventeen. Summoned to Peking, its jubilant architects found an impatient Mao "waiting at the door to greet them." They had gone too far. To "doubt everything and overthrow everything" was reactionary, he said bluntly, and the notion that government by the masses meant doing away with all heads was "extreme anarchism." Rule by the rabble was therefore to give way to rule by "revolutionary committee"—a "triple alliance" of the rebels, the local military, and acceptable cadres of the old bureaucracy, whose members would not be chosen by popular demand but by "democratic consultation" (horse-trading among the interested parties).

Mao may have floated the idea of the Paris Commune in order to mobilize the masses against the hierarchy, but he had no intention of seeing China split into independent city-states under a system so excruciatingly democratic that the mob could sack anyone it pleased, Maoist or revisionist. That would only be acceptable if he controlled the mob, the army supported it, and only his enemies suffered at its hands. But that was not the case. And there was the rub. He might insinuate that once again he had pronounced the magic words that would transform China, and that others had misused them; that he had not been responsible for the contents of Pandora's box—he had only lifted the lid. But the truth of the matter was that the timing was wrong.

The crude attempts of the Red Guards and revolutionary rebels to "seize power" everywhere had yielded a meaningless mosaic of violence instead of a new revolutionary order. Shrill voices from all over China filled the air with tales of the inextricable tangle of enmities as Maoist battled "Maoist" at Mao's behest. Radio stations from Canton to Xian, from Fuzhou to Wuhan listed the endless crimes of a treacherous revisionist enemy that played the doppelgänger, fielding false Red Guards who staged false "seizures of power" and spread false rumors to fuddle the masses, inciting rebel to fight rebel.

When these revisionists then blamed the righteous for all the bloodshed, they merely justified the righteous in shedding more blood, it seemed. "Revolutionary beating, killing, and robbing is very good," Radio Xian protested triumphantly. "Chairman Mao says we must uphold whatever the enemy opposes, and oppose whatever the enemy upholds. Certain Party officials oppose revolutionary beating, killing, and robbing. This proves that we are doing the right thing!" The hatred engendered between local rebels and "Long Marchers" from elsewhere was fanned by wall artists whose scrawled characters screamed imprecations from their posters in the demotic idiom—"You bunch of bastards, how did you get here? You bunch of bad eggs, what are your credentials? You children of landlords, kulaks, counterrevolutionaries, bad elements, and rightists, get out within twenty-four hours."

With double standards fluttering vigorously in all the wind, the mass movements had broken up into countless squabbling factions, for the Cultural Revolution had given the clannish Chinese license to gang up again, and they wasted no time. Rebels who began by accepting Mao's open invitation to throw out their Party bosses were quick to turn on one another. "Maoists" fought Maoists, Peking Red Guards fought Canton Red Guards, and according to one report, workers in a single Shanghai plant were split into a hundred quarreling groups. Managerial cadres in mills and mines everywhere found themselves contending with a kaleidoscope of alliances made up of sharp, mutually hostile splinters that would coalesce to "struggle" against the "local power holders" only when they were not attacking one another. The Cultural Revolution was skidding badly, and having brought in revolutionary rebels to support the Red Guards, the Maoist leadership now had to order the army in to support the revolutionary rebels.

❀ *CHAPTER* TWENTY-THREE ❀

T HE ARMY had been made the right marker of the revolution in 1964, when all Chinese were instructed to "learn from the PLA," and two years later Mao had directed that it should become "one great school" of politics, production, culture, and arms. But the PLA was no mere military machine. Its veteran generals were not simple soldiers who took their orders from the brass hat one rung up the ladder; they belonged to an intricate network of loyalties and rivalries formed in the different Red bases of the thirties and the different field armies of the forties. And now they were the commanders and the political commissars of the thirteen disparate military regions into which all China was divided, "Red warlords" who laid down the law and kept the peace in their great territorial fiefs with the help of up to a quarter of a million troops. They were conservative by nature, more at ease with the pedestrian policies of the pragmatists in Peking than Mao's flights of egalitarian fancy, and their first instinct was to keep the army out of the Cultural Revolution and the Cultural Revolution out of the army.

The Red Guards might be officially labeled "brother fighting units" and a "powerful reserve of the PLA" to which the army was obliged to give technical aid and attach advisers. But when fists and bricks started to fly, the soldiers held back the rebels more often than not, siding naturally with the responsible "revisionist" cadres who stood for order and stability and the status quo in their domains, rather than with undisciplined gangs of scruffy adolescents out to make mischief and change everything.

Towards the end of January 1967, the PLA was given unambiguous orders to "support the left," yet six months later the rebels had gained the upper hand in only four out of China's twenty-nine provinces. For one thing, the regional overlord frequently wore two hats—one as the military commander who was now directed to help the revolutionary ragtag smash the local Party apparatus, and the other as boss of the Party apparatus they were to smash. And no general with half a dozen divisions behind him sees it as part of his duty to encompass his own defeat.

Zhang Guohua, concurrently military master of Tibet and first secretary of the local Party, was a case in point.

February 1967. Faint but ominous, the spectre of open rebellion has risen over the vast outlying autonomous regions of China, where powerful communist warlords are reported to be stonewalling Mao's revolution and sending troops to crack down on the Red Guards. Peking posters accuse Zhang Guohua of conducting a "white terror" in Lhasa against Mao's mass organisations. Earlier this month he smashed an attempt by Red Guards and revolutionary rebels to seize and hold the government, Party and police headquarters in the Tibetan capital. Four hundred Maoists were arrested, 100 are said to have been killed, and Lhasa is virtually under martial law.

Accounts of "bloody and serious" events in Huhhot, capital of the sprawling Autonomous Region of Inner Mongolia, echo those from Tibet. This peripheral violence follows fighting in China's Far West, where seven out of eight army divisions are understood to have sided with Wang Enmao, army and Party boss of the Xinjiang Uygur Autonomous Region, against Maoism and perhaps against Mao himself . . .

Mao had flirted dangerously with the formula for a political fission bomb offered by the Paris Commune, and had the generals agreed to throw their weight behind his militant rebels, he might not have been so quick to renounce it. But the arithmetic was against him. In at least five military regions the PLA commanders were grace-and-favor trusties of Liu Shaoqi and Deng Xiaoping, and up to ten of the top brass in the capital looked to the two arch-revisionists rather than to Lin Biao, who commanded the implicit loyalty of not more than half of the three-million-strong armed forces. If the left wing revolutionaries applied heat too suddenly, therefore, they would risk splitting the PLA wide open along what were already only half-concealed cracks. And the same might apply to the leadership in Peking, where radical Maoists like Jiang Qing were breathing fire into the rebellion, while moderate "Maoists" like Chou En-lai were desperately trying to limit the havoc.

Consequently Lin Biao had recoiled from the hazards of plunging the PLA into an armed struggle on the side of the rebels, and Mao had put the Paris Commune back among his dreams for later. The Shanghai experiment was rejected in favor of government by revolutionary committee, and the army was not to help the masses seize power for themselves, but to forge these "triple alliances" of rebels, soldiers, and cadres in every province—and then keep the peace among the incongruous partners. The time had come for the Chairman to make another tactical withdrawal, and as China moved from zig to zag, Chou En-lai advanced and Jiang Qing retreated, like figurines in a rustic Swiss barometer that presaged fair and foul weather in response to the mental climate of Mao himself.

March 1967. The curtain has now risen on a new act in which the centre of the stage is taken by the champion of compromise, Premier Chou En-lai. The Chinese prime minister is reported to have condemned all past excesses, including the humiliating persecution of senior officials, and to have deplored absurd "revolutionary" situations in which, for example, 100 over-zealous ignoramuses took over the Public Security Bureau of Peking, with the apparent intention of trying to run its 10,000-strong police force themselves.

A new line now emphasizes that China needs her old leaders and experienced cadres. They should be reinstated, provided they formally admit their mistakes. The official target of Maoist enmity has been drastically narrowed to a handful of top-flight personalities, headed by President Liu Shaoqi and the disgraced Party secretary-general, Deng Xiaoping . . .

The "misconception" that all cadres were evil and must be flung out of office was anarchistic and wrong, the press warned sanctimoniously, for it robbed the nation of the "mature political and organizational skills of experienced men." But it proved almost ludicrously difficult to put together the syndicates of mutual distrust called triple alliances, and two and a half more years of turmoil were to pass before the last provincial revolutionary committee could be formed. The rebels were being asked to sit down not only with soldiers who had obstructed them, but with bureaucrats they had ignominiously evicted from office and publicly scourged, since cadres who had been billed as "ghosts and demons" only yesterday were now "treasures of the Party" to be "boldly employed." The revolutionaries were not only disgusted, they were scared—"What will happen to me if he is reinstated?" a troubled comrade might well ask of a superior he had called a "fascist dog" and cuffed through the streets in happier days. And when they were not afraid of the cadres, they were afraid for their own dreams. What would be left for the heroes of the revolution if the old gang of revisionists took back all the plum jobs?

For the cadres, meanwhile, there had been too short an interval between kicks and kisses. They were reluctant to return to their posts, some because they bore a grudge against those who had victimized them, others because they were terrified of being exposed again to the vicious whims of the mob. Mao's China might not be Stalin's Russia, and in the political game of snakes-and-ladders fallen men might rise again, since they were rarely swept from the board. But many of the bureaucrats had been given a bitter lesson in the basic Taoist principle that what goes up must come down. "They made their mistake once, and they never wish to be leading officials again," as one Communist put it to me. The safest place on the ladder was the bottom rung. The government wanted the cadres to be coaxed into facing criticism, to confess and be forgiven their sins. But the cadres did not want to endure the ordeal a second time, and the rebels wanted no cheap absolution for the guilty.

In the triple alliance at the top—where Lin Biao represented the army, Chou En-lai the administration, and the Cultural Revolution Group the rebels—Chou was meanwhile trying to provide an eye in the storm by neutralizing one contrary wind with another. But like all masters of compromise, he had only brought the conflict out of the streets into the house. The three-cornered alliance was in fact a three-cornered struggle, which sharpened ominously in February 1967 when nine eminent veterans from the most rarefied ranks of the Party protested vehemently against the excesses of the Cultural Revolution and the senseless wrongs done to thousands of loyal functionaries throughout the land. This outburst heralded the so-called "February Adverse Current," a pernicious movement to whitewash and restore revisionist cadres to their posts (so the Maoists charged), and to discredit as a gang of irresponsible hooligans the gallant rebels who had fired them in the first place.

Amid the miasma of universal ill will, the mutilated administration—stripped of some cadres, deserted by others—was rapidly breaking down, yet most of the revolutionary committees that were to replace it were no more than headings on paper for incompatible Chinese to quarrel over. As the old structure disintegrated in vast areas of the republic, therefore, military control commissions moved into the vacuum to direct everything from the railways to the media. The army was taking over.

But China was still sick with the "rampaging anarchism" of faction fighting among rebel cliques, so that the passion of the PLA for order and of the revolutionaries for disorder now brought them into ever bloodier conflict. Perplexed commanders unable to distinguish between Maoist and "Maoist" suppressed the unruly even when they were not the ungodly, and where the PLA did "support the left" the rebels still ended up clinging impotently to the nether fringes of any triple alliance that was formed, while the soldiers gave the orders and the cadres did the work. The army had no intention of letting the left-wing militants impose their will, and the day would come when they would be accused of manifold activities possible only to a six-armed Indian goddess of malevolent disposition—"cheating the masses, sowing dissension, undermining the proletariat, fishing in troubled waters, subverting the PLA, and strangling the new-born triple alliance in its cradle."

Alarm bells rang in Peking, and the radicals counterattacked. In April 1967 the powers of the PLA were severely curbed by a directive forbidding the army to "open fire on mass organizations" or brand them counterrevolutionary, and the easy acceptance of bourgeois cadres who came in from the cold was condemned in the revolting idiom of the day as "compromism" and "adjustism." The verbal stoning of Liu Shaoqi was meanwhile intensified in order to give the drifting Cultural Revolution new impetus. The drab old Communist who had steadfastly put the Party before all else was accused of every sin in the calendar, from sabotaging the "socialist transformation" of China to praising an old film that had maliciously libeled the Boxers. The antics of these homicidal ruffians, who had massacred sixteen thousand men, women, and children at the turn of the century in a wide variety of particularly loathsome ways, were then commended to the impressionable Red Guards as the "heroic struggles" of a "great antiimperialist, antifeudalist revolutionary movement," "the pride and glory of the Chinese people" and much "extolled" by the Chairman himself.

"Don't be afraid of chaos," Mao told a group of young militants. "The greater the chaos and the longer it goes on the better. Disorder and chaos are always a good thing . . . but never use weapons." Two months later he was condemning anarchism, three weeks after that he was demanding more revolution, and a month after that once again

denouncing the principle of "overthrowing everything." As the signals
from Peking became increasingly contradictory, all parties in the provinces made free translations notable for their poetic license. But it was
the dedicated advocates of chaos who got their way.

June 1967. China's cultural revolution is now free-wheeling out
of control. Posters and newspapers present a picture of increasing
turmoil and disorder, of confused struggles between pro-Maoists
and anti-Maoists, and between rival pro-Maoist groups, while the
army backs first one side, then another.

This breakdown of law and order is hardly surprising. Of
China's 15 key vice-premiers, only two have escaped heavy criticism or outright dismissal. Of government ministers, only half
appeared with Mao at the Labour Day rally last month. In the
Communist Party, a third of the Politburo and two-thirds of the
Secretariat have not been heard of or mentioned publicly for 10
months, and of 174 members of the Central Committee, nearly
100 have been denounced.

In the army, nine of the top 14 military officers in the Defence
Ministry and the Party's Military Commission have been disgraced
or have disappeared from view, and a question mark must be put
against the names of 23 top-flight generals. Only seven out of the
13 regional military commanders have declared themselves for
Mao's revolution. The Maoists have "seized power" in only four
provinces and two municipalities out of China's 29 main administrative divisions . . .

All attempts to form triple alliances had degenerated into a scramble
by soldiers and cadres and rival rebel groups to "seize power," and
as the more impatient revolutionaries looted arms depots, the streets of
city after city were swept by eccentric tides of shapeless violence.
Workers flooding down to the communes to seize power clashed with
angry peasants converging on the towns, where the more purposeful
mayhem perpetrated in the name of "mass democracy" developed its
own penumbra of workaday robbery and pillaging, murder and arson,
as the contagious lawlessness took over from the law. Calling to each
other across the tumult, urban radio stations were now echoing each
other's harsh cries of "anarchy" and "chaos" as not only Chinese society
but the haggard Chinese economy threatened to collapse.

July 1967. The government is now anxiously warning all revolutionaries to abandon "struggle through force," which tends to

leave behind a trail of sacked and beaten-up technicians, smashed equipment, looted plants and idle, locked-out labour.

In Sichuan province, the richest and most "reactionary" in metropolitan China, exasperated workers have clashed with officious revolutionaries on the factory floor, and when violently suppressed, have retaliated by sabotaging machinery, ransacking workshops, and then abandoning the plant in question, leaving the dead on the ground. It is reported that among many industrial installations they have deserted are a vital aircraft assembly plant and a munitions factory from which the men took enough bazookas and mortars "for a battalion."

There have been major stoppages in China's biggest motor works, in cotton mills and electrical installations, in the oilfields of Xinjiang, and the army has had to intervene in the coal mines of Manchuria and Shanxi to ensure a minimum output. In some provinces industry has been virtually paralysed by politics in the raw, and an astronomical number of man-hours lost in demonstrations and rallies, in strikes and "struggle meetings," in public polemics and poster-pastings, sit-ins and lock-outs . . .

All central planning had stopped. More than forty of China's foremost economic and industrial experts had been purged. Hundreds of thousands of experienced managers and rural cadres had been uprooted by the political storm when the rebels took the Cultural Revolution into the factories and farms, and too often incompetent novices had "seized" their jobs. Iron and steel production had fallen sharply, and coal output had dropped by nearly 50 percent (if one remaining economic vice-premier in Peking was quoted correctly). The railways, which 50 million Red Guards had ridden free in 1966, were again choked with humanity as workers and peasants left home to join the revolution. One year after the first Red Guard rally in Peking, Chou En-lai was to report that China was already "six months behind in production."

But by then tempers had snapped. The army had mutinied.

❀ CHAPTER TWENTY-FOUR ❀

Reports of the "Wuhan Incident" of July 1967 reached the West blurred by its violence, for each excited account contradicted the last. But if the haze of history has not helped to sharpen the detail, the main structure of the plot has emerged.

The military commander of the region was a certain Chen Zaidao, a small, skinny, pugnacious general with a pockmarked face and a revolutionary past that had never brought him close to either Mao Tsetung or Lin Biao. Like many others, he paid lip service to the Cultural Revolution, and, instead of recognizing the four hundred thousand left-wing militants of the rebel movement in Wuhan as the legitimate Maoists, he backed the "One Million Heroes Army," a bellicose combination of workers and militia with suspiciously good contacts at the local "revisionist" Party headquarters and an abiding objection to Red Guards.

Stiffened with a PLA formation of divisional strength equipped with armored cars, the Million Heroes had arrested more than three thousand Maoists by the spring of 1967, after going through the usual formality of branding them "counterrevolutionary." Word reached Peking, and in July the Minister for Public Security and an extremist from the Cultural Revolution Group named Wang Li were dispatched to Wuhan to investigate charges that Chen Zaidao was conspiring with the enemy. But as soon as these emissaries from the capital rashly accused the general of supporting the wrong side, they were given a taste of the prevailing temper in the proud city where a military uprising had triggered the Chinese revolution fifty-six years before.

Their hotel was surrounded in the early morning by an intimidating jam of army lorries packed with helmeted men, and a cursing, club-wielding squad of militants burst in upon them, locking the minister in his room under guard, and giving Wang Li a brutal thrashing before tossing him into a truck and driving him to Chen's headquarters. There he was hauled before a vast press of hostile demonstrators brandishing swords and spears and rifles with fixed bayonets, and marched through the streets wearing a placard around his neck damning him for a revisionist—battered, bloody, one eye closed, his Mao suit a ruin.

With the army on hand to give covering fire, the Million Heroes then set out to capture all rebel strongholds in the three riverine towns that make up industrial Wuhan. Messy fighting followed in which revolutionaries were beaten up and killed and buildings burned, and when Chou En-lai flew down from the capital to rescue the two victims of the counterrevolution, he narrowly escaped being kidnapped himself. Crack troops were rushed to the scene to quell the legions of the mutinous general, who was arrested and escorted to Peking to be confronted with a list of his egregious crimes. Yet all that happened to him was that he was relieved of his command, obliged to confess his errors, sentenced to study the works of Mao—and later transferred to another region. He was not put against the nearest wall and summarily shot in order to encourage the others. For his death just might have done so.

Not all saw the danger in the same light, however. Wang Li was the hero of extremists in the Cultural Revolution Group in Peking, who were not only appalled but morbidly excited by the traumatic episode. Chen had flouted established convention. He had not simply twisted directives from the capital to suit his own provincial convenience in the hallowed tradition of China's imperial satraps. He had flagrantly defied Peking. His unbecoming conduct had thrown into high relief the dire threat to the Cultural Revolution posed by powerful and hostile military commanders. But it had also provided a heaven-sent pretext for tearing the PLA apart in its turn.

Led by Jiang Qing and Wang Li, the radicals organized a strident campaign to "strike down the handful of army leaders who have taken the capitalist road" and "drag out the powerholders in the PLA." If any general refused to support them, even fringe factions of left-wing rebels could now hit back swiftly by charging him with "Wuhan revisionism," and some Red Guard units were secretly armed to attack the more bloody-minded among the soldiery.

The soldiers were not the only targets. As the pendulum swung wildly to the left again, Chen Yi, the bald old marshal who had become China's outspoken foreign minister, came under sustained and vicious fire—and beyond Chen the Maoists had their sights on Chou En-lai himself. In the summer of 1967 extremists seized control of the Foreign Ministry in Peking, and a series of outrages perpetrated against foreign diplomats culminated in the burning down of the British chancery by a mob of well-briefed rebels, after London had failed to kowtow to an "ultimatum" to lift a ban on left-wing newspapers in Hong Kong. Once again, the firebrands had gone too far.

Characteristically, the Chairman was not in Peking at the time, for when Mao flew a kite, he used a long string. In 1966 he had left his adversaries in charge to give them a chance to sabotage the revolution in his absence; this time he had left his vanguard in charge to give them a chance to stimulate it further. If things went right he would come back to claim his victory; if things went wrong he would return to lay the blame for any misplaced "left-wing adventurism" where it belonged. "The enlightened ruler reposes in non-action," Han Feizi had written more than two millennia before. "Where there are accomplishments, the ruler takes credit; where there are errors, the ministers are held responsible . . . Be empty, still and idle, and from your place of darkness observe the defects of others." The two secrets of infallibility were absence and silence.

Until the moment of truth arrived. Returning to Peking in September, Mao declared that Wang Li had made more mistakes in forty days than Chen Yi had made in forty years. Judgment had been passed. The Foreign Ministry was taken over by the army on the Chairman's orders and the ringleader of the left-wing intruders arrested. The extremists had dangerously overheated the revolution, and risked shattering the army and the political leadership. Just as the junior cadres and technical experts had been blamed for the follies of the Great Leap Forward, the radicals were now blamed for the idiot excesses of the summer, and Mao could once more beat a victorious retreat to prepared positions. But the culprits were ultra-leftists of the so-called "16 May" Group, and since they could hardly be morally condemned for being leftist, it was explained that in fact they were the ultra-rightist "black hand" of Liu Shaoqi, a tight ring of reactionary conspirators who had plotted to give the Cultural Revolution the unacceptable face of anarchy in order to discredit it—"waving the red flag to defeat the red flag."

The sacrifice of their expendable friends, tricked out as "freaks and monsters" of the enemy, enabled the principals to slip out through the back door. Jiang Qing made two speeches full of dishonest indignation against moronic extremists who had been so misguided as to attack the PLA—"fomenting trouble against the army is like tearing down the Great Wall," she said, petulantly eating yesterday's words. A directive was issued ordering "all revolutionary masses" to support the PLA and to return their ill-gotten guns. They were warned not to attack troops on any pretext, and soldiers were authorized to disarm them by force—shooting to kill if necessary. The young were told to get off the streets and go back to school.

October, 1967. After a long, long vacation lasting nearly a year and a half, during which Chinese schools and universities were either shut down or ravaged by warring factions of Red Guards, the *People's Daily* was pleading this week for the young to return to their lessons.

In February the government announced that schools would reopen, but Red Guards still on the rampage simply defied it and continued to play truant. Those who returned to the classroom spent most of their time singing revolutionary songs and chanting quotations from Mao. In July the first institute of higher learning belatedly opened its doors, and others began to follow suit. It was agreed, however, that until September students would spend all their time criticising the old order and carrying out political "struggles."

The realisation that the country needs its cadres emphasizes the appalling magnitude of the sacrifice China has made. Peking has lost a scholastic year and more, during which nearly a million students should have attended university and four million more should have studied in secondary school.

Furthermore, it was disclosed last week that in a typical secondary school three periods out of five are now reserved for the study of Mao's works, and for "revolutionary criticism" . . .

And for what had the sacrifice been made? The damage could now be assessed. China was laced with political vendettas as intricate as the lines on a crackleware vase, and for every scar there was a score to settle. Even Chou En-lai had been hard put to protect his own ministers from the iconoclastic rebels, and only eighteen out of fifty-one still appeared in public. Only nine of the twenty-five members of the Politburo had escaped verbal vivisection, and of twenty-eight provincial Party secretaries, only four had survived in their jobs.

It was no different in the PLA, for a provincial chief might have been an outstanding general in the Jiangxi Soviet thirty-five years before, but he could still be "dragged out" by a posse of adolescents for ritual vilification as a "rat in the street," stripped of all his posts, and put under arrest. Revolutionary hatchet men had disposed of four commanders and ten political commissars at the head of the republic's thirteen military regions. Heads had fallen freely even in Peking itself, where in September Xiao Hua, chief political commissar of the entire armed forces, and five of his immediate lieutenants had been axed in a sudden stroke that effectively decapitated the General Political Department of the PLA.

Xiao Hua's crime had been to stand in the way of Madame Mao, for the ambitious Pasionaria of the revolution hankered after control of the cultural—and therefore political—activities of the army that naturally fell within his province. However, like other obstructive soldiers whose fall from grace had been contrived by Jiang Qing, Xiao Hua was a protégé of Lin Biao. The sordid, immemorial conflict of ambitions between the empress and the imperial heir was recurring, Mao's wife and Mao's successor were no longer smiling at each other in private, and more than two thousand years of Chinese history taught that one of them would live (if not for long) to rue it.

The clash of wills had driven Lin Biao closer to Chou En-lai, and now that Mao had made another strategic withdrawal, they were free to counterattack. In March 1968 the chief of staff and two left-wing military "power holders" who had connived at Jiang Qing's machinations were unceremoniously kicked out of office in their turn. The chief of staff was then replaced with Huang Yongsheng, a general who was no lickspittle of the Chairman's wife but had been reassuringly bedizened with all the charges the Red Guards could pin on him as a "black bandit" and "butcher of the Cultural Revolution." The appointment conformed with the times, for dissent that yesterday had been gloriously dubbed "making revolution" was now damned as "divisive factionalism," and the revolutionary masses—the Chinese third estate—were being treated as a public nuisance.

At this point the concentric cycles of the Chinese story begin to resemble those sets of ingeniously carved ivory balls, one inside the other, for which Chinese craftsmen are justifiably notorious. First there is the outer sphere of the empire, with its undulating motif of rising and falling dynasties over the centuries. Within this is the shorter span of the People's Republic, whose vainglorious leaps towards Utopia alternate monotonously with rueful pauses for recovery every few years. And inside that on an even smaller time scale is the Cultural Revolution, in which China shuttles predictably back and forth between near-anarchy and near-order every few months. Were the moderates and the military on top by the winter? The next onslaught from the Left was as foreseeable as spring itself.

> May 1968. The dramatic promotion within the Chinese hierarchy this week of Jiang Qing, Mao Tsetung's wife, responds to a hairpin twist in a zigzag course of cultural revolution which opens up new prospects of political fury ahead. Jiang Qing was listed sixteenth among the Chinese leaders who celebrated National Day on 1 October, but jumped to eighth place on Wednesday, when Mao led the line-up for Labour Day.
>
> In March, moderate policies still prevailed. Last weekend, however, the official communist press swung around and denounced those who attacked "proletarian factionalism" as "bourgeois self-seekers" trying to crush the morale of genuine revolutionaries.
>
> The storm warnings are peculiarly shrill. Radio and press almost hysterically call an ever-lengthening roll of "Kuomintang," "Khrushchevist" and "right splittist" bogies in the provinces who are allegedly attempting a comeback. "Conservatives" in the public security service are castigated by Jiang Qing for arresting 35,000 revolutionaries in Sichuan province alone. In Shanghai the rightists are planning a "second revolution." There is splittism in Peking, sabotage in the steel industry, reaction in the Foreign Ministry.
>
> This carefully fostered mood of suspicion may lead to untidy consequences . . .

The rebels were now urged to "maintain their fighting will" and to demand a bigger say in the new revolutionary committees. But not a single revolutionary committee was formed in the short, white-hot summer of bullying and butchery that followed, during which "Maoist" and Maoist Red Guards stormed into the streets once more to fling themselves at one another. The political visibility was closing down hourly, and by July the trussed and bloated corpses of the losers in the pitched battles being fought out between rival cohorts in Canton were being washed up on the beaches of Hong Kong. The Maoists had given the signal for another attack on the bastions of reaction, but the Cultural Revolution had spun out of control.

> August 1968. In the streets of China's unhappier cities, the power struggle is provoking bloody clashes between Red Guard mobs supporting the local revolutionary committee and the equally ruthless Red Guard mobs inspired by Jiang Qing. In the past two

months bitter fighting has been reported from eight provinces and autonomous regions, especially in the rebellious south, where men are notoriously Nelson-eyed about signals from Peking.

In Guangxi province warring mobs struggling for control of the towns with machine-guns, mortars, and grenades have been supported by rival factions within the army itself . . . Canton is no haven. The city and much of the country around are the battleground for the "East Wind" and "Red Flag" Guards. In this monstrous projection of medieval lawlessness, in which a community of three million people is divided between ideological Montagus and Capulets, hundreds and even thousands of rival red revolutionaries fight it out with everything from bottles and bicycle chains to modern automatic weapons seized from the soldiers themselves. According to wallposters, 20,000 people have been killed or wounded in the province in the past four months . . .

Mao, whose Thoughts were gospel and who could have stilled the destructive tempest by making his wishes clear, publicly and in person dividing sheep from goats, continued to remain silent as the blood flowed and the bodies piled up. "Heaven does not speak," said the ancient philosopher Mencius, and in those words perhaps explained the tragedy of man. "Mao does not speak" could similarly explain the tragedy of China. Faced with stiffening resistance to his revolution, the Chairman addressed the masses not with one tongue, but with many, each suitable for the moment—the tongue of Chou, when it was necessary to pacify; the tongue of Jiang Qing, when it was opportune to incite; of Lin Biao to rally the army; of editorialists in the Party press in order to flash his "instructions" to the millions as impersonally as an Aldis lamp—but never his own. Ambiguous, Delphic at times, he was master of all sides of the argument, and therefore beyond fault.

But the puppets in turn could give their own words authority by attributing them to the grand ventriloquist, and down in the turbulent provinces all rival factions claimed to be the true interpreters of his disembodied directives, which they adapted to suit their own particular "line" in the cutthroat struggle for local supremacy. In consequence, the latest attempt to stoke the fires of revolution had simply blown it apart. Even comrades on the fourteen-man "proletarian headquarters" that had replaced the dismembered Politburo (and to which collective leadership in China was now reduced) were shocked by the so-called "hundred-days war" of futile internecine fighting at Qinghua University in the capital itself, in which many students had perished. It was time for the Chairman to retreat yet again. After the obtuse cadres who had betrayed the Great Leap Forward, and the dissembling "ultra-rightist" ultra-leftists of the Cultural Revolution Group, it was the turn of the Red Guards to take the blame.

In a tearful, five-hour encounter at the end of July 1968, Mao told local Red Guard leaders in Peking that they had let him down, and threatened to impose martial law if they did not stop their aimless faction fighting. Editorials in leading Party organs called upon the army to provide "powerful and firm backing" for the revolutionary committees (the haves) and to "guide" the masses (the have-nots). And the army did not demur, for nineteen chairmen and twenty vice-chairmen of the twenty-nine provincial committees that would be administering all China within a month were senior commanders of the PLA.

Mao had struck a bargain with the inconveniently powerful pragmatists in the army and administration in the provinces, a truce that would restore a semblance of unity to the country. The truce embraced men like the "Black Hand of Guangxi," the boss of the revolutionary committee of that province who had earlier "kidnapped and beaten" Maoist martyrs, "obstinately pursuing the bourgeois-reactionary line of Liu Shaoqi," "frenziedly suppressing the Cultural Revolution," and organizing "general mobilization to carry out massive counterrevolutionary massacres." But he was, after all, no worse than Chiang Kai-shek, with whom Mao had also shaken hands in his day. The revolutionary committees, only yesterday denounced by the Maoists as the tools of ambitious local warlords, were publicly extolled as "fighting headquarters for leading the masses to new victories," and their military chiefs began doing so at once by putting Red Guard factions into voluntary liquidation.

This could now be done with impunity. Whenever Yao Wenyuan picked up his pen, it has been noted, somebody was going to suffer. In November 1965 his malevolent attack on *Hai Rui Dismissed from Office* had heralded a massive exercise in political mayhem; in August 1968 his article "The Working Class Must Undertake Leadership in Everything" was the signal for the first phase of the chaos to end, and tolled the knell of the Red Guard movement. The Cultural Revolution was being taken away from skittish effervescent youth and placed in the steady hands of the honest toiler. "Worker-Peasant Mao Tsetung Thought Propaganda Teams" poured into every strife-torn organization throughout the country to lay down the ideological law and restore peace. But their immediate targets were schools and colleges, and when the first team of all marched into Qinghua University, the rowdiest faction-ridden campus in the country, the Chairman set his personal seal on the operation by sending its members a symbolic gift of mangoes.

Mao was discarding the Red Guards, yet he still remained silent, for he could not offer a word of comfort to these bewildered young people and simultaneously placate their opponents if he did all the talking himself. Instead, Chou En-lai and Jiang Qing acted like certain oriental gods that each symbolize a different aspect of the same higher deity. Addressing a rally in Peking, Chou spoke of the "triumph" of the Cultural Revolution and emphasized the glorious contribution made by the workers, without once mentioning Mao's "little generals," and it was left to a visibly bad-tempered Jiang Qing to even the score by telling the Red Guards they had done a "wonderful job." They were nonetheless being dismissed, if with her blessing. And that would not save them. The deployment of workers and peasants in the classrooms of China was accompanied by an insidious campaign against the "petit bourgeois" young and their intellectual mentors, and workers with "muddy legs but red hearts" were given the task of revising the curriculum and vetting academic staff.

"Young rebels must go to the villages and accept re-education by the poor and lower-middle peasantry," said the Chairman, and another massive *xiafang* campaign shoveled millions of students and cadres down to the country, where schools were being founded "by the poor and lower-middle peasantry" in which instruction was almost exclusively limited to Mao and muckraking. Militant Red Guards who had thrown themselves zestfully into revolutionary action and riotous living in the city streets now found themselves being quizzed about their class origins by self-righteous worker-teachers, or saved from their sins on some distant midden by sermonizing peasants who regarded them as stuck-up and soft. They had been sacrificed in accordance with Mao's ever-changing "strategic plan," so that he could make peace with military power holders in the provinces like the "Black Hand of Guangxi," and exact concessions in return.

September 1968. Fighting the instinct of local commanders to play the warlord, Peking is demanding absolute loyalty to Mao. For with all the provinces pacified—at least on paper—this cycle of the

Chinese revolution should logically be completed by the holding of the long-overdue Ninth Party Congress.

Unlike the first seven Congresses, the last was democratic, and delegates were elected "upward from below." In consequence, Mao found himself facing a hostile clique in his own Central Committee. Part of any deal he has made with provincial leaders must include the stipulation that this time delegates will not be chosen at lower echelons, but nominated from above. It is understood that Mao wants a vastly expanded Congress well-packed with "loyal" military and political cadres who will demonstrate the unity of China by letting him have his way, and the entire assembly is expected to approve the dismissal of Liu Shaoqi and of the execrated Party secretary-general, Deng Xiaoping. In exchange for this, ostensibly repentant men hitherto damned by left-wing Red Guards will just as ostensibly be forgiven their sins . . .

That would not be the last movement of the opus, however, for Mao saw the Congress as the prelude to the rise of a reborn, fire-purged Communist Party in his own spiritual image that would not only replace the old, discredited mandarinate, but take all power back from the hidebound soldiery—once he was again in a position to "fight downhill."

The first results of all the haggling meanwhile began to appear. For two years and more Liu Shaoqi had been reviled as a renegade, traitor, spy, scab, and lackey of imperialism, yet although he had offered his resignation three times, it had been ignored. Blustering Red Guards had thrown out his written self-criticism, he had been frogmarched to a struggle meeting, manhandled and struck, "unmasked and overthrown," dubbed "China's Khrushchev," and put under guard like a criminal after forty-seven years of faithful service to the Party. But he had never been officially damned by name, for the etiquette of the Chinese Inquisition demands that the sinner remain anonymous until he is formally purged for his obduracy.

Now that the military and the moderates had an unwritten contract with Mao, however, the see-through anonymity ended, and in October a rigged meeting of the Central Committee expelled Liu Shaoqi from all his posts as "Liu Shaoqi." Sick, isolated, deprived of essential drugs, he died in November 1969. His family was not told at once, and his body was left lying in the passage of a bank vault for three days before it was loaded on to a jeep and driven to a crematorium. It had been tagged "highly infectious" to keep away the inquisitive, and after incineration a card bearing a false name was put with the ashes. For Liu, this was the end of the "capitalist road." But while Mao appeared to have won the day, it was no more than a false dawn.

April 1969. The Ninth Congress of the Chinese Communist Party which opened this week on All Fool's Day has been widely acknowledged as a victory for Mao Tsetung. Like a victory in some protracted dynastic war, however, it brings no permanent conquest, but only an unhappy truce that will at best endure until he dies.

The latest Peking order shows Mao and his chosen successor Lin Biao at the top of the Communist hierarchy, closely supported by a cosy clique of wives and secretaries, in-laws and former body-guards. This oligarchy appears to dominate the Party executive. Meanwhile, nearly 60 percent of the 176 members of the Presidium have been drawn from the army, while the Congress of more than 1,500 delegates is packed with hand-picked Maoists.

But Mao may be digging the grave of Maoism in his enthusiasm for burying others. This is a gimcrack Congress producing a gim-crack Party, weighted with nominated nobodies, backed by bay-onets, its Presidium adorned with the chairmen of the provincial revolutionary committees. Compared with Chou En-lai and the moderates, the civilians in the group are puffed-up nonentities into whom Mao alone breathes political stature and shape . . .

The Congress—the first for thirteen years—endorsed a new Party constitution that enshrined Mao's Thought as holy writ, and formally named Lin Biao his successor. It also provided that "leading bodies of the Party at all levels are to be elected through democratic consulta-tion"—there was to be no further nonsense about open elections in which the just might risk being outnumbered by the unjust; private bargaining would replace public voting. Mao remained Chairman, Lin Biao was sole Vice-Chairman, and both of their wives and the rest of the "Shanghai Mafia" became members of a new Politburo in which—as in the Central Committee—the mutually suspicious Maoists and military were nicely balanced, with a minority of moderates like Chou En-lai for a fulcrum.

Mao had skillfully put together a pastiche of conniving rivals. But there is only a single stroke of the pen between collusion and collision, and while the new Party leadership might yield endless contradictions for him to exploit, it hardly bore out the promise of the "Congress of

Unity" that had produced it. Nor was he himself aloof from the contradictions, for they began with Lin Biao.

Behind Lin Biao's platitudinous flattery and protestations of subservience ("I ask the Chairman for instructions in everything I do, and do everything according to his orders") was a Chinese Uriah Heep. The first Communist commander to know both the pleasure of throwing modern tanks against the Kuomintang in Manchuria and the pain of throwing under-armed troops against American firepower in Korea, he was unconvincing when he championed Mao's theory of "people's war" and his belief in the superiority of men over machines. He did not embrace Mao's Thought for love of Mao, but because an alliance with the Chairman would enable him to dominate rival military chiefs who saw eye to eye with Liu Shaoqi. With the forging of that alliance, moreover, the army had become the lead horse of the revolution, a role that gave him a unique chance to put the PLA on top—and to wield increasing personal power himself as his septuagenarian master was progressively canonized into political impotence.

As the military moved into ministries and offices and schools and factories, Lin filtered his own men into key posts in the capital and the provincial citadels of distrustful "Red warlords." But an insidious undertow sapped at his success, for Mao was not blind. A draft constitution that would have made the army independent of the Party was rigorously amended, and an ingratiating speech Lin planned to deliver to the Ninth Congress was thrown out (he was obliged to rewrite it under the Chairman's "personal direction," it is said). The "Tiger Cat" was uneasily aware that the narrow shelf of power on which he teetered high up in the hierarchy might collapse beneath him. Jiang Qing and her literary cronies, who had been so quick to cry, "Drag out the powerholders in the army," were now prominent in the Politburo and close to the Chairman, and the possibility that the pen might yet defeat the sword was not to be borne.

The Russians had maliciously dismissed the latest of Mao's Chinas as a "military bureaucratic state," and Lin Biao must have realized that Mao was not amused by the irony. The chaotic years of the Cultural Revolution had produced neither a chessboard of Paris Communes governed by the masses, nor a monolithic Communist party tempered in the furnace of revolution. Utopia was still over the false horizon, and the nearest thing to Mao's new communist man was not a peasant-worker-soldier, but a soldier-worker-peasant in the ubiquitous PLA. No new socialist state had arisen from the ashes of the old, and the net achievement of the upheaval had been to put power into the hands of brass hats and bureaucrats who had deplored the whole business in the first place.

Meanwhile, it seemed that the new Communist Party might die as swiftly as a cut flower, for if it was to have roots, local committees of "old, middle-aged, and young" must first emerge throughout the country. But these could only grow out of the existing provincial organs, from which they would one day take over—the revolutionary committees. And the revolutionary committees were dominated by army commanders who declined to rob themselves of regional power by "rearing tigers to devour them later." By December 1969 only one of the 2,200 counties in China had been able to form a Party committee. Twelve months afterwards the figure had risen to just 70, and there was still not a single provincial committee in being.

But although putting China together after the wrecking spree of the rebels was proving a slow affair, Mao was already pointing the way to Utopia again, and new shills were materializing to shame the masses onwards and upwards. "I apologize deeply to Chairman Mao; from now on I shall vigorously combat self-interest and hand back my private plot," said an old farmer hitherto known for his firm and uncomplimentary views on collective work. Others followed suit, or at least "volunteered" for a general cut in the size of their minuscule vegetable gardens. Plans were laid for bringing back the communal dining hall, for breaking up production teams so that their members could be merged into rural regiments once again, for building more local plants producing fertilizer and farm tools in the struggle for self-reliance. Every county was to have its own "Dazhai," a totally collectivized model for all the neighboring villages. Workers were to farm, peasants to run factories, and articles about the virtues of deep plowing and close planting began to appear in the press for the benefit of both.

Mao was giving the revolution another ideological kick in the flanks. Newspapers stressed the "superiority of the people's communes, which are larger in size and have a higher degree of collective ownership" than smaller units, and hailed the Great Leap Forward of 1958 as a major achievement. Shanghai echoed the Chairman himself in May 1969, warning the people "not to think that after one or two, or two or three great proletarian cultural revolutions everything will be settled." The past might never have happened—in more senses than one. No one would have guessed that China had just emerged, shaken and "preparing for war" from the most dangerous brush with the Russian army across the border since the untimely end of the eternal and indestructible friendship between Moscow and Peking.

CHAPTER TWENTY-FIVE

T HE DECADE which began in 1960 with the sudden exodus of the Russians from China ended with hopes or fears on all sides that they might now return even more suddenly, carrying bazookas rather than blueprints. For while time had further frayed any vestigial threads of fraternal tolerance left binding Peking to Moscow, prejudice had hardened with age. The sixty-eight-year-old Mao who saw the Soviet leaders as a gang of revisionist renegades in 1962 was to call their regime a "bourgeois dictatorship" in 1964, to accuse them of plotting against China with the vile American archenemy in 1966, and finally to brand them "socio-imperialists" even more dangerous than the warmongers in Washington in 1969. Since whatever the Russians did was by definition wrong, Sino-Soviet hostility was a furnace that burned any polemical rubbish, and all reports and rumors served to fuel it.

Abrasive delegates from Peking fought their way through one Communist congress after another, intent on splitting the international movement and isolating the Soviet Union, and in 1963 they began attacking Khrushchev by name. But by then he had given them something to bite on. When the Chinese made a quick thrust into India in October 1962 in order to seize disputed territory the Indians had earlier "infiltrated," Soviet approval was so muted that Peking accused Moscow of siding with the bourgeois enemy—"confounding right and wrong, pretending to be neutral, calling China brother while actually regarding the Indian reactionary group as their kinsmen."

Within days a Soviet bid to put missiles on Cuba provoked an American blockade and a battle of nerves that had the world biting its lip until Khrushchev blinked first and removed them. This enabled Peking to reprove the Russians for their "adventurism" in shipping the rockets to the island in first place, and then for their "capitulation"

in taking them off again, thus catching them quite literally coming and
going. While the gallant Cubans had stood firm against the "monstrous
crime" of the Americans that had "filled the Chinese people with
indignation," the miserable Muscovites had betrayed them by "wilting
in the face of imperialist nuclear blackmail."

In June 1963 Peking addressed to Russian party leaders a document
whose superb arrogance and empty assumptions of god-given authority
were reminiscent of the ludicrous bulls that Chinese emperors had in
the past directed to barbarian vassals. In 1793 a Manchu emperor had
loftily enjoined George III to "act in conformity with our wishes by
strengthening your loyalty and swearing perpetual obedience," and
now Khrushchev and his comrades were instructed in the correct line
they should follow both at home and abroad, so that their conduct
would be strictly in accord with Marxism-Leninism as interpreted by
Chairman Mao. This letter successfully sabotaged impending talks
between the two parties before they even opened, and instead of risking the radioactive consequences of adopting the truculent Chinese
stance towards the nuclear family of imperialists to their west, the
Russians signed a limited test-ban treaty with the British and the
Americans.

The Chinese at once denounced the contract as a "gigantic fraud,
which has jeopardized the cause of world peace and is aimed at tying
China's hands." The Soviet leaders—"gnashing their teeth in their bitter
hatred of socialist China"—had joined the United States in an alliance
against Peking. By the time *Pravda* had struck back at lunatics who
"saw no great harm in a policy that might produce a global nuclear
conflagration," there was nothing much more to be said, and it only
remained for the Communists throughout the world to take sides.
Friction had rubbed Sino-Soviet relations raw.

As pro-Chinese splinters were torn from pro-Soviet parties in a
dozen countries from Australia to Belgium, Peking jubilantly proclaimed a new "inexorable" law whereby revisionists "create their own
opposites who inevitably will bury them." But the illusion that Mao's
China was triumphantly saving the souls of Communists everywhere
by luring them away from the Russian apostasy, that the redeemed
were now turning to the East to pray as naturally as they turned to
the West to curse, was false. The international Communist movement
was in any case shaking itself into a looser "polycentric" form, and
the Kremlin's grip on it slackening to a grasp. In the meanwhile spit-in-
your eye Maoist diplomacy had succeeded in isolating China from the
best of both worlds—imperialist and revisionist—leaving her with a

diminutive Albania for a solitary "staunch ally," and inspiring "closer, wider, and more brazen counterrevolutionary collaboration between Washington and Moscow," as the Chinese press complained in 1967.

By then Khrushchev, the "goulash Communist," had gone and Leonid Brezhnev had come, but for China nothing had changed. In 1968 the Russians shocked the queasier comrades as well as the freer world by pushing their way into Prague and flattening the tender shoots of Czech liberalism with tanks. The Chinese seized the opportunity to enlist sympathy for their Russophobia, and although the temerarious Czechs had in fact out-revised the revisionists, Peking fulminated against Moscow's "atrocious aggression." It did little good. Within a year the Soviet Union was able to call a world conference of sixty-seven Communist parties, at which Brezhnev could condemn the absent Maoists for "political adventurism" without anyone waving a fist in his face, and the final declaration would ignore China and the Chinese altogether.

That was only one side of the Russian problem, however. Nearly five years before, Khrushchev had added a new and dangerous dimension to the Sino-Soviet quarrel by stressing that relations were deteriorating not only between the Soviet and Chinese parties, but between the Soviet and Chinese states. The answer of the Chinese to both the ideological and military implications of this situation could be summed up in one word: fission. They set out to bombard and split not only the international Communist movement, but the atomic nucleus.

Mao's military thinking had been shaped by his dependence on the ordinary mortal in the mass whose substitute for firepower was faith. While boasting of the one weapon he could deploy in almost limitless quantities, therefore, he loudly belittled the weapons he did not possess—man was the master of the battlefield and the atom bomb was a "paper tiger." On paper. However, just as man may despise all tigers "strategically," since he can easily wipe them off the face of the earth, but must respect just one "tactically" if he meets it in the jungle, so Mao scoffed at the imperialists and their bomb in order to sustain the confidence of the Chinese millions in ultimate victory, but was careful to remind them that in the here-and-now their nuclear enemies could prove "living tigers, iron tigers, real tigers that can eat people." And while the dazed masses, jerked viciously to left and right, found themselves roaring through the nineteen sixties on an ideological roller coaster, China's nuclear scientists were largely left to their own nefarious devices in surroundings insulated from the mob and most of the Mao-study.

Within ten years of exploding the first of those devices, in consequence, the Chinese would be able to argue that they already held the balance in a nuclear *Three Kingdoms*. Peking's delivery systems might still be puny, but they were enough to "wrench an arm" off Russia in retaliation if the Kremlin launched a preemptive strike against China—and the Chinese were always ready to demonstrate on the abacus that even risking an arm when you were swapping dead with a nation of 700 million could prove a mug's game. On the other hand, if the preemptive strike were designed to knock out every single one of China's widespread silos and airfields in order to avert that risk, the Russians would find their nuclear arsenal fatally depleted by the operation when they turned to face an American adversary who had not committed a kiloton to the slaughter. And vice versa.

But some of the most cold-blooded generals in Chinese history had found it cost-effective to go for the hearts and minds of their enemies rather than for their throats, as Sunzi taught, and for Mao the psychological value of the crude contrivance detonated in 1964 outweighed the military. Peking at once promised "never under any circumstances to be the first to use nuclear weapons," and proposed calling an international conference to outlaw them. It was a telling gesture. Now that their country was the fifth nuclear power (although possessing neither bombs nor the means to deliver them as yet), the proposal gave the Chinese the aura of righteousness that so unreasonably bathes the countenance of one who demands peace at pistol point, and this further enhanced the fearful prestige they had won in the Third World by breaking a devastating white monopoly. The slightly clownish if sinister image of the backward China that had perpetrated such economic buffooneries as the Great Leap Forward was supplanted in men's minds by that of an efficient socialist state which had, once again, found the right formula.

That was what counted for Mao. In the fifties his vision of the world he never saw was of one divided into warring imperialist and socialist camps. But the axis had then tilted, so that by 1962 he was resectioning humanity again, splitting it this time into "counterrevolutionary" and "revolutionary" groups, with the American imperialists and the Russian revisionists and their running dogs on one side, and China and the rest of the righteous on the other. The battleground for the struggle between them was to be the poverty-stricken terrain of Asia, Africa, and Latin America, while China herself (he later fore-saw) would be the political and technical hub of operations in this global "people's war," an arsenal "able openly to supply weapons marked in Chinese characters to the revolutionaries of the world."

In Asia the Chinese were once more bent on reasserting their lapsed spiritual dominion over what they regarded as their rightful zone of influence, but their wider concern was to persuade all Afro-Asian bodies to blackball their Russian rivals as white interlopers, first cousins to the colonialists, and revisionists in the wrong camp. With their pigmentation as their passport and China's status as an atomic power to add to their height, they again enjoyed some initial success, as they had a decade before. Peking offered more credits and trade and aid, and the urbane Chou En-lai made firm and infirm friends in Africa, Burma, Pakistan, and Sri Lanka during one exhausting political package tour. By the end of 1964, fifty countries recognized the People's Republic instead of Chiang Kai-shek's rump of a regime in Taiwan, and within the Afro-Asian bloc the Chinese had recruited a valuable "neutralist" cat's-paw in the Indonesian president, Sukarno.

They needed one, for after all that, they were far from being universally loved. Their ill-concealed sense of racial and moral su-periority outraged the tender national pride of decolonized peoples, and men mistrusted their ideology. But most disconcerting of all was the strange, chimerical overlay—like a print of some minatory medieval allegory—that Mao superimposed upon their map of the familiar world. His tendency to see it as a blowup of revolutionary China had reached a point where a secret report drawn up in Peking in the early nineteen sixties could compare the stages of political development in different African countries with the Boxer Rebellion in 1890, the Wuhan Upris-ing in 1911, and the May 4 Movement in 1919, and then soberly con-clude, "None has yet reached the Northern Expedition." Because the Chinese had been liberated by the gun, all others were told that their sole road to freedom lay through "armed struggle." War was there-for inevitable. "It is a mistake to say that there are war powers and peace powers," said Mao, "there are only revolutionary war powers and antirevolutionary war powers." By 1966 he was predicting that China would be fighting the United States "within two years at the latest."

At the same time many were perplexed by the idiosyncratic logic of Peking, whereby peaceful coexistence was disreputable when practiced by the Russians, but respectable when preached by the Chinese—who could simultaneously pursue a policy of "mutual nonaggression and noninterference in internal affairs" towards Asian and African governments, while pledging "firm support for all revolutionary struggles" mounted to overthrow them. Peking might protest that whereas coexistence was the business of the Chinese state, revolution was the business of the Chinese Party, but since Chinese state and Party were inextricably interwoven, this failed to mollify politicians from the polychromatic continents who were already steeped in their own sordid sophistries at home—and knew one when they saw one.

During his tour in 1964, even the affable Chou En-lai apparently felt obliged to declare, "Revolutionary prospects are excellent throughout the African continent"—and so furrow the brows of indigenous leaders who fervently believed that the time for overturning governments had abruptly ended when they themselves came to power. Nor was distrust allayed when Peking sponsored a glossy magazine called *Revolution in Africa*, which described its incumbent masters—the men who had so gloriously freed the black man from the white man's yoke by liberating the white man from his burden—as nothing better than "nationalist reactionaries." The opprobrious epithet also expressed the attitude of the Chinese towards Arab rulers in the Middle East, yet they demanded that the men they so unamiably denigrated support China's maverick policies unswervingly, rebuff the intimidatingly powerful Russians and Americans, and join in a chorus of condemnation of the body to which they all proudly subscribed—the United Nations.

For Mao, the UN was "a dirty stock exchange for political deals between the United States and the Soviet Union" which had "committed every kind of evil deed" (including recognizing Nationalist Taiwan as "China"). The People's Republic would not join it until it "evicted the Chiang Kai-shek gang" from all of its organizations, and was restructured to exclude "all imperialist and puppet governments." It would also have to apologize for its ridiculous condemnation of China's alleged aggression in Korea.

But Afro-Asians who saw the United Nations as a peerless platform from which to air their own multitudinous grievances were reluctant to fight for China's entry for fear of being identified with these uncharitable sentiments and sweeping demands. When Sukarno took Indonesia out of the UN in a fit of megalomaniac pique at the beginning of 1965, Chou En-lai proposed the formation of a rival "revolutionary" organization of underdog states to realize the "antiimperialist and anticolonial ambitions of the peoples of the world," but the response was tepid. The Afro-Asians did not care to be browbeaten into striking China's intransigent who-is-not-with-me-is-against-me pose, neutralist states objected to being told that neutrality was a sham, and the nonaligned that all must take sides.

If ever there was jealous god, however, it was Mao, and no bowing down before graven images—Taiwan, America, Russia, imperialism, revisionism—would be overlooked, whether the idolaters were capitalist or communist. In 1964 the Chinese penalized the Japanese for "subservience to Taiwan" by canceling a bulging portfolio of contracts, and in 1965 they punished the Cubans (earlier hailed as the "hope and example" of Latin America) for drawing closer to Moscow by refusing to buy Cuban sugar and savagely cutting exports of rice to Havana. The image of China as a bigot and a bully was hardening once more, for in the same year Peking issued an imperious ultimatum to New Delhi over their border dispute while India was locked in war with Pakistan, and almost simultaneously the Chinese were compromised in a bloody but abortive bid by the Communists to seize power in Indonesia. And then there was Vietnam.

Those who prophesied that the Chinese champions of armed struggle would plunge into the "people's war" that had suddenly escalated just across their southern border in Vietnam misread their Mao, who by then was mesmerized by his own dogma that China was the revolutionary mentor of the world. The "war of liberation" in China had been fought by self-reliant Chinese in order to rid the country of the last vestiges of foreign domination. It was imperative, therefore, that if the Chairman's theory of people's war was to be upheld as a universal truth, the Vietnamese must be ready not only to wage a protracted struggle until they won, but wage it alone. There could be no question of committing the PLA to the fray.

The Chinese sent equipment and instructors to Hanoi, and after the Americans began bombing North Vietnam they deployed antiaircraft batteries and forty thousand railway "engineers" across the frontier in Tonking to keep the narrow-gauge lifeline to China open, for the Vietnamese could not be allowed to lose. But the Vietnamese could not be allowed to owe a quick victory to the Kremlin either, and appeals to Peking from Moscow for an air corridor down which to channel Russian aid, for the use of Chinese ports and airfields, and for the right to route Russian military personnel through China were rebuffed or ignored.

During the Cultural Revolution, Red Guards held up and stripped freight trains of Soviet guns and ammunition before they could cross the border into Vietnam, but the Chinese shrugged this off as provincial hooliganism, and accused the Russians of sending the hard-pressed Vietnamese "damaged and obsolete" weapons. Japanese Communists witnessed an embarrassing scene in 1966, in which Mao reputedly lost his composure when told that the Chinese railways had been carrying Russian arms to Vietnam without his knowledge. Unmollified by assurances that some of the equipment had been sabotaged "to discredit Soviet assistance" in Vietnamese eyes, he shouted angrily that it was all the work of the "weak-kneed" revisionists in Peking.

Mao's purpose was to confound the Russians, not mitigate the sufferings of China's "younger brother" to the south, and he brushed aside all suggestions that Peking and Moscow should act in concert against the Americans in Vietnam. The Americans and the Russians were birds of a feather, the world must join forces against both, and anything the Soviets propounded was therefore automatically to be rejected—including peace. The Chinese denounced the American air attacks on North Vietnam as a conspiracy between Moscow and Washington to "force peace talks through bombing," and when in September 1966 Washington put forward proposals in the UN for ending the agony, they once more linked the United States and the Soviet Union as partners in crime by contemptuously dismissing the American demarche as a "peace swindle in collaboration with Russian revisionists."

They were perversely ensuring that the Soviet Union would win the struggle for the hearts and minds of the Vietnamese. But if mounting exasperation with China seemed to be pushing Hanoi into the arms of the Russians, that was only one twisted piece of the wreckage—now strewn across the face of the earth—of what had once been Peking's high-flying foreign policy. No one could say that Mao was not a man of principle, since for the sake of his principles the Chinese had kicked away their one sound foothold in Latin America by "punishing" Castro, had antagonized India, and had shocked the nonaligned world with a display of left-wing adventurism in Indonesia that had ended with the massacre of the Communists and the fall of President Sukarno. They had quarreled with every country that wanted peace in Kashmir or Vietnam or both, and with all political leaders—capitalist, communist, or neutralist—who leaned towards Moscow,

Washington, or Taipei. And their answer to any insolent outsider who dared to demur when they dictated what all should do and think was not a debate, but a flood of intemperate vituperation.

By 1966 they had reaped their reward. Peking's prolonged struggle to pistol-whip the Afro-Asian People's Solidarity Organization into ostracizing Russia and the UN ended in February of that year, when the disillusioned AAPSO expelled pro-Chinese delegations from a meeting in Nicosia. Five countries broke off diplomatic relations with the People's Republic, and in Africa the number of Peking's embassies fell from eighteen to fourteen, while Taipei's rose from fifteen to nineteen. "China has friends all over the world," the Chinese boasted, but those they could count on were now chillingly easy to count.

However, that did not deter Mao from announcing that the war in Vietnam heralded "a storm of revolution in Asia, Africa, and Latin America," or Chinese propagandists from claiming that the Cultural Revolution was universal because the Chairman was "the great leader of the people of the world" and 90 percent of the human race supported him.

It followed from this that any government that did not accept his guidance was automatically opposing the will of the masses. China might quarrel in quick succession with Burma, Italy, Indonesia, India, and Britain, but "the Burmese people warmly love Chairman Mao," "Italy's genuine revolutionaries support the line of Comrade Mao Tsetung," "the Indian people cherish a boundless love for Chairman Mao's works," "Chairman Mao is foremost in the hearts of the Indonesian people," and 90 percent of Britons were incensed by the "fascist outrages and anti-China crimes" of their execrable government. The "masses of the world" were swallowing Mao's collected works with the thirsty reverence of teenage communicants—"the radiance of his writings now shines everywhere, from the embattled jungles of Southeast Asia to the rugged Andes, from the southern tip of Africa to Iceland near the Arctic Circle. Clearly the sun never sets on the word of Mao," the *Peking Review* was to eulogize ecstatically, paraphrasing more than one ideologically dubious text in the process.

With the whole world behind them, then, the Red Guards went to work, and by August 1967 they had mounted mass demonstrations in Peking against the embassies of ten countries that had transgressed; beaten up and spat on Czech, French, Swedish, East German, Indian, and Indonesian diplomats; attacked the cars of the Hungarian and Mongolian ambassadors; burst into the Mongolian Embassy and belabored the staff; burned down the British chancery in the capital and seized the British Consulate in Shanghai (diplomatic immunity was "bourgeois").

The British were prime targets, for the Cultural Revolution was spilling over into Hong Kong, where a labor dispute had led to left-wing violence and the police had stepped in to arrest troublemakers. The Peking press translated this as "bloody suppression," and the Chinese demanded immediate apologies, compensation for the "premeditated large-scale sanguinary atrocities" committed, and guarantees of good behavior in the future. Token strikes then flashed across the dependency like pent-up static, and the colonial government was peremptorily ordered to "accept at once all just demands put forward by Chinese workers." When the British did not budge, China cut off the water supply, forcing the local authorities to impose stringent rationing; five Hong Kong police were killed in a staged border shooting, and as tension mounted, the colony was disfigured by sporadic rioting and a rash of bomb incidents.

Nearly all the bomb victims were Chinese, the boycott organized by the Hong Kong Communists hit China harder than it hit the crown colony, and as hundreds of local Chinese associations perversely pledged loyalty to the colonial government, fury gave way to sound. The masses had failed to "seize power" from below, for Hong Kong was mainly populated by refugees from Mao's China whose feet had already voted for them, and who only wanted to be left alone to scratch a living in peace.

Like the ordinary man in Hong Kong, the overwhelming majority of the 17 million overseas Chinese scattered throughout Southeast Asia were not susceptible to the scarlet fever raging in the People's Republic. But wherever Chinese were gathered together it was always possible to find a hireling who could be paid to throw a brick, or a hothead who would gladly throw it for nothing. All but one of China's ambassadors abroad had been recalled for "consultation" (criticism and correction), but in many capitals—Djakarta, Kuala Lumpur, Singapore, Moscow, Paris, Baghdad, and Rangoon—a more emphatic Chinese presence was assured by local "Red Guards" goaded into action by the extremists controlling the Foreign Ministry in Peking, for whom diplomacy and revolution were synonyms. Chanting columns of these militant students were ready to fight off the police and beat up bystanders if any indigenous fascist had the impudence to try to disperse them from the streets, wielding on occasion not only the Little Red Book, but brickbats, bottles, hose piping, and dustbin lids as instruments of policy.

The assumption that any mob wearing Mao in its buttonhole was right wherever it rioted could nevertheless evoke brusque responses, and in Rangoon thousands of Burmese surged through the capital, stoning and battering any Chinese they could find and storming the walls of the Chinese Embassy. In Peking the Chinese struck back, cursing the strictly neutral Burmese government for a clique of racist reactionaries and laying down universal law from the heights of China's preposterous delusions of grandeur: "It is the sacred and inviolable right of our compatriots and of the Burmese people to study, propagate, and defend the great Thought of Mao Tsetung, and to express their boundless love for Chairman Mao, the great leader of the people of the world. The reactionary Burmese government must guarantee that in future it will not wilfully obstruct this or intervene in it." The reactionary Burmese government thought otherwise. It was the end of a friendship carefully fostered by Chou En-lai and Chen Yi, who between them had paid seven official visits to Rangoon between 1964 and 1966.

When the Sri Lankans, mindful of the lesson of Burma, seized a diplomatic package containing Mao badges before some mob could flaunt them in the streets of Colombo, the Chinese treated them as they had the Cubans, and ruthlessly cut off their supplies of rice. But at least they had averted possible mayhem. Mao badges and militant propagandists provoked anti-Chinese riots in Katmandu and Djakarta, Indian and Chinese mobs besieged each other's diplomatic missions in New Delhi and Peking, and Chinese Maoists fought it out with French riot squads in Paris. And where fanaticism and fatuity provoked "repressive measures" abroad, there would be retaliation at home. After students returning to China through Moscow clashed with Russian police in January 1967, the Soviet Embassy in Peking was besieged for two weeks by a baying mob of "little generals," who were later to break into the consular section and burn all the files they could find.

China contrived to quarrel with twenty-five countries in the first six months of 1967, but by the end of the year revolutionary rage was slowly ebbing before reason as moderates gained a precarious ascendancy in the capital. Roughhouse diplomacy abated; Chinese water once more flowed to Hong Kong, and Chinese rice to Sri Lanka. There was, however, to be no imperial pardon for the Russians, whose self-righteous bullying of the erring Czechs the following year unmasked them as "socio-imperialists" capable of plotting a second "Czechoslovakia" against China herself. According to Peking, Soviet troops had already thrust their way across the border into Chinese territory at least sixteen times in the previous two years, and on 2 March 1969 the PLA shot thirty-four Russian soldiers dead when they surprised a patrol on a disputed island in the Ussuri River, on the frontier between Siberia and Manchuria.

Like a propaganda shell that explodes in a shower of leaflets, this operation had evidently been staged not to kill the few but to rally the many. Within forty-eight hours ten million people all over China had taken part in mammoth protest demonstrations against the latest "Soviet aggression," and the press was calling upon the nation to "turn anger into energy" and to "defend the Motherland at any cost." With a minimum of bullets and a maximum of ballyhoo, the Maoists were striking at the ideological enemy with the threefold object of uniting the people solidly behind the Chairman on the eve of the Ninth Party Congress, branding the Russians men of violence, and stigmatizing Chinese revisionists as traitors colluding with the barbarous invaders of China's sacred soil.

Two weeks later the Chinese tapped Moscow on the shoulder again, launching an attack in strength towards the same glorified mudbank on the Ussuri, and opening up on it with guns and mortars. But having first withdrawn to lure their provocative enemy on, the Russians taught him a lesson, hitting back on a wide front with waiting artillery, tanks, armored cars, and jets, and slaughtering about eight hundred members of the PLA.

Angry patches of inflammation continued to appear on the long scar of their common border, notably in the far west, but the usual babble of contradictory claims that arose with the dust of each encounter prevented any still, small voice of truth from identifying its authors. One thing was certain, however. The dangerous game of baiting the Russian bear belonged to the dream world in which the ugly ruins of Chinese foreign policy were obscured by a hallucinatory "storm of revolution," the massive array of Peking's enemies could be dismissed as "anti-Chinese scum," and a nuclear war could, with profit, destroy half of the human race.

❀ *CHAPTER* TWENTY-SIX ❀

H E HAD no alternative" is often the simple explanation Chinese offer the obtuse foreigner for the baffling behavior of one of their number. The ritualistic Confucian world that dictated the measured steps of a man's life bred a people to whom it was as natural to have no choice as it was to marry a bride sight unseen. The moment produced the mandatory reflex, and in Mao the reflex was revolution. Once the vision of his socialist nirvana appeared before him, there was nothing for it but to tackle boldly all the obstacles and perils that lay between. Life itself had become the "death ground" of Sunzi from which there was no retreat. He could therefore contemplate the prospect of a nuclear holocaust as an unavoidable hazard on the road to paradise with apparent equanimity because—as he would have said with relief—he had no option.

But the do-good demon in man also inflames him with a lust for the power to do the supposed good, and the terrible irony was that since the moderates were not selfish opportunists but egotistical patriots who, like Mao, thought they knew what was best for the Chinese people, the Chinese people were doomed to be tormented victims of the struggle for supremacy among their rival benefactors. Although Mao did not visit a nuclear war upon the world, he proved that his Thought was indeed his country's "spiritual atom bomb" when he found that he "had no alternative" but to shake all China with a devastating act of political demolition to remove those who got in his way. The Cultural Revolution became inevitable in the nineteen fifties, he might have protested, when fainthearts and revisionists inside and outside the Party slowed down collectivization and began to obstruct him at every turn, until it seemed that Chinese society must be marooned forever in a Sargasso Sea of timidity and reaction.

Any unfortunate consequences were therefore the fault of those who had defied or betrayed him. But in 1981 the belated verdict of the Central Committee read otherwise. The Chairman had "initiated and led" a revolution that had negated not only the "principles, policies, and achievements" of the Party, but the "arduous struggles the entire people had conducted in socialist reconstruction." He had substituted personal control for collective leadership, the cult of Mao had been "frenziedly pushed to the extreme," and he had brought "catastrophe to the Party, the state and the whole people." Responsibility for this "grave Left error, comprehensive in magnitude and protracted in duration, does indeed lie with Comrade Mao Tsetung. . . ."

It was a harsh document that could have been much harsher. Mao had "indeed" initiated the Cultural Revolution, for it had not erupted spontaneously from the masses below. He had let youth off the leash and told Red Guards eager for the barricades that they were "right to rebel against reactionaries," that "whatever the enemy upholds, we oppose," that "the greater the chaos and the longer it goes on the better," and two Canton Red Guard bulletins quoted him as saying that he would like to see the entire public security and legal system "thoroughly smashed" (he had his way).

It must be added that his words were not totally irresponsible. "Wage peaceful not violent struggles," he wrote. "Unite with all with whom you can unite . . . enable those who have committed mistakes to correct their mistakes." But his exhortations to play hard but play quietly were too often ambiguously juxtaposed—and a moment's reflection on what would happen in Europe or America if an idolized political leader *ordered* the young on to the streets, to "make revolution" at the state's expense and overturn established authority, will reveal the enormity of what he had done. His words were a mandate to create chaos, and even if the Canton bulletins were lying, the frightening thing was that the lies were perfectly plausible. They may have quoted Mao out of context; they had not quoted him out of character. He had come to personify the principle that a political egoist is never more evilly employed than when he thinks he is doing others good.

He was astounded by the consequences of his acts. Everything happened so quickly, and events were so violent, he said. He "had not foreseen" that as soon as the first poster went up, "the whole country would be thrown into turmoil"; he had "had no idea" that his own message—"Bombard the Headquarters"—would plunge the provinces into confusion. "There is no basic conflict of interest within the working class, and there is even less reason why the working class must be split into two opposing factions," he was protesting by 1967, seemingly confounded by all the rivalries that rent the land. "Too many were arrested because I nodded my head," he complained the following year.

What did he expect, one wonders (if he did not in fact expect exactly what he got)? He may have recommended "struggle through persuasion," but as one quick to use his fists when young, he could not have believed for one moment that words would not lead to blows. His knowledge of his own people must have told him that in times of stress they would break into factions, that a nod from him could provoke a thousand arbitrary arrests, that his sacred signal to make revolution and "bombard the headquarters" would detonate China itself. Nor could he have failed to realize that as militants and mock militants vied to show their political zeal, a million innocents might go down with the "handful" of guilty, and Maoist and "Maoist" end by fighting their looking-glass war against each other.

He was familiar with the genius of the Chinese for twisting a text to suit all seasons—and he knew young people. The Red Guards and revolutionary rebels took those few ill-chosen words of his—"it is right to rebel against reactionaries"—lopped off the last two, and gave themselves a general license to practice lawlessness. "To rebel is justified" became their talisman, and they rebelled, not only against bourgeois reactionaries and the "four olds," but against orders to avoid using force, to keep out of factories and villages, to stop fighting each other, to surrender their weapons, to go home, to go back to school, to pay for their tickets on trains, and to cycle on the right side of the road. The Chairman had let loose 50 million of these privileged revolutionaries to "destroy every vestige of the old world" and then "seize power," and those were the instructions they chose to obey.

But since the Red Guards and the revolutionary rebels were his shock troops, Mao was reluctant to curb them. "Young people should be allowed to make mistakes," he said in the early stages of the Cultural Revolution, and "We should let the chaos go on for a few months, in the firm conviction that the majority are good and only the minority bad." His whole instinct was to cry, "Don't shoot the masses, they're doing their best," and it was he who first advocated the Paris Commune formula that would have made them sole masters of China.

The trial of the "Gang of Four" in 1981 was nevertheless the climax of five years of collective whitewashing during which the new leaders in Peking placed the blame for the "ten terrible years" of the Cultural Revolution not on Mao, but on the quartet of extremists who had acted as his left hand. "I promise you that the trial will not stain Chairman Mao's memory at all," said Deng Xiaoping, announcing the verdict well before it even opened. The Chairman had only committed "errors," whereas the crimes of the Gang were so numerous that "we don't have to implicate Mao to prove them."

The Four were accused of conspiring "to overthrow the political power of the dictatorship of the proletariat." They had "brought false charges against Liu Shaoqi and persecuted him . . . to death" in what was afterwards described as "the biggest frame-up in history." They had "framed and persecuted" other outstanding revolutionary heroes and national leaders, two of whom died. They had "incited beating, smashing, and looting, whipped up violence, and trumped up false charges, persecuting and suppressing large numbers of cadres and people," and they had instigated armed clashes and plotted armed rebellion.

The indictment was littered with sinister quotations compromising the accused in advance: "Step up the interrogation to squeeze out of him what we need before he dies" . . . "Make it sound as if you were giving me the information yourself, not as if I had directed you to do so" . . . "You are a renegade, I can tell—forty years' experience in revolutionary work gives me this kind of intuition." More than 729,500 people had been "framed and persecuted"—including 80,000 soldiers and 300 high-ranking dignitaries of Party, government, and state—and 34,800 had been killed or driven to their deaths. Jiang Qing had turned like a viper on those who had earlier slighted her, and at least one of them no longer resembled a human being by the time his torturers had finished with him.

Found guilty of "organizing and leading a counterrevolutionary clique," the fiercely unrepentant Madame Mao was given a suspended death sentence. The Four were held up to execration for crippling the Party and economy, the educational system, the arts and sciences, and a whole generation of youth. But no mention was made of the fifth, invisible member of the Gang. Apparently, not only had he committed no crime, but (so it was said) he had seen through his termagent of a wife and her sleazy accomplices from the beginning.

As early as 1966 Mao had warned Jiang Qing not to become "dizzy with success," to remember her "weak points, shortcomings, and mistakes," and in 1967 he had ordered her to make a self-criticism after the ultra-leftist firebrands in the Cultural Revolution Group had excelled themselves while he was out of Peking. During his remaining years, he would tell her not to "flaunt herself," not to write instructions on official documents behind his back, not to try to form her own cabinet. "In my view, Jiang Qing has wild ambitions," he was to say.

When her indiscreet confessions to an American academic in 1972 appeared in print, they disclosed that the zealot who so savagely attacked bourgeois tendencies in others hugged to herself a heretical love of soft luxury and smart clothes. The reformer who had given the Chinese "plain water" on the stage had admitted to a guilty appetite for modern novels and American films. But her biographer also quoted distasteful and slighting references to life with the aging Mao,* and scabrous rumors circulated about the consolation Jiang Qing later found with a vigorous young ping-pong champion.

The *People's Daily* was to report that Mao wrote to her bitterly in 1974, "It is better if I do not see you; you have not carried out my instructions for years past." "She does not speak for me," he told the Politburo, "she represents only herself." At her trial, the Public Prosecutor was to go further: "Jiang Qing represented no one but a handful of schemers, careerists, counterrevolutionaries, criminals, hoodlums, and other dregs of society."

But that was not her story. In court she described herself as an assistant who merely "carried out the orders entrusted to her." Everything she had done had been "with the permission of Chairman Mao Tsetung," or "on behalf of Chairman Mao Tsetung or in accordance with his instructions." "*I was Chairman Mao's dog,*" she finally yelled from the dock. "*Whoever he told me to bite, I bit.*" But the bitch would be put down, not the master who had specifically nominated her to head the "special group" that hustled Liu Shaoqi to his degradation and death.

Where did the guilt lie? It was to be found in the no-man's-land of absences and silences and ambivalent utterances that enabled the Chairman to observe from the safety of his own lines what his wife could get away with, and what she could not. The naive might argue that their estrangement exonerated Mao from all blame for her conduct, but that is to turn the logic of the leader upside down. Like the hero that he was, Mao had always been ready to sacrifice the fourth Madame Mao to his destiny if the need arose, but once the marriage turned sour it was all the easier for him to regard her purely as an instrument for achieving his own revolutionary ends. "Chairman Mao allowed her to usurp power and use his name . . . even later, when he was separated from her," Deng Xiaoping was to confirm.

* Roxane Witke, *Comrade Chiang Ching.*

Furthermore, no one could blame Jiang Qing or the rest of the Gang for the earlier years of swelling acrimony within the ranks of the Party that had burst with the Cultural Revolution, or for the grief inflicted on the Chinese people since they had become masters in their own country back in 1949. For until Mao gave the Shanghai Mafia the contract to liquidate his enemies in the mid-sixties, its members had been political midgets compared with the giants they were to slay. It was the Chairman who had picked them up and plugged them in to his own source of power, galvanizing them into vigorous revolutionary life.

If Mao later came to distrust them, his guilt was all the greater, for they were still at the height of their spectacular political careers when he died. Although he had warned Jiang Qing in 1974 against forming a conspiratorial "gang of four" (his own phrase), she remained a full member of the Politburo. By 1972 the youthful Wang Hongwen had "helicoptered" to become mayor of the municipality of Shanghai, vice-chairman of its revolutionary committee, political commissar of its military garrison, and boss of its trade union federation. But that was only a beginning. One year later he was presenting a revised constitution to the Party congress in Peking as vice-chairman of the 28-million-strong Communist party, the third man in all China after Mao Tsetung and Chou En-lai, and tipped by some to succeed Mao as Chairman when he died.

Yao Wenyuan, who was in 198th place in the Chinese pecking order in 1966, rose to 8th—and membership of the Politburo—in 1969, and to 5th in 1972. He was made "the person responsible for Mao Tsetung's office," and his easy access to the Chairman inspired wild tales that he was destined for great things. As for Zhang Chunqiao, he was to become not only a senior member of the Politburo and a vice-premier, but chief political commissar of the Chinese army.

But position must not be confused with power. It was Mao and Mao alone who held them all in position, so that when he took his last breath in September 1976 and the power was cut off, the Gang collapsed like so many dolls, and within a month they had been swept from the stage.

THE STONE GOD

The higher one is boosted, the harder one will
fall, and I am prepared to crash to smithereens.
(MAO TSETUNG, IN A LETTER TO JIANG QING,
8 JULY 1966)

❈ *CHAPTER* TWENTY-SEVEN ❈

W HILE HE still lived, Mao himself was uneasily aware that the source of his power—his image as the immortal sage of the revolution—could be turned against him, for he was being transformed into a cult, and in danger of being isolated from the Chinese people not only by his age but by his apotheosis. He suspected, moreover, that this was the precise object of the outrageously sycophantic Lin Biao, who hailed him as a genius the like of which China could produce only once in a few thousand years—"everything he says is true, and every word he utters is worth ten thousand words of others." "I'm no genius," Mao objected irritably. "Genius is dependent on the mass line, on collective wisdom . . . and one word is, after all, just one word. How can it be worth ten thousand?"

But although he periodically deplored the veneration that was gradually walling him in, he himself had edited the Little Red Book of his quotations that the millions now reverenced as their bible, and he—not Lin Biao—had been the author of the sixteen-point directive for the Cultural Revolution whose keynote was, "It is imperative to hold aloft the great red banner of Mao Tsetung's Thought . . . the movement for the creative study and application of Chairman Mao Tsetung's works should be carried forward among the masses . . . Mao Tsetung's Thought should be taken as the guide to action. . . ."

The truth was that, as with so much else, the personality cult was to be despised strategically, but respected tactically. Mao needed the adulation and the awe of a people who had worshipped their emperors for more than two thousand years, for the more surely he held the hearts of the millions in fee, the more surely could he rouse them to annihilate the bureaucracy that so sacrilegiously defied him. He did not balk at fostering feudal superstition when the focus was Mao Tsetung, therefore, nor did he flinch from the flattering comparisons

257

made between himself and the despotic First Emperor of the Qin Dynasty. Whereas many ancient tyrants had wanted to be both loved and feared, however, Mao so adroitly garnered all praise to his person (while shifting blame to others) that it was he who was loved by the masses, and the Party that was feared, for what was not right was simply not Mao.

When he swam the Yangtse as an ageless sexagenarian, he left youngsters gasping in his wake; when he wielded a pick, "the great earth trembled." He was an expert in everything from nuclear physics to good food, and impervious to cold, hunger, and fatigue. But the Thought was even mightier than the thinker. A study session with the Little Red Book "supplied the breath of life" to soldiers gasping in the thin air of the Tibetan plateau; enabled workers to raise the sinking city of Shanghai three-quarters of an inch; inspired a million people to subdue a tidal wave in 1969, inaccurate meteorologists to forecast weather correctly, a group of housewives to re-invent shoe polish, surgeons to sew back severed fingers and remove a ninety-nine-pound tumor as big as a football. The entire population of a commune struck by an earthquake was quoted verbatim as declaiming like a Greek chorus, "Quake as you like, earth. Buildings collapse, but not the people's will. As long as we have Chairman Mao's precious books, we have nothing to fear, even if the heavens fall."

It was difficult not to hear the angel choirs of Hollywood as all this robust schmaltz was served up in print, but while the melodramatic, priggish, irremediably phony little fables might repel the foreigner, they were cut to fit the moralizing Chinese mind. "No educated Chinese is really going to believe these fairy tales about groaning men clutching the Works of Mao rather than screaming for morphine," one of them said to me, "but we will still repeat them in order to teach the ignorant faith."

By 1969 daily observance and ritual marked the life of the pious Chinese as he recited the orisons and liturgies prescribed for him in the name of Mao. The rites varied, but an average family would start the day by bowing before his portrait, sing "The East Is Red," and chant selected quotations from his Thoughts before setting off for work. When the day was done, all once again assembled to make an "evening report" to the Chairman, chant more quotations, and conclude by wishing him "Ten thousand years," the Chinese amen. In each household there was a "Precious Book Table" on which Mao's works were stacked; shops sold icons with his image in the center—sometimes complete with golden halo—to take the place of ancestral tablets; and in barracks and factories shrines were set up displaying a statue or picture of him, before which soldiers and workers would make vows of diligence and obedience.

But while faith, even as a grain of mustard seed, may move mountains faster than Mao's Foolish Old Man, it can quickly develop into a morbid growth—especially when watered by the obsessive sense of symbolism of the Chinese. As soon as Mao made a gift of mangoes to the worker-peasant team that was put into Qinghua University in 1968, all China ran riot with mango mania. When "precious gifts" of imitation mangoes were subsequently sent down from Peking to different provincial capitals, ecstatic crowds up to half a million strong flooded into the streets to welcome each pair with gongs and drums and frenzied applause, and the local military commander would then drive the consecrated facsimiles on a tour of the lucky city for the adoring public to see. The train carrying two of these objects to Xian had to stop at every station so that people along the line could catch a glimpse of them, and on National Day in Peking thousands of marching workers escorted decorated floats bearing monster mock-mangoes in the parade. Most of the originals were embalmed in formaldehyde, encased in glass, and enshrined at Qinghua University, but two were seen on display under armed guard in the waiting room at Peking Airport, holy relics imbued eternally with the "Invincible Thought" of Mao.

It was not surprising that with the Chinese lured into a mood of mass hysteria from which the last vestiges of common sense seemed to have evaporated, imagery should make the subtle transition to idolatry, and man to myth. Disciples might have claimed with reason that the stimulating aphorisms of the master put new heart into the patient and a new conscience into the doctor, but now a cancer victim on the point of collapse rallied on catching sight of the "lofty image of Chairman Mao," and a sailor with half his brain shot away recovered consciousness when a volume of Mao's works was pressed into his hand. The Chairman's Thought was curing the blind, the deaf, the mute, and the mad, and men trapped in wrecked trains and foundering ships saved their lives by invoking his name. Paper charms pasted up to ward off evil bore his sayings instead of prayers to the gods of the past, for his doctrine had become a "magic weapon," and Mao himself a sorcerer who cast out revisionist demons in a world in which Chinese hyperbole had translated his sensible advice into senseless incantation— "the nine planets revolve around the Red Sun—The Red Sun is Chairman Mao and his Thought. . . ."

Corrupted like a "Buddha blackened by the incense of his worshippers," Mao was tacitly exploiting the predilection of the Chinese for converting their philosophies into religion and their thinkers into gods, so that over the centuries a crop of gaudy temples had risen even to Confucius. "Mao liked to make fun of gods and idol worship," Edgar Snow wrote in 1965, "but he was well aware that the supernatural holds great attraction for many ingenuous people. Among them, the cult was a powerful weapon."

It was so powerful that for apologists to protest that Mao could not control the destinies of the gang of four pygmies into whom he himself had breathed political life was manifestly absurd. It could still be argued, however, that a question mark hung over the degree of his responsibility for their actions, for not only the narcotics of power, but the numbing years could have been eroding his mind and atrophying his conscience. In 1964 one visitor thought he had had a stroke, a second that he had had a heart attack, a third that he saw signs of incipient Parkinson's disease. And Mao himself told Snow the following year that he was preparing to "meet God soon" (although he was in fact preparing to meet the Shanghai Mafia and launch the Cultural Revolution). In 1966 there was more talk of a heart attack, high blood pressure, cancer. As in every fat old man, there was a skeleton struggling to get out.

Even his health seemed to zigzag, however. In July he appeared to confound pessimists and optimists by swimming nine miles down the Yangtse at the age of seventy-three, "with glowing, ruddy cheeks . . . chatting with those around him," yet when towards the end of the same year he appeared on television, he was supported by a nurse on either side. By 1973 the "Great Helmsman" was describing himself to President Pompidou of France as "shattered . . . weighed down by illness," but two years later his mind was evidently still very much at the helm. Henry Kissinger, who saw him in 1975, noted that he "could barely speak . . . yet even then, in the shadow of death, Mao's thoughts were lucid and sardonic." They were together for little more than an hour, but when Kissinger reread the transcript of their exchanges long afterwards, he found that "every single thing we discussed in subsequent conversations with Chou En-lai was previously mentioned in that single talk with Mao."

"Talk" was presumably a figure of speech. Television shots showed an octagenarian seemingly turned to wood in mid-word, his mouth half-open for eternity. Visitors reported that three women read his lips, and if there was any confusion he would write down what he wanted to say. "But they can't possibly make out his grunts," a skeptical Asian leader told me after seeing Mao. "And when he writes, his hand shakes so much that the result is an illegible scrawl. No one could read it. In my view, they know in advance what he wants to say, and they are simply going through the motions of asking him." It was another Chinese charade, he implied, the last conspiracy between Mao and his minions.

The Chairman's mind may have been crystal clear, but he had been trapped and quarantined by the degeneration of his body. For the last five years of his life the world outside his book-lined study saw nothing of him, the silence and absence he had used as tactical weapons in the past were now thrust upon him by an ironical fate, and when no foreign witness was present, his incomprehensible "instructions" were at the mercy of those who interpreted them for the Chinese millions. "Chairman Mao says" was no longer necessarily what Chairman Mao said. He was to end life on earth as a stone god through whose hollow mouth conniving high priests might issue commands to the awed natives to suit their own disreputable purposes. Even so, the time had not yet come when he could evade all responsibility by fading into senility and death, leaving nothing but his Thought, like the smile of the Cheshire cat.

❉ *CHAPTER TWENTY-EIGHT* ❉

Physically wrecked, mentally "lucid and sardonic," Mao now received a long string of foreign dignitaries. For if in his philosophy it was necessary to smash first in order to build afterwards, the time had come to gather up the fragments of China's shattered foreign policy and give it a new shape.

The Sino-Soviet border clashes of 1969 had sharpened the perception of those leaders in Peking who declined either to blink away inconvenient facts, or outstare them. After the ravages of the Cultural Revolution, the Chinese state and the Chinese army were as decrepit as the Chinese Chairman, and the Chairman himself had come to believe that the powerful and immediate Soviet Union was an even bigger threat to the People's Republic than the Western imperialists, for all their unsleeping malevolence.

While making noisy "preparations for war" that justified further dragooning of the tired masses, the Chinese therefore set out to stall the Russians while they mobilized the world against the "new czars" in the Kremlin. Sino-Soviet talks on the navigation of border rivers opened, and Peking affirmed that the two parties should be able to maintain normal state-to-state relations "on the basis of the five principles of coexistence." The Maoists were still not inclined to be conciliatory, and when in September 1969 Chou En-lai conferred hastily at Peking Airport with Premier Kosygin, *de passage* between Hanoi and Moscow, the Russians gained the impression that the Chinese premier had been able to arrange the meeting only after a bitter argument within the Politburo. None of the Chairman's personal circus attended it. Ritual border negotiations were nevertheless to pursue their tenuous course to nowhere through the seventies, for although the object of both sides seemed to be to score points on paper, they helped to keep in a holding pattern a quarrel between two powers that, in the last analysis, recoiled from the prospect of a costly conflict.

The standoff suited the more paranoid Chinese, for they saw themselves menaced by a trio of potential enemies locked in a satanic ring specifically fashioned to encircle them. The thievish Japanese—"resurgent militarists" bent on new conquests—had a security treaty with the United States that gave the Americans military bases in their islands, yet at the same time they were brazenly flirting with the Russians, who could entice them with promises of an alternative source of oil to the unstable Middle East. Professional alarmists in Peking therefore jerked to attention when Moscow and Tokyo started to discuss the joint exploitation of mineral resources in Siberia, including the laying of railways and pipelines that could also serve the Russian divisions on the Sino-Soviet frontier, and promptly denounced this fumbling for handholds as "Soviet collusion with the Japanese reactionaries to oppose the people of China." But even more disconcerting was the gravitational pull that was simultaneously closing the distance between Moscow and Washington, as North Vietnamese and Americans met in Paris for "a fraud jointly devised by U.S. imperialists and Soviet revisionists"—that is to say, peace talks.

Clearing away the rubble of their "revolutionary diplomacy" of the sixties, the Chinese now raised a starkly functional structure on the site which bore little resemblance to the romantic folly it replaced. Courting bourgeois governments came before arming Communist insurgents to overthrow them, since the immediate aim of Peking was to rally the rest of the planet behind China. The shift in emphasis implied no betrayal of the hunted guerrillas in the wilds of Asia and Africa, it was argued, for Mao had already laid down that armed struggle à la chinoise was a strictly do-it-yourself affair. The Chinese could not turn their backs completely on "people's wars" without letting the Russians slip in behind them to fill the gap, but their unequivocal support was reserved for respectable insurgencies of blacks against whites in Africa, and Vietnamese against Americans in Indochina.

The political map was meanwhile redrawn to show China at one pole, the unholy alliance of superpowers at the other, and an "intermediate zone" embracing everyone else—honorary "people" who were to be drawn into an international version of Mao's united front. The Chinese set out to mend their fences with the community of nations they had so affronted at the height of the Cultural Revolution, and between the boorish excesses of 1967 and the politesse of ping-pong diplomacy in 1971, they were to prove that they could slap the world in the face and then seduce it within four years. Like a man stooping briefly to duck through a low doorway, Chou En-lai conceded in June 1971 that Peking's impossible conditions for joining the United Nations could be reduced to one—the expulsion of Taiwan—and in November he could straighten up again, for China was admitted as the one and only "China" to the organization he had earlier dismissed as "manipulated by U.S. imperialism and only capable of mischief."

Chinese envoys fanned out into foreign capitals again, and Peking began negotiating new ties with hesitant neighbors in Southeast Asia in a drive to undercut the thin topsoil of Soviet influence. The odious evangelism of the Red Guards gave way to the "smiling diplomacy" of Chou En-lai, and hot gospeling to cold calculation. China offered generous government-to-government aid to the developing continents, and in 1970 overtook the Soviet Union to become the biggest philanthropist in the socialist camp. Peking exchanged ambassadors with countries like Canada and Italy that only agreed to "take note" of China's claim to Taiwan, and hailed with enthusiasm the news in 1972 that four more countries (including Britain) would be joining that dubious capitalist syndicate of the "Second World," the European Economic Community. The Chinese were no longer fighting reaction, but wooing it against Russian revisionism.

Mao the revolutionary purveyor of people's wars was eclipsed by Mao the strategist engrossed in the international power game, and kings, presidents, and premiers—empty-handed heirs of the more manageable barbarian vassals who had brought tribute to the Chinese emperors—were now ushered into his presence as part of the operation to win over the world. Any file of their photographs—facing the camera, turning to talk to Mao—could be mistaken for a collection of mug shots for a rogue's gallery of feudal despots, fascist dictators, and bourgeois bosses taken from China's antiimperialist archives. They included the Emperor of Ethiopia and the king of Nepal, President Marcos of the Philippines and his wife Imelda ("product of a corrupt capitalist system"), President Mobutu of Zaire ("that imperialist puppet"), the military master of Nigeria, and anti-Communist diehards from Greece to Thailand.

Mao was once more joining forces with a lesser evil to destroy a greater, just as he had joined forces with Chiang Kai-shek against the Japanese, and he trusted the predictable pragmatism of conservatives more than the "sentimental oscillations of the liberals," as Henry Kissinger put it. "I like rightists," he had said. To him, they were practical men with an eye to profit, they did not challenge the true faith by peddling dangerous ideological heresies of their own, and they were doomed anyway.

During the seventies the Chairman was to welcome visits from the Conservative Edward Heath and the Republican Richard Nixon both in and out of office, from the ultra-rightist West German opposition chief Franz Josef Strauss before the socialist Chancellor Helmut Schmidt, and from the hawkish Senator Henry Jackson rather than the doves in the Democrat loft. He had never been afraid to soil his hands to pan gold, and he saw traces of the stuff in men like these. They were opponents of "false détente" between Western Europe and the Soviet Union, and they viewed Moscow through narrowed eyes. They could be convinced that while the deceitful Russians "made a noise in the East" they would "strike in the West," that Soviet militarists saw Europe as a tender morsel but China as a potential bone in the throat, and that the NATO powers must therefore put up a stiff, uncompromising front to the common enemy in the Kremlin.

While pointing one finger at the Russians, the Chinese had been crooking another at the Americans since 1969, in accordance with the same antique principles of strategy that inspired the courting of Western Europe. The Chinese defense against the two superpowers was shaped by the tradition of "vertical" and "horizontal" alliances forged in the cutthroat era of the Warring States before the days of the First Emperor, when China was a heptarchy of rival kingdoms playing a seven-sided war game. The "vertical" alliance was designed to unite six weaker states against the might of Qin; the "horizontal" riposte of Qin consisted in breaking up the alliance by "befriending the distant and attacking the near" (much as the French once made allies of the Scots in order to threaten their English neighbors on two fronts). These alternatives were now combined—a "vertical" alliance was to be forged by mobilizing the world against the superpowers, and a "horizontal" strategy initiated that would pin down most of the Janus-faced Soviet army in the West by making "distant allies" of the Americans and Europeans at Moscow's back door.

The USSR was identified as the immediate enemy, the parallel of Mao's tactical collusion with the bourgeois-reactionary Chiang Kai-shek unblushingly evoked, and by 1972 China would have made her peace with both the "militarists" in Tokyo and the imperialists in Washington. But the rapprochement was not simple, for obvious reasons. The agile Chinese were following up a backflip away from their Russian comrades with a somersault towards their American enemies, and this display of political acrobatics jogged the memory as well as jolting the system.

The American memory was one to inspire a daydream of fond reminiscence—of selfless Protestant missionaries striving to save the heathen soul of nineteenth-century China; of a morally upright Washington that had stood aside when greedy European colonialists plundered the Celestial Empire, endowing it instead with the Open Door policy; of a generous administration that had lavished military aid and moral counsel on the Chinese during the war against Japan; and of a culture that had given them the precious message of democracy and the American way of life.

The Chinese memory was essentially the same, for there is only one history, but it had been scarred by all the love bites. These were the same Americans whose missionaries had practiced their questionable arts under the protection of extraterritorial rights illegally extracted from the Celestial Empire by bullying barbarians. They were the tricksters who had filched all they could from China by invoking the high-sounding Open Door policy, scooping out their share of the loot without putting anything into the country, and demanding the same privileges as the other robbers without taking the same risks. Finally, they were the arch-imperialists who had played big brother to the bandit Chiang Kai-shek, defended his regime of ruffians in Taiwan with their fleet, and then tried to encircle and "contain" China, invading Korea to her immediate north and Vietnam to her immediate south.

Even after they agreed to re-open the Sino-American dialogue in Warsaw at the turn of 1970, the Chinese opened a barrage of abuse against President Richard Nixon, calling him a liar and a gangster and announcing that the nineteen seventies would be a decade of worldwide struggle against imperialism—American and Russian. When the Americans put more men into Vietnam, Mao himself inveighed against the President's "fascist atrocities," and when they started to withdraw men from Vietnam, they were accused of concocting a "vicious scheme to Vietnamize the war."

But under cover of this noisy routine and similar conventional displays of antiimperialist fury, the Chinese were prepared to talk. The Americans would not only make the most powerful of "distant allies," they would offset the Russian menace in the Far East itself if China could quietly persuade them to keep a firm foothold in the region (while loudly demanding that they "go home"). And there was no doubt about the menace. The Kremlin had trebled the number of troops along the Sino-Soviet border since the days of Khrushchev, and deployed missiles in Mongolia after concluding a military alliance with Ulan Bator.

In December 1970, accordingly, Mao told Edgar Snow that he would be happy to see Nixon, for it was with Nixon that he would have to solve the problems that separated their two countries. And when they parted, he described himself to the American writer as a "monk under an umbrella." This was the first line of a Hunanese couplet of which the second ran: "No law and no Heaven." Mao the rebel, concealed from the eye of his Marxist god, was ready to sup with the devil.

So was Nixon. Within twelve days of taking office, the President had asked Henry Kissinger to attack the problem of moving the U.S. nearer to China, and by 1969 the first crack had appeared in the twenty-year-old American ban on trade and travel between the two countries. In April 1971 the Chinese invited an American table-tennis team to Peking and magnanimously inflicted upon it no more than a marginal defeat. Ping-pong diplomacy had been born.

Almost simultaneously, Chou En-lai sent a note to Washington through Pakistani intermediaries confirming that the Chinese government would be glad to receive a high-level official "or even the President himself for a direct meeting and discussions." Kissinger paid a preparatory visit to Peking in July 1971, Richard Nixon took his first step on Chinese soil on 21 February 1972, and within four hours he was talking to the seventy-eight-year-old Chairman. Chou En-lai had apprised Kissinger of the prompt summons from Mao almost curtly, "without the usual banter." It was a solemn moment for the polished and indefatigable Chinese actor—now a gray, strained, drained-looking seventy-three himself. Revolution had yielded to realpolitik.

To the Chinese the show was a hit even before the curtain went up. The subtle overture of détente had already yielded Peking a seat at the UN at the expense of Taipei, and the United States was to recognize that Taiwan was an integral part of China in the Shanghai Communiqué issued at the end of the trip, abandoning the infamous proposition that there could be "two Chinas." The visit would confound Peking's enemies, real or imaginary—the Soviet Union, Japan, India, the South Vietnamese, the South Koreans, the Kuomintang, and all of America's other running dogs from Laos to Lisbon. At the same time, it would enhance China's prestige as self-appointed champion of the Third World in the United Nations, for it would show the small and the weak that Peking was ready not only to stand up to the super-powers in their defense, but to bargain with the bosses on their behalf. It was not easy to placate North Vietnam, but it was reportedly put about that Nixon had come to Peking to kowtow and talk peace because his bid to encircle China had failed, and this meant that the Vietnamese and all other revolutionary peoples could "win new victories against their imperialist oppressors."

Chinese foreign policy was to remain slippery with ambiguities, but after 1972 Sino-American détente was a fact of life—confirmed, if anything, by the unfaltering stream of invective Peking aimed at the imperialists in Washington. For the less they spurned the capitalist enemy, the more the Chinese had to be heard to be doing so—they were obliged to preserve their revolutionary face, and they could not leave all the barracking to the Russians and the Vietnamese.

A concatenation of disconcerting developments had buttressed Mao's belief that the American card must be played against Moscow, and the ring around China broken. These had included not only the Russian military buildup and diplomatic moves beyond her borders that threatened her with "encirclement," but the evidence of the plot that was unfolding in Peking itself even as signals began passing between the Forbidden City and the White House—the damning text of "Project 571." This document revealed that Lin Biao, categorically assuring his accomplices that "our action will be supported by the Soviet Union," proposed to murder his master.

❊ *CHAPTER TWENTY-NINE* ❊

T HE HEIGHTS of Lushan are covered with forests so dense, says the *China Handbook,* that the tall trees "prevent most of the sunshine from reaching the ground." For Mao Tsetung, who described in defiant verse how he had "twisted and turned four hundred times" as he pushed upward through the green maze of mountains, it was always to be a place of political shadows and enemies in ambush, it seemed. "At the 1959 Lushan Conference," he was to say of the sudden, searching memorandum on the blunders of the Great Leap Forward that he was then forced to face, "Peng Dehuai colluded with a foreign country . . . Peng wrote a letter which was an open declaration of war. His intention was to seize power, but he did not succeed." Eleven years later, "At the 1970 Lushan Conference they made a surprise attack and carried out underground activity . . . a certain person was anxious to become state chairman, to split the Party and to seize power."

The "certain person" was Mao's "close comrade-in-arms and successor," Lin Biao, who had urged that the position of head of state be revived and offered to the national genius, Mao Tsetung. Lin had good reason to believe that he would refuse it ("I don't want to be state chairman; I have said this six times already," Mao was to protest), whereupon he himself would be elected. It would be the last rung on the ladder to power. Why not wait until Mao died and he could step into the old man's patched slippers? The constitution that named him his heir was perilously like Mao's own will; wills could be revoked, amended, superseded—and the Chairman was no longer smiling upon him.

Chen Boda seconded Lin's proposal, for the Cultural Revolution Group was already broken up, and vengeful men were demanding Chen's blood as nominal director of the Grand Guignol it had staged in the sixties with China as the mangled victim. He needed protection, and Lin Biao could provide it. But Lin failed him. Their proposal was thrown out, and Mao's secretary became the next sacrifice to be flung to the wolves, to the usual chorus of minatory voices damning all "sham Marxists and political swindlers" who had secretly conspired with Liu Shaoqi. Chen Boda, now dubbed the "black puppet master" of the "ultra-rightist" ultra-leftists, fell precipitately from grace and ten years later found himself standing trial with the Gang of Four.

Mao was obliged to handle Lin Biao and his powerful friends in the PLA with more circumspection, however. They were to be "educated"—cured of the disease so that the patient would be saved—and Lin Biao himself was to be "protected" in the interests of unity. But Mao's idea of protecting the Tiger Cat in the interests of unity was to isolate him—his clique of army generals within the Party was compelled to denounce Chen Boda and renounce the "theory of genius," commanders in Peking Military Region loyal to Lin were posted elsewhere, and his following in the powerful Military Affairs Commission was diluted with newcomers. Cheated of his chance to become head of state, Lin Biao was haunted by fears that if he waited patiently for the "peaceful transition" of power, he would be dropped down some convenient political oubliette before Mao died. He therefore opted for a policy of sudden and violent change.

The result was the so-called "Outline of Project 571" drawn up in March 1971, an improbable scenario for killing Mao and seizing power in an armed coup that read like a penny dreadful for under twelves, and was executed with outstanding incompetence long after it had been hopelessly blown to the Maoists. The first the outside world knew of this black comedy was a version of questionable authenticity put out by the Kuomintang in Taiwan, allegedly based on a top-secret document circulated by the Central Committee of the Party in Peking. This purported to reveal to skeptical outsiders that as the targets of a conspiracy singularly lacking in the most elementary security precautions, the Maoist leaders were to be "bagged in one sweep" at a high-level meeting in the course of an improbable operation that could involve "extraordinary measures, such as poison gas, germ weapons, bombing, car accidents, assassination, kidnap, and small urban guerrilla teams. . . ."

". . . catch all in one net, using special means such as bombs, guided missiles, traffic accidents, assassination, kidnapping, and urban guerrilla squads," read the official Communist version published in Peking ten years later, just before the survivors of this lurid comic strip were put on trial. The unbelievers had been effectively silenced. But the script was still a disaster. "What we cannot do with words we can do with the gun," one of the conspirators is alleged to have said after Lin's ploy at Lushan had fallen flat. While they moved around the country to "drum up support for their counterrevolutionary plot," however, Mao Tsetung went on an inspection tour by special train, dropping broad hints that—not surprisingly—he knew there was something shady afoot. His remarks were reported back to his enemies, who were filled with alarm and decided that he must be liquidated without delay. Lin Biao thereupon "wrote an order for the armed coup d'etat with a red pencil on a sheet of white paper," and his son relayed it to his accomplices.

The killers had decided to give themselves six chances. They were going to have officers on hand at both Hangzhou and Shanghai to assassinate Mao in his train, to attack the train with flamethrowers and bazookas, to shell it "with reassembled 100-mm. antiaircraft guns firing point-blank," to blow up an oil depot in Shanghai at the point where it would be halted, or to dynamite a bridge as his coach passed over it. On 11 September 1971 the leaders of the conspiracy assembled "at a secret center" at Peking Airport, and "with a murderous look" Lin Biao's son called for action, "encouraging his followers with promises of high posts."

But the first assassin appointed to dispatch Mao at Hangzhou while bidding him good-bye lost his nerve, the miscellaneous salvos that were to annihilate him were never fired, the oil depot was not blown up, the second murderer detailed to kill the Chairman at Shanghai was not even allowed to board the train, and the train crossed the fatal bridge while the plotters "were still preparing the dynamite."

In despair, the ineffectual villains elected to set up a rebel regime in Canton ("We can obtain foreign assistance: Lin Biao still enjoys a high reputation in the Soviet Union"). But the suspicious movement of a Chinese Air Force Trident that had been flown out of Peking for the use of Lin was reported to Chou En-lai, who ordered it to be grounded, whereupon the Tiger Cat decided that the game was up and they should all make for Mongolia instead. "As the bullet-proof Red Flag limousine sped away from Lin Biao's villa, the guards motioned the car to stop. . . ." The inevitable last-reel car chase followed, and shots were fired as the miscreants raced for the naval airfield where the jet—and freedom in the U.S.S.R.—awaited them. "Lin Biao and the others rushed up to the Trident in the limousine," eyewitnesses later reported. "Before the car had come to a standstill, they had tumbled out . . . the plane was ordered to start taxiing without waiting for the co-pilot, navigator, and radio operator to board." Not surprisingly, the Trident crashed in Mongolia, and all in it were killed.

Melodramatic treatment effectively diminished the credibility of what seems to have been a very real plot, and as a mechanical solution to the embarrassing problem of unmasking Mao's chosen heir as an incompetent regicide, the denouement could not have looked more contrived. Lin Biao was dead, and two years could be allowed to pass before a new Party Congress purged of his supporters need write his epitaph as a "bourgeois careerist, conspirator, counterrevolutionary, double-dealer, renegade, and traitor." But once he was identified by name, the evidence against him—as always—was piled as high as a house of cards.

The dry, dedicated Liu Shaoqi had been transmogrified into a guzzling scion of the exploiting classes who had "never been a Communist" and tried to sell out the PLA to Chiang Kai-shek. Lin the "ever-victorious general" was now unmasked in his turn as a coward and a cretin in the field who had consistently pursued a "bourgeois military line" in defiance of Mao (who had won all his battles for him). His transparent perfidy—like that of Peng Dehuai, Peng Zhen, and Chen Boda—could be traced back to the nineteen twenties. This was routine re-editing of history and all part of the charade. No one was foolish enough to ask how Mao could have been blind for so long to the treachery of these "freaks and monsters" around him. Yet another deer had turned out to be a horse. That was enough.

But until Lin Biao was officially damned in 1973, the warier Chinese felt they had excellent reasons for not giving up their seats on the fence in order to stand up and be counted against him. For one thing, Mao himself was mum again—he did not say a single word for or against the Tiger Cat. For another, the Party was saddled with the incongruous by-products of the Chairman's exercise in political cannibalization at the Ninth Party Congress held in April 1969—a Central Committee varicose with old soldiers (too many of them lieutenants of Lin Biao), a gap-toothed Politburo more than half of whose members had disappeared, vacancies for the vital posts of defense minister and chief of staff, and a draft constitution that still proclaimed Lin Biao to be Mao's successor. Attempts to decide who and what should end these anomalies were provoking sharp disagreement among the Maoists, the moderates, and the military. Nor could the shadow of Lin Biao be ignored, for commanders of nine out of China's thirty-odd armies had given their allegiance to the Tiger Cat or his chief of staff at the moment of his eclipse.

However, Chou En-lai was painstakingly putting the pieces together again, exploiting the mutual interests that made the moderates and the military natural allies, and seducing Lin Biao's former followers with live-and-let-live contracts that could bring them back into the fold once they conceded that the "small handful" of guilty conspirators at the top were out of the game for good. Shaking hands with him at a banquet in the Great Hall of the People in November 1972, listening to his laconic, professional backchat, I saw that his coal-fired eyes no longer danced as they had in the fifties and that he was carefully rationing his movements. But at seventy-four he still radiated controlled tension and mental vigor, and one sensed that while Mao's was the glory, his was the power. He was the man—if not the master—of the moment.

Twenty senior soldiers and cadres who had fallen from sight during the Cultural Revolution had reappeared like so many Banquos at the feast, and that was only a beginning. Within a few months Chen Zaidao, the truculent little general who had defied Peking during the "Wuhan Incident" in 1967, would materialize at a similar function, and early in 1973 Deng Xiaoping himself—the revisionist renegade "overflowing with evil" who was second only to Liu Shaoqi. It was as if the Maoists had talked of the devil once too often.

Mao personally sanctioned Deng's return, it seems, as part of a hard-faced understanding. A balance had been struck between the "lines" that left the peasants their private plots and the production teams control of their affairs, that gave the workers "reasonable rewards" for harder work, and that put formal examinations back into the schools. There was more talk of expertise and less of egalitarianism, "making politics" was quietly demoted, and so were dreams of a new leap forward.

It was even agreeable to squelch through the mud of a commune amid the all-pervasive reek of "indigenous fertilizer," for now the cadres were allowed to be sane, and the target for the year was 4,500 kilograms of rice for each hectare of land dosed with 50 kilograms of mixed manure. In the sad, whispering rain I heard once again the mad voices of 1958, gabbling meaningless statistics ". . . twenty-five thousand kilograms this year, and next year thirteen times as much, using a hundred fifty times as much green fertilizer, planting ten seeds where we used to plant one . . ." A family of five had one-twelfth of an acre on which to raise four pigs annually, a clutch of scruffy hens, and a few disciplined ranks of vegetables. Did they all eat in a communal mess hall? I asked the mother. "A what?" she laughed and took me through two plaster-walled rooms into the kitchen. It was primitive enough, but it was still home. Fourteen years before they might have been consigned to a single mud-floored cell in a jerry-built barrack.

Mao buttons were on the breasts of many, but far from all. The Chairman's teachings were no longer memorized from a little red missal, but studied along with those of Marx, Lenin, and Engels. His Thought was now the product of history, not of individual genius. There was a move towards collective leadership in the Politburo, and Chou En-lai talked deliberately of "the Party Center and Chairman Mao," whereas in 1966 an entire issue of the *People's Daily* had been withdrawn for this blasphemous inversion of the order of precedence. The days when families bowed to a portrait of Mao on rising from their beds were gone. "What do you do when you first get up?" we asked an elderly housewife in Shanghai. "Listen to the weather forecast," she replied promptly. With Chou En-lai in charge of day-to-day business, China had once more taken a sharp step back from the brink of lunacy, it seemed.

But wise men still preferred to wait and see, for nothing had yet proved permanent in China. Those who said the country was unified held only one-half of the truth, and those who said it was divided held the other, for in a dualistic world even unity had two sides. Pragmatist and radical could sink their differences only by playing a subtle game of give-and-take that saved faces all around, but sometimes left Jiang Qing the thin end of the deal, and sometimes the thin end of the wedge.

While the moderates might loosen restraints on profit, Mao's wife could simultaneously tighten the corsets on culture. Compromise was in the air, but the left was still inveighing against the "counterrevolutionary and revisionist black line in literature and art," echoing the Red Guards by condemning old customs and traditions as "a national heritage that is like a malignant tumor," denouncing material incentives and demanding more collectivization. "Professional" generals might clamor for a modern army equipped with computerized weaponry, but a squad leader raised on people's war was still to give me a lecturette on the ideological value of bayonet practice—and then demonstrate how to beat the bayonet (in case you hadn't got one) with a shovel. Everybody echoed everybody else, however, and as smiling women cadres sent down to the country from their offices in

Peking sang us a lively little number entitled "We pig-maids love the Party," it was clear that no outsider could guess how deeply the iron had entered into the Chinese soul. He only saw the haft.

Having called upon all factions to unite and not split, moreover, Mao failed to make a single appearance with Chou En-lai at his side or to proclaim his support for the prime minister, as he had so frequently done for Lin Biao. Instead, he bypassed the leadership in Peking yet again, opening his own direct channels to the provinces through Jiang Qing, and the man who would be photographed standing at his right hand when the Party held its next congress in 1973 would not be Chou, but the cadet of the Shanghai clique, Wang Hongwen. The Tenth Congress, which was supposed to end the anomalies of the Ninth—the era of empty chairs, the struggle between the "two lines"—simply exacerbated its contradictions. For under the aegis of Mao not only did the entire Shanghai "family" remain in the Politburo, but this radical nonentity was made second vice-chairman of the Party.

Mao was pushing eighty. He had become increasingly querulous with Jiang Qing, who was to set up her own establishment in the state guest house after being forbidden free access to his own quarters. But it was not Jiang Qing who was the target of his next mass campaign. It was Chou En-lai, the man who threatened the "perpetual revolution" by holding the whole ramshackle Chinese structure together and was slowly dying of cancer as he did so. For Mao was in more of a hurry than he had ever been before.

❋ *CHAPTER* THIRTY ❋

T HE LONGEST JOURNEY, say the Chinese, begins with one short step, and now that he seemed just one short step from the longest journey, Mao's sole concern was to perpetuate the revolution since he could not perpetuate himself, to see his ring of radical apostles firmly entrenched in the Politburo while he was still there to champion them.

As time was inexorably compressed within his diminishing life span, the Maoists reacted with a fierce campaign against the "soft" policies of Chou En-lai like the final flare-up before the fire dies, for they knew that they were working with waning assets, that once the Chairman was gone the moderates would have no compunction in cutting them out and destroying them. If the moderates controlled the gun, the Maoists still controlled the pen, and the press opened an offensive against "bourgeois ideology in state organs and the government," ominously demanding a "revolution of the superstructure." Once again, the hierarchy was under siege, and the fears of those who foresaw a second phase of the Cultural Revolution—this time directed against the prime minister—were fed by ominous turns of phrase that stood out like swastikas painted on a synagogue.

"Chairman Mao's Red Guards forever in battle," ran a headline in the *People's Daily* over an article which commemorated the first rally of these "valiant trailblazers" in August 1966. Dropouts who rebelled against the paper chase in schools were praised as "young generals" who "defended Chairman Mao's revolutionary line," and eerie echoes carried on the wind of all the wordy propaganda denounced "bourgeois careerists and conspirators" who had "wormed their way into the Party to steal state power." "Chairman Mao has taught us rebellion is justified," blared a big provincial radio station, while the Peking press thundered, "You must have the revolutionary spirit to go against the tide. . . ." New radical publications called for "revolutionary violence" to "overthrow the rule of the bourgeoisie and smash the old state machine."

An angry rash of wall posters spread across the country, and China was pitched into the confused cut-and-paste of another paper war. But it seemed to many that the Chinese might simply be exploiting the therapeutic properties of sound and fury. With Lin Biao gone, the Maoists had no champion who could put the PLA behind another Cultural Revolution, most of the military were aligned with the moderates, and those with a long, sour aftertaste of the insolent antics of Red Guards in the sixties were not going to stand by and see it all happen again. The radicals were screaming away their frustrations, and the world was watching a war dance, not a war.

Was it? The underlying proposition that China was once more falling into the arthritic hands of narrow-minded Party bureaucrats was thrown into relief by a campaign scarifying Confucius, who now served as a combustible effigy of all that the Maoists abominated, from traditional Chinese customs to the pragmatism of Chou En-lai. Appeals for Party solidarity inspired by the prime minister were denounced as a manifestation of the ancient philosophy of the Golden Mean, a treacherous attempt to "reconcile the contradictions and abolish the struggle" between proletariat and bourgeoisie, and so enable "smiling political swindlers" to hoodwink the masses and "hide inside the Party."

In 1974 it appeared that Chou had successfully deflected the movement, for it was now linked to a drive to eradicate the ideological poison spread by Lin Biao, and since the antique saint and the modern sinner were both under fire, the target—and the target behind the target —depended on who was doing the talking. The moderates had not lost their voices, and while the Maoists carried the "criticize-Lin-criticize-Confucius" campaign down to farm and factory in order to attack the pragmatists through Confucius, the pragmatists riposted by using it to attack the radicals through Lin Biao. Lin Biao's tactics had destroyed the unity of the Party and the PLA, ran the argument and now other irresponsible "opportunists" and "class enemies" were sabotaging that unity and inciting the masses to fight the masses, brazenly disobeying Mao's orders to "consolidate the great revolutionary alliance."

By mid-year what might have been a harmonious chorus of hatred against dead men who could not answer back had become an acrimonious public debate among the living, in which it was fatally easy for the ideologically tone-deaf to sing the wrong note to the wrong audience. As the accusatory big character posters multiplied in response to the radical battle cry, "Go against the tide," the prudent among the proletariat began to stay away from work to keep out of trouble. Dormant antagonisms from the sixties had surfaced in the factories, and old scores were being settled as the mounting discord divided men into quarreling factions that "made revolution" on the management's time, frittering away millions of man-hours at mass rallies and interminable political-study sessions. There was a protracted stoppage at the giant Wuhan steel works, a go-slow at major ports, and provinces began signaling shortages of coal and power and fertilizer, a falloff in farm work in the fields and a breakdown of discipline in the foundries, a standstill in gross industrial output in this region, sabotage and unfulfilled targets in that.

Troops were called in to "mobilize" stalled industry and transport in mines and ports and marshaling yards, and orders then went out from Peking for workers to "make revolution only in spare time," to restore discipline, "grasp production," and give output priority. The moderates were again exploiting the damage the Maoists had done, and Mao himself withdrew once more behind the screen of his left-wing pickets (Jiang Qing "does not speak for me"). He had "approved the launching" of the criticize-Lin-criticize-Confucius campaign, runs the retouched official history, but when he found that the Shanghai clique were "turning it to their advantage in order to seize power, he severely criticized them. He declared that they had formed a gang of four and pointed out that Jiang Qing harbored the wild ambition of making herself Chairman. . . ."

The Four were nevertheless to remain his confederates as long as life remained, for they were his court cards in a complicated hand that he was now playing from weakness. When the Fourth National People's Congress convened in January 1975, a thin, hard gloss of compromise barely concealed the underlying victory of the moderates. The fact that it was the first NPC to be held for eleven years was in itself a silent comment on the illicit rule by mob, clique, and decree that the Chairman had imposed on China for so long, and that was now to end.

The Congress itself was not so silent on the subject. It approved a "revised" constitution pointedly identified with the original charter of 1954 that the Shanghai radicals had so flagrantly violated in the name of Mao. This document was to provide the foundation for a new era of economic sanity, collective leadership, and lawful government. It established the prerogative of the individual to work for himself, and it protected "the right of all citizens to ownership of their income, their savings, their houses, and other means of livelihood." "A state must have rules," the deputy who presented the draft emphasized virtuously. But this deputy was no die-hard pragmatist. He was Zhang Chunqiao, oldest member of the Gang and the hero of its most unruly act, the formation of the Shanghai Commune. His dubious conversion to constitutional practice (and subsequent appointment to be chief political commissar of the PLA) was the key to a tactical truce, one end of the bargain that had made the Congress possible.

But at the other end of the bargain was the arch-revisionist Deng Xiaoping, who was promoted to be a vice-chairman of the Party as well as vice-premier of the government, and would shortly be appointed chief of staff of the army. It was Deng who read to the congress the report on the work of the government submitted by its chief, Chou En-lai, and it was quite clear to whom the dying mandarin proposed to pass his seal of office. The report performed the ritual kowtow to revolution that protocol demanded, but then outlined a purely practical program for the future, whose object was to "accomplish the comprehensive modernization of agriculture, industry, national defense, and science and technology before the end of the century." To achieve this, all Chinese must "unite still more closely, and adhere to the Party's line and policies," and "work hard to increase production and speed up socialist construction."

To Mao, this was all in execrable taste. Leaving Zhang Chunqiao to play the constitutionalist in Peking, the Chairman went south, boycotting the Congress yet making sure that all knew he had been fit enough to attend it by receiving Franz Josef Strauss of West Germany while it was in session. He then treated the NPC as an invalidated rubber stamp, as he had in 1955, by issuing an "important instruction" to the masses to "dig up the soil of revisionism" and root out the "bourgeois style of life." Provincial radio stations began talking yet again of a "new leap," and "bourgeois rights" guaranteed by the new constitution—like the private plot of the peasant—were denounced once more, as inspired articles in the press fulminated against the "vile wind of capitalism" and stressed that "unceasing revolution must be carried through to the end."

The moderates hit back by stigmatizing as "ultra-leftism" the revolutionary urge of the radicals to strip peasants and workers of their private pickings "in one morning," striking out at all those "afraid" of stability who were ready to sabotage social order in their eagerness to take the corners to communism too fast. Once again, a paper compromise was reached. "Bourgeois rights" were to be "restricted." They would not be bloodily excised, but slowly drained. They must not be allowed to expand, but nor must they be rudely snatched from the masses, for it had been proved that when facing a nervous peasantry it was unwise to make any sudden or unexpected move. China must not slide back into capitalism, but discriminatory wage scales, private ownership, the profit motive, and money itself were meanwhile to be accepted for what they had always been—necessary evils.

Like the double image in the viewfinder of a camera, left and right seemed to have slipped into focus for the moment. But a single twist of the argument could split them into two again. In Peking, the fixed smiles of solidarity on the faces of moderate and Maoist Party chiefs concealed ruffled relations constantly in need of ironing. In the provinces, the unresolved contradiction between the revolutionary conscience of the cadre itching to "restrict" material incentives, and the natural instinct of the more industrious worker to defend his legitimate "bourgeois rights," became even more acute. For the compromise had created a condition of maximum conflict: zig and zag were now simultaneous.

Strikes and violence flashed erratically across the country once more as labor unrest fomented more faction fighting. The resort of Hangzhou, to which Mao had withdrawn when the National People's Congress was held, was shaken by confused strife which escalated murderously after thousands of workers who had poured out of the factories to join the fray were recruited into the urban militia to keep order. Given access to rifles and submachine guns, they promptly took to the streets again, and the city was cut off from the outside world for weeks on end as the armed mobs of warring left and right reduced it to near-chaos. Allotted the task of stopping the tumult, Wang Hongwen predictably failed. Deng Xiaoping then forestalled any bid by the "revolutionary masses" to "seize power" with the connivance of the Gang by sending in ten thousand crack troops to restore order. The moderates might play the Maoists with care in Peking for the sake of solidarity, but by the same token they were not going to risk the unity of China by pandering to anarchy in the provinces.

The radicals had not exhausted their ammunition, however. Jiang Qing, allegedly speaking in the name of Mao, was reported to have launched a venomous diatribe against "intoxicated" Chinese ambassadors who devoted their time to "doing business" with the imperialists. The Maoist press had already started to attack the "unbridled quest" for foreign equipment and technology promoted by the "chieftain of the revisionist line." Chou En-lai had in effect warned the backward Chinese that self-reliant modernization would mean they would have to pull themselves up by imported bootstraps, and the radical howls grew louder as Deng Xiaoping duly "squandered China's precious resources" by contracting to pay for plants purchased abroad with Chinese oil and coal. Meanwhile Mao reputedly issued an instruction to all Chinese to study the great bandit saga *Water Margin,* which was presented as an allegorical tale about the iniquities of those who tore up the principles of their revolutionary chief after he died.

Mao or "Mao"? By 1975 the Gang appeared to be using Wang Hongwen and the younger, more malleable members of his own family to feed the insulated Chairman a predigested diet of half-truths calculated to evoke the "instructions" they wanted from him. "He only saw the people around him," Deng Xiaoping was to confirm later, "people belonging to the Gang of Four." Much of the time, no one could be sure who was calling the shots.

Much of the time. But it was Mao—and certainly not "Mao"—who had used his personal authority at the end of 1973 to order a shake-up of "Red warlords" of the PLA settled too firmly in their provincial fiefs, and in doing so cross-posted the commanders of Canton and Nanking Military Regions. This move took Nanking out of the hands of a ranking member of the Politburo sympathetic to Deng Xiaoping, and confided its 220,000 troops to Ding Sheng, a loyal disciple of the Chairman from the days of the Long March. The effect was to soften significantly the hostile attitude of the local army command towards the radical masses manipulated by the Gang of Four. And that was crucial, for Nanking Military Region included their main revolutionary base—Shanghai.

The timing was suggestive. Shortly before the transfer, a left-wing journal had called for the formation of an "extensively armed" urban militia under the evocative headline, "The Paris Commune and the Arming of the Workers." Just two months after Ding Sheng took over the military region, official broadcasts disclosed that a new "armed defense group" had been created in Shanghai to help keep law and order. It sounded innocuous enough, but later in the year Party cadres and militia commanders in the city met to pledge themselves to "carry out military training and master skills in combat," and to maintain close links with the workers so that they could "rely on the revolutionary masses in fighting a people's war, and make every street and factory a military stronghold."

Not a single army officer was listed among the 4,300 people invited to that meeting in the summer of 1974. Ding Sheng did not trust the local garrison, it was later disclosed, and the PLA was deliberately excluded. The Shanghai militia was to be built into a force of armed, combat-ready workers with its own "antiaircraft, antitank, and explosive squads," commanded by left-wing Party cadres, cooperating with the Maoist public security services—and outside the control of the army.

Seven years after all China had been told to emulate the "January Revolution" of 1967, when the mob seized power in the city, all China was again being told to "Learn from Shanghai"—and what all were to learn was to "arm the working class," to forge the urban millions into a great fighting machine independent of the PLA in order to perpetuate the revolution. Mao was coming very close to fulfilling his threat at Lushan in 1959 to "go out and organize another liberation army" if he were thwarted, it seemed, knowing that if that led to a showdown with the PLA, it could make the haphazard violence of the Cultural Revolution look like a pillow fight.

Was he guilty—or had he been tricked, misquoted, ignored? It is significant that the men who outlived the Chairman did not try to make the Gang of Four scapegoats for his most arbitrary acts. They could hardly do so. For just as Mao alone (and never "Mao") had the power to uproot from Nanking Military Region one of the two most powerful generals in China without fear of mutiny, so he alone could impose a glib nobody like Wang Hongwen on the Party as the third man in the hierarchy. And now he was to flout the real powerholders again, with all the disdain of an emperor who could ignore his mandarins when unscrupulously disposing of a "meritorious dog" or promoting an incompetent favorite. In January 1976 Chou En-lai died, and Deng Xiaoping read the eulogy at his funeral. But Mao Tsetung not only failed to attend the obsequies for the subtle revolutionary who had been his political kedge anchor since 1935, he dishonored his dying wish and defied the majority of the Politburo by passing over Deng and making a certain Hua Guofeng acting prime minister instead.

Hua Guofeng (then Minister for Public Security) was not an incompetent, but he was a cipher compared with the brilliant, irascible, and hard-bitten veteran he was supplanting. Deng had commanded an army in the Jiangxi mountains in 1927, risen to be chief political commissar of the 2nd Field Army in the legendary struggle against the Kuomintang for the Central Plain, and become secretary-general of the Chinese Communist party by 1953—when Hua was still running a rural district. Sixteen years his junior, Hua was a lightweight from the far side of the generation gap, a patient plodder who had made his way up the provincial Party ladder in Hunan and had only reached Peking and the Politburo in 1971. While he was no ultra-leftist, however, he was personally loyal to Mao.

The Chairman had made his choice, but there was to be more to it than that. "Comrade Mao Tsetung could not bear to accept systematic correction of the errors of the Cultural Revolution by Comrade Deng Xiaoping," was the Party's finding in 1981. He had therefore "triggered a movement" to criticize Deng and what he mistakenly saw as a right deviationist trend in the ranks, "once again plunging the nation into turmoil." Both his guerrilla instinct, and the Chinese principle of *li si*—"dying force"—which teaches that a man near the end has nothing to lose by exerting all his strength for a final blow, seemingly persuaded Mao that the moment had arrived to shatter Deng beyond repair. Wall posters went up attacking anonymously the "unrepentant capitalist-roader" who had shamelessly put unity and stability before class war. Press and radio called him "China's Khrushchev," cursing him for a renegade who had plotted to restore capitalism and make China modern instead of Maoist, and the sudden flash of ideological fury that illumined the country seemed to turn Deng overnight from future premier into nameless outcast.

But in a significant show of dumb insolence, all but a handful of the twenty-nine provinces ignored promptings from Peking to organize rallies in a drive to hound Deng to his political death, and in April the "Tiananmen Incident" exploded in the capital itself. A vast and defiant crowd pressed into the Square of Heavenly Peace to raise a great pyre of wreaths to the memory of Chou En-lai in angry protest against the betrayal of his protégé, and placards appeared execrating Jiang Qing and demanding an end to the reign of the "First Emperor of Qin." When next morning Peking awoke to find that the wreaths had been torn down during the night, about a hundred thousand demonstrators streamed into the square again, and violent rioting broke out in which an army barracks was fired and cars were overturned where once Red Guards had gathered to glorify Mao.

The disorders were savagely suppressed, and as the official account later put it, "Comrade Mao Tsetung wrongly assessed the nature of the Tiananmen riot and dismissed Comrade Deng Xiaoping from all his posts inside and outside the Party." A reduced Politburo summarily sacked Deng for being responsible for the "counterrevolutionary" disturbances, confirmed Hua Guofeng in his post as prime minister, and appointed him Vice-Chairman of the Party—solely "on the proposal of our great leader Chairman Mao," and without any constitutional authority whatever.

Once again, Mao was saving the Chinese millions from themselves by giving them what they did not want and—as the shock waves hit the country and the static accumulated—exploiting the loyalty that, in the last analysis, was his safety net. China's mandarins were all Chinese and all Communist, and they hesitated at such an inopportune moment to rebel against their master. For the second time, Deng Xiaoping was bowing to his fate and going down before the Chairman rather than risk a head-on clash that could split the country, and his supporters agreed that the powerful and abrasive vice-premier should temporarily "step aside." He would retreat now to advance later, for there was an alternative to confrontation: they could all bide their time, if only because they had more of it than Mao Tsetung. Decay and approaching death provided a pretext for ostensibly inclining to his will and conniving at his errors as long as he still lived.

The contract concluded and the conspiracy intact, florid messages flowed into Peking from the provinces hailing the choice of Hua Guofeng, pledging support for Chairman Mao and his proletarian revolutionary line, and promising that the crimes of the fallen Deng would be relentlessly exposed. "Several hundred million Chinese were highly elated" by the changes, mammoth rallies bringing the masses together "in a jubilant mood" were held throughout the country, and the army declared itself "boundlessly loyal" to the Party and ready to "do whatever Chairman Mao says." This was lip service on a lavish scale, even given a hundred million more or less in the claque, few of whom had heard of Hua Guofeng one year before. But it was, of course, a meaningless rite. Four months later the Central Committee formally asked the eighty-three-year-old Mao to "retire," and although he was to continue to be "busy with national affairs," it was clear that he was fading into history.

The residual strength of the radicals now rested on the credibility of a Mao the masses never saw. There was no meeting of minds, for all that was left was the dog-eared script of the anti-Soviet antirevisionist "proletarian revolutionary line" which everyone knew by heart. Chou might be dead, and Deng an outcast, but the Chairman was no more than a touched-up photograph gazing blankly into the middle distance.

Increasingly desperate as they felt time and the ground slipping away from them, the Gang of Four began to incite the young against the veterans in the hierarchy, urging junior commanders in the army to defy their hidebound revisionist superiors and "carry out the political tasks of the revolution." Their voices became ever more strident as they strained to promote the proletarian pillars of wisdom of their dis-integrating Chairman—all power to the masses, total collectivization, class war without end—and there were renewed calls for "protracted struggle," for the Shanghai mob to "seize power," for youth to re-member that "rebellion is justified." Reports of "bloody disorders" and "beating, smashing, and looting" multiplied like the tremors before an eruption, and when the radicals found few allies in the PLA willing to provide them with firepower, they turned to the "Shanghai experi-ence"—the urban militia trained to "make every factory and street a military stronghold."

In 1981 the "Jiang Qing counterrevolutionary clique" were arraigned before a special court, accused of plotting "armed rebellion in Shang-hai" as Mao lay dying. Wang Hongwen was quoted as having said, "We must be prepared for guerrilla warfare." Ding Sheng, described as "a confederate of the Lin Biao clique who had thrown in his lot with Jiang Qing," had gone to Shanghai from Nanking in August 1976, when "74,220 rifles, 300 artillery pieces, and more than 10,000,000 rounds of ammunition were issued to the militia." But the powder was damp. The rest of China had declined to "learn from Shanghai" and connive at more criminal irresponsibility by raising a heavily armed "people's army" for the next exercise in chaos. On 9 September 1976 Mao died, Hua Guofeng became Chairman, and three weeks later the Gang were under arrest. The worst was over.

THE LEGACY

An exalted, wilful Dragon—cause for regret.
A host of dragons without a head—good fortune.
(THE FIRST HEXAGRAM OF THE "I CHING":
LAST LINE)

❀ CHAPTER THIRTY-ONE ❀

T HE WORST? Mao Tsetung had not usurped power from a political paragon beloved of the millions when he proclaimed the People's Republic in 1949. Whatever the merits of Chiang Kai-shek, he had been master of a noisome midden within which the Chinese people were abused and callously exploited as the greedy and the corrupt picked over the sorry mess for the last ounce of personal gain.

The profiteers around the Generalissimo made huge fortunes by rigging the money market, hoarding vital commodities in order to create false shortages while millions starved, and running tentacular monopolies that ruthlessly squeezed out the small man. The peasant, the shopkeeper, and the scholar alike were the prey of local bosses who could skin them alive by putting a tax on everything from hogs to coffins, "requisition" their grain and goods only to sell them off for gold, even confiscate their property by labeling it "Japanese." Military commanders forcibly recruited their sons for "pig soldiers," whom they traded among themselves like cattle. To all this Mao had offered an alternative, and—as Chinese history foretold—the misery and poverty could have only one end. The Mandate of Heaven passed.

By the seventies the average Chinese might seem to be confined to a big, overcrowded bird cage, but then what—he might have asked—did the West mean by freedom? Freedom to feel insecure, to be stripped and starved? He was fed, housed, clothed, treated when ill, provided with schooling for his children. He paid no income tax, and if wages were frozen, prices were stable. Not only the evils of the Kuomintang, but hijacking, parcel bombs, traffic snarls and terrorists, porn, pot, rack rents and racial strife were all a far cry of agony from the order around him.

Yet appearances were deceptive. Under the Kuomintang even the impossibly high standards of venality had been fixed points of reference that enabled a man know where he stood. But now he was not only trapped between Mao's exotic ethics and his own acquisitive instinct: he was obliged to ride "two lines" that did not run parallel but crisscrossed to trip him as Maoists and moderates fought for supremacy. And the "contradictions" caught him young. Children might be molded for the Maoist way of life while their bones were still soft—some production brigades held "preparatory Red classes" for four-year-olds and upward in which the first faltering steps in "revolutionary mass criticism" were taught, and it was claimed that results were encouraging. Mao's world nevertheless remained a bewildering place in which it was easy for a boy to blunder.

Temples and shrines converted into schools were hung with portraits of Mao, yet the sacred ancestral tablets had been painted over for use as blackboards, since they were relics of "feudal superstition." But if worship was superstition, why worship Mao? He learned not to ask. He had only to accept a few cabbages from a revisionist rich peasant to be scolded for lack of "revolutionary vigilance," and if he picked wild blackberries and proudly brought them home for his parents to eat, he could be rebuked for not handing them over to the collective. When he refused to touch a bowl of grass served up one day in place of his usual rice, he was severely reprimanded, for the whole family had to eat this unappetizing dish to keep fresh in their minds the bitter memories of the years of oppression before Mao arrived to save them.

On the other hand, if his parents were among the ungodly who neglected such rites, he was in trouble if he did not report them to his political mentors. He could not plead that they were his own father and mother—a family production team had been held up to public shame for "babbling that since everyone in it was called Ma, there was no class struggle." This lapse was known as "preaching the reactionary theory of human nature," he was told.

Once at school, he was caught up in the conflict between the two lines on education, for although conventional studies and academic standards had been restored, the radicals had again launched a ferocious counterattack against them. In 1974 colleges were scathingly criticized for choosing students solely on the basis of a 60 percent pass mark, for "not publishing examination questions beforehand," for "forbidding students to refer to books, exchange opinions, or copy from others" during the tests, and for discriminating against proletarian candidates in favor of bourgeois swots in defiance of Mao's dictum that the laborer was worthy of his higher education.

It was a grave mistake to pick a bourgeois for a father, for a political sin like that could be treated as a crime by a regime that treated crime as a political sin. Men who committed "murder, arson, hooligan gang-sterism, thefts, and speculation" were branded class enemies, revisionist renegades undermining society and therefore accomplices of the Liu Shaoqi clique. Radical propagandists would convert the commonest fiddle in the book into "sabotage" or some other heinous ideological felony as automatically as a cipher machine will convert plain language into gibberish. A cadre who used a tractor as free transport within his commune was guilty of "incorrect political thinking" and of "employing tools for the revival of capitalism."

Every day was a hazard, whether a man was a peasant, a worker, a cadre, or an intellectual, for he had to pick his way through a mine field sown with heresies, and to put a foot wrong could prove fatal. Even to say "men must eat" could be construed as an insinuating revisionist argument, a plea for production to be given priority over politics—when Lin Biao stressed the importance of providing food and clothing for the masses he was accused of "bringing back the parasitic life of the exploiting class."

Did a misguided playwright try to amuse his audience? He was pandering to the "reactionary theory of entertainment" and distracting them from his socialist message. Did he, on the contrary, keep the story stark and simple in order to bring out the virtues of his revolutionary heroes? If so, he was failing to put the message across by boring people with a dull plot. That did not mean that he should indulge in empty invention, however, for then he would be dreaming up drama behind closed doors instead of "going deep into life" among the peasants and workers. On the other hand he should not "write about reality" either, of course, for then he would be tempted to show up the shortcomings of great revolutionaries and the mistakes committed by the Party.

If the intellectual appeared to be walking a tightrope, the cadre was caught on a knife edge between orders and counterorders that were the projection in the provinces of the unending war of ideas in Peking. Since the Chinese ideogram for an official contains two squares connected by a vertical line, he was said to be "one who speaks with two mouths." But now a cadre had to be ready to speak with two Maos as his authority—Mao as interpreted by the radicals to justify one policy, Mao as interpreted by the moderates to justify another. That did not save him, however. When he tolerated lucrative peasant enterprise, he was damned by one faction as a "political swindler," and when he stamped on it, he was accused by the other of erroneous ultra-leftist adventurism, of driving the exasperated farmer into a fit of unproductive sulks by not allowing him to cultivate his own garden.

There was no safe middle course between the heresies of right and left. Faced with enigmatic directives from Peking to distinguish carefully between "proper domestic sidelines" and "spontaneous capitalism," to allow the peasant to cultivate his private patch to a point where it boosted his output *but* did not impair his "socialist activism," a cadre had no difficulty in getting both of them into trouble.

The difference between orthodoxy and heresy could be as small a matter as one porker. Disdaining communal pig herding as profitless and even degrading labor, peasants tended to devote their energies to rearing pigs on their own private plots. They might buy two at first, and expand later by adding a third, perhaps a fourth. As we have seen, however, in 1975 the radicals mounted one of their seasonal hates against the anachronistic bourgeois rights that allowed farmers to indulge in "small production" at the expense of collective work. In consequence the peasants took fright, fearing they might be dubbed class enemies and their porcine assets confiscated. They stopped breeding pigs, and output slumped.

But the pig loomed very large in the Chinese ministerial mind—in 1958 Mao himself had propounded the ideal of the one-man-one-pig people's democracy as a "great and glorious task" to be achieved in one or two five-year plans, for apart from its "meat, bristle, hide, bones, and entrails," the pig was a "small chemical fertilizer plant." New directives were therefore sent out, telling the local cadre to assure the mistrustful peasant that his private plot was safe and his vigorous pig raising much admired. But neither could be certain how many private porkers he could fatten, how much time he could spend on them, or how much money he could make from them before "proper domestic sidelines" became "spontaneous capitalism," and honest farmer Jekyll was reclassified as bourgeois-reactionary Hyde.

Most men played safe—as always—by leaning to the left, and since the Chinese have an outstanding talent for pushing matters to their illogical conclusion, something of the bizarre enthusiasm that had inspired the freakish facts and figures of the Great Leap Forward reappeared in the seventies. Power-station workers ignored "absurd bourgeois warnings" and again souped up old and tired foreign equipment in a bid to improve performance 25 percent, leaving others to put their fingers to their ears. Shipbuilders in Shanghai ran up a ten-thousand-ton freighter on stocks meant only for a three-thousand ton vessel and overcame a shortage of wood by using cardboard to enlarge the mold for an oceangoing hull. Men with no experience whatever were making generators in a bucket-and-spade farm-tool factory, while others constructed steel windlasses and tube-drawing machines from unconsidered trifles retrieved from the trash heap to prove that they, too, were "industrial guerrillas" who treated a production problem as a "political battle."

Or a surgical problem, where doctors were concerned. The official press reported in 1974 that a woman suffering from an abdominal tumor had been cut and restitched twice before the ideological dispute that raged over her reclining form ended in the defeat of a surgeon who had protested that the operation was too dangerous. He was inevitably exposed as a revisionist, and only then was the patient opened up for the third time and the tumor removed. She was finally tacked together again sixteen hours after the debate had begun.

"Politics"—meaning the arbitrary rearrangement of life on earth by Mao Tsetung—was "in command," and it was as if the laws of the universe itself had been changed by the intrusion of a strange new dimension that left nothing as it had been. The peculiar misery and nausea that afflicted the disoriented Chinese as even good and evil acquired alien, shifting coordinates during the "ten terrible years" have been poignantly brought out by the so-called "wounded" school of writing of the victims. Far more striking than the sometimes clumsy plots of the authors are the mental processes of the characters—like the father who tears all pictures of Mao out of the comic books of his four-year-old son, for fear that he may accidentally deface one with a crayon. They are the frightening reflexes of a people who have not been shaped, but warped, by cultural revolution; the living legacy of Chairman Mao.

Within a year of the Chairman's death, the gerontocrats who now ruled China were questioning much of their heritage—the "newborn things," as the radicals called them, that Mao had bequeathed the Chinese people in place of the bad old ways. People's communes were "newborn things," as were the model farming brigade at Dazhai, the model "revolutionary" operas of Jiang Qing, workers' colleges and peasant universities, institutions of higher learning packed with proletarian youth, the mass line in science, the spirit of self-reliance. They included *xiafang*, which thinned out the cities and mingled man with man; the exchange of roles that taught deskbound officials the meaning of manual labor, and nurses to remove an appendix while surgeons hurried by with bedpans; the barefoot doctor, the much-needed paramedic armed with the Thought of Mao and some ten months of basic training who tended the sick where none had tended them before.

One is tempted to add the Red Guards, of whom the well-known authoress (and confrere of Lao She) Han Suyin wrote before Mao died: "Everyone praised the Red Guards whose conduct was excellent, and who were very clean, well-behaved and polite"; they applied "democratic methods of reason and debate," it seems, and there was "no hasty impulsive action opening the gates of hooliganism as reported so erroneously in the Western press." The last sentence is characteristic of the writer, who dismisses the foreign interpreter of China as irredeemably purblind while arrogating to herself a familiar infallibility. It is, however, the infallibility of the wind sock. By 1980 she was describing in vivid detail the "absurd and ugly things" the Red Guards had done: how they ransacked houses, and took turns to beat their victims—"the worst not only burnt books and destroyed historic monuments, they also killed and tortured."

A very different tale, but then by 1980 the wind had indeed changed. Mao was gone, Deng Xiaoping—thrice-risen—was back in power in Peking, and the Cultural Revolution was a write-off. "Nothing was correct or positive during those ten years," said Hu Yaobang, the future Chairman of the Party. "The whole thing was negative. Tremendous damage was done to our economy, culture, education, political thinking, and Party organization. The only positive factor, if we may say so, is that we have learned something from the mistakes made during that decade." The supreme irony was that Mao's own actions in striving ceaselessly—not for his last ten, but his last twenty years—to mint a new and shining China in which ideological virtue would be its own reward had left his unhappy heirs facing the reverse side of the coin.

Their most urgent problem was how to inject life and logic into a mechanistic economy in which output was governed by ambitious targets fixed by the state, often with a ludicrous disregard for demand. Their solution was to halt production for production's sake and gear it instead to sales, to encourage managers of provincial enterprises to conclude their own contracts and measure their success in terms of turnover, not tonnage.

They had set themselves no light task. Mao's exhortation to be "daring" in spirit had yielded an army of cadres frozen into bureaucratic rigidity by fear. Reinvested veterans who had been crucified by the mob once were too cowed to risk arousing the ire of "rebel" workers again by enforcing discipline or checking the quality of output, let alone talking impiously of profit. On the other hand, the rash of young radicals that the Cultural Revolution had pushed into positions of power had been promoted for their Maoism, not their managerial skill. They were keenly aware of their incompetence to survive in a new China in which the orderly suburbia of state planning gave way to the savage law of the marketplace, and their instinct was to block their ears to such heresy anyway. In consequence, mountains of shoddy goods that nobody wanted continued to pile up in the state-run shops as mindless factory officials, mesmerized by their production quotas, churned them out in spite of empty order books—in 1980 Fujian province alone boasted a surplus of more than twelve million unsold ping-pong balls.

Where the manager preferred his fixed quota, moreover, many of the men preferred fixed pay. The egalitarian system whereby all bench hands of the same grade drew the same wage whether they turned a lathe or played cards had transformed workers into shirkers. By 1979 some of the industrialists in Hong Kong who had opened up factories across the border in China were pulling out again, having quickly discovered that cheap labor that does not labor is not cheap. The famous Chinese work ethic had vanished, it seemed. Deng Xiaoping's slogan "less talk, more work" might please the diligent, but it made the lazy and the incompetent nostalgic for the days when the Gang of Four had urged the millions, "Don't be afraid to stop production . . . if an iron furnace goes out, this is a victory." When productivity was the enemy of politics, millions of man-hours could be whiled away on poster polemics and psittacine denunciations of Deng and the rest of the revisionists. There was no way of punishing the absentee and the idler then, since there were no bonuses and they could not be sacked.

The bitter feud that had split the Chinese Communist Party from top to bottom continued after Mao died, for the Gang had padded it with their protégés, and half of its members were raw radicals inducted during the "ten terrible years." The country was suffering from a glut of blind dogmatists, of "whateverists" whose creed was "whatever Chairman Mao decides, we firmly uphold; whatever Chairman Mao instructs, we resolutely obey." In 1980 the press was still accusing Party and managerial officials of factionalism, anarchy, and stultifying bureaucratic behavior, of sometimes taking six months to solve problems that could have been settled in a "two-minute telephone conversation." The public works division of Peking was about a billion dollars in debt; houses had been built without water, gas, or electricity; the roads had been dug up and filled in so often for the haphazard laying of pipes that cynics were saying the authorities "should put zippers on them." Millions were crying out for accommodation, yet buildings lay empty.

The "Great Teacher" had left something even more distressing in his entailed estate, however—a broken school system and a lost generation of youth. Mao's mass line in science and technology might have set China back ten years, but his "line" in education had set it back twenty, Deng Xiaoping was to say. It was estimated in Peking that 120 million Chinese under the age of forty-five remained illiterate, but more tragic had been the fate of those who could put pen to paper—or poster: the millions of students who had been lured out of the classroom to be Red Guards.

They had been incited to rebel against their parents and teachers and established authority, excused from school in order to smash society, and left free to cut one another up in bloody faction fighting, often seizing weapons from soldiers who had been ordered to "support the left." They had then been brusquely consigned to the country to do mortifying penance in the pigsties and among fermenting tanks of human excrement, shoveling manure and "learning from the peasants." They were true creatures of the Cultural Revolution, whose only escape from endless bucolic drudgery seemed to lie in flight. Disenchanted with their down-to-earth existence on the farm, so-called "wandering sons" therefore made a break for the forbidden city, drifting back to Shanghai or Canton in their thousands.

But in the city they were illegal "black persons" with no official existence, and since they could not register for rations or jobs or residence in their family homes, their only recourse was to crime. By the early nineteen seventies whole rows of houses in slatternly quarters of Canton were devoted to gambling and girls, and the territory was carved up among secret societies or "spectaculor organizations" whose thugs fought and killed to keep their pitches, ran underground factories and flogged stolen goods on the black market, robbed, burgled—and peddled and "protected" their women.

Whereas the ordinary "roadside chicken" could be signaled with a banknote sticking halfway out of a man's pocket, these superior "motors" could only be met through their "organization man." They charged their marks five *yuan* instead of the usual two, and diversified their activities by stealing and swindling for the mob. The prostitutes of Canton included "educated youth" who had either dodged *xiafang* altogether or slipped back into the city from the country, and the worst of these "wandering daughters" were those who had been primary-school students during the Cultural Revolution, according to one escapee.

Why? Because at that time their teachers "didn't dare speak out about anything . . . they really didn't receive any education . . . they learned about all the bad ways of doing things then—the fighting and killing—and they became bad themselves." Sometimes the girls organized their own *xiafang*, going down to the villages to escape a residence check and do a little incidental business; but when in Canton itself one of the favorite beats of "roadside chickens" was the Park of Culture, where they would often indicate their availability in an appropriate manner by sporting the red-and-gold lapel button of the man they might have said had put them there—Mao Tsetung. Few respectable people wore them anymore, so there was little danger of confusion.

The "right to rebel" was being turned against society in general, the Red Guard factions had become criminal gangs, and the guns taken from the PLA the weapons of armed hoodlums. "They were continuing to fight Cultural Revolution style," as one eyewitness put it, but they were fighting "for territory"—the political motives had disappeared into the mists of modern history. Crime in China, where formerly no one even carried a key, was by now commonplace. There was ten times as much juvenile delinquency as there had been fifteen years before, and Peking laid the blame for most of it squarely on the Cultural Revolution, when the young were "brought up in an atmosphere in which beatings, smashing, and looting were considered revolutionary actions," and the hole torn in the economy provoked an explosion of unemployment.

By 1979 despairing young men and women who had been sent down to the country ten and fifteen years before were clamoring to return to the teeming cities, where the jobless already numbered 20 million. Thousands of "rusticated youths" from Shanghai who had been allowed to go home for the Chinese spring festival went on the rampage, smashing trains and disrupting rail traffic, refusing to leave, and demanding work in a conurbation already morbidly swollen with more than 300,000 workless truants.

This was one consequence of Mao's determination to beat 800 million-odd Chinese into the shape of a single selfless archetype, but there was more to the inheritance. The struggle between the "two lines" had pulled countless other threads from the fabric of Chinese society, leaving a hopeless tangle of vendettas, of guilt and injustice, distrust and resentment. In 1979 the body of the Chairman lay in its pretentious mausoleum in the center of Peking to evoke ritual tears from those who filed past, but true misery was to be found just two minutes away around the corner, where shabby petitioners from all over China were camping on the pavement like a colony of beggars, waiting for the procurator-general's office to right the wrongs committed in Mao's name. The Cultural Revolution had claimed 100 million political victims who were now demanding redress, it was said. The country was maggoty with grudges from end to end, and the official press was imploring everybody to forswear revenge; for otherwise the sores would take a century to heal.

For one thing, the weak-kneed economy could not take the strain. Mechanization of agriculture had been neglected in favor of collectivization, industry starved of foreign know-how in the interest of self-reliance, experts kicked out of their jobs to make way for "red" ignoramuses, and a generation of potential scientists and technologists simply thrown away. The economy had been merely stumbling along, growing old without growing up like a victim of progeria, the tragic and obscure disease that can make a sixteen-year-old look sixty.

Much the same could be said of the armed forces. The PLA had fissured badly when the single focus of its allegiance—Chairman-and-Party—had split traumatically into Chairman and Party. But its defense program had also been split in two by a dichotomous strategy based on "people's war" and the H-bomb that had left the conventional army twenty years behind the times, at a moment when Maoist foreign policy had successfully bracketed China between a hostile Soviet Union to the north and a hostile Vietnam to the south. National security depended on a sea of under-armed soldiery and militia at one extreme, perhaps three hundred nuclear weapons at the other, and little in between apart from about one hundred jet fighters that might still qualify for the international league—just.

Mao had once more withdrawn, leaving the mandarins to pick up the pieces from his last experiment with a quarter of mankind. But the most daunting obstacle to recovery was not a practical problem of education, justice, economy, or defense. It was distrust. The Chinese were sick of sudden change, but Mao had taught them that the shortest distance between two points was a zigzag, and they were persuaded that nothing would ever run straight again. The resurrection of Deng Xiaoping was therefore no more convincing in this decade than his damnation had been in the last, the current censure of Mao no less artificial than the adoration lavished on him earlier. Socialism was like the Yellow River, "China's Sorrow"—the course never remained stable, and to build on its banks was to court possible disaster.

"He who has once been bitten by a snake, jumps at a piece of string," the Chinese say. Mao Tsetung had succeeded in destroying the very thing that he had insisted a thousand times was the key to the revolution—the faith of the masses. In 1979 the *People's Daily* was complaining that peasants still suffered from the "morbid fear" that the pragmatic program of modernization would sooner or later provoke a radical antirightist witch-hunt. Whatever Peking promised, the people assumed that the recurring nightmare would continue to recur, and that there could be another Cultural Revolution tomorrow.

And the danger was there, in the fermenting discontent of the unwanted—the semiliterate lost generation, the crass "proletarian" teachers, the unskilled radical cadres, the senescent veteran generals, the new left-wing Party members—all the anachronisms left by revolution that would be hit by whiplash when China accelerated towards an elitist technological society under the "four modernizations" program. If Mao cast a long shadow across the past, his legacy cast a long shadow across the future. But like all shadows, it was only one side of reality.

❊ *CHAPTER* THIRTY-TWO ❊

T HE THOUGHT OF MAO was still his most hallowed bequest to the nation, but it was interpreted to meet the temporal needs of the modernization program, for while God might be God, the day-to-day business of the church was now in the hands of its cardinals. Radical voices might cry in the wilderness for the dead Chairman's egalitarian utopia, but the talk of the town was of the "emancipation of ideas," of freeing culture from its sectarian fetters, of democratic practice and the rule of law, of foreign funds and joint ventures, and of the paramount importance of science and technology in a computer age.

In 1980, as in 1958, China seemed to have burst into recognizably human life. The traffic in Peking had thickened, and new Japanese buses and taxis blared a path through the great flocks of bicycles spinning sedately past the Gate of Heavenly Peace. Trim women cadres dressed in smart, dove-gray tunics even in the capital, breaking into sky-blue suits, colored blouses, and finally cotton frocks as one moved south. People crowded hungrily around window displays of clinging cheongsams, Western wedding gowns, or a wall-to-wall stretch of bras. Bookshops were doing a fast trade in Chinese fiction, technical texts, and translations from English and French, while counters piled high with the *Selected Works of Mao Tse-tung* were deserted. At the stripped Democracy Wall idle Chinese listened raptly to an amplified rendering of "Auld Lang Syne" played on Hawaiian guitars. The mood was tangible.

Peasant families and even individuals were now cultivating not only their private plots but part of the collective land of the commune, and selling any surplus for personal profit. In Chungking some factories were free to market everything they produced above the state quota on their own account, and workers were getting bonuses that could add 50 percent to their pay packets. At the same time, the government was struggling to reduce the formidable unemployment figures by opening up private opportunities for young people. In Shanghai one-man "cooperative" street enterprises were drawing customers at every turn—a pavement shoemender, a tailor cutting out a suit on a collap-sible table, a carpenter knocking together a wardrobe in an alley. In Peking thirty-four small teams of photographers were tapping the tourist traffic, and at least one of them was making a thousand dollars a month. At the other end of the scale, a syndicate of former capitalists who had been given back the assets confiscated from them under Mao had set up a building-construction company—after raising $25 million from subscribers.

"Capitalism is not all bad, you see," one cadre told me, echoing her superiors, and the *People's Daily* confessed that the new enterprises were "superior to those run by the state because they are flexible and efficient." This was the other side of reality. The muscle-bound Maoist cadres who recoiled from the exacting heresies of the economic rat race were matched by irrepressible ordinary Chinese glad to be back in business, it seemed. Socialism might be in danger of becoming irrelevant, for the trouble was not only that money talked, but that it talked politics.

And yet. And yet. Hu Yaobang had said that the Chinese had at least "learned from the mistakes" made in the last decade of Mao's life, and in this respect they had indeed enjoyed all the advantages of an expensive education. But if the painted face of Peking had con-cealed peculiarly Chinese blemishes in 1958, it concealed the same blemishes in 1980, and history could almost unnervingly repeat itself, as if one had passed through a time warp.

The dust and the deadly driving, the hotels more remarkable for their plush than their plumbing, the prissy protestations of diligence in the factories (and the card playing around the corner), the frustra-tions of foreign businessmen, the often appetizing food and the always indigestible propaganda—these were all part of a timeless China. The déjà vu started to disturb, however, when diplomats told stories of jerry-built apartment blocks with collapsible floors and lift shafts out of true that had been run up only the year before, for I had heard precisely the same complaints twenty-two years earlier. I had also heard how the Chinese had broken a diamond-point rock drill after refusing to allow its Swedish manufacturers to supervise its use on the site—and now British mining experts in China were telling me how they had run into exactly the same trouble.

In 1958 I had met a foreign biochemist in Peking who was convinced that the Chinese would find a cure for cancer within five years, because "Party and state committees can call out all women between thirty and thirty-five for weekly tests, and the mass of statistics available cannot be obtained anywhere else." He was wrong. But in 1980 the interpreter for a visiting British medical specialist passed on to me his considered opinion that as the Chinese could carry out mass tests on millions of women to order, they might well "find a cure for cancer within five years."

Twenty-two years before a cadre had solemnly declared that in China there were "no prostitutes, but only women who do it for money"—to be complemented by another in 1980 who said that there were virtually no hardened juvenile delinquents in China, but only young people "who don't know how to abide by the law" (there were also youths guilty of gang war and murder who were "unaware that they were committing crimes"). If in 1958 a compost heap had been a "fertilizer plant," and a peasant scavenging for scrap iron an "industrial element," now profit-sharing partnerships with a strong whiff of capitalism were "collectively owned enterprises," a man in business for himself was "individual labor," and the millions of workless were "awaiting employment."

These were new trimmings on all the old hat, but history was also being rewritten again. It was not simply that when Deng Xiaoping became the latest wizard, Jiang Qing became the last witch. While muted homage continued to be paid to the memory of Mao, a cult had developed around the dead Chou En-lai. And not only Chou. The dying Mao had allegedly told Hua Guofeng, "With you in charge, I'm at ease," and soon after he was gone, the obscure Hua was being presented to the dazed masses as a semilegendary figure, their "wise leader" and "worthy helmsman," the hero of a hundred edifying if apocryphal tales.

The new Chairman suddenly stood revealed as a fearless guerrilla and the implacable enemy of landlords, an ingenious administrator who had taught the Hunanese how to make everything from nitrogenous fertilizer to television sets, a tireless worker who had tilled the soil alongside the poorest peasants, who had sold toothpaste ("actively introducing customers to the various kinds available"), eaten "wild vegetable soup" so that his rice ration could go to a sick grandmother. His writings were published, a film was produced about him, an enormous portrait put on display inscribed "Boundless love for Chairman Hua." Hua, once rumored to be the son of Mao, had become the earthly manifestation of a trinity with two Holy Ghosts.

But Hua Guofeng was also the most glaring anomaly in the Chinese leadership, for he had joined the radical chorus that denounced Deng Xiaoping in 1975 and then usurped his position as prime minister. He was not the only one, however. The country was again ruled by a catchall of discordant elements, as it had been in Mao's day, and Deng's handling of this awkward package was to be strongly reminiscent of the old guerrilla.

Deng was seventy-five and in a hurry, as Mao had been before him, and just as Mao had turned to youth for his revolution against the entrenched revisionist bureaucracy in Peking, Deng turned to younger men for a new generation of leaders mentally geared to modernization. They were often younger in ideas than in years, but as he eased these sexagenarian whiz kids and aging technocrats into positions of power, he nonetheless threw into an incongruous alliance against him the revolutionaries who were now threatened with eclipse as has-beens—from the vintage generals of the thirties to the militant radicals who had blackened their names in the sixties. This opposition decried the unseemly haste with which Deng was trying to push through his pragmatic reforms, to create a cold new world in which they would have no place, and to discard the doctrines of Mao which they identified with their own fortunes. And at the pivot of the protest was Hua Guofeng.

Paradoxically, Deng Xiaoping had already started to outflank Hua in the manner of his master—with the masses. Instead of Red Guards, thousands of peasants converged on Peking in 1978 and 1979 to demonstrate—sometimes outside Hua Guofeng's home—against poverty and persecution, while in place of the poster artists who had decorated Peking University in 1966, organized dissidents plastered the Democracy Wall with hard-hitting broadsides demanding human rights.

Except for a lunatic paper fringe, the posters were part of an orchestrated propaganda campaign to corner Hua and his supporters. The evils exposed by this public outcry were ascribed to the "fascist" and "dictatorial" days of the Maoists, so that everything from the muddle and penury in the countryside to the muzzling of the masses could be laid at the door of Hua's radical friends. The peasants and bill stickers were briefed in advance to clamor for what Deng wanted to give them, so that the noisy expression of their prefabricated popular will could reinforce his own proposals to the Politburo.

When mosquito magazines and placards on the Democracy Wall began to call for political freedoms beyond the framework of the socialist system, however, the culprits were arrested and savagely sentenced, the Wall was proscribed, and the "four big rights" were struck from the constitution—the prerogative of the people "to speak freely, air their views fully, hold great debates, and write big character posters." Like the heroes of the "Hundred Flowers" before them, the rebels had gone too far.

Deng was already attaining his objectives, moreover. Hua Guofeng was progressively isolated within the Politburo, until in June 1981 he lost his post as Chairman of the Party and dropped to seventh place in the hierarchy. He was accused of serious errors as a "whateverist," of fostering his own personality cult, and of foolhardy economic planning reminiscent of the Great Leap Forward. Deng had neutralized his radical "Liu Shaoqi."

The charges were not groundless—least of all the last. By 1977 responsible Party members were again beginning to ooze optimism like bubble gum. A senior official assured me that the damage done by the Gang of Four would be repaired within three years and that "so much has been achieved that we are ready to launch a new Great Leap Forward." As if to confirm all fears, a minister in Peking then predicted that the new leap would "certainly surpass that of 1958 in momentum, scale, and scope," and the *Peking Review* declared that China must "overtake the United States economically" by the end of the century. Chairman Mao, it reminded readers, had "laid down the general line of going all out, aiming high, and achieving greater, faster, and more economical results."

The incurable Chinese were once more in the grip of a paroxysm of exotic figuring, but in March 1978 Hua Guofeng made the figuring official. Presenting his report to the National People's Congress, Hua outlined a modernization program that would "achieve 85 percent mechanization" of farming and give China not only a light industry producing "an abundance of first-rate goods," but an "advanced heavy industry . . . with iron and steel, coal, crude oil, and electricity in the front ranks of the world in terms of output"—all within ten years. "By 1985 we are to produce four hundred billion kilograms of grain and sixty million tons of steel . . . the increase in our country's output of major industrial products in the [next] eight years will far exceed that in the past twenty-eight years," he announced triumphantly. But success would still depend on the "do-or-die" spirit of the people.

Within a year of that exercise in euphoria, the government was obliged to confess that its blueprints for modernization were as wildly impractical as anything Mao Tsetung had dreamed up, and must be drastically "readjusted." By the end of 1981, Peking had suspended or canceled foreign contracts running into billions of dollars, capital investment had been cut to the quick, and construction plans for heavy industry shelved indefinitely or simply torn up.

China was zigzagging again—taking a "big ax" to boastful economic plans after another great leap in the dark had threatened to prove as foolish as the first, clamping down on dissent after allowing a "hundred flowers" to bloom on the Democracy Wall, excising freedoms from the constitution after calling for the "emancipation of ideas." Mental flashbacks to the days of Mao were stimulated by other similarities. The opprobrious babble of anti-Soviet propaganda continued unabated. The in-and-out thrust of the PLA across the southern border in 1979 was designed to "teach Vietnam a lesson" that China had taught India in 1962. The trial of the Gang of Four—branded a "counterrevolutionary clique" in advance and arraigned before hectoring judges who had been their victims—had all the impartiality of the kangaroo courts of the Cultural Revolution for which they were themselves to be condemned.

And human rights? Human rights were guaranteed by ending man's exploitation of man, abolishing poverty and privilege, and making the masses master of the country, I was told in Peking in 1979. Since all this could only be accomplished by practicing "socialist democracy" under the leadership of the Communist Party, it followed that those calling for the overthrow of the system in favor of "Western democracy" (which had so contemptibly failed to end exploitation) were not defending human rights, but threatening them. Like the Gang of Four, they, too, were indictable as "counterrevolutionaries" under the new legal code, and when one of them was given a fifteen-year jail sentence, human rights were not violated, but upheld. "Freedom is not abstract," noted the *Liberation Army Daily*. "Without dictatorship there can be no true democracy."

The era of Mao and the post-Mao era mirror each other imperfectly as if through water, but although the image is refracted, the features are inevitably alike—as idiosyncratic as the epicanthic fold that narrows the Chinese eye and makes it "Chinese." For what his successors inherited was not just the legacy of Mao, but the legacy of China and the Chinese character—the idiom of the Chinese mind by which Chinese men and women live and die, and which molded Mao even as he was molding the millions.

Mao was not the father, but the child of the same guerrilla instinct that persuaded the mandarins and the masses to connive at his vision, of the tradition of peasant revolution, of the monkey-paw grip on power once grasped, of belief in the one true ruler and the one true doctrine that made all others heresy, of a black-and-white world of "two lines" in which the emperor was always right and the dissident always a bandit.

He may have wanted to create a society in which men would freely practice their own "lively style" of debate within the framework of socialist discipline, but the Chinese seemed doomed to oscillate forever between anthill and anarchy. They were a people of extremes, and although Mao might offer them Utopia, his very insistence on perpetual revolution was prompted by his knowledge that it was by definition only a matter of time before an hourglass was turned, top became bottom, and all things "reverted to their opposite."

The tight knot of spivs on the Shanghai street corner who eyed me speculatively in the summer of 1980 revealed just how far the Chinese had "reverted to their opposite." Beyond their sharply cut Mao suits, they had no visible connection with the Chairman's China—that land of pious sermons in which a floor waiter would not accept even a cigarette from a foreigner—nor even with the days when a misguided youth would paint a watch on his wrist to look trendy, and a rather more misguided "roadside chicken" would walk with a bounce to imitate the high-heeled shoes she could not possess. Now the heels were real, and the flashy digital gadgetry on the young men's wrists would tell them not only the time, but how much they should pay for the black-market dollars they vainly hoped to buy from me. Their dark glasses still bore a tiny label, "Made in Hong Kong." It was (for some) a sign that they were in business.

They were not the only ones. The government was soon to complain that within the administration "kickbacks and bribery" had become "open practice." Factories were seducing buyers with under-the-counter gifts of electronic paraphernalia, and enterprising officials in a position to supply plants desperate for scarce raw materials were squeezing thousands of dollars out of their hapless clients. Rival provincial corporations were ruthlessly undercutting one another for overseas orders, while on their side foreign firms found they could blatantly bribe their way into contracts by paying "compensation" to the negotiating cadres.

The compensation often took the form of a free trip abroad which

would give the Chinese an opportunity to stock up in bourgeois comforts—one cultural group visiting Japan was "investigated" for bringing back to China 69 color television sets, 30 refrigerators, 68 tape
recorders, 57 cameras, and 138 watches. Smuggling had become a major
industry, the black market flourished, and as far back as 1978 one
syndicate of six Party officials had set a stiff pace in straightforward
embezzlement by appropriating $100 million in the form of construc-
tion materials, relief funds, and state income to build luxurious homes
for themselves and their cronies.

The masses meanwhile found themselves being ripped off by shady
operators all down the line from factory to fruit stall. Manufacturers
were caught illegally raising prices or lowering the quality of their
products, or both. State-owned shops had begun selling short weight,
falsifying their scales, switching labels and trademarks. Peddlers in
the south had reverted to their ancient habit of stuffing poultry with
sand and vegetable hearts with rotten leaves to make them heavier.

These were the consequences of a more enlightened and liberal policy
that had allowed the Chinese to become human again. Hotel guests
were being robbed, handbags snatched in crowded stores, watches
torn from the wrists of unfortunate victims caught with their pants
down in public lavatories. Greater freedom of religious belief prompted
sorcerers, geomancers, palmists, fortune-tellers, magicians, and similar
recondite riffraff to crawl out of hiding. But if loving God was legal
now, so was loving one's family, or even the opposite sex. There was
a boom in marriage-brokering, and the country was alive with the
scuttling of professional matchmakers. The venerable custom of buying and selling brides was revived, and parents were once more ruining
themselves to give the betrothed a stylish send-off. Even freedom to
die in comfort provoked its own bourgeois backlash, as extravagant
funeral and memorial services in the Chinese tradition became more
costly than the extravagant weddings.

This was the face of the anti-Mao, and there were those who
lamented the death of the Chairman's dream of a selfless and frugal
utopia, grieving that China should slip into the vortex of the materialis-
tic consumer society, with its built-in incentive of spiraling discontent.
Between the two extremes, it might nevertheless be possible one day for
Deng Xiaoping and his supporters to find their own Golden Mean, to
establish a socialist state with an acceptable face that took account of
man's acquisitive nature and his innate sense of insecurity, but from
which demoralizing "bourgeois liberalism" would be banished. For
the difference between Deng and Mao appeared to be that Deng

had never forgotten what the downtrodden Chinese peasant—the father of the downtrodden worker and the downtrodden soldier—really wanted.

Mao had. The almost untranslatable expression *Fanshen* implies to overturn the world as one may turn the soil with a spade. For Mao, it meant the Communist revolution that would lead to the perfect collective society. But the Chinese were too numerous, too wretched and too ignorant, too steeped in the tradition of despotic rule that oppressed men overthrew in order to replace it with more despotic rule. For the average underdog, *Fanshen* simply meant becoming the overdog, reaching for revenge and riches and land for family and clan. Talk of a profitless paradise left most men cold.

Yet Mao tried to force them into his uncongenial mold with all the callous insistence of Procrustes, and was ready to destroy friends and enemies (and Party and state if necessary) in order to hug to himself the power to achieve his end—"the ten bitter struggles on the question of our line," as he called his ruthless elimination of all those with other ideas about the future happiness of the Chinese people. Accused of "feudal absolutism" after his death, he had provided a Confucian negative example for his heirs, and so pushed China towards the opposite pole himself—ably supported by the ultra-leftist Gang of Four, who had unconsciously outdone all others in "waving the red flag to defeat the red flag."

At the time, however, "the Party failed to prevent Comrade Mao Tsetung's erroneous tendency from growing more serious, and instead accepted and approved of some of his wrong theses," Hu Yaobang admitted in July 1981. It was the collusion of the mandarin and the millions that had given the Chairman his mandate to practice the art of the impossible. The resulting debacle had been a truly collective effort, a product of the "mass line."

The collusion was symbolized by the painted face that was all men saw of his imperfectly embalmed corpse as it lay rotting secretly in his mausoleum in Peking, for it both concealed and hastened his moral decomposition. But he had already been corrupted by a vision, by the conviction life wrote on the "blank sheet of paper" of his mind that he alone was right, and by the advance of age that turned conviction into dogma. A young hero's desire to do good had become an old villain's desire to dictate, and the vision a vice. By the nineteen sixties his Chinese translation of Marxist-Leninist theory was simply a weapon in the power game that he used when it suited him, and eternal class struggle was a formula for purging friends and enemies. Those who did not bow to his will were arbitrarily branded ultra-leftist or rightist or both, as he alone defined the terms. And where Lenin's instrument for the liquidation of adversaries had been the Cheka, and Stalin's the MVD, Mao's was the mob.

It may be argued that there was a touch of the sublime in the way in which Mao ignored the frail nature of the human race when he laid down his formula for its future, for all great teachers had told men what they should be, not what they were, whether Confucius or Christ. But where others taught, Mao enforced, and while his message may have been unexceptionable, his methods were not. He often spoke with great insight, displaying a breadth of vision matched only by the length of his perspective, yet despite that perspective he was betrayed by his impatience. As a molder of men, he tried to shape without a proper care for the material to be shaped; as a teacher, he set the people tests before he had educated them to take them; and his hasty experiments with the economy led only to muddle and disaster.

His romanticism, his idealization of man and moral strength, his love of stratagem and ruse, his distrust of foreigners and his contempt for intellectuals all suggest a fatal immaturity. There was something incomplete about a man who could encompass the misery of those he professed to love to prove himself right, about an obsession that seemed to lie on the borderline between genius and madness, about his very single-mindedness—it is the single-mindedness of war that makes the art of peace so much more difficult, and more than a Mao Tse-tung can handle. But if he was no Cincinnatus, content to return to the plow after saving the country, it is nevertheless difficult to disentangle his egoism from his altruism, the nerve ends of patriotism, political conviction, personal ambition, and the itch for power (*per se* or *pro bono publico*) that governed his reflexes.

It can be said that had it not been for his destructive instinct, China would now be twenty years ahead, and the immediate future already in the immediate past. But then, without that urge to shatter the bad old world in order to build a brave new one, there would have been no China as it is today, a "people's republic" united and at peace, a power in the world, a country that has "stood up."

"Chairman Mao had high goals even when he was advanced in age, wishing to do within a few years things which need a hundred years to accomplish, and this led to trouble in the end," wrote an eminent Peking commentator in 1981. "He really meant to do what would benefit the people and promote the advance of the revolutionary cause, and he devoted his whole life to this ideal. Chairman Mao's mistakes are mistakes made by a great revolutionary . . . to defame and distort him will only lead to defaming and distorting our Party and our socialist motherland, and this will harm the basic interests of the Party, the state, and the thousand million Chinese people." To deny the Chairman would be to deny the Chinese revolution itself. He was a founding emperor comparable to Qin Shi Huangdi or to Liu Bang of the Han Dynasty.

But it was still true to say that if China came before all else in his thoughts, he put his Thoughts before China, that if he was Brahma, he was also Shiva, the single embodiment of Creator and Destroyer. Had he echoed the brilliant strategist in *The Three Kingdoms* who lamented, "Unhappily I am dying and leaving my task uncompleted; I am injuring my country's policy and am in fault to the world," he would have been mistaken. He was the right man at the right moment, but if he was not born before his time, he did not die before it either. A flawed giant, the personification of a monumental irony, a ruthless champion of both right and wrong, he leaves us with one dominant image of himself that he would perhaps have wished above all for an epitaph—he was a very *Chinese* hero.

❊ SOURCES ❊

TRADITIONAL CHINESE REFERENCES:

Blofeld, John, tr. *The Book of Change*. London: 1964.
Chuang Tzu. *Basic Writings*. Translated by Burton Watson. New York: 1964.
Han Fei Tzu. *Basic Writings*. Translated by Burton Watson. New York 1964.
Legge, James, tr. *The I Ching: Book of Changes*. New York: 1963.
———. *The Chinese Classics*. London and Shanghai: 1935.
Lo Kuan-Chung. *The Romance of the Three Kingdoms*. Translated by C. H. Brewitt-Taylor. Tokyo: 1959.
Shih Nai-an. *Water Margin*. Translated by J. H. Jackson. Hong Kong: 1963.
Sima Guang. *Zushi Tongjian (The General Mirror)*. Shanghai: 1920–22.
Sun Tzu. *The Art of War*. Translated by Samuel B. Griffith. London: 1963.
Watson, Burton, tr. *Records of the Grand Historian of China*. New York: 1961.

IMPERIAL CHINA:

Bodde, Derk. *China's First Unifier: Li Ssu*. Hong Kong: 1938.
Collis, Maurice. *Foreign Mud*. London: 1946.
Cottrell, Leonard. *The Tiger of Ch'in*. London: 1962.
Cranmer-Byng, J. L., ed. *Embassy to China: Lord Macartney's Journal*. London: 1962.
Dawson, Raymond, ed. *The Legacy of China*. Oxford: 1964.
Eberhard, Wolfram. *A History of China*. London: 1958.
Fitzgerald, C. P. *China: A Short Cultural History*. London: 1958.
Gernet, Jacques. *Daily Life in China*. London: 1962.
Goodrich, L. Carrington. *A Short History of the Chinese People*. London: 1957.
Hudson, G. F. *Europe and China*. Boston: 1961.
Latham, Robert, tr. *The Travels of Marco Polo*. London: 1958.
Needham, Joseph. *Science and Civilization in China*. 5 vols. Cambridge: 1954–1970.

MODERN POLITICAL HISTORY:

Clubb, O. Edmund. *Twentieth Century China*. New York: 1978.
Fairbank, John K., and Reischauer, Edwin O. *China: Tradition and Transformation*. London: 1973.
Fitzgerald, C. P. *Revolution in China*. London: 1953.
McAleavy, Henry. *The Modern History of China*. London: 1967.
Mende, Tibor. *The Chinese Revolution*. London: 1961.
Pelissier, Roger. *The Awakening of China, 1793–1949*. London: 1967.
Wheelwright, E. L., and McFarlane, Bruce. *The Chinese Road to Socialism*. London: 1970.

MAO TSETUNG:

Chen, Jerome. *Mao and the Chinese Revolution.* London: 1965.
Chang Kuo-sin. *Mao Tse-tung and His China.* Hong Kong: 1978.
Paloczi-Horvath, George. *Mao Tse-tung: Emperor of the Blue Ants.* London: 1962.
Payne, Robert. *Mao Tse-tung.* New York: 1950.
Schram, Stuart R. *Mao Tse-tung.* London: 1966.
Siao, Emi. *Mao Tse-tung, His Childhood and Youth.* Bombay: 1953.
Siao-yu. *Mao Tse-tung and I Were Beggars.* London: 1961.
Snow, Edgar. *Red Star Over China.* London: 1963.
Wilson, Dick. *Mao: The People's Emperor.* London: 1979.
Wilson, Dick, ed. *Mao Tse-tung in the Scales of History.* Cambridge: 1977.

The Selected Works of Mao Tse-tung, Vols. 1–5. Notably:
  "Analysis of the Classes in Chinese Society." March 1926.
  "Report of an Investigation into the Peasant Movement in Hunan." March 1927.
  "A Single Spark Can Start a Prairie Fire." January 1930.
  "On the Tactics against Japanese Imperialism." December 1935.
  "Problems of Strategy in China's Revolutionary War." December 1936.
  "On Practice." July 1937.
  "On Contradiction." August 1937.
  "Problems of Strategy in the Guerrilla War against Japan." May 1938.
  "On Protracted War." May 1938.
  "The Role of the Chinese Communist Party in the National War." October 1938.
  "Problems of War and Strategy." November 1938.
  "The Question of Independence and Initiative Within the United Front." November 1938.
  "On New Democracy." January 1940.
  "Rectifying the Party's Style of Work." February 1942.
  "Talks at the Yanan Forum on Art and Literature." May 1942.
  "On Coalition Government." April 1945.
  "The Foolish Old Man Who Removed the Mountain." May 1945.
  "The Hurley-Chiang Duet Is a Flop." June 1945.
  "On the People's Democratic Dictatorship." June 1949.
  "The Chinese People Cannot be Cowed by the Atom Bomb." January 1955.
  "On the Cooperative Transformation of Agriculture." July 1955.
  "On the Ten Major Relationships." April 1956.
  "On the Correct Handling of Contradictions among the People." February 1957.
  "Comrade Mao Tse-tung on 'All Reactionaries are Paper Tigers.'" November 1957.

Mao Tse-tung Unrehearsed. Edited by Stuart R. Schram, London 1974. Notably:
  Speech at the Supreme State Conference. January 1958.
  Talks at the Chengtu Conference. March 1958.
  Speech at the Group Leaders' Forum of the Enlarged Meeting of the Military Affairs Committee. June 1958.
  Speech at the Lushan Conference. July 1959.
  Speech at the Enlarged Session of the Military Affairs Committee and the External Affairs Conference (on learning from mistakes). September 1959.
  Talk at an Enlarged Central Work Conference (on democratic centralism). January 1962.
  Speech at the Tenth Plenum of the Eighth Central Committee. September 1962.

Remarks at the Spring Festival (on education). February 1964.

Talks with Mao Yuan-hsin. July 1964.

Speech at a Meeting with Regional Secretaries and Members of the Cultural Revolution Group of the Central Committee (work teams obstruct the revolution). July 1966.

Talks at the Report Meeting. October 1966.

Talk at the Central Work Conference. October 1966.

Talk at a Meeting of the Central Cultural Revolutionary Group. January 1967.

Talks at Three Meetings with Comrades Zhang Chunqiao and Yao Wenyuan (on the Shanghai People's Commune). February 1967.

Talk at the First Plenum of the Ninth Central Committee of the Chinese Communist Party. April 1969.

THE COMMUNIST ERA: GENERAL

Bloodworth, Ching Ping and Bloodworth, Dennis. *Heirs Apparent*. London: 1976.

Cheng Chu-yuan. *The People's Communes*. Hong Kong: 1959.

Chesneaux, Jean. *China: The People's Republic, 1949–76*. Sussex: 1949.

Contradictions: China in Ferment. Hong Kong.

Daubier, Jean. *A History of the Chinese Cultural Revolution*. New York: 1974.

Elegant, Robert S. *Mao's Great Revolution*. New York: 1971.

Fan, K., ed. *Mao Tse-tung and Lin Piao*. New York: 1972.

Fraser, Stewart E., ed. *Education and Communism in China*. Hong Kong: 1969.

Goodstadt, Leo. *China's Watergate*. New Delhi: 1979.

Greene, Felix. *A Curtain of Ignorance*. London: 1965.

Hughes, Richard. *The Chinese Communes*. London: 1960.

Lethbridge, Henry J. *The Peasant and the Communes*. Hong Kong: 1963.

MacFarquar, Roderick. *The Origins of the Cultural Revolution*. Vol. 1. London: 1974.

Schwartz, Benjamin I. *Chinese Communism and the Rise of Mao*. Cambridge, Mass.: 1952.

Snow, Edgar. *The Other Side of the River*. London: 1962.

Vladimirov, P. P. *China's Special Area, 1942–1945*. Bombay: 1974.

Wilson, Dick. *The Long March*. London: 1971.

POLITICS:

Lewis, John Wilson, ed. *Party Leadership and Revolutionary Power in China*. Cambridge: 1970.

Liu Shaoqi. *How to be a Good Communist*. Peking: 1962.

———. *On the Party*. Peking: 1951.

Schram, Stuart R. *The Political Thought of Mao Tse-tung*. New York: 1969.

Yao, Wu Teh. *Politics East–Politics West*. Singapore: 1979.

MILITARY:

George, Alexander L. *The Chinese Communist Army in Action*. London: 1967.

Liu, F. F. *A Military History of Modern China, 1924–49*. Princeton: 1956.

O'Ballance, Edgar. *The Red Army of China*. London: 1962.

INTERNATIONAL RELATIONS:

Clubb, O. Edmund. *China and Russia: The Great Game*. New York: 1971.
Crankshaw, Edward. *The New Cold War: Moscow v. Peking*. London: 1963.
Fairbank, John K. *China: The People's Middle Kingdom and the USA*. Cambridge, Mass.: 1967.
Fitzgerald, C. P. *The Chinese View of Their Place in the World*. London: 1964.
Frankland, Mark. *Khrushchev*. London: 1966.
Huck, Arthur. *The Security of China*. London: 1970.
Kissinger, Henry. *The White House Years*. New York: 1980.
Klein, Sidney. *The Road Divides: Economic Aspects of the Sino-Soviet Dispute*. Hong Kong: 1966.
Larkin, Bruce D. *China and Africa, 1949–1970*. Berkeley: 1971.
MacFarquar, Roderick, ed. *The Sino-Soviet Dispute*. New York: 1961.

BIOGRAPHIES:

Current Scene profiles of: Jiang Qing
                       Yao Wenyuan
                       Zhang Chunqiao
                       Wang Hongwen
Dr. Sun Yat-sen: Man of the Ages. Taipei: 1971.
Chi Hsin. *Teng Hsiao-ping*. Hong Kong: 1978.
Chung Hua-min, and Miller, Arthur C. *Madame Mao*. Hong Kong: 1968.
Hensman, C. R. *Sun Yat-sen*. London: 1971.
Hsu, Kai-yu. *Chou En-lai: China's Gray Eminence*. New York: 1969.
Witke, Roxane. *Comrade Chiang Ching*. London: 1977.
Wolf, Margery, and Witke, Roxane, ed. *Women in Chinese Society*. Stanford: 1975.

MODERN CHINESE FICTION:

Barmé, Geremie, and Lee, Bennett, trs. *The Wounded*. Hong Kong: 1979.
Chen Jo-hsi. *The Execution of Mayor Yin and Other Stories*. Taipei: 1978.
Han, Wu. *Hai Rui Dismissed from Office*. Translated by C. C. Huang. Honolulu: 1972.
Stories of Not Being Afraid of Ghosts, selected from *The Man Who Sold A Ghost*, Peking: 1958.

OTHER DOCUMENTARY SOURCES:

Beijing Review, Peking.
China News Analysis, Hong Kong, notably Nos. 1031, 1034, 1037, 1046, 1201.
China News Summary, Hong Kong.
China Quarterly, London, notably Oct./Dec. 1961, Oct./Dec. 1963, July/Sept. 1973, March 1977.
China Reconstructs, Peking.
China Reporting Service, United States.
China Topics: Documents taken from the press and radio of the Chinese People's Republic, United Kingdom.

Current Scene, United States.
Far Eastern Economic Review, Hong Kong.
Foreign Broadcast Information Service, United States.
Major Current Events as revealed in the press and radio of the Chinese People's
     Government, Hong Kong.
Monitoring Digest, Singapore.
New China News Agency (NCNA), Peking.
Observer Foreign News Service, London.
Problems of Communism, United States.
Reuters.
Summary of World Broadcasts, BBC.
The People's Daily, Peking.
Translations from the Mainland Press, United States.

LEFT-WING CHINESE PERIODICALS, Hong Kong:

Cheng Ming
Contemporary Monthly (Dangdai)
East and West (Dong Xi Fang)
Look Fortnightly (Janwang Banyueh Kan)
Ming Pao Yueh Kan
Nanbei Ji
The Observers (Jianchagia)
The Trend (Dong Xiang)
Zhongbao Yue Kan

SPECIAL DOCUMENTS (as published by Peking unless other sources given;
listed chronologically):

Eighth Congress of the Chinese Communist Party, September 1956.
Speech by Mao Tsetung to the Supreme Soviet of the USSR on the fortieth
     anniversary of the October Revolution, 6 November 1957 (from *Mao Tse-tung
     and Lin Piao*).
Conference of the Central Committee at Wuhan, Nov.–Dec. 1958.
Conference of the Central Committee at Lushan, July 1959.
   Peng Dehuai's memorandum (from *China Quarterly* Oct.–Dec. 1966 and *Party
   Leadership and Revolutionary Power in China*).
   Speech of Mao Tsetung (from *Mao Tse-tung Unrehearsed*).
Liu Shaoqi's speech to an enlarged conference of the Central Committee (7,000
     cadres), January 1962 (from *Party Leadership and Revolutionary Power in
     China*).
"Long Live the Victory of the People's War," by Lin Biao, Sept. 1965 (from
     Mao Tse-tung and Lin Piao).
Sixteen-point Charter for the Great Proletarian Cultural Revolution, adopted by
     the 11th Plenum of the Central Committee on 8 August 1966.
Draft Constitution for the Chinese Communist Party, October 1968.
Ninth Congress of the Chinese Communist Party, April 1969:
   Composition of Presidium and Central Committee.
   Lin Biao's Report.
   New Party Constitution.

Tenth Congress of the Chinese Communist Party, August 1973:
  Chou En-lai's Report.
  New Party Constitution.
Fourth National People's Congress of January 1975:
  Composition of the Presidium.
  Report on the work of government by Chou En-lai (read by Deng Xiaoping).
  Report on the revision of the Constitution by Zhang Chunqiao.
  New Constitution of the People's Republic.
Report by Chairman Hua Guofeng to the NPC on the work of the government
  (new economic plan), February 1978.
Indictment of the Special Procurate under the Supreme Procurate of the People's
  Republic of China (against Gang of Four and Lin Biao conspirators), Novem-
  ber 1980.
Hu Yaobang interview to Greek editor, stating there was "nothing positive" about
  the Cultural Revolution, reported by *Ta Kung Pao*, 18 December 1980.
Judgment of the Special Court under the Supreme People's Court of the People's
  Republic of China, January 1981.
Resolution on Certain Questions in the History of our Party since the founding of
  the People's Republic of China, passed by the 6th Plenum of the Central
  Committee on 27 June 1981 (assessment of Mao Tsetung's contribution and
  errors).
Speech by Chairman Hu Yaobang on sixtieth anniversary of the Party, July 1981
  (admitting Party had allowed Mao Tsetung to commit errors).
Speech by Huang Kecheng, published in *Beijing Review* of 4 July 1981, assessing
  Mao's mistakes as "mistakes of a great revolutionary" (see pp. 309–10).

MISCELLANEOUS:

The quotations from the works of Han Suyin on the Red Guards were taken from:
  The Wind in the Tower. London: 1976.
  China in the Year 2001. London: 1967.
  My House Has Two Doors. London: 1980.
Quotations from *Utopia* of Thomas More were taken from the translation by Paul
  Turner, London 1965.

❀ INDEX ❀

DENNIS BLOODWORTH *was born in London in 1919. After service in the Second World War, he joined* The Observer *as an assistant to the chief Paris correspondent. After five and a half years in France, he was transferred to Saigon to cover the end of the French Indochina war, and thereafter became Southeast Asia correspondent and then chief Far East correspondent of* The Observer. *Based in Singapore, he covered regional events from the subsequent fighting in Vietnam, Cambodia and Laos, to the overthrow of Syngman Rhee in Korea, the civil war in Indochina, coups in Thailand, Communist terrorists in Malaysia, as well as, of course, events in China.*

*He is the author of two main selections of the Book-of-the-Month Club—*The Chinese Looking Glass *and* An Eye for the Dragon—*as well as four works of fiction and two other books on China written in collaboration with his Chinese wife, Ching Ping, whom he married in 1957.*